Also by Enid Saunders Candlin

The Breach in the Wall

A
TRAVELER'S
TALE

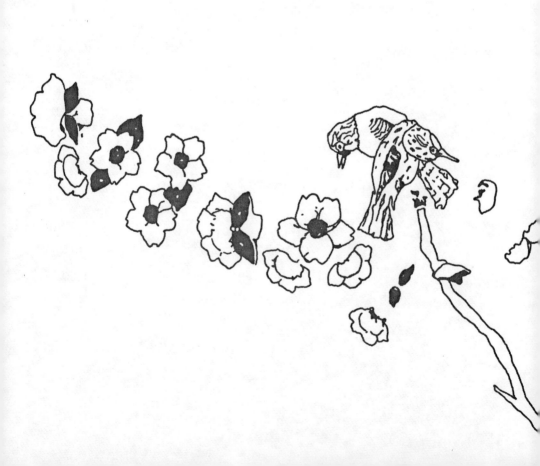

A
TRAVELER'S
TALE

Memories of India

ENID SAUNDERS CANDLIN

MACMILLAN PUBLISHING CO., INC.
NEW YORK
COLLIER MACMILLAN PUBLISHERS
LONDON

Macmillan Publishing Co., Inc.
866 Third Avenue, New York, N.Y. 10022
Collier-Macmillan Canada Ltd.

Library of Congress Cataloging in Publication Data

Candlin, Enid Saunders.
    A traveler's tale: memories of India.

    1. India—Description and travel—1901–1946.
I. Title.
DS413.C23   915.4'04'35   73-20045
ISBN 0-02-521110-2

FIRST PRINTING 1974
Printed in the United States of America

Acknowledgments

This book was started a very long time ago. I hoped then only to sketch some small part of our Indian years and send the result to my mother, whom I was unable to visit. Gradually it grew and gathered weight, but only at the bitter end was it ever properly typed. I am extremely grateful to my friend Elizabeth Heimerl, who performed this task, paring away repetitions and redundancies as she went along, always tactful and helpful. My thanks are also due to Neil Millar, who was most obliging and kind in looking up curious data for me in his large collection of encyclopedias and dictionaries.

A Note to the Reader

The Romanization of Hindustani, and particularly the spelling of place names and people in this book, are not consistent. That would be difficult in the best of circumstances, and more so here, as it seemed appropriate in some cases to follow the forms in common usage in British India, and at other times to employ those in favor today. For instance, I write "Cawnpore," whereas now this is spelled "Kanpur." *Cawnpore* is the way you meet this name in almost every old history and record; *Kanpur* is, in any event, a variation of the Mohammedan *Khanpur* (or *pore*). You can find variations of form for the majority of the names encountered in this book, just as you will in the anglicized renditions of Chinese and Cyrillic, of many languages. The best answer seems to lie in flexibility.

To Stanton

Contents

Contents

Preface

There is an old tale from the deserts of Sind of a beautiful princess who was held captive in a fortress with a sorcerer for her guardian. With his dark arts he encircled her prison with a rushing river, in which all the suitors who came to her rescue were drowned. At last the right prince appeared, who recognized the spell. There was no river there; it was only an illusion, and walking dryshod across the sand, he claimed the lady. (He was, of course, already married, but that made no odds in this context and the princess joyfully exchanged the fort for his harem.)

The lady could be taken for India in those centuries when encircled by her own deep currents of illusions she was wooed by many European suitors. The successful aspirant, Britain, seemed, however, to have soon entered the aura of the illusions himself. Caste was certainly the strongest element of the spell—and who did not bow to it? It seemed a web as strong as steel, but was, in fact, only part of the insubstantial pageant that was India.

Myriad myths ringed both countries: adamant traditions, conventions which were cherished, however harmful. But it is easy to be wise after the event. The long association brought, in spite of much friction and many mistakes, a rich harvest to both sides. For Britain it brought immense opportunities and the cornerstone of an empire. For the Indians it brought—for a considerable number—education, better health, an entry into a larger world of thought. Today the assumption of the right to govern another country as England did India seems preposterous, but it must be viewed within the context of its own times—and those were centuries of great achievements, not to be lightly dismissed.

To try to summarize one's impressions of a country, to distill its essence in the understanding and to express that understanding in words—to recapture the charm, the color, the scents, to remember the heat and the rains, the kindness and the choler—is a baffling pursuit; one is caught up in a world of dreams. It is particularly difficult if it is an oriental country drawn into the crosscurrents of vast world changes. Thinking of India I become so enmeshed in details that I can hardly discern the pattern. But the main design stands out sharply—the climax of the struggle for self-government. The problem was fraught with so much passion and moment that it dwarfed the issues of the Second World War as they affected the country, though they were always uppermost in the minds of the Europeans. But we were so few.

I see our first Bengal garden, still in the hot noon. A mongoose runs swiftly across the lawn, a gray horizontal line, a controlled shadow, its long tail held straight out on a level with its body. I watch it from the deep shade of the veranda, behind the blinds. Then I turn back to the high rooms of the old bungalow where the flickering revolutions of the ceiling fans are reflected all day in the red mirrors of the floors.

I remember the bearded Mohammedan waiting by the wall for the bus which was to take us to Aurangabad, that ancient capital of the Deccan, and his astonished: "What! You have passed three days in Khuldabad, and you have not yet seen the tomb of Alamgir!"

Then the dry plain, which lies between the Western Ghats and the sea, stretches out, and in Bombay we are watching the whiteclad ratings of the Naval Mutiny as they go through the streets shouting "*JAI HIND!*"

One has only to say the words "East India Company" to be carried into another world of merchant princes and nabobs, of fantastic profits and trials which brought colossal figures down to ruin—trials which are debated to this day. The Mutiny, the somber tragedy that cleft the dark people and the pale, brings to life the most vivid memories of all—the ordeal at Lucknow, the unforgiven sorrows of Cawnpore. I cannot summarize India, I can only tell a little of what I saw, of scenes played before the constant backdrop of the heat, the labyrinths of the bazaars, the interminable Bengali ballads, the gold mohur trees, the choleric and weary people, the sacred cattle with their magic eyes.

Life, like a dome of many-coloured glass,
Stains the white radiance of Eternity.
                                    Shelley

I To India

Many a green isle needs must be
In the wide deep sea of Misery,
Or the mariner, worn and wan,
Never thus could voyage on
Day and night, and night and day,
Drifting on his weary way, . . .

Ay, many flowering islands lie
In the waters of wide Agony:

SHELLEY

PERIODS OF INTENSE ACTIVITY and drastic change often contain within their turbulence long, easy pauses. Between the *con fuoco* and the *con brio* lies an *andante;* it is not the eye of the storm—it holds no foreboding—it is that moment when one rests on a chord, letting the pedal carry out the long resonance, till there comes that impulse from the music which tells the player to go forward.

It was a long time before I became aware of this pattern, before I came to expect these moments of stillness which make more bearable gruesome experiences like packing and moving (of which I have had far more than my, or anyone's, fair share). I can at last reassure myself that there will be many hours, even days, when everything is in suspension, most of the books packed, the dishes in crates, when suddenly I will find that I have complete leisure. There are then more of these *andantes* than in ordinary life; nothing has been arranged, everything is in flux, what time now appears, pouring from its mysterious crystal source, lyric, cool, inviting, is one's own. Then I can sit down on whatever chair is left, with a book in my hand, or I can open the typewriter and put down the ideas that came to me as I was sorting the linen.

The watershed year 1941 was for me a time of many such delicious pauses. After that year we were all keenly aware that a great deal both good and bad had passed, never to return. The emphasis of life had shifted, but it was not yet clear to what—other than, of course, the war. And we were used to the war; we had had it with us since 1937 and Marco Polo Bridge. After Pearl Harbor we seemed to be dimly groping in a haze, knowing that once past this gigantic hurdle of total war, not only would there be, as Shaw was saying, "wigs on the green," but an entirely different framework for our lives. As the year went on, though, that year and the next and the next, we were all preoccupied with *petits détails*. In spite of what we had read in *The Art of Thinking*, there still remained the question of what to have for dinner, should the park be camouflaged, would we use the air raid shelter or just stay in bed?

World War II had begun for me in 1937 when I was in Nanking. On a hot August evening I managed to get out of the city on one of the last trains, reaching Shanghai late the next night to find it stunned by its first bombing. More people had been killed from the air on that fatal day—and by accident!—than in London during the whole of World War I. Ignorant of what was to come in the way of death from the skies during the next decade, we were staggered by Shanghai's two thousand casualties. We could only compare it with the horrors of the Spanish Civil War; but we soon had plenty of firsthand knowledge of raids over undefended towns. The tempo of the Japanese War was at that time very fast; one city after another was destroyed or captured, and the vast population began to move inland—resolute, patient, deserving so much more than it was to receive in the years ahead. The Westerners—and there were thousands of us—scattered or stood our ground as we could. It was during this time that Stanton and I met and became engaged. He was a metallurgist in a Hong Kong shipyard, and I had been sent down to the Colony to carry on the work I had been doing in Nanking and Shanghai.

The outbreak of the European War in 1939 hastened our marriage. We remembered our parents' tales of the effect of the 1914–18 war on the China Coast, when most of the young Western men volunteered in August and sailed away, full of enthusiasm, never to return. Many of them fell at Gallipoli. The Allies had pushed the Germans out of the International Settlements; it was a long time before the old patterns of trade and diplomacy were resumed. But World War II produced a very different design; this time, in Hong Kong it was decreed that no man of military age might leave the Colony. That strange phase called the "phony war" in the West—when the Japanese were as active as ever in China—increased the political awareness of many Occidentals, whose position had become ambivalent. Their emotions had been primarily involved with Europe and America, but now for the first time they became keenly aware that the oriental conflict would not necessarily leave them always on safe, neutral territory. The shock and dismay when Norway was seized by the Nazis, and then, so soon afterwards, the almost unbelievable fall of France, had a tremendous effect all over the Far East. The Axis powers seemed much more formidable to the Orientals than they ever did to the Allied nationals, who never for a moment considered the possibility of ultimate defeat, whatever the present setbacks.

Never was this more evident than the summer of 1940, when on the receipt of alarming intelligence it was decided to evacuate "the women" from Hong Kong. This meant, however, "those of pure white descent" who would be able to go ashore in Australia without difficulty and whose numbers were small enough to manage easily. Several ships were commandeered and the exodus began. Many of us looked upon this act with shame and disgust. Some refused to go, though it was an order; to others it was a devastating experience, breaking up families. The humbler residents of Hong Kong were furious and outraged that they, holding British papers and paying taxes, had no chance to leave, and were even asked to pay for the cost of this evacuation. It was an extraordinary affair; it proved not "smart" to go, except for those with young children. The leading citizens' wives generally stayed on under one pretext or another of being "essential to the war effort," which naturally caused further resentment. "My dear! You're not *going?*" became one of those important social questions. Still, many left innocently and thankfully, and those who did go did not have to spend several years in prison camps.

I was not obliged to leave because I still had my U.S. passport. Certain others stayed from very admirable motives, several spirited ladies even bringing the whole evacuation question to court and airing their right to refuse to comply with the government's proclamation. One of these Portias explained that she was not eligible because she was not "of pure white descent," being Jewish. (This was before the state of Israel existed, and Jews were not in the way then of so openly declaring their origin—her family, one heard, was not pleased.) The government was embarrassed. The defendants won, but by then the ships had long since gone, and Hong Kong had become more of a fortress than ever. It was felt that the Colony should be able to hold out for a considerable time in case of attack, and there was great reliance on Singapore, which was looked upon as a tower of strength, a real bastion. How illusioned we all were!

About the time of the evacuation storm there was a conference held in Delhi to see what could be done in the way of a concerted Far Eastern war effort. As a result of the plans drawn up there, and the demand for metallurgists and chemical engineers, Stanton was put on a list, and we were sent to India to work in the Inspectorate of Armaments. This took precedence over his work in Hong Kong and gave him a permit to leave the Colony. As I had successfully resisted evacuation, we were felt by our friends to be leading an almost incredibly charmed life. Most of them had seen their families off to Australia (for which, of course, they were to be more than glad in the years to come), and knew well that they were just sitting ducks. At least, a lot suspected this, but up to that time the Oriental had hardly ever worsted the Westerner in a serious open fight, and the thought of being even temporarily defeated by the Japanese was difficult to entertain seriously.

In this way, Stanton and I were plucked up from Hong Kong like a brand from the burning and sent to the banks of the Hooghly, outside Calcutta, to the area then known as the Arsenal of India. Stanton was to work in the Inspectorate of the huge Metal and Steel Factory, then expanding and intensely busy. In the next years India would arm and equip an army of two million men.

We left the doomed colony in February, very easily, on a coaster. We were even able to take our baby grand with us, though we left behind a good deal of our furniture, something I was after-wards bitterly to regret. But freight was expensive and we were favored in being able to take as much as we did, and people said, "You'll find everything like this" (looking at our new Hong Kong wicker, our Bilabed chair, our bookcases) "in India; that's the country for hot-weather furniture, for verandas," which sounded reasonable. So we left behind our couches and long chairs and tables, and never saw their like again, except, long after the war was over, abroad and at fabulous prices. India, we were to discover, was an expensive country for people on modest government salaries. Compared to China it had few craftsmen, few skilled artisans. To us, accustomed all our lives to the marvels of Chinese artistry, it soon seemed the land of the *kutcha*—the temporary, the ill-made, the costly.

Still, Pearl Harbor was coming nearer every day, and though not exactly foreseen, we knew well that we were fortunate to leave Hong Kong, to get round the point from Singapore. It was not a time to moan about leaving pretty new chairs, even though, as it turned out, we were soon to live in a bungalow which had the most graceful veranda in all the world, the most deserving of such furniture—but who can care about that as the world falls? Our world had been falling for some time anyway, yet that Bengal veranda did indeed give us a wonderful haven, a long green pause, a green isle, between bouts of storm and wind.

Our small coaster took a fortnight to reach Calcutta, stopping at Singapore and Penang, pleasant places drowsily enjoying their last months of tranquility. At Singapore we took on great numbers of Indian troops as deck passengers, and blackout precautions became very strict. All the bulbs were removed from our deck cabin—we decided that we would rather have no light at all than close the shutters in the heat. Then the concern was only for German or Italian submarines—we would have been incredulous if we had heard that in a year the Japanese would render these waters almost impassable for Allied shipping. But even in 1941 the risk was great enough for us never to go down to the dining room together—one always stayed with the baby.

In the Bay of Bengal there were constant light breezes, the air was clear and salty, and the blue beauty of sea and sky made every hour enchanting. But as we drew in towards the land, passed the Sunderabunds and entered the delta of the Ganges, a steamy damp heat, unrelieved by any clarity at dusk or dawn, enveloped us and the world seemed suddenly labored and dull—the sullen shores of Bengal extend their gloomy influence far out to sea. The blue waters gave way to muddy currents, and the shoreline became flat and ugly, unlike the sleek Malayan coasts we had so lately passed where the jungle comes down to the waves in a classic wall of tall palms. Here heavy undergrowth and isolated shaggy trees made an uneven, graceless line on the horizon. There was little shipping, and that seemed hard-pressed to make its way against the tide. In most Eastern harbors hordes of picturesque native craft come out to meet liners, but not here—the river is too treacherous, the people too dispirited. Near the city the banks are lined with drab factories, and over everything hangs a pall of lifeless heat. Most ports are a pleasure to enter, but not Calcutta.

The passengers ceased to be a band of brothers and became again preoccupied individuals. We were a dozen persons from China who had come to join the forces in one way or another. Some of us knew our destination, some did not; a few of the men had been told to report to Fort William in Calcutta, and their wives did not know whether they would be able to accompany their husbands beyond the city. The cares of the land fell on these couples as we docked in the early twilight. But we were all glad to have left China; we sensed that the coming years would be terrible ones there and none of us could have done much to help. As it turned out, we would probably all have either been killed or interned by the Japanese.

We were among the fortunate that night—someone from the Inspectorate had come to meet us and to help us pass our formidable luggage, with many crates of household goods, through Customs. I sat waiting on a long table in the Customs shed, holding the baby. It was hot and dim, everyone was in white, the cold weather was over. Soon we had left everything in the hands of an agent and started on the drive through the city and out to Ishapore. Calcutta was not really blacked out that February of 1941, but it was not well enough lit to disclose itself as more than a vast city, and all the way out to the factory the roads were in darkness. It seemed a far, black goal that first night, till at last we went through the iron gates of a park and up to the compound of the head of our inspectorate, who was to put us up till our own bungalow would be ready. There was no hotel in the station, and no guest bungalow.

Our hosts showed us our room, dinner was waiting for us, and when they were assured that we had everything we needed they went out, as there was a dance in the station that evening. Upstairs, outside our room there was a long veranda, the outer wall composed entirely of shutters. The old *ayah* of the house, enveloped in a rose-colored sari, rustled in, full of curiosity to see the infant guest, bending over her with loud, flattering cries in Hindustani. A folding cot was arranged beside our bed, all under an immense mosquito net—there were no screens. *Ayah* withdrew, salaaming, and we went down to dinner. After the simplicities and isolation of our days at sea, the recent dark uncertainties of the drive, this strange little station, where a dance was in progress, made a sufficient contrast. Outside the lit circle of the table beturbaned bearers waited in obsequious silence.

We had hardly sat down before awful howls broke out all around us and I sprang up to run to the baby. But William, our escort, told us that it was only the jackals roaming through the park, and that their screams were a part of every night. They did no harm unless one was mad. Soon afterwards everyone went away, the lights were put out, we went to bed. It was a wild night of wind, not rain—there would be no rain for months—the shutters banged from one end of the veranda to the other, and Stanton, getting up to try and secure them, was attacked by the house dog. The great white net, swinging from a high frame and enclosing our bed so invitingly, contained, we discovered to our dismay, innumerable mosquitoes. We put on the lights and tried to catch them with our hanads, but they eluded us. At last we fell asleep, too worn out to care, resigned to being consumed. So passed our first night in India.

II Ishapore

There is nothing ugly; I never saw an ugly thing in my life: for let the form of an object be what it may, light, shade, and perspective will always make it beautiful.

The world is wide: no two days are alike, nor even two hours; neither were there ever two leaves of a tree alike since the creation of the world; and the genuine productions of art, like those of nature, are all distinct from each other.

JOHN CONSTABLE

WHEN IN ISHAPORE you had to keep thoughts like Constable's very much in mind, so dispiriting was the juxtaposition of a dreary British industrial complex upon a poverty-stricken Bengal village area. We were delighted to find that all the ordnance bungalows in Ishapore were occupied, due to the press of wartime recruitment; we were to live four miles downriver in Barrackpore, an old cantonment, which, though certainly limited enough, was at least not confined to persons of one basic industry, with one employer, and almost wholly drawn from an industrial background.

Nearly all the British Ishaporis had come from the factories of the United Kingdom to oversee the labors of the thirty thousand Indians who worked in the Metal and Steel and the Small Arms factories, which lay side by side. The only exceptions were a few military persons stationed there: an officer commanded the station and some of the Inspectorate personnel were officers. The O.C. was a genial Irishman who, holding the most important post, naturally had the best house, one I like to remember—unlike nearly everything else in Ishapore, which I only want to forget.

This riparian settlement had long ago, in the lighthearted early days of imperial snatch and grab, belonged to the Dutch, who had left behind them a conical tower they had used both as a powder store and as a shot tower, a pyramid of smooth gray stone pleasing to the eye. Near it was the splendid old white house always occupied by the garrison commander, and still, after two centuries, far and away the best in the station. Though delightfully habitable with its immense rooms and high ceilings, its clarity and atmosphere, its elegance of line, its air of secure dominance, tied it to the past, not the present. From the veranda which ringed the second story, at the back, an immensely long stairway led from the outside of the house to the ground—a narrow hypotenuse, very pictorial. This severe line, complementing the right angles of the house, was no doubt less attractive to the *jemidars* who had to carry all the hot water upstairs in buckets on its narrow, steep stairs. During the monsoon rains they were always soaked. But these poor people were still bred to an uncomplaining endurance of the intolerable and the unnecessary. Not that their present employers were unkind—the contrary—but no one went against custom, and *jemidars* were still plentiful in 1941.

The Netherlanders had been harsh enough in their day. This ancient house had even a Dutch ghost, an unusual attribute in India. She was sometimes seen, by those given to supersensory perceptions: she would drift, sad and bemused, through a wall, trailing her long skirts, the victim of a cruel story of passion and intrigue. The station was proud of its white ghost.

But nearly all of the two hundred or so bungalows in the Ishapore Park were modern and very hideous indeed, scattered about a wide and grassy area. There was a club where people played tennis and drank pegs; altogether it was a homely place with many young families in which the parents were experiencing with mingled pleasure and annoyance the ministrations of a great number of servants. The transition from places like Manchester or the Clyde to Ishapore was not very happy or rewarding to most people, whose outlook was generally still confined to the two places. A few of the houses had in their gardens small iron cannon and ball from the old days—a dramatic background to herbaceous borders. The love of gardening was a redeeming feature in some of these rather pitiful, uprooted establishments. Where we first stayed our hosts were setting out a great number of rose bushes in their garden, which lay on the river (our host, being the head of an Inspectorate, had drawn a house in a coveted position). The care lavished on the

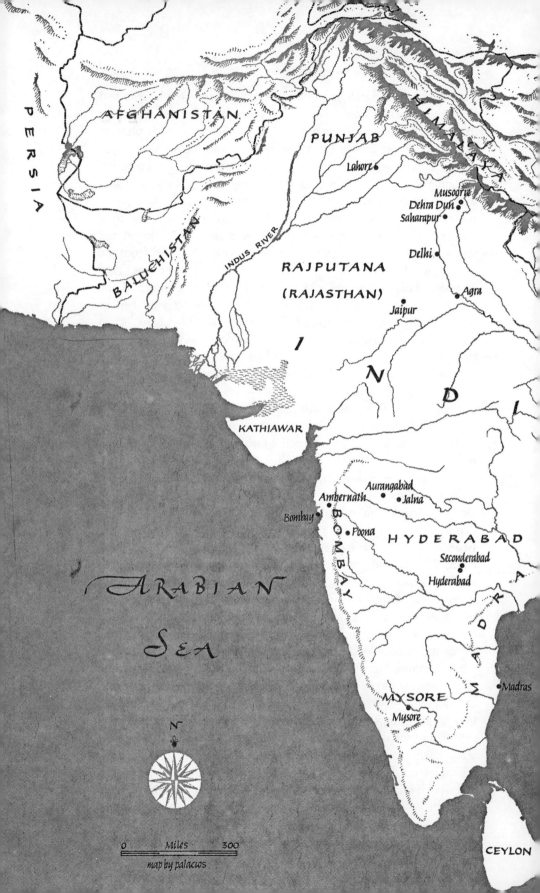

PERSIA

AFGHANISTAN

BALUCHISTAN

PUNJAB

Lahore

HIMALAYA

Musoorie
Dehra Dun
Saharapur

Delhi

Agra

INDUS RIVER

RAJPUTANA
(RAJASTHAN)

Jaipur

I
N
D
I

KATHIAWAR

Aurangabad
Amhernath
Jalna
Bombay
B
O
M
B
A
Y
Poona

HYDERABAD

Seconderabad

Hyderabad

M
A
D
R
A

ARABIAN

SEA

N

MYSORE
Madras

Mysore

CEYLON

0   Miles   300

map by palacios

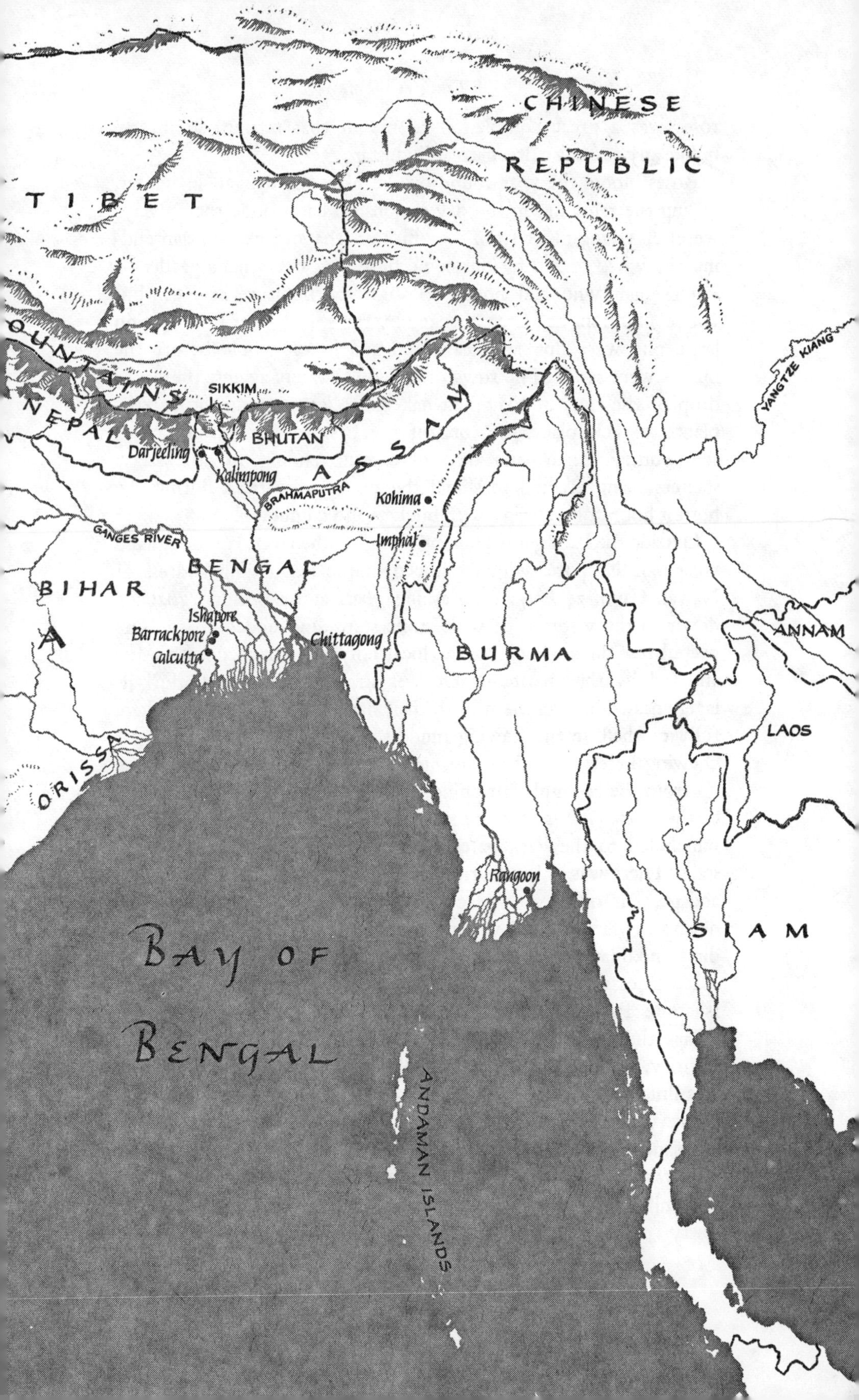

CHINESE

REPUBLIC

TIBET

YANGTZE KIANG

SIKKIM

NEPAL

BHUTAN

ASSAM

Darjeeling

Kalimpong

BRAHMAPUTRA

Kohima

Imphal

GANGES RIVER

BENGAL

BIHAR

ANNAM

Ishapore

Barrackpore

Chittagong

LAOS

Calcutta

BURMA

ORISSA

Rangoon

SIAM

Bay of

Bengal

ANDAMAN ISLANDS

roses was a great consolation to me in that setting, so utterly unlike any romantic dreams of Hindustan.

Roses bloom the year round on the plains in Bengal—in winter, during the rains and in the dry seasons. What a boon they always were! A young clerk from the office at Ishapore was superintending the work of setting out some bushes in our chief's garden—a young man who had hoped to study horticulture at Kew but whose ambitions had been checked by the war. Under his direction large pits were dug and leaves burned in each hole before the bushes were set in. The rows of smoking craters against the backdrop of the river and the half-naked coolies carrying the narrow plants to their places was one of my first strong impressions of the country. Then came days of careful tending, of little straw shelters being erected to shield the young rose trees during the hottest hours, of watering with buckets and bamboo pipes.

Outside the Park gates, running along by the river, lay the squalid village of Ishapore, which rejoiced in the resounding address of Nawab Gunj, 24 Parganas. Bathing *ghats* and a burning *ghat* led down to the water with wide stone steps, and under a large fine peepul tree on the bank sat the local holy man, daubed with ashes and fed by the charitable. He was strategically placed; the villagers passed him on the way to their daily bath (which was taken, fully clothed, in the flowing muddy water). Near him people sat chewing betel nut and discussing their affairs, while women came up from the Hooghly, dripping with water, as were their brass or earthenware *chattis*. A few sacred cows passed slowly up the road which led to the Park gates, picking up vegetables at the open stalls. There was only one rich house, an imposing affair of marble and great mirrors, with peacocks in the garden. Long afterwards, during the famine year, we once entered it and found it extremely dirty and dilapidated for all its brave front.

It was easy to condemn the drab and commonplace elements of Ishapore Park, but once inside that desperate poverty-stricken village the world beyond seemed a world of marvelous order and security, of prosperity and health. To pass from one to the other was almost like a blow.

Every evening the gates were thrown open, and out streamed thousands and thousands of workers on bicycles. In the winter this was something to see, as the Bengali winter overcoat was a Kashmir shawl, provided the man could possibly afford to put out thirty rupees on such a thing. That was expensive, the pay ranged from something like one rupee, eight annas a day to perhaps three rupees, eight annas. Overtime and increments might raise this, but a Kashmir shawl was a serious outlay. The *babus* and workers wore white *dhotis* and shirts and Western-style leather shoes. The shawls (and most of the bicyclists had them) they swathed about their shoulders and arms and over their heads, wearing them high lest they get caught in the chains of the machines. Both wide and long—perhaps two yards long by over a yard wide—these shawls are of the most delectable and melting colors, with deep embroidered borders, and are very warm, very soft. The Bengalis are a dark people with a mournful cast of countenance. Their large sad black eyes looked out from wrappings of rose or turquoise, old gold, orchid, pale green—the shawl covered their mouths, ears, and arms right down to the wrists which, dark, thin and knobby, stuck out from these luscious colors. As the light began to go, these swooping, fast flocks of Kashmir shawls on wheels sped through Ishapore's narrow road, armed against the chill, hastening home to their evening curry.

It was never really cold, but it seemed frigid in comparison to the ten months of heat, and there were no proper provisions against the few weeks of winter. One felt the cold bitterly as night fell. But the days were warm with the constant sun.

Servants

Hindustan is a country that has few pleasures to recommend it. The people are not handsome. They have no idea of the charms of friendly society, of frankly mixing together, or of familiar intercourse. They have no genius, no comprehension of mind, no politeness of manner, no kindness or fellow feeling, no ingenuity or mechanical invention in planning or executing their handicraft works, no skill or knowledge in design or architecture: they have no good horses, no good flesh, no grapes or musk melons, no good fruits, no ice or cold water, no good food or bread in their bazaars, no baths or colleges, no torches, not a candlestick.

BABER, 1530

Poor India has never lacked critics! Critics as severe as those who attack the United States. They can't stand the country, that's what it is. Four hundred years after Baber relieved his feelings in this summary, many people would still have agreed with him. I didn't agree, but I soon knew what he meant.

Our hosts in Ishapore told us that the first necessity of life for us was to engage servants. There was no progress to be made, they insisted, until we had at least a bearer and an *ayah*. Our hosts, the Stoddards, had the usual staff for people of their rank in the factory hierarchy—seven—but not one of them would wait on us except at table, and even that they did unwillingly, realizing that we would be in the house for some time and that Stanton was junior to their master. Abdul, the bearer, obviously considered making our bed a monstrous imposition, but had I done it, it would have been an unforgivable gaffe. I could not leave our baby alone, nor could I take her with me through the dirt of the bazaars under the strong sun if I went out; and the old house *ayah*, though amiable enough and pleased to see the baby guest, was not going to put herself out one inch for any newcomers. For harmony to be maintained in the house we had to have some servitors of our own, and immediately.

As soon as it was known in the bazaar that a new home was to be set up in the neighborhood, a score or more of Indians waited upon us. We sat under the fans in the cool, darkened drawing room while three lots of men came in, in turn—the bearers and *missolchis;* the cooks; and lastly the sweepers, who were outcastes. They were all dark, villainous, and secret of countenance—wonderfully pictorial, but from the standpoint of becoming members of our own household they awoke in me a certain uneasiness and I lamented our inability to read character in these faces. They all had glowing letters with them, at least half of them patently borrowed or hired in the bazaar. Some of the candidates did not even answer to the names on the chits and their own accounts of where they had worked previously often did not tally with their references, but these trifles disturbed no one but ourselves.

The bearers were the best-looking, in their long, full-skirted coats with wide sashes, wearing turbans if they were Hindus, fezzes if they were Muslims. The *missolchis* wore the same costume but were rather shabbier. We had been told that according to the dictates of custom we must have a *missolchi*—no respectable bearer would work for us if we were not to have a *missolchi*, his underling as well—though in such a modest household as ours this post was a sinecure and a racket. The *missolchi* helps to serve and to wash the dishes, and, depending on his caste, he will undertake certain other duties. He will dust; sometimes he will even be so good as to wash windows. Caste is a wonderful evasion, far better than any picayune trade union rules, for there is no possible argument about it. If a man's caste would not allow him to wash windows, the subject was closed, forever, to the fuming *memsahib*. Was he to descend in the scale of creation for the sake of a few panes of glass? The division of labor can be carried to a fine art on this exalted religious basis where, it seems, the opponent must always lose. So that all would be fair and aboveboard, the Mohammedans accepted all the caste barriers of the Hindus as far as work went, so no one was better off in employing a staff which was wholly Muslim.

At that time we were ignorant of all this; we only realized that we must start somewhere. We hired Santu as our bearer, or majordomo, and Allah Bux as the *missolchi*, because their references seemed to belong to them and they both looked intelligent. Santu was a Hindu from Lucknow; handsome, with acquiline features and soft eyes, he had a good manner and had evidently been trained. We did not see that he was recklessly temperamental, and that above all persons in the district he hated and loathed the Muslim Allah Bux, who cordially returned this sentiment. Allah Bux, though we were too dense to perceive it, was furiously angry at being chosen as a *missolchi* and not a bearer. He proved, under Santu's aegis, to be dirty, lazy, and mendacious. Perhaps on his own ground he would have made a better showing. We were innocently entering upon one of the most difficult fields of life in India. Chinese servants had been so good, so easy to deal with—here everything was to be much more complex. Years later a missionary lady of angelic nature, who had lived twenty-five years in the country, told me that every year the mission sent them forms on which one of the questions was "What is your hardest problem?" To which she replied, "Dealing with Indian servants."

The odd thing was that the third man we hired that morning was another bosom enemy of Santu. Afterwards I wondered if any other three men would have fallen into such a triangle, so violent and choleric are the denizens of Bengal. Or did the chief fault lie with poor Santu? At that hour, as far as we could see, none of them gave the slightest hint of his feelings. The third character, the sweeper, was called Jummoo. Here we were really stupid in our choice, as this strong young man turned out to be a proper *budmash*, a word that conveys the quality of being cross-grained.

But if it had been hard to look into the faces of the more fortunate servants, it was doubly difficult to assess the wretched *jemidars*, who came in in a long file, men bred in the conviction that they are outcastes.

As befits their valuation of themselves, they have all the most disagreeable work given them. They must wipe over the red stone floors of the bungalows twice a day so that no dust rests on the mirrored surface; they must heat the bathwater on a stove built outside the house where they will intrude on no one; and if the houses are without sanitation they must deal with the consequent problems. I was ashamed to associate myself with the system but on a short-term basis there seemed no alternative—someone had to sweep, evidently. The men who came in were unkempt and of savage mien, with downcast looks. Their turbans were of diverse colors and roughly wound, loose shirts hung over their coarse *dhotis* (the length of white cloth, so draped as to form trousers, and which may, according to the artistry of the wearer, be a graceful garment), their big bare feet were horned and dusty. But poor and ignorant men in any society are outwardly marked by like characteristics; nothing more separated these outcastes from their fellows than their own unquestioning acceptance of an obsessive cruel belief.

The cook came in with great assurance, showing in his confident bearing that he considered the interview a matter of form only. His lean, shabby rivals could not compete with his powers and it was evident that any serious competitors had been refused entry. This big fat man in his snowy shirt and flowing *dhoti* was a brother of the Stoddards' cook; we hired him without ado and were, for a brief period, to be his victims.

I was more interested in finding an *ayah* than in acquiring any of these men servants, most of whom we did not need until we got into the house. Abdul, however, having now provided us with a bearer, did not care at all if we ever had an *ayah*. This ancient Muslim, with his large white turban and straggling white beard, considered our descent upon the Stoddards much as we would have looked upon a cloud of locusts coming down on a promising field. Stanton was junior to his *sahib* and therefore deserving of little consideration, and as for me—no Muslim was in a hurry to put himself out for any woman of any color if he could possibly avoid it.

All leave from India was stopped during the War and there were probably more British families than had ever been there before at one time. As more troops came out there were more new house-holds and more European babies, and consequently fewer *ayahs* to go round. The caste prejudice against the work is too great to permit the majority of women to undertake it, poor as they may be. Attending to the needs of small children involves duties which can rightly only be done by an untouchable, or, of course, by that personage born outside the circle of life altogether—a *memsahib*. For a respectable woman it was better to beg than to be an *ayah*. In the field of labor, Muslim and Christian women, like all the other servants, were just as adamant in their ideas of what they would or would not do as the Hindus. Though we would employ *jemidars* to sweep, from the point of view of cleanliness, we did not want their women handling our babies.

Still, Abdul did eventually round up a string of candidates and usher them in to me one day. I was aghast when I saw this line of slatterns slouching against the wall. Dirty, ingratiating, evasive, their saris soiled, their hair rough, loaded with nose-rings, bracelets and anklets! Not one spoke a word of English. After the shining clean, able, tranquil Chinese *amahs* we had always known, they were a discouraging if an interesting contrast. Their faces seemed as secret as the men's and it did not take us long to choose Aknis, the Nepali, whose Mongol features were familiar, at any rate. It seemed romantic to have someone from that (then) secret, for-bidden country in the house.

Though in the end she left us under a cloud, we never regretted our choice. It was not long before I was very fond of her, though she was always untidy, careless, unpunctual, and in her own home life startlingly unconventional. But she was so affectionate, honest, anxious to please. Being a hill woman, she had a happy nature, un-like her sisters of the plains, to whom life is ever a sad burden.

A Hindu bathes every day as part of the ritual of his religion. For a poor woman, this means that she walks fully clothed into a river, if there is one within a possible distance, or else she crouches under a tap in a compound, still dressed for modesty's sake. But if her mistress will provide her with enough saris, she will gladly put on a fresh one every day—fresh to the extent that it has been wet and then dried in the sun. She has no soap, she has no iron, no electricity. She anoints her long black hair with coconut oil till it shines with a blue light, she does her best, and in the end one be-comes accustomed to her limitations (so few of them her own fault) and forgets them in welcoming her smiles, her fidelity, the grace of her draperies, the tinkling of her glass bangles. Sometimes we had *ayahs* who were really clean, an achievement won in the face of great odds. Be it acknowledged to our shame that they had almost no facilities for being so, that all the conditions of their lives militated against the pleasure and comfort of cleanliness.

Aknis had one outstanding characteristic: she was grateful for everything we did for her. I sensed in her, as in many another oriental woman, great latent intelligence and strength. So far life has given few opportunities to these potentially able and gifted women—once they can awake to their own capacity what a difference it will make to the country!

III Barrackpore and Calcutta

Ah, many flowering islands lie . . .

. . .

To such a one this morn was led
My bark, by soft winds piloted . . .

SHELLEY

Barrackpore

BARRACKPORE WAS an old cantonment, a garrison town as its name implies, and once a residence of the governors-general of Bengal. One of the earliest incidents of the Mutiny* took place here, on the Parade Ground. The native troops had heard many

---

* The causes of the Mutiny of 1857 were social, economic and military, but not nationalistic—that element came along afterwards, in our own century, when the country had been welded into a nation. In the middle of the nineteenth century it had yet to develop a national consciousness, being then composed of many different states and confederations, ostensibly under the sovereignty of the old Mogul Empire. This had, in fact, become a facade, and the British were filling the power vacuum in the name of the East India Company, which was gradually absorbing more and more of the sub-continent, either by arms or by purchase.

The Westernization of India was by then arousing great opposition among the traditionally-minded sections of the country: the native princes and rajahs, the great landowners, the priests. Many of the less fortunate, those outside of the circle of vested interest, welcomed the new education (which even extended to women), some reforms of taxation, Christianity.

The rising was almost entirely on the part of the sepoys; the people of the country remained largely spectators. The army believed (mistakenly) that the cartridges issued to them were greased with cowfat, and the annexation of Oudh had aroused bitter resentment upcountry. The East India Company was certainly an aggressive, sometimes a predatory instrument. Fighting broke out simultaneously in many places, notably Delhi, Meerut, Cawnpore and Lucknow. Some of the troops remained loyal to the British; there were sieges and fierce battles with heavy casualties. After it was over, the Company reluctantly gave way, and the Crown took possession of India—it soon became part of the Empire.

wild rumors from the Dum Dum Factory, which was only a few miles up the river, but as the high command took notice of this immediately there was no rising here—the troops were disarmed at once and Bengal took no part in the insurrection. But whereas Ishapore felt new and alien to the country, Barrackpore did not; it was a true part of India, for good or ill.

How green it was that first morning when we drove over to see it, leaving Ishapore Park behind us! The gardens by the water were lovely, full of flowers; the Governor's Park was green, with its wide lawns and great trees; the lodges, high-columned, elegant, were brilliantly white against them. It was Kiplingesque, just as people imagined India to be in the old stupefied days, when facts and figures were more easily pushed from the mind. Even that morning, simply driving in to look at the house which had been selected for us, life seemed to be proceeding at so leisurely a tempo that the whole cantonment almost gave the impression of being in a dream. But we were immediately captivated by its charms and the respite it promised from the hideous modernities and industrial aura of Ishapore.

Our bungalow was the first on the Riverside, lying next to the Governor's Park. Between our garden and the park a short lane, deeply shadowed by heavy trees, led down to the water, and we were told that this was an active link in the smuggling trade which was carried on between the French settlement of Chandernagor, across the Hooghly, and the English side. It did not seem possible that morning that anything in Barrackpore could come under the heading of "active," nor indeed did it seem desirable—its sleepy grace, under the strong light, was part of its flavor. We drove from the lane through some gates and stood waiting under the wide portico of the bungalow till an old watchman had fumblingly unlocked the doors and thrown open the shutters.

Georgian and pre-Mutiny, like all the other bungalows of the cantonment, ours was built round a central room which was rounded at the far end and led through high French windows onto a veranda with a wide and sweeping curve that overlooked the river. All the walls, even between the inner rooms, were eighteen inches thick to help ward off the heat, and over many of the wide inner doors were still the marks of a slight depression in the plaster, showing where the ropes of the old pull *punkahs* had passed. Metallic green lizards sported on the high stained walls with slight, flicking movements, suddenly assuming alert, curved positions in their play below the cobwebs. The rooms seemed permeated with memories, sun, heat, silence, and dust. We stood in the echoing dimness—the old watchman being drowsy and lazy, unwilling to throw open more shutters than he must—and loved it, loved it.

Outside the garden, on the side towards the river and under the shade of an immense banyan whose many trunks formed an arcade over a wide area both within and without our own compound, stood a little round shrine of Grecian design, domed and mossy, having within its columns a black stone tablet which bore this legend:

To
Perpetuate the Remembrance of
Professional Gallantry
Manly Character and Private Worth
This cenotaph is inscribed
By his brother officers
To the memory of
CAPTAIN N. P. GRANT
of the 15th Regiment of Bengal Sepoys,
Who Whilst Employed in the Service of
HIS COUNTRY
Was Slain by Banditti,
Near the City of Kureemabed
IN PERSIA
In the Month of April A.D. 1810
At the early age of 26 Years.

Man cometh up and is cut down
like a flower,
In the midst of life
We are in death.

Under it was a verse in Arabic and the bas-relief of a lily. This young officer had played a part in the dream of Napoleonic conquest of the East and had been in Persia opposing French penetration. His solitary memorial faced the wide, muddy, deserted river, here running strongly between flat banks.

The next morning we went early to the office of the garrison engineer to see what could be done to put No. 1 Riverside in order as quickly as possible. This personage was a genial Irishman who readily promised all we asked. The landlady unfortunately had other ideas. She was an old rich widow, a Hindu of tractable disposition (so we were told), but most unhappily her affairs were in the hands of a wicked agent whose intention was to give as little for as much as possible. With him our Irishman waged constant and not very successful battle. We had first to convince the black-hearted agent that the place was not fit for habitation, which required much persuasion as he contended that it was now in good condition. It possessed two fittings: a mounting block under the portico and one tap, which constituted the entire water supply for the house other than a tank for the servants in the garden. The agent thought it quite unnecessary to paint, to plaster, to put in plumbing, but he did want to rent the house so there was some basis for bargaining—the long, slow bargaining of the East, where only the impatient Westerner cares for the flight of time. The mildewed walls, the peeling paint on the shutters, the cracked panes, were of no consequence to these Bengalis; and with some justification, as the usual Hindu or Muslim tenant would not have made much objection to them. But there were no Hindu or Muslim tenants wishing to rent the bungalow—this was our trump card.

We endured five weeks till the bungalow was partially prepared for us and our patience exhausted to the point of moving into it even though it was not ready. We could no longer presume on our chief and host and we imagined that the remaining work could be finished while we were there—though we were warned by the experienced that this would not be so. The landlady was wearing us down by attrition, deliberately. And in fact, as soon as we went in all work on the place stopped abruptly and for all time.

Before we moved I often went to the bungalow, worried the garrison engineer and prodded the workmen, but the results of everyone's efforts were pitiably meager. There would generally be as many as fifteen or twenty painters and carpenters in No. 1 Riverside when I visited it, a dozen lying asleep on the cool stone floors and the rest lounging against the walls, watching two small boys. These children would be perched on a bamboo scaffolding arranged lightly against a wall and always on the point of collapse, the poles being only very loosely tied together with coconut fiber. High above our heads (for the rooms were over twenty feet high) they would be dipping rags very, very slowly into old cans of color-wash, their hands and wrists cream-colored above their thin brown arms. At last the house was done in a streaky and uneven fashion, and the army of languid idlers moved out to the verandas and started dipping their rags into green paint for the shutters. As they did not take off the old coat first, the new one went on in a series of lumps and blisters, which they did not mind in the least. Then they extended their perimeter to the wooden slats, the jilmils, which connected the upper sections of the columns that ringed the beautiful veranda and contributed to its shade. It was when half of these were finished that we moved in. At that very instant the workmen left. I was surprised to find them capable of such speed—they vanished into the dust before our eyes. They knew that from the day we came the rent would be paid, whatever the condition of the quarter, and that was all that mattered to their employers, who had clearly left instructions that the moment we arrived work was to stop. This was, in any event, only normal practice.

During these weeks of waiting I had made several excursions to the great bazaar, Crawford's Market, in Calcutta. This was a miniature, roofed city containing hundreds, perhaps thousands, of booths, with lanes for the rug sellers, the silk shops, the sweetmeat makers, the fruit *wallahs*, the toy shops (which were particularly enchanting with their large red plush elephants and beturbaned dolls). In this famous and fascinating labyrinth I had bought such unromantic items as the outdoor stove which would heat the bathwater, the pails to carry the hot water into the house, the mosquito nets, the incense sticks whose smoke would, we hoped, discourage mosquitoes, and the curry stone, which were all listed as imperative requirements. The furniture we hired on Wellesley Street was brought in from the city, and our own boxes came out of storage. The piano was carried all the eighteen miles to Barrackpore on the heads of coolies, this proving the cheapest means of transport.

The servants moved into their quarters, and the eyes of Santu, Allah Bux, and Jummoo began to glitter as they took up their positions on their triangle. The cook went to the Barrackpore bazaar to arrange his campaign for taking immediate advantage of my innocence and preoccupation.

On one of the early visits to the house we had acquired a mad gardener, whom we found waiting by the gates hoping for employment. Like most gardeners in Bengal, he came from Orissa—an "upcountry" area—and was a strange, deerlike figure with liquid eyes and shy, timorous ways. These gardening Uriyas, as I was soon to discover, are by our standards almost unbelievably stupid—but I always suspected they felt the same way about us.

From their point of view, for instance, we were so unbelievably stupid that we did not see that this man was mad. No one enlightened us either. How is one to understand people who cannot tell the mad from the sane? So the other servants must have thought. Santu and the rest of the triangle no doubt felt this accounted for the way we had picked the staff. However, it was not very long before even Stanton and I realized that our Uriya knew nothing of gardening, though he was full of wild and grandiose schemes and wanted to make beds in the shapes of tigers and elephants. Having been thwarted in these plans, he stopped being a man of thought and became one of action, seizing the shears and cutting down a magnificent hibiscus in full bloom.

But in spite of these shortcomings, we had a home we loved and we could really begin to live in India.

Calcutta

A handful of tradesmen, who in their nature are like foxes, have pretended to put themselves on a footing with tigers.

> *A letter from the* NABOB NIZAM UD DOWLAH *to*
> FAZEL BEG CARON, 1780

It is in this ignorance and apathy that our strength consists.

> SIR HENRY STRACHEY, 1802

Prosperity withers in our shade.

> *A* GENTLEMAN *in the service of the* EAST
> INDIA COMPANY, *examining land tenure in India,* 1829

Ishapore, Barrackpore, and half a dozen other little places, somnolent and preoccupied beside the river, depended on Calcutta—that was our city, our center, our great bazaar, our contact with the world. It had then a population of about four million, and was dismissed by most of us as dirty, corrupt, wicked, unhappy. All our acquaintances assured us that no one could like Calcutta. William warned us of the Victoria Memorial on the Maidan: when an Italian architect was shown it, he burst into tears and cried out, "And such beautiful material, too!"

Still, I was unconvinced. You can't really dismiss a city, any city.

All the way in on our first visit I felt caught up in its spell, in its European past. It was for me then the city of Clive, of Warren Hastings, the *mise-en-scène* of the East India Company; I was too ignorant of Bengali history to see it in any other way. Coming from families long settled on the China coast, Stanton and I had grown up in the warlord era and were accustomed to many comparisons between India and China. British textbooks were then frankly, unashamedly, imperialistic. It was natural in British circles to believe that India was admirably run and had had the greatest good fortune to have been administered for so long by an incorruptible civil service devoted to the general welfare.

Certainly, in all those long voyages we took, passing back and forth between Europe and the East through the Suez Canal and anchoring at Bombay and Ceylon, India did give an impression of stability and calm compared to poor torn China. Enlightened self-interest was the British guideline; a quality which includes much elasticity of interpretation. What Pendrell Moon has summed up as the choice between being a missionary or a mercenary was not apparent to many people forty years ago. Of course the firms were there for profit; how could their men have lived otherwise? But then, there were the missionaries too, the schools and hospitals, the scholarships, the great kindness of the few.

This delta of the Ganges had for centuries reflected the turmoils of European wars. The first early "factories," the narrow strips of land by the river, were entangled in the struggles of the Portuguese and the Dutch, of the French and the English. To this remote and difficult corner of the world all these nationals had come, and the Danes and Germans as well, hardy adventurers and missioners, absorbed by a few uncomplicated ideas—trade, the sword, conversion. Today, with the West everywhere withdrawing from its old vantage points, it is startling to remember with what apparent lightheartedness these small European countries threw their wide nets of intrigue and conquest, undisturbed by their lack of communications, scorning danger. A world in which Bombay could be given away as part of a European dowry!

The ugly, flat, unhappy stretch of ground over which we were driving had been the scene of momentous English triumphs; here the other countries had given way, leaving England most of the riches of the delta and, ultimately, of the whole country. The East India Company, that shameless royal cartel, had derived its wealth from this apparently wretched setting where, that morning, there was little in evidence but decay, dirt, and terrible poverty. Macaulay said that the directors of the Company came to have the motto: "Thou shalt want ere I want," and, superficially, it looked that way. Down this very road had passed the muslins of Dacca and many another precious cargo which would lead to such ostentation among the rich nabobs in England. But to have lived here among these dark strangers, to have survived when so many succumbed to illness or the sword, must have given those who finally returned with great fortunes to England a sense of elation, of being specially favored. No wonder they played the fool, tried to redress the balance of their lives by thrusting themselves forward, by overemphasizing their achievements in the East.

Our way led along the Grand Trunk Road, lined by heavy trees overhanging traffic which spanned centuries. In the West we move more or less in the same time blocks, but here we encountered figures which might well have been there in the fifth century. Under the welcome shade of banyans and mangoes went bullock carts drawn by beautiful animals with wide, curving horns and great eyes, moving deliberately as though in a trance. Herds of shining black water buffaloes lumbered along, contemptuous in their vast bulk of the lorries and motors which swooped past each other but were obliged to wait often enough for these prehistoric beasts. The passersby were a slow-moving frieze, barefooted, burdens on their heads, their dark limbs accentuated by their white draperies.

After passing Barrackpore the road goes through half a dozen villages built on the river bank whose whole existence was bound up with jute, and therefore with Dundee. Their direction and their managers came from Scotland, and there went their profits. Titagar was the largest of these places, and a terrible sight it was. Its slums (and, indeed, save for the factories themselves and the compounds of the Europeans, it was just one vast slum) were said to be among the very worst in the world. Over the greater part of it sanitation was unprovided, and hundreds drew their water from one tap. We were glad to get past the jute district.

Near the city, on each side of the road, were old neglected gardens with an air of ancient splendor about them, though the high, elaborate gates were falling and the walls ruined; the glimpses we caught of the mansions standing far back in their parks showed them to be sinking into decay. They were homes from the days of the Company, now either empty or in the hands of Indians who had no interest in maintaining them—even though they might have been financially well able to do so. This process of deterioration had clearly been going on for a long time.

After the shattering climax of the Mutiny, Bengal became much less dominant as a province. The Company had overreached itself and the political and economic tangles of India, much of it still nominally ruled by the Moguls, had become impossible for it to deal with. The servants of this unique and uniquely profitable instrument must have regretted in many ways to see it disappear, absorbed by the British government and replaced by a bureaucratic administration. With the end of John Company, an era was closed in India, and especially so in Bengal, even though in that Presidency there had been no actual physical strife. But it was a long time before Delhi finally became the capital of British India; the old magic, the aura of command, hung over Calcutta, which remained the seat of power till 1912. After that it was only the capital city of the Presidency and the chief commercial center of the country. Hence the building, the mansions, the parks.

India was architecturally blessed in that two of her conquerors— the Moguls and the English—brought with them their best traditions of building. The cantonments which were constructed all over the country were Georgian. After that era there was little more building in the small places. When the Company was growing to its full strength and the number of merchant princes fast increasing, the houses built for them were of such grace and purity of line that not even the ineptitude and carelessness of the native carpenters could seriously mar them. Calcutta in those days must have been, in its European quarters, of a marked elegance. The ancient houses on Chowringhee, Loudon Street, Russell Street, even now retain beneath their crumbling plaster and mildewed facades the best of eighteenth-century English proportion—India's third legacy from Greece (the first came directly, with Alexander). Bombay, a hundred times more happily situated on the bright blue waters of the Arabian Sea, with a climate less enervating than poor Bengal must endure, cannot compare architecturally with Calcutta—Bombay is the flower of India's Victorian Gothic, while Calcutta, torn with riots, stricken by famine, ridden by municipal corruption, yet built in a time of good taste, remained under her shabby misery a city of quality.

Not having realized any of this before, I spent my first day in the city in a state of great surprise. I knew that there had been here, before the Europeans arrived, a village called Kalikata,* dedicated to Kali, the goddess of anger and destruction—and a singularly appropriate deity for the city she has proved herself. William drove us in that day, and proved as usual a good and cheerful guide, showing us Chowringhee, the green Maidan, Dalhousie Square, and Clive Street. Even here, in front of the modernity of the banks, strolled sacred Brahminy bulls, the incarnation of idleness, privilege, and complacency. Then we had lunch at Firpos, certainly one of the most agreeable of all the Calcutta landmarks, before plunging into Crawford's Market.

Gradually I saw more and more of the less fortunate aspects of a city which since that time has become always more crowded, more desperate, more unmanageable. This seems today to be the fate of many of the cities of India, but none perhaps has problems so terrible, and solutions so apparently unattainable, as Calcutta. There are just too many poor.

---

* Kalikata was the old name for the village around which Calcutta grew, and must not be confused with Kalicut, the Madrassi city on the Malabar Coast (from which our word "calico" is derived).

IV No. 1 Riverside

But when the mistress of a house is to be selected, a single individual must be found who will combine in her person many diverse qualities. It will not do to be too exacting.

. . . Then there is the zealous housewife, who regardless of her appearance, twists her hair behind her ears and devotes herself entirely to the details of our domestic welfare. . . . This is apt to be very trying.

The Tale of Genji

WE CAME INTO the bungalow in March, when the plains were beginning to work up in a crescendo towards the great heat of May. Even with a fan turning over us, the spring nights were inexpressibly sultry and we were genuinely glad to get up early. At that season there was no wind from the river, and the bungalow seemed to be perfectly airless. There was a sort of iron grill which the old-timers had had fitted into their French windows so that they could leave them open all night, but by the time we arrived none of these were to be had. Indian thieves are a legend: greasing their dark bodies, their bare feet making no sound on the stone floors, they are supposed to be able to glide into a bedroom and, not content with removing clothes and pocketbooks, even take the very sheets from under the sleepers. This sounded plausible, but even so we had to open the windows; and we had no thieves.

Aknis arrived before seven and took the baby out into the garden while the sun was still gentle. The servants would all come up to the pram and salute the child in deep tones—"*Salaam, Baba! Salaam Huzoor!*" Like all Orientals they loved babies.

The gardeners also started work early, as a concession to the schedule they had arranged for their day, which included a siesta

29

lasting from eleven to five. According to custom the head *mali* arranged the flowers himself. When we came out onto the veranda we would find our beturbaned gnome crouching before heaps of freshly cut blossoms which he had acquired by some sort of barter (certainly there was very little in flower in our garden) and earnestly putting them into vases. He had arranged a circle of these around him on the floor. That first mad *mali* was, in his gaudy, deluded manner, something of an artist, and for his short stay I let him daily startle us with his creations of scarlet hibiscus and golden laburnum, with marigolds alternating with pink zinnias and red roses. He selected yellow bowls for red flowers and loved huge bouquets belling out from small silver vases. It all went with the bizarre flavor of the day and induced me to forego the pleasure of doing the flowers myself.

In that early, buoyant mood, we sometimes played golf on the course near us, starting at six. It was lovely in the early light, the green fairways and immense trees standing out in the pearly air, tempered by river mists; but after a little while it seemed too hot to be worth it. We were becoming fast metamorphized into Bengalis: "Never stand up if you can sit down, never sit down if you can lie down." On our first Sunday we even went to play in the middle of the morning, and were astounded to find ourselves the only Occidentals on the course, while at four-minute intervals keen Japanese golfers teed off. Forty percent of the membership was Japanese! It was nine months before Pearl Harbor, and here to this little unfashionable course well out of Calcutta (where they all worked) but near the armament factories and the waterworks, these enthusiasts came unhindered. The whole area was under their steady, silent, trained observation till November of that year when they quietly melted away. Fresh from the China theatre, we were horrified to find these people our fellow-members, but no one else seemed sensitive to the danger nor did they feel any particular antagonism towards the country which was destroying China.

Every morning, as soon as Stanton had gone, I went to see the cook. Next to the bungalow a long arched arcade led to the kitchen, a huge hall with a lofty, pointed ceiling and walls colorwashed to a soft yellow. In one corner, eighteen inches from the floor, was a tap, under which a hole led out to the garden. This was the only taint of modernity in the room. In a corner twenty feet away from the tap stood a large mud stove, with a small niche built into its high back to hold the image of whatever god the presiding cook might find helpful to his art, and who might usefully be implored to keep the soufflés from falling. It was always shady here and relatively cool—the windows looked out upon a jungly part of the garden, so that the light came through a translucency of vines and palm leaves. Here there was a restful feeling of space and time for deliberation—it was the pleasantest kitchen I have ever seen.

On the floor stood the large rough stone on which the spices were ground—little red chilis, cloves, nutmeg, garlic, cinnamon, saffron. The cook had produced a miserable *chokra*, or apprentice, who cleaned the pans with a handful of ashes, fanned the charcoal fires of the stove with a wide palm leaf fan, pounded spices, and beat eggs, crouching on the floor. He was the cook's servant, not mine; we revolved in different orbits. This first cook assumed that I was new to the East and did not know the ways of oriental cooks any more than I understood Hindustani, and proceeded to bleed me at a more reckless pace than was prudent. At first Santu came with me as an interpreter, but very soon I had enough command of the language to go alone, *Hindustani Self Taught* in my hand.

I was to realize as time went by that this morning call on the cook was a significant event in the lives of the Westerners in India. To many it was a major contact with the people of the country and their ways—and this applied not only to the housewife and her servant, but to many a young officer, chosen to take care of the affairs of his mess. Later, as the army grew and new regiments came in, we made friends among the young men who were struggling with the domestic problems of their peers and many told us of their struggles with the cook, their rage and despair over the most absurd details. John, a debonair, highly intelligent young man whom we came to know, told me that to his surprise (for he was a mild-mannered person) he would find himself in a towering rage, screaming, even bursting into tears; and all his friends, in their turn, had the same experience. As for the *memsahibs*—it was the same story very often. Why? The choleric nature of India, the Western fury that arose when there seemed no way to stem a flood of tacit robbery?

Though not very mild myself, I did not feel this. Chinese servants being adept in the art of the squeeze, I had long acquaintance with the usual dodges, which I recognized were in play from the outset. But they are easier to recognize than to check. One had to pay for peace, but not too much or one would not only be robbed but be taken for a fool as well. And in many ways it was not robbery. It was a recognized (recognized to a degree) cut, exacted by a relatively poor man—in fact a very poor man—from a relatively rich (however that person judged himself) employer. The scale of wages was low because of the division of labor; there were no benefits, no insurance. It was unreasonable therefore to expect a more strict accounting. It was a case of what the market would bear, and the scales were so loaded in our favor that no sensitive conscience could really think this thievery.

The cook and his *chokra* would both salaam, after which the bazaar book, a small grubby affair, would be produced. In it all the morning's purchases would have been written out in English (of a sort) by a bazaar scribe, for which amenity I was daily charged six pies. I was also asked this sum for the services of the coolie who carried the day's provisions home, as the cook was too noble for such work and had to be followed by someone of lower status bearing a large, flat, shallow basket on his humble head. The *chokra* could not be spared from the kitchen at that hour, for it was his task to kindle the charcoal fires in the flat depressions on top of the clay stove. Electric stoves, refrigerators, and supermarkets may lack romance, but through them and like agencies how much individual degradation is obviated! My English neighbors usually did not agree with me: they contended that the coolie who carried the basket was fit for nothing more and was perfectly contented in his humble role, that "it doesn't matter what you do," and so on. A life spent on the lowest level of poverty, with real danger of starvation and no opportunity to raise oneself or one's family, did not seem a disaster to most of them. It was picturesque, it was convenient (while it lasted), it was cheap—and it was the custom. Were factories with their great numbers of laborers in the West (all of them literate) really instrumental in creating a happier state of society, they would ask. It was futile to argue that that was not the point.

The bazaar list was not a formality—it had to be checked. It seemed absurdly long, but every item was fully justified by the cook, who contended, with reason, that he had to buy small amounts every day in the great heat because the Frigidaire was so small it held very little. (After this first year we never had another; I was never able to count on keeping food at all.) Both the cook and I tacitly understood that he made a commission on every item. It seemed to me that I should not be so mean as to quibble over so many tiny sums—six pice for parsley, one anna for salt (didn't salt keep in the heat either, I wondered,) one anna for curry spices—but the total was rather surprisingly large. That is, however, the nature of totals. It was awkward to add up, as everything had to be divided by sixteen to compute the rupees and there was the further complication of pies and pice. There are four pies to a pice and twelve pice to an anna—or the other way around, I have forgotten now. A rupee was then worth a little over a shilling, and I was ashamed even to care about pies. It always ended by my accepting his arithmetic. Our salary, of course, was based on a cheap bazaar. In the spring of 1941, though prices had risen, it was still a workable basis.

The weights were computed in "seers," or two pounds, and I had not bought scales. The day's eggs were produced, and with them another little book of reckoning, entirely devoted to egg statistics. (How many decades of disputes between cooks and *memsahibs* had led to these records?) If I thought it impossible that we had used eighteen eggs yesterday, here it all was in black and white: so many for breakfast (do not forget the guest, *Memsahib*, who had two), so many in the soufflé, so many in the cake, in the *baba's* pudding. They were very little eggs, and cheap, but we did seem to use a staggering number. With the egg book in my hand, it was difficult to fence—perhaps he really had used them. Meanwhile the freshly scrubbed vegetables lay on the clean kitchen table, the pots and pans shone with cleanliness. I did not want to change my servant. It was evident that we could not possibly have eaten what he credited us with, but I was not a practical housekeeper. I had moved too often, and had had too many Eastern kitchens under my theoretical eye, to be wise in the minutiae of "just how much." This the cook understood, and he hoped to placate me by sending in meals which were always very good indeed.

All this bazaar intrigue was negotiated during our breakfast. In India the cooks did not get up early and do the marketing in time to cook the *sahib's* breakfast, as they did in China. Surprisingly enough for such a hot country, they were late risers—it was part of the general indolence. Here, too, a manservant might sometimes arrive quite late every day because he had to do the family shopping before his own work could claim attention, the women of his household being in strict purdah in spite of their straightened circumstances.

There seemed also to be a law against cooks making toast or

preparing sandwiches, these duties falling to the bearer or the *missolchi*. The *chokra*, however, might fry eggs, or the bearer would do it if his caste allowed it. Hardly anyone could even touch bacon—moving it from one shelf to another in the Frigidaire might be enough to lower a man in his next life cycle. The whole question of cooks was so intense, so involved, and varied so much from one individual to another that one rapidly became its victim and deep in the River of Sind in no time. For Hindus the most important thing about a cook is that he must be of a caste that will not defile his master's food by touching it. Thus a low-caste Hindu family might even have a Brahmin for their cook, if they could afford one, as in this way they are perfectly safe. Food is a major concern, often a major problem, in any country, but in India the complications surrounding it are so tremendous that sometimes one almost forgot that it was much ado about nothing and wasted time arguing over the details of this "turbulent and dangerous lunacy."

It was like being obliged to fence with shadows. If the cook, for instance, in the temporary absence of the bearer, announced that he could not bring a dish to the table as such an act would defile him, one had to defer. Shadows literally played a part in this vast mesmerism. The fear of the shadow of a man of lower caste contaminating food is so great that when the educated clerks in Stanton's office ate their lunches they retired each one separately to some secluded corner of the room and there would huddle in a hot cranny, even under a desk. An experienced and able engineer, who had for ten years worked in the Ford factories in Detroit, did the same as soon as he reentered the hypnotic web of Indian opinion. So much of the social life of the greater part of the world is played out round a table that one can hardly overestimate the effect of this teaching which forces men apart instead of drawing them together at such an hour.

One solution to the practical difficulties would seem to be to employ Muslim cooks, but, strangely, they are seldom as proficient as Hindus. Muslims were often thought to be, in general, less intelligent and were certainly in the main less educated than Hindus—but neither of these qualifications need apply to a cook, who should be a being of a rare order, beyond education in the ordinary sense, and who, if he is a true cook, receives his gift from on high. Perhaps the austerities of the Mohammedan faith are a drawback to the development of this art—though certainly even Islam has its soft and glittering aspect. But if it be supposed the

True Faith will interfere with the carnalities of the table, what of the Hindu who in his profession as cook makes nothing of cooking beef—his own sacred cow—or mutton or chicken for his master, though he himself may not even crush a mosquito without imperiling the passage of his soul? I would look about the kitchen, its low, creamy arches, its soaring ceiling and big yellow stove, while the little dark-legged boy stood before the glowing mounds of charcoal, slowly waving his palm-leaf fan, and have no inclination to spoil the scene by asking what had happened to all the mangoes and pomegranates he had bought yesterday.

The first month I did not lock up our few stores; that is a detestable business and I hoped I could dispense with it. But at the end of four weeks we found that we had used forty pounds of sugar and over ten of tea. The baby was still on a bottle and could not be deeply implicated in these figures; the cook claimed with unruffled poise that all this had been consumed by the lean *sahib* and thin *memsahib* and our few guests. After that I locked up everything and these amounts fell with astronomical swiftness to a more normal rate, but the cook was neither abashed nor discouraged. He just had to try some other system now. Every day after tiffin he went away, leaving the bearer to make tea. In the cool of the afternoon the artist returned to prepare our late dinner.

Having discussed the menus for the day with this sleek ruffian and yielded to his dubious accounts, I went back through the arcade, stopping at a side room to count clothes with the *dhobi* who came every day to wash in our house and wield his extremely large, high charcoal iron, scorning the electric one I offered him as beneath his powers. I did not wish to expose our embroidered Chinese linens and our clothes to the *dhobi ghats* where clothes are trodden out in common. There tanks, each about a yard square. were set under a high roof, and with a maximum of soda and a minimum of soap the clothes are beaten and stamped upon, the *dhobis* standing in the water, which rises above their thin, dark knees. I was as amazed to find that most Europeans patronized these places as I had been to find that *ayahs* were accepted; but while I did conform in the matter of *ayahs*, I held my ground about the *dhobis*. Washing was a serious problem—there was an immense amount to be done, with all the white trousers and shorts. *Ayahs* would only wash out some baby garments; a *dhobi* seemed inevitable, and in an ineffective country their efficiency was remarkable. Everything was put out in the brilliant sun to bleach and some care exercised that cows did not wander over the drying fields; the ironing, with the heavy old irons, was very good. *Dhobis* are necessarily of a very low caste or they would not undertake the work. We found them nearly always very quick and very intelligent, even though they believed themselves to be degraded. Our first *dhobi* was clean, honest, and quick; with any education he would have been quite formidable—had he been able to lay aside his caste.

Caste, caste, this invisible burden pervaded the very air—we could not forget it, we seemed unable to shake anyone's convictions about it. In our household I discovered that Santu was considered to be of a very mean caste for a bearer—he belonged to the leather-workers and came from Lucknow, a center for this craft. The *missolchi*, Allah Bux, was out of it all, being a Muslim, but he stood on his immunity from any work he did not wish to do as fiercely as the best. It was, for instance, beneath his honor to wash any windows save those in the drawing room. Aknis, being nominally a Roman Catholic, should not have felt any labor unworthy, but even she could not resist giving part of her work to Jummoo, the sweeper. I could not hand him a packet of seeds and ask him to give it to the gardener, because the latter could not have received it from his hand. Every simple act of service all day long had to be assessed from this preposterous attitude.

I found that my awareness and my distress in these caste enormities were not shared to any great degree by most of my acquaintances. They disapproved of the rigidity and the religious basis of caste but they lived with it calmly and generally accepted it without much demur. The British in India were seldom of a democratic turn of mind; in fact democracy itself was suspect in many circles in British India. I was appalled, time after time, to hear persons otherwise kind and fair repudiate democracy, not because they thought it unworkable, but because they did not want it. They did not consider it desirable in India and other countries which were largely illiterate and underprivileged—an arguable point of view—but even in England and the West in general they felt a better solution would be to have a governing élite, some form of benevolent dictatorship.

It was a momentous point in history when the British, repulsed in the West by the American colonies, turned eagerly, naturally, to the East—and entered another mental climate. The American Constitution embodied the great principles of law, liberty, and respect for the individual which had matured in England: this was the mother country's great legacy to the rebellious colonies. But the reactionary elements in England, always predominant in her long tradition, were nurtured by what they encountered in India, a country of extreme contrasts in the human condition, very autocratic, dominated by ferocious priesthoods in many regions. Caste seemed inevitable. The conquest of India demanded courage, imagination, physical bravery, and abstract justice, as well as mercantile adventurousness—all these qualities the British had and to spare. They had too, on occasion, much kindness. But social justice is something else again, and we are barely struggling towards it even now, anywhere.

England's Empire was not brutal, savage, or evil. But the terrible conviction of the innate superiority of the few, the tradition of a ruling class always given every advantage of education, opportunity, and position, had insensibly resulted in something like a *Herrenvolk*. It was a circle hard for the outsider to enter without wealth or genius. Persons who had grown up in this stratified society did not find the Hindu concept of a few privileged beings and the rest hopelessly and forever menial shocking. The Church of England had for centuries been telling their poor to be content with the lot to which God had called them.

It was not altogether in jest that the Indian Civil Service men called themselves "The Twice-Born"; they felt themselves in every way Brahmins, *The* Service.

The scornful Allah Bux, having dusted the drawing room, came towards me, salaaming, and gave me the book which held our orders for the local store, a list so artfully contrived that every day there was something fresh we had to have. This gave him the chance to go out and hear the bazaar rumors. It was an errand which always took him at least an hour though it might have been done in a quarter of that time—he had a bicycle and the bazaar was not far away. But in a country where time was of little or no consequence my viewpoint was held silly and womanish. Allah Bux liked to be away because he knew it irritated Santu, who would have set him to polishing silver or brushing clothes.

During this time the sweeper had gone over the stone floors, wiping the white dust away, and polishing them till they shone like cold mirrors, dark red and gleaming. The cool austerity of the floors was wonderfully refreshing to those coming in and out during the heat of the day, and were a shining surface for the bare brown feet of the servants. They afforded no cover to the myriad insects which haunted us; but they set off the rich colors of the rugs. It was easy to see why there were so many rug shops in Calcutta. We had only a few small Chinese carpets; I thought it impossible for us to buy Persian rugs on our salary. Then.

I was much more concerned with the sweepers themselves. Our landlady had promised us sanitation, but had not put it in. If we had stayed, if we had not been so out of pocket I would have installed a septic tank, but that was out of the question for us. I was constantly appalled with what this involved, as the sweepers' work included keeping the bathrooms clean. None of our neighbors in Barrackpore had proper sanitation. "Oh Charles doesn't mind," said the local military doctor's wife. "The sweepers are so good, we don't care if we have flushes or not." I looked upon these unhappy beings as men and brothers and could not bear to see their passive acceptance of their occupation, their deep, automatic resignation to their alleged inferiority.

The cities, and places like Ishapore with government buildings, now had proper sewage. American missionaries had furthered this work, installing septic tanks in their upcountry stations, often to the indignation of the local diehards, who first had to see sweepers become unavailable for this task before they approved the new sanitation. But many handsome, even luxurious, government bungalows a little off the beaten track had no sanitation. It took the war, inflation, and the threat, at last, of sweepers' strikes to force the authorities to consider the situation in all seriousness. The very humane major who administered the Barrackpore cantonment in our time could not understand my point of view. "Why," he said, "what else could they do? They would be unemployed if we put in sanitation!"

The mosquitoes would have been unemployed too, I suppose, if the houses had been screened: so we struggled with nets, punk sticks, and flit guns, slapping at our ankles and arms. The servants, most of whom slept on the ground wrapped up in their clothes like mummies, face and all, to avoid being bitten, took these trials stoically. The bearers could generally afford a *charpoi*, a wooden-framed bed with strings laced across it—not uncomfortable, but it gave them no advantage when it came to mosquitoes or the other insects which raged even more freely through their quarters. These were bare rooms in outhouses, rough and poor, but to them better than the homes they had had.

For their only light they used little earthenware lamps shaped like shells, very shallow and brittle, of a dull red color. These were filled with oil and had a floating wick; though they radiated only a dim light it was enough for people who could not read or sew, and in an archaic, humble manner they were beautiful. Under the courtyard tap which served their quarters was a stone tank, three feet square, and here they filled their big round earthenware *chattis*, plunging them under the surface till the air ceased to bubble up out of their long and slender necks. Being porous, they kept the water stored in them surprisingly cold. (Once on a train Stanton shared a compartment with an Anglo-India employee of the railways who had among his many pieces of baggage a *chatti*, neatly fitted into a wooden frame. Stanton remarked to him that this was a rather cumbersome arrangement, whereupon the gentleman replied that so it was, but how else was one to take drinking water with one?) None of the servants brought much more with them than a *chatti*, a lamp, and a few brass vessels to hold food.

The newer, government-built quarters were a little better—the floors of these places were often of stone and sometimes a small veranda with a brick stove would be built onto each room, but the Barrackpore bungalows were very old and primitive. But whether old or new we all had about ten quarters. Most of us did not have so many servants and there was quite a little business done in the matter of subletting rooms by the more lively of the staff. Workers coming in to the expanding factories found it hard to find anywhere to live; strangely enough the situation seemed to be exploited by the seemingly stupid *malis* more than by the other domestics—they were always asking permission to let a "friend" use an empty godown. William, who lived behind us in Barrackpore, had a number of empty quarters; being a bachelor he was able to engage fewer servants. He had, however, a large dog who was attended by a dog boy, a youth who appeared to be almost incredibly obtuse. One day the police called, complaining that this character had established a brothel in our friend's unused godowns. It became more and more evident that we were ourselves incredibly obtuse.

Aknis, however, did not live in our godowns—to my regret, as she was more needed as a resident than any of the other servants from my point of view. She was a Barrackpori herself and had a baby of her own, so when she first came to us in Ishapore I had not insisted on her living in the godown which the Stoddards offered her. She told us that she would stay with us when we came to Barrackpore, which seemed fair enough though it meant putting up with an arrangement by which she came late and left early.

A day or two after we had moved into the bungalow a caller was announced, a dapper soldier, very neatly turned out in a khaki uniform with highly polished boots and a Gurkha hat. He spoke good English and had such an impressive manner that I was half-wondering if he might possibly come from some southern European country, when I suddenly realized that he was Aknis's husband. He was, he explained with great dignity and respect, the head *durwan*, or guard, of the Governor's Park next to us where he had been allotted a whole compound to himself, quite large enough to house a number of his relatives (of whom the most important was clearly his mother). The ground surrounding his house, he told me, was sufficient for his cows and goats. This establishment he could not give up, obviously, yet Aknis equally could not come and live alone in one of our godowns, with menservants quartered near her and he only half a mile away. Would I therefore waive the custom of having the *ayah* live in? She would stay as long as we liked, and come at any moment. His request appeared so reasonable, his manner so polite, and I was already fond of Aknis so I could not refuse, although I knew that all this would prove a great nuisance to us, which indeed it did. I also realized that they had never intended Aknis to conform to the usual practice but had duped me. She had got her foot in the door—I would not have engaged her on these terms. Today, in a different world, any servant for a baby is so welcome that these terms seem sufficiently generous—but that was not true of the prewar world. Aknis therefore continued to come late and go early; she was not on hand in the evening if any impromptu plan arose, and she had no notion of time in any case. But I liked her so much by this time and I was pleased that she had so impressive a husband. As a soldier he had seen something of the world and had, besides, the proud and unconquered air of the Nepali, who speaks with assurance, in contrast to the plainsman, so often ingratiating or servile. Here was another individual, another situation, about which I was entirely stupid.

Aknis used to stay till the baby had had her lunch, after which she sang her to sleep with the time-honored *ayah's* lullaby, chanting it over and over again without any impatience or hurry to be away, till the child was still:

No. 1 Riverside

Nini, Baba, nini,
Machan, roti, chini,
Machan roti hoggia,
Chota Baba soggia.

This, as I well knew, was supposed to be a classic mistake; it would spoil Posy, who would always insist upon someone doing it for her. But it had no such effect and I rejoice that I never interfered with so pretty a scene. The little tune would reach me faintly through the high, darkened rooms, till Aknis slowly gathered herself up from the floor where she had been kneeling, and with a "Salaam, *Memsahib*" would slip out of the house onto the hot dust of the road which led to the Park, to her sons, her husband, her mother-in-law, her problems.

When I knew enough Hindustani for us to talk together I discovered that Aknis herself was not impressed by her husband's courtly charm. He drank, she complained, and so did his old mother. What they were really interested in was palm toddy. This man was Aknis's second husband; the first had been killed a dozen years before in the great Darjeeling earthquake. That man she had loved. He had left her with an infant son, and it was then that she had turned to the work of being an *ayah* and had become also a Roman Catholic. I could never find in her the faintest trace of any Christian doctrine (though she practiced many of the virtues), nor did she go to church, but some mission had, presumably, baptized her. She had then drifted about—not alone, I fancied—and eventually had married the *durwan*. Her second child, also a boy, was now a year old. She was certainly unhappy in this new marriage and, though I did not realize it, did not intend to put up with circumstances which she found uncongenial. Nepal has more men than women, who are accordingly highly valued. The "naughty Nepali" has as much spirit as her brother, the fighting Gurkha, and is something of a legend in those parts.

V The Green Veranda

Verde que te quiero verde
Verde viento. Verdas ramas.
El barco sobre la mar
y el caballo en la montana.
Con la sombra en la cintura
ella suena en su baranda.
Verde carne, pelo verde.

LORCA

IT WAS STILL quite early when these chores were over, and I would then go out onto the veranda, whose sweeping, liberal curve always gave me such pleasure, where long green bamboo blinds hung from the jilmils, and where the ceiling fan at least kept the air moving in slow hot spirals. The servants withdrew to their godowns to drink tea. There was a long interval of repose.

The true and just proportions of that minute corner of Bengal exerted a calm and stable influence on me—the world was spinning but here there seemed always to be peace and grace. Everywhere one turned there was shade, romantic color, and scent. The air was surcharged with heat and damp, with strong sunlight, with the fragrance of gardenia and neem, all muted by contact with this shadowy arcade. The foliage of the trees and vines was as green as glass, the hibiscus were scarlet, a row of young trees near the wall was veiled with wide, blowing mauve blossoms, and orchids grew on the boughs we had hung from the arches of the portico. The cicadas kept up an incessant din, till, suddenly, for just a moment they all stopped together and a span of true silence burst upon us like light.

Here I read, studied Hindustani, and began to get the feel of the country. The *Calcutta Statesman* revealed a great deal, not only in its news—and it was an excellent newspaper—but in many other columns. Under "Poultry and Livestock" it carried wonderful advertisements: "Wanted—Young female elephants. Staunch to tiger shooting." "Wanted—tame pure white Albino female Deer or Antelope with pink eyes." Tutors were in great demand, too: "Wanted—a Hindu first class or a high second class M.A. in English for the son of a nobleman in a hilly country." "Wanted—A tutor strong in Persian and Mathematics."

At appropriate seasons long regulations were published concerning the *hadj* pilgrimages, which came under the Government of India Commonwealth Relations Department. Great numbers of Indian Muslims made the journey to Mecca, returning with their hennaed beards and their assurance of a Paradise to Come; but first they had to fill in endless forms—even this pious journey was hedged about with paper. Prices were announced for Deck Pilgrims traveling by camel through the Hejaz. This was the cheapest way, and even so, costly enough, considering the poverty of many of the Faithful—it could not be done under a hundred and fifty pounds. "Name and address of the legal heirs of the applicant," "Signature or thumb impression of the applicant," "Applicants should send, preferably by money order, the following amount, being Jedda Sanitation Dues, Boat Hire and Kamaran Quarantine Fee. . . ." My ideas of that country being based chiefly upon *Arabia Deserta*, I found it difficult to envisage this journey connected with anything so prosaic as money orders, but so it was.

There used to appear from time to time accounts of the passage of a long and famous lawsuit over the case of one Kumar Narayan Roy, a very rich man who had been ill and had been finally considered dead. The funeral pyre was prepared, the body laid on it, and the torch was just to be applied when a violent storm broke out and the mourners ran for cover. When they returned the body had disappeared. Roy was not dead, and coming to his senses during the tempest had climbed down from his pyre. But he was not in his right mind. Somehow, in his confused state, he joined a troop of dancing dervishes, with whom he journeyed for twelve years. At the end of this period he happened to come back to his own district where he was recognized. Eventually he recovered his reason; then commenced a long struggle to recover his estates. The heirs contended that the plaintiff was an imposter. This fantastic case continued till 1946—right through the war. At last it was won by the man who had been laid on a pyre, had roamed the country impoverished and of unsound mind for over a decade, and then had to fight for nearly as long to establish his identity.

When a chance wind from the river blew the blinds away from the columns I could see the huge banyan at the far end of the garden in the black pool of its own shade, its long, tangled roots stretched out yearningly towards the earth, and behind it, through the brilliant light over the water, the Canaletto landscape of the far bank. Occasionally a big gray monkey would jump suddenly down from a tree onto the garden wall, where chipmunks scampered. Inside the house lizards disported themselves, green and dextrous, of a darting grace, and spiders wove their webs over the high ceilings. These were immense creatures. The sweeper had a twenty-foot pole with which he attacked their handiwork, but spiders never give up. Sometimes a small red scorpion made its way over the floor. Barefooted persons in hot countries are quick to see something like this—I never was. Loud shouts would ring out and he would be no more.

Lucy, an army bride who lived on the other side of the Riverside Road, used to come over to see me at this hour. She had been born in the country, of a family with a distinguished service record and many proud names. Her father had been killed in World War I and she had been sent to a school for officers' daughters in England. Now she was married to a man in an English regiment who was stationed briefly in Barrackpore. They were a lively young couple and we saw a good deal of them for a few months. Then Alec was sent over to Quetta to the Staff College, so they moved away forever. We saw him once more, on his way through to Rangoon in the early part of 1942. He was one of the first to fall in the city.

Lucy knew a great deal about cantonments and enlightened me in many ways. She was pretty, with beautiful eighteenth-century hands. She spoke good Hindustani, and together we considered how we could economize. With her I made an early morning trip to the bazaar and priced the eggplants and mangoes, the rice and curry spices directly, something the cook thought extremely under-handed of me. We also talked of the local wives' war effort and compared notes on how we thought things might be done in the cantonment. Everything in Barrackpore went on a traditional system based on the leadership of the *burra Memsahib,* who attained this eminence by being married to the man with the largest salary in the station. At that stage most of the activity was confined to knitting and work parties, which rested on talk of the kind that goes "and I said, and he said, and she said," so neither Lucy nor I went to them.

Stanton and I found our housekeeping very expensive as prices were steadily rising, the beginning of wartime inflation. Fifty rupees a month seemed a great deal to pay for rented furniture which we did not even like, so we decided to return these pieces to Calcutta and rent ours locally. There was a Mr. Nundy in the bazaar who engaged in this business and one hot Saturday we set out to find his shop. Barrackpore, in common with most Bengali villages, had a bazaar which was wholly dirty, hideous, and poverty-stricken, without any trace of the picturesque to lighten its misery. There was a large foul pool of stagnant water in it where *dhobis* were always washing, though to what end I am ignorant, and from there it extended in long wavy lines of narrow, dusty, ill-smelling lanes, past rows of shabby, flimsy tenements, till it worked itself out into the countryside and faded away. In these roads were naked children, thin women in dingy saris, and hostile-looking men. Mr. Nundy's shop and storerooms fitted easily into this background, and it took a good deal of subtracting in our checkbook before we could bring ourselves to furnish our beloved bungalow from his establishment.

Mr. Nundy himself received us, very amicably, in his shop where he sold provisions and drink. He was a large fat Hindu, speaking good English, dressed in a shirt and *dhoti*, his feet in loose leather slippers. We asked to see his furniture and he led us to his godowns, of which there were several some few doors away down a lane, to be reached only after successfully bypassing a few sacred cows who were almost blocking the way. The godowns were very evidently never swept, never dusted, never aired, and cobwebs and cockroaches had here full play. I shrank from the thought of having anything in the house which had come from this loathsome quarter, but Mr. Nundy supplied all our needs for a third of the Calcutta figure, and the military families went to him without a tremor Lucy had told me, so we steeled ourselves to find the less revolting pieces stacked in the gloom of the dark rooms, which were piled to the ceiling with dirty chairs, couches, wardrobes, and bureaus. Those we pointed out were dragged into a courtyard by some lean coolies who wiped the surfaces of the dressing tables and desks with black and noisome rags. I asked Mr. Nundy why he did not keep his shop clean and make the furniture look more attractive. He replied, "Why?"

The furniture was all old and had probably been hired out by three or four generations to their contemporaries in the Indian Army, but it had never been any good—the firm had battened on short-term customers in a desperate market. The wood was poor and shoddy, the designs heavy, ornate, and Victorian. Against the walls of the godowns leaned large black oval tabletops, this potentially lovely curve so mishandled that the effect appeared misshapen. But we took one, and some of the cane chairs with the extending arms for the cavalry leg. The cupboards and wardrobes were frightening "great big black things" and the upholstery of the cane couches was so dreadfully grimy that we almost weakened. Mr. Nundy was perfectly unmoved at our dismay; he knew very well it made no difference—we would hire his things. A tailor was called in from nearby and new covers were ordered, and Mr. Nundy solemnly promised every single piece of furniture would be washed before it was carried to our house on someone's head. (Washed in the pond, I wondered. I knew it would be useless to ask.) And after a few days we got used to the effect of the pieces, which were in their way very suitable, and we became reconciled to them. We forgot about the godowns. This was, of course, the secret of Mr. Nundy's success with all his customers.

With this dark furniture in the rooms the floors looked peculiarly bare. It was hopeless even to think of buying rugs, but I decided I could at least be informed so that I could recognize those I saw in our neighbors' bungalows. I took some books on oriental carpets out of the Barrackpore Club Library and even made a chart for myself as I read, the better to remember the borders and medallions, the knots, the chief places where they were made.

Everything fits together, ultimately. One morning, when I had a few designs and colors firmly in mind, a vendor stood under the portico, calling out that he had Persian rugs to sell. I told Santu to send him away. But the rug *wallah* was already insinuating himself through the wide open doors and in beguiling tones urging me only to look at his beautiful wares. There was no need to buy, had I no pleasure even in looking at Persian rugs? I assured him I could not buy. While these few remarks passed between us he had crossed the entrance hall, entered the drawing room, and placed a few long dark rolls on the floor. What could be more tempting? A rug in that situation cries out to be unrolled.

The rug *wallah*, a master salesman in his long fitted Muslim jacket and red fez, bent and lightly unrolled a Prince's Bokhara, a Shiraz, and a strange and beautiful rug, dark purple with a diamond pattern of dull old gold, tawny and rich. I asked him what it was and I was lost. We were soon deep in animated conversation. He told me the third rug was a Yakub Khan. I knelt and counted borders and knots, reiterating that I had no money and could not buy anything. Money, said he, who wants money? Money was of no interest to him, he said. But did I have anything to exchange perhaps for a few carpets? What, for instance, I asked. "Baldwin *Memsahib* at number X," he replied, "has just given me five silver tea sets for some rugs." I was naive enough to be startled by this intelligence. How could Mrs. Baldwin have had five silver tea sets to exchange? I had never even heard of anyone owning five, except perhaps the Queen. We had all been earnestly cautioned in the Inspectorate against ever accepting any gift, receiving anything at all, even if it appeared to be the most innocent and friendly offering. Of course the Baldwins were not in government service, and they had been long years in the country . . .

Anyway, I was not going to part with any of my silver. The servants were very expert at cleaning it and I had more use from my wedding presents in India than I have ever had since—generations of polishing army accoutrements and mess silver, let alone brass bowls from Benares, had produced *missolchis* and bearers who were able to extract the last gleam of light from a Georgian bowl. The rug *wallah* read my thoughts, and cocked his head to one side. "An old car?" he asked.

We had bought an old car, a very old car, when we came and it was already a dismal failure. It was an Armstrong Siddeley which drank our (rationed) petrol like a fish and generally refused to go. Stanton was now bicycling daily to the factory on a machine rented from Mr. Nundy, who was becoming the essential prop of our lives. I agreed that perhaps he could have an old car, but that we would have to wait till the *sahib* returned for lunch and entered into our arrangements, which, in principle, were that the car was to be exchanged for three rugs, one of which would be the Yakub Khan.

Soon afterwards Stanton appeared with William, who had driven him back. They were surprised but enormously amused to hear of the scheme the rug *wallah* and I were hatching and William pointed out that Stanton could use the rugs as flying carpets for transport. Stanton's pleasure in these lovely objects, particularly the Yakub Khan, was only tempered by his fear that the Armstrong Siddeley would not start. It so seldom did; probably the deal would fall through. We warned the rug *wallah* that he was bargaining for a very battered object but he said that his nephew knew all about cars and would soon put it in order. To everyone's delight the old car roared like a tiger and shot out of the garage on our first attempt to start it. The rug *wallah* stipulated only that he should have just a little something more and I generously threw in Posy's pram—she had just begun to walk and scorned it now anyway. The baby who appeared the next year never had a pram on this account. But we are still using the rugs, which have given us thirty years of beauty and comfort.

In the brief twilight, after Stanton had come home, we used to walk on the foreshore and watch the boats. Sometimes Aknis and the baby came with us, the hill woman striding along on the low bank, holding herself regally, the blond child on her shoulder, both intently watching the sails. When the tide and the wind worked together a line of wooden country boats would ride up on the flood like Roman galleons, their wide square-cut sails bellying out above the brown water with rich and subtle colors—tangerine, yellow ochre, burnt sienna, ultramarine. The vessels were clumsy and unadorned—seen at close quarters they had neither craftsmanship nor line to admire—and to our eyes, accustomed to the carved and shining beauty of junks, they were pitiable affairs; but seen sweeping the water in this bold diagonal of color, they partook of the glory of all ships, being wedded to the wind, and its unseen, fickle strength.

The wide grassy river margin, sparsely planted with thin and brittle tamarisks, ghostly and gossamer by moonlight, offered an open and lonely place for our promenades—it was surprising how few people ever wandered there. It afforded a fine, distant view of the heavens, and as the season drew on towards the rains, it was from this vantage point that we could best watch the towering cumulus clouds piling themselves up in vast edifices. Cattle sometimes grazed on the meager pasture by the water and at the far end, beyond the cantonment, were often herds of blueblack water buffaloes. Up in the high trees of the neighboring gardens, overlooking the scene, sat vultures, waiting in a horrible, keen-eyed patience. Sometimes we came upon the newly-shed skins of cobras, the pouch that had held the hood still firm and round. At night packs of jackals coursed here, howling.

Behind this strip lay the white-columned bungalows of the cantonment; set off by their splendid trees, their wide lawns, and deep flower beds, they appeared the very beau ideal of Southern homes. Seen from this angle, nothing could have been prettier in the way of a town, less involved with cobras, vultures, jackals, and appalling, insoluble human problems.

From Government House and the Park this green foreshore extended for nearly a mile, confronting the once Danish settlement of Serampore and long stretches of jungle across the river. Further upriver came Chandernagor, then under control of the Free French. Someplace here there had once been a Portuguese settlement which had been destroyed by the Moguls and seemed to have left no traces at all. Serampore still had certain fine old buildings from its colonial days—a church, a handsome theological college with many columns adorning its facade and guns at its portals and a good entrance to its main *ghat*, whence steps led down to the water. These, seen across the river, gave us much pleasure, though they seemed rather incongruous in that hot and languorous setting.

Most of us had no idea of the significance of this town or realized what a role it had played in its day. For it was here at Serampore that the Baptist missionary William Carey worked—here the presses had been set up that issued over forty translations of the Scriptures into oriental languages. To those who knew this the place had an almost Pentecostal aura.

Carey, a poor and humble cobbler with a genius for languages, entirely self-taught, came out to India at the end of the eighteenth century, burning with evangelistic fervor, and in spite of every imaginable obstacle. The Company wanted no missionaries and at home Non-Conformists had no encouragement from anyone. He was entirely without influence and almost penniless; but everything gave way before his faith, his genius, persistence, and industry. Though even now not really widely known, he was one of the great men of his age.

Unable to sail in a British ship because the Company would admit no missionaries, he came out on the Danish East Indiaman, the *Kron Princessa Maria*. At first he supported himself and his family by growing indigo, while rapidly mastering Bengali. He had, while at his bench in England, taught himself Greek, Latin, Hebrew, French, and Dutch; before he had been many years in India he knew Sanskrit, Marathi, Gujarati, Oriya, Persia, Arabic, and a number of other tongues and dialects well enough either to teach them or to supervise translations into them.

A Danish trading company had in the middle of the seventeenth century bought twenty acres of land on the west bank of the Hooghly, naming their property Frederiksnagar. Eventually it was absorbed into British India but during its long era of independence it earned its own immortality. It had already been renamed Serampore by the time Carey arrived and was under the aegis of a pious governor. Due to the kindness and practical help of this official the band of missionaries which gradually collected on the shores of the river was able to settle on Danish soil and there erect a paper mill, a type foundry, and presses.

Carey was followed by the master printer Ward and another able and God-fearing individual, Marshman, who arrived on the *Criterion*, a vessel whose American Captain Wicker also did all in his power to help them. These men plunged into the study of languages, the translations of the Bible, and the founding of schools and churches. They met at first with great opposition from the British, but with interest and sympathy from many Indians. Their cause prospered amazingly and came to receive recognition and support. Lord Wellesley, the Governor-General, was so furious when he learned that the Bible had been translated into Bengali that he determined to have the presses destroyed forthwith (arguing that British rule could not be maintained if the natives were taught that they were the equals of their masters); yet he eventually became so amiable and friendly that he eagerly supported Carey as a teacher of Bengali, Sanskrit, and Marathi at the newly-formed college at Fort William established to train Englishmen to become administrators. Most of the pupils were young, recruited in England for the East India Company, and had had very little education.

The astonishing Carey interested himself in a score of fields. Horticulture fascinated him; he laid down a famous garden at Serampore following Linnaean principles; he advocated scientific forestry in India; he urged the establishment of savings banks for the rural poor; all the while pressing on with translations not only of the Bible, but simultaneously putting the Ramayana and the

Mahabharata into English. Because of him, even while Sydney Smith was fulminating from the pulpit of St. Paul's in London against "these ignorant and low-born preachers," the first missionary societies were founded in London, in America, and in the Netherlands.

Carey was so modest and self-effacing that he wished no mention of himself to remain, no monument, no personal traces. In a way, he had his wish. Almost no one in Barrackpore, I am sure, had ever heard of him, and even in Serampore one could wander through the small settlement quite ignorant of these great events. It was martial glory and administrative skill that interested the conquerors of India. In Barrackpore Park there were many monuments to commemorate heroes of old battles and there was even one for a favorite horse—this was not the sort of place that cared about men like missioners.

VI The Turning Year

Under the connecting feeling of tropical heat
and vertical sunlights, I brought together all
creatures, birds, beasts, reptiles, all trees
and plants, usages and appearances, that are
found in all tropical regions, and assembled
them together in China or Hindustan.

DE QUINCEY

. . . Laburnaum, rich
In streaming gold

WILLIAM COWPER

THE SPRING and the fall are Bengal's two hardest seasons and of
these two the spring is the more difficult, as the earth has then
for so long been unvisited by any rain. In the fall at least the
monsoon has left its traces. By March the poor cattle stray mournfully over the *maidans*, searching for the least blade of grass. Sacred
they may be held, but they are generally quite uncared for, and in
these seasons reach a pitch of emaciation which sickens the heart.
Every bone stands out and their beautiful eyes shine only with
mild despair. However, we found that though we were truly sorry
for these beasts, we were unprepared to sacrifice our garden to
them.

One night soon after we had moved to Barrackpore I was
wakened by strange sounds in the garden, heavy, muffled noises.
Going to the French doors and peering into the dark, I was
astounded to see cows everywhere, wandering about and tearing
up the borders. It did not seem possible, the gates were shut; was
I dreaming? I woke Stanton and it was evident that we were

sharing the same dream. He rushed out and began driving them out of the garden, or trying to, as they were far from eager to go. There were about ten of them. The gates were still shut.

The servants heard his shouts and emerged from their godowns. This was quite normal, they implied. Someone had driven them in to feed. This incident was repeated several times till we found the way to stop the unknown owner—we arranged with the local pound to collect the animals and not to give them up till a fee was paid. This was the only method open to anyone who had a garden he wanted to preserve.

Not that ours was anything to boast of then. It was already too late, that first March, to try and do much with it till the rains began. It was in a pitiable state, the jungly grass sere and dry and a few wretched zinnias drooping in hard beds. That our *mali* was an absolute failure held us back further. After our first rapid plunge into the domestic market we became much more cautious in hiring servants. A trained gardener, we found, was a rara avis and quite expensive, and an untrained *mali* as a rule was untrainable. Aside from their phenomenal stupidity (from our angle), these gardening Uriyas are excessively given to leisure and are miracles of slow motion—they could easily spend a whole hour in potting one small plant, and that not the one you wanted to have in that flowerpot. But somehow we managed to keep some thin and aimless figure wandering among the luxuriant bushes and watering the borders. And the trees were always beautiful. The Governor's Park, which was next to us, was beautifully tended and planted with rich and marvelous borders and I used to study these, wondering what small sections of them I could emulate.

It was a lovely place and open to us all. In the old days it had been only for the governors-general and their circle, and after Pearl Harbor the army got it—but for this brief hour we could all enjoy it. Some of the lodges were occupied by civilians in war work. They had been intended for aides-de-camp and were very fine, elegant places indeed with their white columns and pediments. Many records exist of the Park, Emily Eden's and Curzon's probably the best known.

The official who managed this charming place was an eager botanist and kept it in remarkable condition, every tree cared for, nothing wild or jungly—it was like an English park. He particularly hated palms, with their ragged, disorderly silhouettes, and told me once that if he had his wish he would uproot every one in Bengal.

Still, he had to endure the presence of a few of them in his own domain, but they were not noticeable beside the vast banyans, the gold mohurs, the mango trees, the famous clump of feathery bamboos, and the wealth of laburnums. These last are much lovelier in India than in the West, much more golden. They framed the monuments. The most beautiful of these was the replica of the Maison Carrée—but much more perfect here than in Nimes, as here it was white and embowered in trees, a perfect Greek temple. It had been put up by the Earl of Minto as a memorial to the heroes who fell in the conquest of Mauritius and Java in 1810 and 1811. (True to the manners of the times, those remembered were all officers.)

In a remote part of the estate, screened by a sheltering copse, was the grave of Lady Canning, a high white marble sepulcher, heavy still with an atmosphere of deep grief. She and Canning had been devoted to one another and together suffered from the censure of public opinion during the Mutiny. Everyone was quick to condemn the Governor-General for his slow start and his early sanguine telegram: "Take Delhi with all despatch." His insistence that vengeance should not prevail at the end was unpopular; people called him "Clemency Canning" with a sneer. The British soldier has seldom felt much personal animosity after the fighting is over but during the Mutiny that was not true and for a time every one of them was eager to butcher every Indian he encountered, in memory of the women and children who had been thrown down the well at Cawnpore. Canning restrained this passion. Afterwards he returned to London and was loaded with honors; a few months later he was buried in Westminster Abbey. One could sense his sorrow at leaving his wife, as he felt, alone there in India under the dark circlet of the trees in that great imposing tomb.

Barrackpore was, in fact, a mortuary little place. On the outskirts of the cantonment, set far back from the road behind a green *maidan*, was an old walled enclosure. Bicycling past one evening, we went in wondering what it was—and found an old cemetery, pitiful, forgotten. It was fully tenanted by the former occupants of the Riverside bungalows—chiefly young wives and their infants who had passed away a century or more earlier. The average age carved on the elaborate tombstones or on the tablets set in miniature Greek temples (for the grace and elegance of this sad garden equaled that of the bungalows) was well under twenty. It was a rarity to come upon an inscription for anyone over twenty-five. Here were also many subalterns—boys fresh from England—most in their teens. All were eulogized after the style of the times, without restraint, with unbounded grief.

One family had lost a baby, aged from a few weeks to a few months, every single year for six consecutive years—I remembered the soldier's wife in *Cranford* telling of losing six babies in "Cruel India" and finally parting from her husband that she might rear the seventh safely in England. It was a terrible little enclosure, still full of desolation and grief, so much so that I could not profane it by even copying any of the inscriptions.

It is not generally known that it was Florence Nightingale who changed the whole pattern of life in India, once fraught with such hygienic hazards. She was too late to affect graveyards like this one in Barrackpore but at last her recommendations were accepted and put into effect in all the cantonments. She came to this enormous task (without ever visiting the country) through her overwhelming interest in the lot of the British soldier, first in the Crimea, then in England and other places where he served—which meant, so often, India. After she had won her immense position in the Crimean War she used the power it gave her to continue pushing through reforms, pressing on with her battle against official resistance and red tape. She interested herself in the (then) new field of statistics and sent out letters and questionnaires to all the military cantonments, realizing that it would be necessary to strike at the root of the problem by, as much as possible, cleaning out the bazaar areas. Her patience and perseverance, her amazing grasp of detail, her capacity for organization, at last resulted in such improvements that the conditions of life for the troops were radically altered all over the subcontinent—and even the more fortunate, the civilians and the officers, benefited.

Then service abroad virtually meant service in India. The conditions in the barracks were appalling—as they had been in England before Miss Nightingale turned her attention to them and investigated the reasons for the high degree of mortality in the London barracks. The dormitories were terribly crowded, unventilated, dirty; the men had no place to go in their free time—no opportunities for sport or recreation. Their only respite was to go to the bazaar and drink. Their uniforms were hot and tight, their food was bad. Their officers generally thought them fit for nothing else—the common soldier was then not respected. It was the Crimea which had forced public opinion to acknowledge his worth, his heroic patience, his immense bravery.

Through Florence Nightingale's years of labor conditions in India improved so much that the troops began to return to England after their service in much the same numbers as they went out. Everyone became aware of the importance of pure water, fresh food, ventilation, sewage. Insects were at least discouraged (though even in our time the houses were not screened). Tolerable barracks were built and the quarters for married men, though often still mean and dingy (as they certainly were in Barrackpore in 1940), were at least sanitary. John Lawrence was one of the men who worked with Miss Nightingale in this; a difficult and tyrannical figure, he was here, as always, distinguished for his essential common sense.

And yet, in those decades of sudden death and sorrow, how pretty Barrackpore had been, and it was still charming in its favored district, with those bungalows of classic design and noble facades whitewashed every year by administrative order (till Pearl Harbor, after which they were covered with an olive green paint, dreary indeed!). Each one was different, yet they were all of the same vintage, all Regency, all flat-roofed, laid out from a central room, high-ceilinged, with porticos and columns. Some were very large—one near us had a drawing room sixty feet long and was locally known as Buckingham Palace. They were ill-made and uneven in finish if you examined them, but it never showed, it seemed to make no difference. Bengalis are in general not craftsmen, the carpenters could not keep pace with the designs in detail, but in spite of that the effect was perfectly harmonious.

We came to know a little—not much—about some of them: that No. 6 Riverside, in our day belonging to a mission school, had for many previous decades been the officers' mess for whatever regiment had been quartered in the cantonment; that No. 7 belonged to the Maharajah of Gwalior and nearly always stood empty, with its long lane of tall royal palms leading up to the veranda columns, seeming to correlate with them architecturally; and then there was No. 14, the queen of them all, truly a beautiful house.

Like Gwalior House it had a curved drive, lined with lofty palms, astonishingly matched in height, going up to the entrance portico which was supported by ten magnificent Corinthian columns. The bungalow was very large, with many great rooms—one oval—and there were elaborations here not found in the other houses, such as carved and molded doors and cornices, treated with delicacy and restraint. For whom had it been built? It had certainly gone up before the Mutiny, more we could not discover. People came and went and left no traces. It was one of the most stately and imposing houses I ever saw anywhere in the world, yet there was a certain sweetness about it. The servants' quarters stretched away in a long creamy line of arcades and arches, delightful to gaze upon, though impossible to defend as dwellings.

Inherited jointly by three Bengali brothers whose mutual antagonism overbore their avarice, the property had been so desperately contested that its value had become of minor importance to them. In their jealous struggle they could not agree to put it in order, to rent it or to sell it, nor would they live in it themselves. We knew an Englishman who had offered to pay a substantial sum towards its repair if he could then rent it, but the brothers could not agree on any arrangement. In the end, lamentably, the army commandeered it after Pearl Harbor and dismantled the most ruined portions (we had been almost afraid to go into it, the columns appeared so shaky it seemed quite possible that our passing might bring one down). They turned it into a storehouse. The lovely drawing rooms were filled up with crates; the Corinthian columns and the noble facade were knocked down.

March went into April and May and the days grew ever hotter and dryer. Santu and Allah Bux sparred, Santu and the sweeper fell out, but Aknis was unruffled, serene, even happy. She used to come back to us in the afternoon with bouquets of red roses, which she arranged in vases in the nursery—afterwards I was to ponder upon those crimson clusters but then, as she slipped in through the shutters and, smiling with relief at being out of the sun, began to sort out the blossoms, I was still quite innocent of what they might imply. If the *baba* was still asleep, Aknis would throw herself down on the stone floor beside the cot and fall asleep herself, stretched out under the fan. I did notice that she often seemed very sleepy but I attributed it to the heat. The heat was the great excuse for everything—an all-embracing cause for any distemper of mind or body. The climate of India is very useful in this way.

I love heat and, as the Chinese put it, have "experienced great heat" many times and in many different places, from the Red Sea to the dog days in the Yangtze Valley; but I found no pleasure in the heat of the Bengali spring. It is not as hot and certainly no more humid than a China summer on the Yangtze or in Canton, but it possesses a destroying quality, enervating, dank. As the cicadas grind on and on, one understands just how the grasshopper becomes a burden. There seems no air to breathe, no song to sing; the piano is unopened the whole day long. One is caught in a heavy web of inanition, it is an effort of will to pick up a book; from outside a hot wind, not strong enough to sway the blinds, blows in the white dust. And yet, though half within the trance myself, I knew in my heart that this was all nonsense. The men worked as hard (the Europeans, that is), the children played as actively as they would have done anywhere. Munitions were pouring out of the factories, all over India production was rising. The children were full of ideas and games, creating little gardens by sticking bright flowers into the earth under the trees, chasing each other, pretending to be monkeys. And one did not suffer from the climate as one can in the cruel northern winters—nor did it create parallel anxieties.

One morning Santu came to me in a black rage. Either he or the sweeper, he said, would have to leave—and immediately. The sweeper would not obey him. Santu was proving himself a good and agreeable servant and the sweeper an indifferent one; though we did not like being presented with an ultimatum it was unquestionably serious. Stanton accordingly found Jummoo a job in the factory, which certainly meant progress for him, and thither he betook himself. We ourselves had had no passages of arms with him, but he was a surly, strong-willed man and between him and the softer-seeming but imperious Santu there was some irreconcilable element. I had pity for the sweeper, I did not see how any young, vigorous man could endure such employment. A new sweeper was produced almost out of a hat, and had obviously been waiting in the wings for this denouement.

I hope we did not deserve some of the servants we had in India, but I do not dare to assume either that we ever deserved Jai Dyal Sefaz, an old man with a truly saintly character. He was tall and strongly built, with big gray military moustaches, and came from a village near Delhi. After a few days his extreme reserve melted away before our friendliness and he revealed himself as an astonishing expression of many virtues—he was good, patient, devoted, industrious, honest; from him one could see how noble the outcaste (or any hopelessly oppressed person) can be, rising above the miseries of his earthly experience into a spiritual gentleness which asks nothing and gives all it has. He was with us a year and became a sort of marvel to me—a Superior Man in the Confucian sense. He was never angry, never resentful, always willing. In that Bengal setting he shone like a star; quite unaware of it himself—indeed one had the impression that he never thought of himself.

Meanwhile Allah Bux, the *missolchi* (a being of quite another sort but considering himself naturally infinitely superior to any sweeper), proceeded rapidly towards his fall from grace. He stood as jealously on his rights as any trade union man, fencing continually with Santu. Santu, for instance, would bring in the tea tray but would not take it out—that was for the *missolchi*. They were maddened by their dislike of each other. We knew that we would have to let one or the other go, and Santu was much the better servant. But we delayed in taking the fatal step, so horrible is it to sack anyone, till Santu again came to us with, "Either Allah Bux or I goes today." Alas, Santu's second success turned his head; he felt now that he was master of the ship. But for a season we had peace.

The older son of the Santu family, a lad of fourteen, came in as *chokra* to his father and soon was doing twice as much as Allah Bux, and that more deftly. He was, moreover, overjoyed with his work and extremely proud of it. Santu beamed on his docile, handsome child and harmony reigned. There was no question of the boy going to school—for such poor persons there was no opportunity and it was better to have him employed with us than idle. It was then that I became friendly with Mrs. Santu, a fat and amiable woman with a gold nose-ring who lived in the quarters and spent her long hot days contentedly doing nothing. It seemed to me that it would be a good thing if I taught her to knit: she could then make khaki scarves and pullovers as her gentle contribution towards the war effort, besides gaining a useful accomplishment. She did have some vague idea that there was a war going on somewhere and was in any case used to the idea of soldiers and garrisons, having lived in many cantonments where her husband had found work—the Santus came from Lucknow and he had more often than not been employed serving officers.

Every morning after she had swept out their room with a bunch of twigs she came to the veranda, giggling, embarrassed, and shy but clearly very pleased with this new exciting development in her life. She was a betel nut enthusiast, her teeth and gums stained bright red by this mild narcotic and her person and clothes smell-ing of it, but otherwise she had a good appearance though she looked very much more than her age—she was probably about thirty and looked forty-five, so quickly do poor Indian women age.

Like most women of her walk of life in India she could not sew, and her hands were so stiff and rough, even though her housework had been negligible, that the gestures necessary for moving the two slender knitting needles nimbly—and especially that of throwing the wool over one of them with an extended forefinger—seemed for many days quite beyond her powers. Babu, her younger son, came with her and picked up the art in no time, which was evidently just what his adoring mother expected. He immediately fell in love with knitting and made great progress with a scarf. Mrs. Santu and I persevered; she had an attractive doggedness. While her fingers slowly became more dextrous, Santu would come out onto the veranda and discuss knitting with me; purling, shaping, casting off, and then go over all my remarks with her. Before we left Bar-rackpore she had made by herself a khaki pullover, to the family's immense pride.

The Barrackpore *memsahibs*, when they learned that I was train-ing a native woman to do the knitting I should morally have been doing myself, they thought, were scandalized. It was a matter of principle, they felt, to knit oneself and most of them were so ex-pert that they could knit in the cinema, turning heels in the dark without even thinking about it. I had been told in Hong Kong by the director of a great firm that all this amateur knitting was not necessary, as a few machines could turn out an equal volume of garments in a very few hours, but the ladies in the Colony insisted on doing it anyway. It made them feel they were actively par-ticipating in the war; they had servants, they had ample leisure, they did not read. I understood their point of view, provided they did not demand that everyone share it. Anyway, Mrs. Santu did acquire in this way one small weak weapon between herself and dire need should the case arise.

Early in June swift storms began to blow over us but no rain fell—how we longed for the great, beautiful clouds to break! But day after day, night after night, brought nothing but more heat, more dust. The clouds were magnificent high above us. To watch clouds is one of the pleasures of life, and cumulous clouds in pale hot blue skies are particularly evocative and lovely. Little tender clouds lay along the horizon, swelling up as the day advanced into an ever-changing, shifting pageant of white billows. The colors of the earth became intensified; we seemed to be in the midst of some gigantic change of scene in a titanic play. At the horizon the sky was the most bewitching shade of greenish-blue, the color of a shell; at the zenith it lost this subtlety and was a strong pale, burning blue.

At last the rains broke, and with them the tenor of life changed. I loved the rains, that year and every year, though the house leaked like a sieve and everything streamed and steamed with dampness. Storms broke over us, bringing torrential downpours and sharp breaths of Himalayan air—cold, pure, and free. Sheet lightning flickered over the gardens and bazaars. The dusty lanes became rivers of mud, and the *maidans* and paddy fields and gardens turned as green as emeralds overnight. Vast rafts of flowering purple water hyacinths swept down the river and grew on pools and tanks, almost choking the surfaces. In a few days the cattle had lush grass to eat and their poor bones began to be covered.

Little deadly kraits lay between the slats of the jilmils, taking shelter. Men were called in to repair the roof but their work was never effectual and buckets stood all day in the rooms catching the noisy drops—in rooms made dark by the heavy clouds outside. For months everything that had been washed was dry in an hour or two—now it seemed that the clothes were always wet. But nothing mattered anymore, everyone was so much better tempered, everyone had relaxed.

In that first monsoon we went through a Pharaoh's curse of frogs. Scores of them hopped wildly into the bungalows in the evenings. This struck me as an astonishing phenomenon; there was, however, a risk that they might be followed by hungry snakes, so we could not stop to wonder in what way we resembled the Egyptians—we chased them out as wildly as they had entered. We had to evolve a technique for putting sackfuls of leaping green creatures out through the long windows—it is not easy to drive frogs as you will. Happily the visitation did not last long. "And the river shall bring forth frogs abundantly, which shall go up and come into thine house, and into thy bedchamber, and upon thy bed, and into the house of thy servants, and upon thy people, and into thy ovens, and into thy kneadingtroughs." This was an exact picture, evidently drawn by an eyewitness.

It was during one of these days when the rain was pelting down in bucketfuls—within and without—that we learned that Hitler had broken his Russian pact and had started to invade the Ukraine. Like most people then, we believed that the Russians could put up only the weakest resistance—had not Finland shown us how feeble the Russians really were? As the summer went on and the Russian front held, or at least did not collapse, we were as astonished as the rest—astonished and grateful, for now the pressure on England was eased. We were encouraged, at last the war was turning, a little. When I think of that first monsoon, the picture that comes to me is of groups of white-clad men sitting on verandas in the evening, with the rain streaming in long streaks on the green gardens (the kind of rain Hiroshige painted), while we all read the papers and discussed the swift advance of the Germans across those far-off plains of Eastern Europe.

For years in China, long before 1937, the danger of the Japanese had been with us, constant, menacing, but here in India it was the European and African theatres which occupied our anxious attention. The U-boat campaign, the raids on London, America's hesitancy, made us half-forget the Japanese War—a luxury we were not to enjoy much longer.

Aknis

When I needed to go into Calcutta for a day's shopping I was loath to leave my baby alone with all the unknown people in our house, and as we had friends in the city I often took her and Aknis with me, leaving them in a cool flat while I went to the bazaar. Aknis loved this and was always delighted to see the city, making herself as smart as possible in the new saris and blouses we had given her. Our friends' flat was several flights up in a building which had an automatic lift. I did not explain this miracle before we went there together for the first time and she followed me with docile, quiet surprise into the windowless little box, obviously wondering what I was going to do this time, as I was always astonishing her in one way or another. When I pushed the button and we started up, her eyes stuck out like organ stops. She had never even heard of a lift before, any kind of lift—to her this was clearly magic, an extension of the rope trick. She found the whole flat almost unbelievable, with its electric stove and hot-water geysers, but once having accepted the lift she was beyond surprise and could have met Aladdin's genii with perfect aplomb.

On one of these excursions Aknis fell ill and on the way home we took her to a hospital. The doctor informed Stanton that she would be having a child in two months and it was this which was upsetting her. We were astonished at the news and I was particularly impressed by the possibilities of the sari as a maternity costume—also by Aknis's excellent figure, which had so completely concealed the situation. There were more surprises in store. The husband, the handsome *durwan*, who was hastily summoned, arrived in some anxiety but when he heard the good news he became livid with fury and swore that the baby was not his. Aknis remained perfectly calm throughout, her flat face impassive—she was quite silent, as though outside the storm. I remembered the red roses and a stalwart Gurkha who had very occasionally come for a few moments to the nursery door from a little settlement by the Park gates, but I said nothing either. There seemed nothing for us to do but to deposit her and her raging husband at the gate of their compound. Later that evening she appeared at the bungalow with both her boys and a small suitcase, asking if she might spend the night in one of our godowns. She was still perfectly serene but now that the secret was out she had altered her way of wearing her sari so that her condition was plainly evident. I marveled at my simplicity. All that drowsiness, too—why of course. She had changed to a black sari with a narrow gold border in which, after her accustomed white or pale blue, she looked older, a little worn, mysterious. She had changed, too, in another way—she had returned as an individual engrossed in her own affairs and not as a servant, though I had not suggested her leaving us—I had not thought of such a thing. I did what I could to make a godown habitable, found a mattress for the little boys, and gave them some food. We did not question her concerning her private affairs, only telling her that she could stay with us as long as she liked, though she would not now be taxed with the care of our baby.

After I left her she went into the Santus' room and stayed there a long time, talking to Mrs. Santu. This chamber was of a quite reasonable standard; though it was outside the house, it was nearest it and had large glassed-in windows (the godowns had no glass) and a stone floor—perhaps it had been intended as a study. The Santus were delighted with it and kept it in good order. Mrs. Santu and the Nepali woman had never been intimate but this evening Aknis evidently did not want to be alone with her thoughts. Some errand took me to the pantry; from that archway I saw them together and could hardly turn my eyes away from the picture they made. Aknis sat cross-legged on one of the low rope-strung beds. A little lamp burned on a low table between her and the *charpoi* on which crouched Mrs. Santu, her legs drawn up, swathed in her white sari, fat and bunchy, chewing betel nut, radiating curiosity and sympathy. The dim light from the little bowl of oil softened Aknis's rather harsh Mongolian features as she nursed her little naked son who lay across her knees—they made an almost allegorical picture of the beauty of motherhood. Very likely many of those beautiful Renaissance madonnas had as complicated and dubious home lives as did poor Aknis, I thought, and in spite of that the pictures seem to indicate an ideal relationship, the world seems to be kind and fair, as fair as the woman; Aknis looked so calm! so mild!

The next morning I was kept very busy running after my own baby and did not concern myself with much else. Early in the afternoon someone burst into the compound, announcing that the *durwan* had been found dead—he had been hanged, or had hanged himself, and near his body was some white powder, presumably poison. Everyone in the household seemed to think, even to take it for granted, that Aknis had done the deed herself and that the Gurkha was not implicated. And no one thought one whit the less of her on this account—indeed her prestige rose. She appeared unmoved, though when I saw her a few minutes after the word came I did feel that she had a cat-after-the-cream expression. She made no pretense of grief but she did ask me, a few days later, if I would please tell the police that she had spent the forenoon and early afternoon of the fatal day in our compound. As I did not know where she had been during those hours I could answer in no such way, and I was relieved when no one ever came to ask me. As far as I could see, the police were quite uninterested in the case —there was no investigation. I wondered how many murders in India came off so lightly and passed into the limbo of time. After a few days Aknis moved with her children into the nearby Nepali settlement and in due time a daughter was born to her. My own ideas of justice by this time had become so confused that all I remember of this is buying some clothes for the new baby and being particular that they were especially pretty.

We now wanted another *ayah*, immediately, but they seemed almost nonexistent in that country of wretchedly poor women, who are both idle and hungry. More and more Europeans were arriving and there were fewer and fewer nurses. Our Rosalind was a baby of wild energy. At the beginning of her tenth month she staggered alone, one evening, across the floor. The next morning she awoke with new resolve and began to run, a sport she pursued for the next year and a half. We used to remember, as we panted after her, the stories of wan white children drooping under a pitiless Indian sun. Actually babies thrive in India, in the hills or on the plains, and are generally quite unconscious of the heat. It is not till they pass the age of six or seven that they acquire the pallor of the plains and sometimes develop faster than is considered healthy for the European—an arbitrary dictum. Our child could not have been more vigorous in any country and she was never ill. It was a disadvantage, however, from our point of view that she had to spend most of the day indoors in order to avoid either the sun or the rain, and that we could not close up any room and leave her playing inside because it would have been too hot, and anyway the doors had no handles and could not be shut. They were wide, double doors, arranged with wooden props in the hinges so that they would stay open.

The servants went to look for *ayahs* and by the time a candidate had been unearthed in the bazaar I was so exhausted that I engaged her, though from the first I was repelled by her lean and witchlike visage and her whining mendicant ways. She was a Mohammedan whose husband was at that time pulling a rickshaw. I have forgotten her real name but we always called her Jezebel, though she did not have enough spirit and dash really to resemble that infamous character. Rosalind liked everyone and made no exception of her new *ayah*, who indeed rather fascinated her at first, as she put her on her knee, stroked her blond curls, and murmured, in the manner of the perfect sycophant, *"Hamara Baba! Hamara Baba! Huzoor!"* Aknis had never tried any of these tactics but had considered Rosalind her companion and peer—the Nepali does not go about groveling and saying *Huzoor* which means "my lord." Though she was engaged on a strictly temporary basis, so that Aknis could come back if all went well, Jezebel decided to make herself absolutely indispensable and foil her rival.

Jezebel's plan of campaign was to be as ingratiating as possible. With this end in view, she cut short her afternoon siestas and would float into my bedroom early, while I was still resting or reading, and massage me. I was astonished the first afternoon when she glided into the darkened chamber and took hold of me with her thin brown claws, but I rather enjoyed this novel and entirely unsolicited service until I realized that it was only the prelude to a premeditated scene. Jezebel had no tact at all. When she had me passive and relaxed on the bed, she felt the time was ripe to let me know what I could do to show my appreciation. She was a poor, poor woman, she would moan, she needed new saris, new petticoats, new blouses, clothes for her two boys, a job for her husband, and she would let me know later what else I could do.

I had intended to get Jezebel some new clothes but having just outfitted Aknis I was not very enthusiastic about starting all over again in an extensive way with a temporary *ayah*. In contrast to Aknis, who had never asked for anything (except for possible protection from the law), Jezebel did not wait twenty-four hours before starting her assault. Soon I had to shoo her away when she advanced upon me with her brown arms lifted high in the attitude of a praying mantis; since she could not massage without the epilogue there seemed no point in being rendered limp and soothed only to be snapped into irritation with the oft-repeated bars of I am a Poor Poor Woman, *Memsahib*. Besides, I now knew I was not really fond of being massaged.

The first cook had gone long since. I had sacked him myself over some matter of stores. We were more than fortunate in his successor, a pleasant and good-mannered Mugh, one of those big-eyed, gentle men who live in the Chittagong area between India and Burma and whose ancestors used to be pirates. The British Raj first pacified them and then turned them into cooks, so the legend ran. The standard of their cooking was surprisingly high for persons trained in British kitchens—the war, the disappearance of cooks, the meager rations, forced the islanders to change their outlook on food and the old days of rice-pudding and cabbage have now greatly changed, but in 1941 we still thought British cooking about the worst in the world. I wondered then if the international character of the Bengal invasions in the preceding centuries was responsible for the feathery desserts we were given, the creations of spun sugar, the delectable chickens. The Danish settlement across the river and the French town next to it, the Dutch and the Portuguese—these people had brought more to India than guns and rosaries. It must have been the French, whose tenure was widespread and quite lasting, who left so welcome a heritage. Our new cook had an air of grandeur hidden behind a modest mien, and when he produced a mass of chits, which were clearly his own, we found that he had once worked for the Commander-in-Chief in

Delhi. He was expensive but it is not often that a Master honors one's kitchen and we never regretted the extra rupees he cost us. He was honest and altogether of a different stamp from his predecessor. I enjoyed my conversations with him, his manner was courtly and he was genuinely anxious to please. To this day we remember his snow puddings, his mocha desserts, his stuffed fish and grilled duck with great emotion. Possessed of all this art, our new domestic was diplomatic and had no passages with the Santus.

Jezebel was then our only domestic thorn but we were not to be free of her till she had extracted from us a trousseau of warm clothes, which she needed when going up to the hills with us. Our first leave was due, we were going to Darjeeling, and we were so stupid as to take her along, though, as we should have known, she stayed there only two days before returning to the plains with her loot.

VII Sandakphu

"What's o'clock?"—
"It wants a quarter to twelve,
And tomorrow's doomsday."

T. L. BEDDOES

THE DARJEELING MAIL left Calcutta in the evening and went through Barrackpore on its way to Siliguri, at the foot of the hills. This was the train the tea planters took on their way back to their estates and it had been made immortal by the men of the Everest expeditions, all of whom used to use it for themselves and their stores in the days before air travel. We had arranged that it would stop and pick us up, and fervently hoped that it would as we waited on the station that November night surrounded by mountains of baggage. Jezebel stood beside us, holding the baby, and moaning over the trials she foresaw like a dusky lugubrious White Queen, enveloped in a dark green shawl of the correct Muslim shade.

But after the train had thundered in and the red-turbaned porters had hurled our impedimenta on the floor of our dirty compartment and rushed out, I realized that Jezebel had not been far out. No warnings about the condition of these Indian Railway compartments had prepared me for the miserable accommodation they offered. They had taken refuge in the problem of dacoity. The Indian Railway thieves, we were assured, had an expertise shared by few other professional bodies in the country and because of them the trains had decided not to install corridors, hooks, or any comforts: the passengers had to bring with them their own bedding, towels, drinking water, and service. The traveler's bearer was supposed to enter his master's compartment at a suitable station, unstrap the bedroll, make up the bed, and get off at the next station, entering his own even more unattractive coupé. This was the system on all but the two air-conditioned carriages which crossed the country twice a week, and possibly one or two others going south—otherwise everyone put up with the inevitable. As the war progressed and the trains filled up, everyone was constantly urged to Travel Light. Ha! How was that to be done?

Jezebel, happily, had been put into her isolated coupé, so at least we were spared her wails as we struggled with the unwieldy bedrolls we had borrowed for the trip and spread them out on the extremely narrow, slippery, grimy leather benches. In principle, the railways were one of the great blessings of British rule, opening up the country, making travel relatively safe, in spite of the dacoits. The Thugs had found the railways a deterrent, for instance. No ordinary trains had corridors, as these were too difficult to guard. As it was, we were told, long poles would come into the windows at night and whisk away your clothes and wallets.

The financing of the railroads had been notorious, most having been built by companies which guaranteed a high rate of interest (for the times), a guarantee backed by the government, which had already granted them free land. Any profit went to the companies, any loss required the dividends to be made up from Indian taxes. Most of the shareholders were domiciled in England and were sure of their five percent whatever happened. This reckless policy removed all sense of responsibility and the stories of the construction of the lines make startling reading. One source described the East Indian Railway, for instance, as "the most extravagant works ever undertaken. . . . All the money came from the English capitalist, and so long as he was guaranteed five percent on the revenue of India, it was immaterial to him whether the funds that he lent were thrown into the Hooghli or converted into bricks and mortar."

However, we did manage to fall asleep in spite of all our disgust with conditions past and present, and at dawn Stanton woke me with a great cry: "I can see the snows!" and after that nothing else mattered. The pure shining peaks seemed to have risen straight out of the absolute flatness of the plain. Far above the earth was a startling line of celestial light, rose-colored, transfigured, where the summits had caught the first rays of the sun. A mist hid the foothills and approaches, so that nothing intervened between the onlooker and this magical vision. Then the violent jolting of the train reminded us that we would be in Siliguri at half-past six and had to do up our bedrolls before we could get off.

These horrible bundles had been bad enough to undo but were much harder to pack and strap up, and the compartment looked even more awful by day than it had by the light of its one weak bulb the evening before. The poor baby fell off her bench into a mysterious and horrible pool of water which had seeped in during the night, and had no compensation for her miseries in the beauty of the snows as we did. We dressed as fast as we could and never abandoned any train with greater enthusiasm than we did that Darjeeling Mail. Jezebel met us on the platform, complaining with all her soul over her sufferings of the night.

We took a car and started up the mountains. The road, beginning in dank, jungly country, going past palms, bamboos, banana trees and stretches of paddy, soon climbs into a clearer air, while the plains begin to fall away beneath. The leaves became smaller—a phenomenon which gave us the greatest pleasure and elation, we felt we were entering a sphere where life was less intense, less dark-toned. Darjeeling is hardly seven thousand feet up, a contemptible altitude in Himalayan circles, but even at this paltry height the snows seemed startlingly near—the shimmering glaciers appeared to lie just above the oaks and cryptomeria. Everywhere on the hillsides were high bushes of scarlet poinsettias, making an extravagant background for ubiquitous files of women porters who were cheerfully carrying immense burdens on their backs, the loads strapped to their foreheads. Their woolen shawls could be seen far over the ranges—brilliant daubs of cerise, turquoise, and clear yellow ascending in impressionistic clarity under the bright sky. These poor but lighthearted hill people put our sober mien and dress to shame—they know poverty but they have no bitterness in them. As we drove past Nepali bullock-drawn carts, I recognized the source of Aknis's courage and gaity—life had not conquered these confident, humorous people.

The road leads through Ghoom, a village set about with wonderfully symmetrical cryptomeria, so perfect that they are the very model trees for a toy estate. Darjeeling lies four hundred feet below; above hangs enormous, dazzling white, threatening, powerful, Kanchenjunga. It was extraordinary that a town with so astonishing and compelling a backdrop could be so banal as Darjeeling. Its contact with the West brought it a confusion of schools, hotels, boardinghouses, cafés, visitors, and ugly houses built far out over the ranges. Yet once it must have been a charming village with its triangular marketplace, its weekly fair, and the beguiling hillmen who made up its citizens—the Nepalis, Sherpas, and Bhutias of the Terai. We found it quite intolerable and on the second day of our leave determined to trek out into the hills, walking as far as we could towards the superb, fascinating Kanchenjunga.

Trekkers should, of course, plan everything well ahead, choosing their route, engaging *dak* bungalows, hiring porters and ponies, buying stores, getting proper clothes. We could do none of this and had, besides, to reckon with a hotel bill. But we were bent on shaking the dust of Darjeeling off our feet and getting nearer to the beauty on the horizon, which proved to be incentive and means enough, though obviously we had to make our journey rather uncomfortably. Still by our precipitancy we avoided the very considerable burden of preparation, something not to be entirely despised. We visited the District Officer and found that by great good fortune there would be a string of *dak* bungalows vacant in the hills beginning on the very next night and immediately put our names down for this sequence of houses, which meant that our trek took us exactly as the bungalows lay—to the isolated, compact little stations where we would sleep each night. All over India, in the hills and on the plains, these bungalows had been put up to accommodate travelers and government officials on tour, offering everything necessary save food, bedding, and servants. Each bungalow had a caretaker, or *chokidar*, to bring in wood and water, and to keep the mail, the *dak*. All through the years in India I loved these little homes of brief tenure.

The bungalows we booked led us in a wide clockwise circle of about a hundred miles, climbing at first, till we had reached nearly twelve thousand feet and were constantly in sight of both Everest and Kanchenjunga, then dropping down through the forests till we were well below the level of Darjeeling on the homeward arc. November, before the real cold of the year sets in, always holds a promise of fine weather in the Terai and on this passage we had ten days of unbroken sunshine, without one cloud to mar the serenity of the heavens. The other favored season for this adventure is in May, when the rhododendrons are out and the hillsides a blaze of color; but then one runs the risk of an early monsoon, which would not only make the paths difficult but would obscure the snows. And they were the real goal, the treasure we went out to find.

We took with us six porters and, according to custom, an Indian sweeper, a gloomy youth who carried only a large tin of kerosene for the oil lamps of the bungalows. His melancholy was the more apparent beside the radiant good humor of the Sherpas who, jauntily carrying their eighty pounds apiece, seemed not to have a care in the world. The three men were Everest "tigers," who wore still the European climbing suits they had been given when they took part in those expeditions. Djalgen, our head porter, had not only been on Everest but had also taken part in the assault on Kanchenjunga under Smythe, in whose book on the mountain he receives honorable mention. Ajeeba, second in importance in our little journey, had been up to Camp VI on Everest, carrying at that great altitude sixteen pounds—a tremendous feat. These men knew all the great climbers and would talk to us of General Bruce, of General Norton, of Somerville and Mallory—they were true mountaineers, always longing for fresh attempts on the peaks which they might join. In spite of their immense strength and real mountaineering ability, they showed no impatience or superiority at our amateurish efforts and were consistently helpful, friendly, and resourceful. For them caste did not exist; we met as equals, an enormous relief to the spirit.

The three girl porters, with their flat Mongol faces and long thick braids hanging down their backs, had the appearance of jolly squaws. Dressed in padded jackets, full striped skirts, high felt boots, and with plenty of jewelry, they moved, as did the men, with a lithe economy of action which, in spite of their thickset physique and short limbs, made their swift unwearied passage over the high hills resemble that of animals rather than people. Every line of their bodies followed the direction of the paths, sinuous and rapid, not a movement wasted. Pempa and Sona Laru carried our bedrolls, which were swollen with borrowed blankets and our extra clothes, but Djalgen's wife, Pemparita, was the happy possessor of a sinecure. While her companions trussed bedrolls and boxed food to their patient foreheads, she had only to bind on her back the lightest but most precious burden of the march—she came to carry the baby.

Rosalind was by this time sixteen months old, and taking her on the trek was, by usual standards, highly unorthodox. But we had no one with whom to leave her and could not see that the fact that babies were not normally taken on such expeditions was, per se, any argument. Our fellow guests in the Darjeeling hotel seemed to suspect we might be taking her into the hills to abandon her. The manageress was so distressed over the plan that she even offered to keep the baby herself, convinced that no child could endure the rigors of the journey. No one, alas, gave the adults of the party a thought or suggested that without a pony it was not the child but the mother who might have to be abandoned on a hillside. And we, so excited over leaving Darjeeling and drawing nearer to the snows, were so ingenuous that we did not consider what the walk might involve or realize that to climb up to twelve thousand feet would require more than enthusiasm. On my part this disregard was staggering stupidity, as I heartily disliked walking. But it was all bound up in the hypnotic effect of the snowy peaks, coupled with the horrors of the town. The baby returned from the expedition in perfect condition, having passed a restful holiday tied securely to Pemparita's warm back by a strong shawl. But her mother survived only because the alternative to reaching the *dak* bungalows each night was to lie down on the trail and expire.

On the first morning, though, when we walked in glorious sunshine up to the beautiful cryptomeria of Ghoom, exalting in the clear, pure air and the freedom we had won, nothing shadowed our delight. There we sat down and looked out over the hills, green and wooded before us, and up to the immense mass of Kanchenjunga—the long snow slopes, the fierce raking contours—and felt that the world of ordinary dimensions had fallen away. In a sense that proved to be true, for when the trek was over and we returned to the plains it was December, 1941, the bombs fell on Pearl Harbor, and nothing was ever the same again for Europeans in the Far East. It was a Grand Finale to our old life.

Our first *dak* bungalow was at a point called Jorpokhri, nearly ten miles from Ghoom, along a forested road. The porters raced ahead, but my pace—and hence Stanton's also—became slower and slower. Kanchenjunga dominated our field of vision above the evergreens and the rhododendrons, larger and larger rose the white peaks of the mountain. Already it had begun to assume a personality for us, as it does for those who attempt to climb it. The heavy trees we passed between were hung with Spanish moss, the dark forest through which we labored rose in sheerest contrast to the gleaming summit we saw when we lifted our eyes, as though we were moving in two dimensions of vision. At last, in a cleared glade, lying under the full aegis of the mountain, we came upon our little stone house already full of bustling life—the sweeper preparing the baths, the *chokidar* bringing in armfuls of logs for the deep fireplaces, the porters preparing tea. The baby, after her first day of trekking, was in tremendous spirits, red with the sun and perfectly at ease in the company of the Sherpas, who looked upon her as a toy brought for their amusement. These heroes of the high altitudes were only too ready to pull up the child's leggings, mix her milk, and squeak her bear for her.

We were alarmed at how much we ate that first night, consoling ourselves, as we called for more toast and eggs and bacon, with the thought that it was really a kindness to the porters—the more we ate, the less for them to carry. The bread was new, the vegetables and fruit fresh, and everything tasted wonderful. We need not have concerned ourselves; though we never went really high, our appetites soon failed and we ate so little that we tightened our belts every day. The porters' diet was abstemious: chiefly rice and tea, which they provided themselves—they asked us for nothing.

The trek divided itself into two stages: the first was of an epic nature, as we went up towards the bewitching, elusive snows, leaving the forest for higher ridges which bore only grass and low bushes. Kanchenjunga was always with us and at first without a rival, but soon we came into the presence of that other, greater mountain, which the Tibetans call "The Goddess Mother of the World"—Everest—compelling but serene, far more impressive, though less spectacular, than fierce, defiant Kanchenjunga. This first stage took us to a high plateau called Sandakphu, which commands a vast stretch of country and lies between the two massifs. Further on this same ridge is the bungalow of Phalut. There we left the high hills and went down into the forests, losing for a time the snows in the romantic glades of the deep woods. Here the bungalows were light and summery, the marches shorter, and, upon our finding ponies, the adventure became idyllic rather than herculean.

Every morning the porters brought us tea very early, while we were still in bed, and then made breakfast. Stanton and I started off first on the day's march, feeling the pioneer's eagerness to press on, though we were loath to leave our little homes, so welcome and glowing a few hours earlier. The bright sun beat down on glittering icicles, which stiffened the grass in the compounds as we strode across to the path leading up the ridge before us. The way was always clearly defined. There was seldom more than one path to take and often we could see our objective, the next *dak* bungalow, ahead of us for most of the day—a little white box, crouching under a snowy peak, and steadily withdrawing itself before us in a malicious manner as the hours passed. Compared to me, the *dak* bungalows made good time.

After we had gone the porters rolled up the beds, packed the stores, made the sandwiches for lunch, and fastened the baby's washing to someone's pack to dry. Then, tying her firmly to Pemparita, they dashed after us. In spite of all these chores, and their loads, they went so fast and took such hair-raising shortcuts that they soon passed us and we could see their rapid progress on a ridge ahead as they bounded upwards, as untired and sure as chamois. I never felt a moment's concern for the child, warm and secure on that friendly back and always beaming and gay when we met in some meadow at lunchtime. It was wholly delightful to go out into the golden sunshine for another long day in those solitary hills, the snows hourly nearer, and not one dwelling place to break the silence.

But if "upon the bosom of the air" the snows were sovereign, the glory of the hillsides themselves lay in the rhododendrons, with their rich promise. In groves and singly, these strong, vital, long-leaved bushes were on every slope, making us long to see them in bloom. Gradually the oaks, the cryptomeria, the bamboos fell away behind us, but the rhododendrons, though in sturdier, shorter proportions, never failed right up to the bleak heights of Sandakphu where, debonair and stalwart, they flourished in the snow. They constituted a basic chord in the score of each day's passage.

Though the hills are untenanted, they form, nevertheless, an ancient highway where men of many types mingle—Mongolians, Tibetans, even Circassians and Turkomans. These people had been through some melting pot which had given them a certain similarity in dress and some speech in common, but physically they showed great diversity. Some even looked Japanese, with their bow legs, short faces, and matted hair, and it is possible that they were—this border region was known to be the pathway for much espionage. Others were tall, dark, aquiline, as though they had come from the West and over the edge of the world. They were here together because they were all porters, carrying a very stolid and unromantic cargo—potatoes! Yet even this was strange, as none of these people are potato eaters to any extent—they depend on rice. Whence the vegetables came and where they went, to whom and why, we never learned; we had no conversation with these earnest carriers, who seemed generally in great haste as they passed down the hillsides under the high crown of the snows. They were dressed in light yellow jodhpurs of a loose, fairy-tale cut and wore black, embossed kaftans on their heads. Very occasionally we would receive a smart salute from one of them, sometimes a smile, but most of them responded to our friendly gestures only with an uncomfortable half-glance.

In the beginning of our ascent the porters were of one distinct type. As we went higher they became more diverse. The men of the lower reaches seemed stunted and half-human. They had clearly shouldered their loads when they were too young for such burdens and probably had always been underfed. They were like gnomes or little old men of the mountains, like figures in a Japanese fairy tale. Their dust-colored tunics were bound low on their hips with russet sashes into whose folds they had thrust the charcoal-black sheaths of their *kukeris*—the daggers of the Gurkhas. Barefooted, they made no sound as they went, and if we were passing in the woods, they appeared without any rustle of warning. When he saw us, the leader of a file would give a peculiar, low, soft hissing whistle, at which signal each man would take the short thick staff he used on his way, put it at his back, and rest his huge basket on it. Then he could lift his head, showing the deep creases his cruel work made on his forehead. The baskets were of an open weave and from a very wide opening tapered to a point at the small of the back; each probably weighed seventy pounds. Everyone on the hills, save our two selves, carried a burden; we were the only pleasure-seekers. Between ourselves and these poor mortals lay an immense barrier—too great to bridge with smiles. Pausing on the narrow paths and watching us, the carriers looked at us in manner neither friendly nor unfriendly but like persons of another framework of space-time. Sometimes we would hear the sibilant whistle in the bamboos but not see anyone, though the silence was eerie with watching eyes. Very infrequently came a man alone, a dusty, bowed, hurrying figure. If a troop was too pressed to stop, they would give us a quick, sideways, bent glance in passing, as quickly turning their dark eyes down again to the steep, twisting mountain path. But after a time we met no more porters; they only worked in the lower hills; as we climbed higher we were alone.

On the open hillsides we sometimes came upon great boulders carved with Tibetan inscriptions and long oblong heaps of stones called *mendongs*. Besides these gray monuments prayer flags waved from immensely high poles—long, narrow, white banners printed with black characters. Here and there on the meadows were others, without the more solid background of the *mendongs*, seemingly unwatched and unheeded, placed haphazardly to the uninitiated eye, blowing lightly—ghostly and strange. We were coming into the sphere of influence of the Tibetan monasteries.

Kanchenjunga was the dominant mountain of our trek, as we were far nearer it than Everest and it was in view for the greater part of the time. But there was a majesty about the Goddess Mother and her "strong toil of grace," a magnetic quality which her role in the thought of that part of the world gives her, and we began to feel it. This played its part, with the prayer flags waving, waving in the constant wind on the ridges, with the figures of the Tibetan carriers, with the rhododendrons, in turning our minds to Tibet, the great magnet of the region, the forbidden country. But there were no temples here, no priests to be seen, nor were we conscious that anyone was stirred to reverence by the sight of the banners fluttering mournfully on the crests of the hills.

Though the long marches through the hills under glittering white peaks were wonderfully inspiring, though the air was sweet and gilded by the brilliant sun, yet the hills themselves were, we thought, disappointing. They were handsome, in a conventional wooded manner, but they did not charm the heart and mind with the subtle, spirit-invoking, romantic joy of the mountains of a Chinese landscape. Those narrow peaks, those twisting hillsides half-wrapped in mist whose "spirit resonance" the Sung painters so exquisitely rendered, bore the same relation to these sturdy hills that the rich, complex history of China has to the lesser annals of these hills of the Terai. Here, meeting these Mongol peoples on the high crossroads, blown by the thin wind, I found myself actively missing temples. In China their fantasies and tinted walls, their curled roof tips, the windows cut in the shapes of peaches and quinces, the vermillion of their decor, the welcome one received in their easy courtyards, were a part of the countryside: I was always subconsciously on the watch for their low walls, for the sound of a gong—but there was nothing, nothing, but the prayer flags waving aimlessly, empty, mocking, without bounty.

We gained height rapidly on the first days, when the climbs

were long and, for me, very arduous. Early on the afternoon of the third day we came to a narrow path which ran along the edge of the hills on the Nepal side of the border. The afternoon sunshine was warm and lovely, and a little stream meandered by the way, purling and sweet. We sauntered by the water, loath to leave this gentle prospect, reveling in a few easy paces, for we could see our road leading sharply over a gap between two hills to the summit of a far-off ridge, where lay Sandakphu and our bungalow for the night. From a fold in the hills before us came the unexpected sound of a river's heavy pounding, which so captivated Stanton that he went on to see if he could glimpse it, leaving me resting on a wide, warm rock, sheltered from the wind. Groups of smiling Nepalis, the first unoccupied people we had seen for three days, were walking towards the sound of the rushing waters, swinging lightly forward with buoyant step as though it were the Promised Land. The porters had not warned us of any difficulties for the day, but I had a presentiment about the final climb to Sandakphu—each day seemed more severe than the last. (After the Nepali Road we met no more porters.)

As soon as we left the shelter of the Nepali Road, a sharp wind blew upon us and it began to be very cold. The path led steeply upwards, first over a stony section, then through a burnt-out area where great black tree trunks stood bleakly in the cold air or lay in long charred lines on the gray earth, incongruous and unnatural. Every step demanded a conscious effort and but for Stanton I think I would never have reached the summit. Struggling through that wilderness of black sentinels while the darkness deepened, gasping for breath, stumbling on the harsh earth with my shaking knees almost giving way, I understood how the superstitious could imagine that the spirits of the place were gathering behind the ashen trunks—it was a very haunt for "night's black agents." When at last we reached the bungalow, we found it standing in snow.

Sandakphu had one, very superior, new *dak* bungalow which had been presented to it by an Indian gentleman, as well as the old original hut which was fairly dilapidated but still standing behind it. We at once decided that we would spend two nights here, as we could move for the second into the old bungalow and would thus gain a day of rest. Here on the summit, just as we arrived, we met an Indian policeman who was on the point of starting down the valley and who, seeing my fatigue, offered to send up a pony for me, which would arrive during our day's halt. A pony then seemed to me to represent the sum of all earthly good and I was soon stretched out by a blazing fire, wrapped in deepest content, the perils of the day almost forgotten.

Stanton, entirely revived after tea, decided that we should tempt our appetites by having a real meal. We had not taken a cook-*sirdar* with us in order to economize, and the porters, though entirely willing, had no clear idea of how to prepare European food. Since once we reached the bungalows, my small remaining energies were fully absorbed in taking care of Rosalind and in my own survival, we seemed to be living on toast and sardines. Stanton then told the porters that he would himself come out to the cookhouse and make some soup, but concealed from them that he had never done such a thing in his life. Carefully coached by me, who also had never made soup but who was well versed in the theory, he went out into the night to find that the gentle and solicitous Sherpas had brought a large armchair from the bungalow across the snowy compound and drawn it up beside the stove, that he might direct operations in comfort! It is no wonder that so many have sung the praise of these Everest "tigers"! They were full of concern for me every day over the difficulties of the journey, always encouraging at the noon halts, always assuring me that the worst was over. In the bungalows, though they were in no way obliged to do any domestic work, they washed socks, tidied the bedrolls (or did what they interpreted as tidying), and minded the baby, prompted only by their own generous hearts.

The next morning we found that Sandakphu consisted of a small plateau just big enough to support a meadow, which lay in a slight hollow protected from the wind by a grove of rhododendrons. Here, lying on the short, brown grass, warm under a strong sun, we passed a day of bliss, gazing at the almost incredible view the place affords. On the northern side, above the wild, forbidding, dark ridges of the Sikkim heights, lay the whole panorama of the snows. A long line of snowy summits, all over twenty thousand feet, leads to enormous Kanchenjunga, a mountain system in itself, after which the horizon drops to another series of lesser peaks, all ice-crowned, till Everest rises above them, majestic, awe-inspiring, dominating all the far ranges. Glittering white, high in the upper air, this radiant pageant, splendid with light, rose above the somber, shadowy valleys which lay between us. On the south were the mountains of Nepal, serene, verdant, gentle, with glimpses of the plain far below. On our right, over Bengal, mist rising between the ridges of the deep-cleft hills transmuted that unhappy province into an exquisite vision, the earth and air like Lalique glass. Far beneath us, we could see tiny pony caravans traversing the slopes. All day long the little meadow held the sun and we lay and looked at the great world. I felt as though it were a note to which I must listen so carefully that I could never forget its tone, though I might never hear it again.

In the afternoon we took the baby up to the rhododendron grove and formally introduced her to Real Snow, scooping up handfuls of it from between the strong lithe roots of these heroic bushes which thrived in such exposure. It was impossible to realize that a week ago we had been languishing on the hot plains, unaware of this rich spectacle which the alchemy of time was to give us.

The perfection of the day was slightly marred by the lamentable failure of the pony to materialize, but the long hours in the meadow, the elation the heights produced in us, made it impossible to be gloomy over anything and the noble porters assured us that the next day would not be a hard one for the *memsahib*, as there would be little climbing. We were, they explained, to follow the ridge, walking straight towards Kanchenjunga, till we came to Phalut and our last mountain bungalow, almost at the very point where Nepal, Sikkim, and Bengal meet.

The way led through a parklike jocund country of brown and springy meadows, set off with pine, bamboo, and russet-leafed bushes. Everest was on our left, Kanchenjunga on our right—we walked between them all day. With ponies, it would have been a glorious day, but as it was often I almost despaired of ever reaching the bungalow, which we could see far ahead under the summit of a high knoll. That this march, like the others, ended happily was again due only to the support and sympathy of my companion who, though a good walker and himself untired, accommodated his pace to mine, while together we mourned the false pony. Kanchenjunga, the fickle witch, on this day assumed the form of a leviathan with a fine tail taking up a third of the great white body. Everest, the Goddess, was her usual mild, deceptively benign self, almost the conventional mountain of a child's fancy, with three smooth and graded humps. To pass thus between them was almost too wonderful for me—I turned my head from one to the other all day, like a nodding doll at a country fair.

The bungalow was particularly inviting when we at last achieved

it, as in it were several bound volumes of *Blackwoods* of the
eighties! How we wished that we could linger here an extra day
and night also—but the knowledge that another party was hard on
our heels was inexorable. It was our last evening in this high terrain,
our last to be spent between the thick stone walls of the mountain
bungalows, in the absolute silence where not one leaf whispered in
the darkness.

Before we turned away from the snows in the morning we
climbed a hundred and fifty feet above the bungalow to the summit
of the hill that sheltered it and stood with upturned, wondering
eyes gazing at Kanchenjunga, thirty miles away and sixteen
thousand feet above us. It was not possible to be complacent over
having conquered twelve thousand feet when confronted by
twenty-eight thousand! Fierce and jagged, deep purple, uncompromising, the Sikkim heights lead up to the base plateau. On this
bright, blithe morning the wanton mountain assumed a new role
with which to mock us, becoming suddenly theatrical, turning itself into a stage setting for a puppet show of *The Black Brothers*.
The enormous central plateau became the stage, sloping slightly
forward and as though well sprinkled with icing sugar, and on it,
heedlessly arranged, were what looked like a number of purple
wigwams, also thickly powdered with snow. Above, the sharp sides
of the mountain rose strongly into the intense blue wings of the
sky. The summit, far above the little stage, was so brilliantly white,
so resplendent, that it seemed to cut off the visible world, as the
facade of the stage in the theatre, with its footlights and the curtains, cuts off the world of the audience from the world of the
actors.

It did not seem as though anything could lie behind that summit
—or even that it could have another side—it arrested one's conception of the tangible world. It was a masterly definition of the rim
of the world, apparently final, inevitable, absolute. One appreciated how the men of the mountains were hypnotized by this great
mass, until they felt it a living personality and an incarnation of
power. But it was equally possible to wonder if it had any existence
at all—would it be there if we turned our backs? Diderot and his
counterpane—"I wonder what you look like when I'm not here?"—
come to mind. Everest, far behind us, seemed in contrast more gentle, beguiling, and mysterious than ever as she bade us farewell,
while the gallant peaks of Sikkim, rising from their sea of white
mist, were only a lovely conceit in that transhifting vision of

"Nature's infinite book of secrecy." Three eagles circled above and below us in a perfect stillness which was only broken, far, far down, by the soft, thin voice of a little stream.

We now entered the beautiful glades and deep dells of the forest regions, losing eight thousand feet in four days. At first it seemed to me a blessed respite to be going *down* rather than struggling *up,* but even with this advantage, by noon of that day I felt that I could no more. We were then some seven miles from Phalut and had come quite suddenly upon a small river running through a clearing where some jungle folk were engaged in building a bridge, watched by Djalgen, Pemparita, and the baby. Attached to the engineering party, in some miraculous capacity, was a pony. Overwhelmed, I sank down upon the dark, moist, leafy ground while Djalgen entered into a long and involved negotiation over its hire. To our infinite joy they agreed to let us have it for two days, assuring us that we would then be in the world of men where we could find others.

The lovely Tilloria was a little furry gray to the casual eye, but to me she was the true color of the nutmeg, and I felt as the Dauphin—"When I bestride him, I soar, I am a hawk: he trots the air; the earth sings when he touches it; the basest horn of his hoof is more musical than the pipe of Hermes."

Djalgen threw his own pink and white padded quilt over my palfrey's nail-studded wooden saddle, I pulled my skirt over my knees and mounted. The *syce* was a lean Old Testament type—not a prophet, but the material prophets had to endure—who seemed pleased to find this unusually profitable burden for his pony. Seizing the bridle, he pulled the reluctant creature straight through the river, till the crystal waters rose to the girth and my feet, hastily pulled out of the stirrups, were almost over Tilloria's ears. The clear, cold water of the ford was dark, reflecting the heavy foliage which ringed it, and when I looked back on it, it seemed entirely familiar, being a perfect Courbet except that it lacked the fleeting stag. But its essential spirit was that of St. Christopher. Now the trials of the journey were over; ahead lay the Arcadian days, warm, easy, and golden.

Though the jungle people working here were few, they seemed to us to make the forest ring with sound, accustomed as we had become to the silence and solitude of the upper hills where no porter would waste his precious breath on talking. We went on for some time before we found a rushing stream beside a grove of

strange oaks where we ate our lunch. Afterwards our path became
the merest track but Tilloria proved so nimble and surefooted that
I did no more than slip my feet from the stirrups for better balance. When we went down gulleys which were little more than
channels for boulders, the *syce* hung boldly onto the patient animal's tail, yelling wildly to encourage himself. In this gallant manner we came to the end of the day's journey, finding ourselves
before a little house of light and shining wood—our first forest
bungalow—very sweet and intimate after the stony huts behind us.
The garden was lovely with flowers in bloom, roses, fuchias,
cosmos, and marigolds, and from it we could see once more the
white sides of Kanchenjunga, but Everest was lost to us—we never
saw her again.

The next morning, going down a steep slope towards a stream,
we encountered a lean Rosinante coming uphill with two sacks of
the ever-present potatoes dangling on his brown sides. Stanton
decided that this was to be His Horse and after very little persuasion the amiable nag was induced to turn around and the
potatoes abandoned by the path. We went on feeling more Chau-
cerian every moment. Before we had reached the stream one of
his stirrup leathers broke, so, picking up the baby and her attendants at the bridge, we clattered into the little village beyond it
for repairs. I put Rosalind up in front of me and we waited thus
in the street (the one street of the hamlet) while I looked into the
open shop of an Indian cloth merchant which was directly in my
path. I had turned Tilloria's head, and if we had gone on we
would have entered the shop itself, mounted. The merchant's
beautiful wife, heavily bedecked with ornaments, showing that
their sojourn here must be profitable, was greatly excited to see
strangers and hurried her little boy into a shirt in my honor.
Though out of the sun it was very cold, this hardy child had
been simply dressed in a silver ring, which hung round his neck.
Now resplendent in a white cotton shirt he came forward to stare
at us, while his mother stood behind him holding her naked baby,
whose large dark eyes were heavily ringed with black paint. I reflected upon all the woolen garments I had found it necessary to
procure for Rosalind before we came up to the hills and which
were now being carried up and down the ridges for her, while a
silver ring and a pot of paint would evidently have been enough.

The deep woods were rendered romantic with cedars—the beautiful spreading cedars of the Himalayas which I saw with a nos-

talgic pang, as two of these magnificent trees had stood on the entrance drive of my parents' home in Shanghai, guarding two stone horses. There they had been something of a rarity—this was *their* home. There was also a great deal of tall bamboo and many hemlocks, as well as the oak which is peculiar to this region, called the *sungri katus*. It had shed its big, pale, improbable acorns all over the hills. The Forestry Department was very active in this section, planting tree nurseries and reforesting burned-out areas— there had been many fires. The little bungalows had been designed so that forestry officials could stay in them comfortably for days at a time, and near them were quartered the *babus* who directed the ordinary work, as well as men who had been trained by the Forestry Department and whom we found very knowledgeable in their field. It was one of the best effects of British rule that we saw anywhere in India.

So passed five days. We changed mounts at the villages; we arrived early each afternoon at our destined bungalow, where we would explore the neighborhood and talk to the porters, luxuriating in the holiday insouciance which we had not been able to indulge in the heroic days of the climb upwards. The marches were short, as the officials needed to inspect their territory closely; this gave us time to lie in the sun in the gardens, poring over the registry books and whatever else there was for compulsive readers like ourselves. The records in the high bungalows were suitably austere, though many an exalted name was to be found among them, but the visitors tended to become personal. "Dog ate our ham," one party had remarked censoriously at Rimbik, but the Princeton couple who went through a few days later had entered, "Dog behaved O.K."

Near one bungalow was a commercialized *gompa*, or Lama temple, which appeared to have been set there as a tourist trap, though it seemed an unlikely place for such a villainy; certainly there were very few inhabitants and they would hardly have wanted such a showy setting for their devotions. We were led through it by a go-getter type of priest, magnificently dressed in the Roman helmet and flowing robes of his calling, who set his prayer wheels in motion, lit incense, and made his gongs and long trumpets boom for us, all for a proper consideration which he entered in a book, requesting us to sign it.

For one whole day, as we ambled past terraces and infrequent hamlets, we were astonished to see that almost every house had a man sitting cross-legged on the floor before a Singer sewing machine, busily stitching. These machines must have been carried in one by one, strapped to strong foreheads, to these wretched little mud-floored huts. Whom were they working for, I wondered? The local people, sartorially not conspicuous, surely needed few tailors, and it seemed a notably inconvenient center for the clothing trade. The mystery remained unexplained. By this time, drenched with the sun (which was of the kind I can bear, as it was warm but not hot, and one met it with covered limbs: my red hair has always kept me away from the sun that others seek), dreamily looking out on the world from my saddle, I felt it was no good asking questions—I had too many and the answers seemed always so vague and unrealistic.

These villages of the Terai have wide wooden couches built out over the hillsides, as resting places for the wayfarer; here people of the same somnolent, contented mood as ourselves reclined in the sun, gazing out over the hills and taking life calmly. I can think of no Western parallel to this symptom of village life, which included nearly everyone. These persons were genuinely easy in spirit, though not idle—they had no wish to dream in the *dolce far niente* of so much of mankind—what leisure they had they gave to a cheerful contemplation. They did not bustle about in the vacuity of sport, nor seek the solace of a glass of wine. Even the children would sit amiably on benches near their parents' homes and though the little terraces often overhung steep hillsides there was no danger that these self-controlled young persons would leap over the low confining sides—they had an innate dignity and good sense.

Another feature of the landscape in the low valleys—we came down to almost four thousand feet—was the air-borne system of drying maize. Three or four very long bamboos were stuck into the ground in such a way that they crossed some five feet above the earth and in this support the bright ears were piled, where each could receive the maximum amount of sun and air. They made delightful golden-orange patches against the green hills. There were here, too, enormous spider webs, hanging between the trees in great profusion. These ghostly curtains went well with the high aureate cones from the point of view of valley decor, though they could hardly have accorded with good agricultural conditions.

When we were nearly at the end of the trek we came upon a village with a wide cobbled street where the inhabitants were so wonderfully pictorial and romantic that I felt they must be in disguise. The merchants, smoking hookahs, sat cross-legged by their copper wine jars or the few handfuls of red peppers which they had artfully disposed on wide leaves, silent and watchful, apparently totally uninterested in their trade, hardly of this world. Slim deer-eyed maidens, trying to keep modestly and becomingly out of sight, were peeping round every curtain at the back of every shop. A baby, dressed only in a shawl of white cotton lace which had been carefully arranged round his head, lay on a booth, howling and ignored. Three Tibetan travelers passed, all wearing one large turquoise earring, their pigtails hanging below heavy fur caps. There seemed no sequence to anything. We did not know what anyone we encountered thought or did, they knew nothing of us, and we all passed on our several ways with absolute determination, dodging cobwebs.

The nearer we came to Darjeeling, the more persons we met: porters, merchants, travelers journeying between the hills—Indians, Tibetans, hill people, occasionally Chinese. We never saw Europeans, with perhaps one exception. Riding along the road late in the afternoon, we encountered a motley group of people going in the other direction who seemed to have joined forces by chance— most of them were porters, poor folk. Among them was one tall, thin young man who compelled our glances. He did not appear to us to be an Oriental; his bearing was easy and assured though he wore a porter's dress and was as unkempt as the others. Our eyes met—I could have sworn he was an Oxonian.

On the last day big strong ponies were sent down from Darjeeling to bring us up the long pull through the tea gardens. Hour after hour under a hot sun, leaning forward in our saddles, we went past plants laid out with geometrical precision— the hillsides looked as though they had been combed. Many workers were busy among the bushes, the whole impression was one of methodical organization. The leaves struck me as being both large and coarse, and the entire *mise-en-scène* unsuitable for the production of anything so ceremonious and elegant as tea, the cup of the scholar. It is more than a hundred years since Robert Fortune went to the tea country of China and, in disguise and some danger, succeeded in studying the cultivation of tea and in smuggling out young plants. The venture certainly proved a financial success for the Empire—but what a contrast between this mass-produced, indifferent, rank product, intended to be adulterated, *miserable dictu*, with milk and sugar, and the small individual gardens of the China trade where the delicate leaves were cherished. There the profession was enriched with legends and fantasies—the tender leaves, fine as phoenix's eyebrows, must be plucked by young virgins by moonlight that they may not be bruised or profaned by rough and impious hands. (I remembered a friend's comment: "Much they know about young girls!")

By the next night we had left the Himalayas and their windy grace far behind us and were once more on the sad plains of Bengal, resuming with reluctance the old ways of life, the vestments we had worn before we had seen the eagles wheeling in the high blue air under the icy garland of the snows.

VIII The Impact of Pearl Harbor

Antonio: What a blow was there given!

The Tempest

THE BARRACKPORE garden looked green and lovely, a "caprice," though the *mali* had planted few of the seeds I had left with him and answered only with reproachful looks when I asked him where he had put the larkspur and snapdragon seedlings. But after Sandakphu trifles seemed only trifles, even in Bengal, and I began to plan our first winter garden with enthusiasm, so that by Christmas we could have pinks, hollyhocks, and poppies in our borders.

On the morning of the eighth of December Santu, as usual, brought the Calcutta *Statesman* to the bedroom and put it under the net. Stanton sat up and opened it, waking me a moment later with the news of Pearl Harbor. We knew our world would never be the same again. Long as we had recognized the potential menace from Japan, we had no more dreamed of this disaster than had the rest of the overconfident, sanguine West, and we were equally deceived in thinking that our newly-declared enemy would quickly regret his rashness. We knew, of course, that the Japanese would lose but not that they would destroy in the process the old Far East which the white man had so enjoyed, where his position had been so dominant. To that extent we would lose: if that were a loss.

The inevitable advance upon Hong Kong and its vulnerability were no surprise, but we were dismayed that it did not resist longer—it had been hoped that the Colony could hold out for three months, not three weeks. It was not the fault of the local garrison, but the horrifying realization that all over the coast Allied nationals were being killed, imprisoned, herded into camps, was a bitter thing to endure. The stoppage of news was an obvious accompaniment to the war, but always comes as a shock; what had happened to our friends, our relatives, to the White Russians in Shanghai who were stateless? What were the Axis nationals doing? What of the hundred thousand German Jews who had fled to Shanghai from Nazi persecution? The terrible silence that falls when total war comes is as absolute as the deafening noise that accompanies it physically.

The Barrackpore Club, following the traditions of the stiff upper lip, had its usual gathering on its lawns on Christmas afternoon. The Club was on the Riverside and very reminiscent of the old days—it had hardly changed in half a century. It was a treasury of ancient trophies, of lances and military insignia; and the gardens were at their best, full of flowers and mild sunshine. There was outwardly perfect calm, inwardly unbelief and consternation. We had just heard that Mark Young had surrendered Hong Kong. Not one of us doubted the ultimate outcome of the war, but it was unpleasant to see in Indian eyes that they expected, even partly welcomed, our defeat. Then came the sinking of the *Repulse* and the *Prince of Wales*—shocking news. These great ships had spelled the supremacy of British seapower in Eastern waters, they guarded the approaches to Malaya and kept Burma and India safe—or so we had thought. Soon Singapore fell and we were waiting for news of the Battle of the Coral Sea. Even though an air battle over Ceylon had been a victory for us, we had become pessimistic as to immediate events. People began to say, "When Rangoon falls . . ."

The West Yorks, the regiment then garrisoned in Barrackpore, was one of the first to be ordered eastward. The military families were hastily sent to the hills and, in theory, the men made ready for battle. The equipment they needed was not there and there was no time to repair deficiencies. The officers of the regiment were assembled when it was still a question to the civilians as to whether "our" regiment would be sent to Singapore or to Rangoon. Alec was recalled from Quetta and the Staff College; his new daughter was only twelve days old when he had said goodbye to Lucy.

Barrackpore changed very quickly from its placid and drowsy state; we did not know what would happen to the cantonment but we realized very well that it was not going to stay as it was. Alec came to a cheerful dinner with us and told us, in a rollicking mood, of the regiment's difficulties and improvisations. There was a lot of joking over the transport of some unfortunate mules—about two hundred of them—which through an error of paperwork had to make a sea journey to Burma three times and finally were to end up working for the Japanese. But we did not know the end yet; we still imagined the British Army would use them. Alec asked me for some soap and went off, debonair and excited, into the night.

A few days later the regiment landed in Rangoon where it fared ill at the hands of both the Japanese and the Burmans. The men had no opportunity to make a stand, it was all over almost at once. Alec was killed among the first. Confused reports filtered back to Barrackpore, sobering the cantonment, already serious enough. The abandonment of Rangoon and the loss of Burma were a particular calamity for the British in India and in Bengal we were flooded with rumors. Disgraceful accounts of official incompetence and bureaucratic collapse began to pour in to the bazaars. High officials and their wives, their baggage, and their pets had been flown out, we would be told, while thousands of the underprivileged had been left behind with no means to escape. Sometimes this was true enough—it is an old story—but we felt it was un-British. That happened with the Fall of France, certainly, but not in the outposts of the Empire. Nor was this basically like the French picture, but there did seem to be some unfortunate elements the two debacles had in common. The public had been repeatedly assured that a stand would be made, the civilian population was told to stay quietly in their homes, the government would remain—but almost as the pronouncements were being issued the government started north. Both Wavell and Alexander encouraged vain hopes and many were lost who might have saved themselves had there been a more realistic policy. But, of course, that is war. If civilian morale is maintained, it is hoped, the enemy will pause on that account. Just before the Japanese actually took Rangoon the keepers of the jails and lunatic asylums decided that their duty lay elsewhere and opened the doors of these places. Their inmates ran wild about the streets, mingling with looters. That is to be understood. The administration had broken down. It was war. But how did this strike the Indian gossiping in the bazaar?

At that very moment tens of thousands of civilians—British, Indians, Anglo-Burmese—had started to walk north out of Burma by the Hukuang Valley, carrying their children and bundles. This dreadful journey took many months for the greater part of the travelers, but at the time we in India knew nothing of it. Long afterwards a day did not pass when the Indian papers did not publish obituary notices like this: "In loving memory of Samuel and Mabel Brown, with their children, Patrick aged 11, David aged 9, Rosemary 8, Eileen 5, and baby John, who perished in the Hukuang Valley in the summer of 1942."

After the Japanese had swept north of Rangoon and were on their swift passage up Burma, it seemed as though the next disaster on the list must be Bengal. The Tanaka Memorial had included India in the scheme of Nipponese dominance, and so far things seemed to be developing according to plan. Few people in India had read that Memorial and we China refugees realized now that we had not taken it sufficiently seriously. India was unprepared for this enemy at her gates: her armed forces were small for a modern war and the "Frontier" to the Indian Army had always meant the Northwest and the Khyber Pass—not the Bay of Bengal and the Burmese jungles. The army was encumbered with conservatism and red tape, there were not enough mechanized formations, and the majority of the "thinking" population of the country was hostile to Britain.

How carefully had the Japanese prepared the soil, while the British had continued to take the Raj more or less for granted! It had not been difficult to spread the doctrine of "Asia for the Asiatics" among an illiterate, dreadfully poor people. The privileged classes, many of whom found the status quo to their advantage, often were pro-British—the princes being the outstanding example. Never in history had life been made more secure for autocrats than for these men under the protection of the Raj—naturally they were "loyal." And some among the humble, who sensed that beyond the pretensions of Empire there lay much righteous government and rule by law, still held to the British. But what the proportion was was hard to assess—the questionnaires which went the rounds in our factories found 5 percent pro-British, 60 percent pro-Japanese, and the rest without any reactions either way.

Among the privileged who were not pro-British the most famous was Nehru. Yet he was personally pro-British in his easy, genial way, though politically all his work was devoted to ending the Raj and instituting self-government. He and Rajagopalacharya, with others who were felt to be the giants of the Congress Party, risked their own prospects and the easy life they could have led for their stand—but they were not typical. Many of the Congress leaders were not, though, men of wealth or any particular standing—for instance Subhas Chandra Bose and his brother were not privileged. And then there was Gandhi, quite outside any ordinary reckoning and the most powerful of them all.

There was a medical officer who lived not far from us at that time who had at one station found it a part of his curious duties to be the jailor of Jawaharlal Nehru. Though he had little inclination to sympathize with his prisoner's aims and activities, he had nothing but good to say of him as an individual—his courtesy, his intelligence, his genial manner.

In Bengal now we all began to think, very personally, about civil defense, which was, as one might have expected, in a state of awful confusion. Hardly any country manages to do a good job on civil defense in peacetime: it's intricate, irritating, very expensive, and, it is always hoped, unnecessary, so why bother? In the Presidency* there had been only a little air raid protection work, not nearly enough shelters had been built, people were unprepared for blackouts. When the eleventh hour arrived there was a mounting sense of confusion, coupled with an increasing contempt for the commands—even the advice—of the white man, who was going down like paper before the Oriental in the Burma campaign.

The difficulties in the way of organizing the civilian population for an emergency were enormous. Most were illiterate, almost entirely uninformed about the war, knew no European, American, or Japanese history or geography, and had no conception of the great struggle then in progress in the world theatre. Calcutta and its environs were intensely overcrowded and the shelters which had been put up were too hot to be long endured. It seemed impossible to maintain any sort of sanitary standard in them. There were not enough men of goodwill and education among the Indians who could be entrusted to form working parties to take care of the streets and bazaars of this vast city—disinterested amateur effort (though it certainly existed) was not generally understood—and it assuredly would not be possible for the relatively few, overworked Europeans to superintend each district personally. This tremendous task was not really seriously undertaken, even at the planning stage, until the moment when, to Eastern eyes, the game was al-

* The regions adjoining the cities of Bombay, Madras and Calcutta were known as the Bombay, Madras and Calcutta Presidencies. (This term was a survival of earlier usage.)

ready up. Within volunteer organizations the affair was rendered more difficult and delicate through the many discrepancies in stores. Indians would offer to help in the sorting of drugs and bandages, which then mysteriously disappeared—for the unscrupulous the temptation could not be resisted.

In the spring of '42 the menace of invasion seemed very great; indeed, had Japan so wished, she could probably have marched up to Delhi almost unchecked. The moment bore a marked resemblance to England's position after Dunkirk, without the faith in a righteous cause, the strength of a united country fighting for itself and its ideals, the supreme confidence of victory. Here was a country already conquered, resentful, dispirited. Those were miserable months, the discomforts and dangers of the time accented by the general pleasure of the dark peoples that the arrogant *sahibs* were being so thoroughly dispossessed.

The more hostile Indians openly gloated over our approaching downfall, and even among the others, the friendly, there was a subtle change of manner. How could it have been otherwise? It was impossibly difficult to explain that it was inconceivable that the Allies should lose the war, that these setbacks, though serious and causing us great chagrin, were nevertheless temporary. I wanted so much to be able to explain to nearly every Indian I encountered that many of us looked upon our record in the East with mixed feelings, but the Japanese would not improve matters, they would prove cruel masters wherever they conquered, and "Asia for the Asiatics" only meant "Asia for the Japanese." Honestly meant, many of us knew this slogan had a sound and righteous basis—but it was not honestly meant. But it was past the time for words.

Yet words were tried. In March Sir Stafford Cripps arrived in Delhi with a proposal which seemed to the British so reasonable and progressive that through the days of deliberation we were ingenuously sanguine of its acceptance, and were astonished when the Indians finally refused it—but we ought not to have been.

When the European War broke out in '39, the Indians were not particularly dismayed—in fact many of those who understood what had happened were rather pleased. They remembered the boom which the 1914–18 war had brought them, and though they were not pro-Nazi (Hitler's race theory had seen to that) they realized that England was bound to suffer from this new conflict and for that they were not altogether sorry. They did not wish her to lose it, but they had endured too much from her rule, either actually or in imagination, to regret at least a temporary shock to her pride. Many viewed the war from the point of view of self-advancement, hoping for good jobs, and some—a few—truly wished to help England. Congress declared its sympathy for the Mother Country and for France, the princes came forward with expressions of loyalty, as did the premiers of the Punjab and Bengal.

But all this passed almost unheeded by the home government. There was no immediate effort to recruit men, no war loan was started, no assessment of technical aid—the period of "phony war" was as marked in the East as in the West; but in the West, though we may chafe under delay, at least we understand to some extent the virtues as well as the faults of our slow-moving systems of administration. In the East where the European is considered a hustler, this inertia which characterized the beginning of the war was psychologically unfortunate—the Indians assumed that their sympathy was unwanted and took offense. A blunder of the first magnitude was committed when the Viceroy issued a proclamation of war on India's behalf before gaining the country's support through the Indians in government.

The Indians did not wish to make things worse for the Raj but they did have an understandable human inclination to bargain— and, after all, why should they have felt just as Britain did in these circumstances? On the 19th of September, 1939, the Congress stated, "India cannot associate herself with a war said to be for democratic freedom when that very freedom is denied to her." They asked if they were to be included in a future scheme for the elimination of imperialism and if they would be treated as a free nation, they wanted to know how soon such a policy might take effect—and for a whole month they had no answers at all. Finally they were told that India was to work towards Dominion status and at the end of the war the position would be reconsidered; that a consultative group representing the major parties was to be formed to ensure that the country was fully informed on the progress of the war. The Congress Working Committee resented these slight overtures, the Congress ministries in the provinces resigned, and a possible ally was turned into an unfriendly neutral. But if the Cripps offer had been made at this time, in 1939 instead of 1942, it would probably have been accepted.

The Muslims, suspicious of the Congress Party, also wanted to bargain, to be sure that the Muslim League would be heard. They protested their loyalty to the Allies but did not commit themselves to the war any more than had the Hindus. Everyone disagreed; nothing went forward in the early months of the war. When France fell, though, India became somewhat alarmed—she disliked the Empire but was accustomed to its shelter, and was impressed, too, by England's courage in that dark hour. Nehru cried, in all sincerity, "England's difficulty is not India's opportunity."

Gandhi, meanwhile, with his immense influence, remained consistently pacifist, advocating nonviolence, wanting to keep India entirely out of the war. Most of the Congress did not follow him in this, so that for a time he stood apart from it.

But after the Japanese attack everything altered in Indian eyes. It was in this atmosphere of discredit that Sir Stafford unfolded the new offer—that as soon as the fighting stopped a properly elected body was to frame a constitution; that India could remain with the Empire or leave it as she wished; that the Muslim provinces could stay out of the Indian Union if they so desired. The leaders of the principal sections of the Indian people were invited to join at once in the councils of India, as well as those of the Empire and the Allies. It could not have been a fairer offer, nor have come at a more disadvantageous moment. The Indians did not believe that anything so just, which they had so long and so ardently desired, could now at last be sincerely offered. When England was stronger, they implied, she might go back on these proposals. They were convinced that there was a catch in it. So they refused it.

They argued that if India did nothing and the Allies lost the war, the dependent country would be in a better position than if she had willingly helped her former master. If England won, the offer would still stand. India would have her independence anyway, whether she fought in the war or not; it was easier and safer to do nothing in the judgment of both Congress and the Muslim League. There was the terrible question attributed to Gandhi—"Why take a postdated check on a failing bank?"

It was painful and disquieting to realize the extent to which England was mistrusted. Yes, yes, it's a good offer, they said, but it's a desperate gesture, made at a moment of extreme peril—if the crisis passes the terms will be subtly altered and the old bondage will continue. Rightly or wrongly, the Raj no longer inspired confidence. It is terrible for a nation which feels itself to be honorable to be so mistrusted.

While all this was going on, the tempo of our lives accelerated. The men were busier than ever, the ordnance factories worked at top speed, the military struggled to make up for lost time, civil defense tore ahead, emergency hospitals were set up. The Maharajah of Gwalior gave his elegant Riverside bungalow to be used as a hospital in case of need, and there we local *memsahibs* assembled to help prepare it. As we tore off lengths of cotton for sheets and rolled bandages we wondered about the structure of our homes and thought of shelters. When would the raids begin? And what would we do? Those were the questions in our minds. We were all horrified at the thought of the reactions of the enormous untrained civil population.

If there were bad raids, who was going to remove the dead, for instance? There is a special caste in India for this task but there would certainly not be enough of these super-untouchables to deal with any serious catastrophe. About this time there was a municipal sweepers' strike in Barrackpore, making everyone aware of our dependence on these unfortunates. What were we to do about sanitation if an invasion took place? Our local administration had no answers to these questions and it was obvious that the *jemidars* would not "carry on"—why should they?

Those who could began to leave the Presidency. But where to go? To the hills? And perhaps be cut off? The poor Indians wanted to go where they would not only feel safer but could find work, and that would hardly be in the hills. Should the Japanese advance to Delhi, as they threatened, and with the Germans now pressing triumphantly towards Stalingrad, it seemed not impossible after this disastrous spring that these two Axis powers might really carry out their schemes and join forces in India or Afghanistan. No one wanted to be isolated on a mountaintop, cut off from the sea by hundreds of miles of parched plains, surrounded by hostile Indians and by the Japanese! These alarms were not too fantastic after the incredible misfortunes of the year. Refugees from Malaya and Burma poured into Bengal with the minimum of belongings, all bemoaning that they had left so late and telling sad stories of friends who had gone up to the hill stations and had not been heard of again. The American Consulate issued warnings advising its nationals to file lists of their property and announcing the arrangements it had made for a few rare steamers to take away those who wished to leave and risk the submarine-infested seas.

Everyone seemed to be packing. Thieves flitted in and out of the bungalows, picking out useful articles from half-filled trunks. The servants seemed suspiciously light-fingered in many a home and the police scarcely tried to keep pace with such activities, even when the garrison commander's house in Ishapore was robbed of its silver. Everyone was too preoccupied, a little silver was not that important.

Painting squads invaded the Park and Government House and the elegance of the bungalows and lodges was soon lost under coats of chocolate-colored distemper. Military huts were put up under the trees and on the lawns. A new cemetery was made and soon strangers were to lie near Lady Canning, some of them American Negroes killed in raids on the Calcutta docks. Government House was partitioned into offices and turned into a Headquarters for Eastern Command. Almost the whole cantonment was requisitioned for the army; civilians permitted to stay often had officers quartered with them. Most of the bungalows were turned into officers' messes and huts were built in the gardens. All these changes came about astonishingly fast.

I knew all about the light fingers that flitted over open boxes because we, too, were packing. As soon as China had become our ally, Stanton and I longed to find some sort of work connected with that country where we had so much experience and where we could speak the language. We offered our services to the government and at first thought we might well be accepted; we had, though, to go to Delhi, where these appointments were being made. Before we left we were allotted another bungalow, out of the Barrackpore area, so we had to pack up, uncertain as to whether or not we would be returning. In any case, we could store our things in the new house, in a place called Palta, down on the river nearer Ishapore, and we decided that I would not come back, whatever happened, till our new baby, expected in August, had arrived.

So I was packing. In the midst of all these great events we had had our own small domestic storms that winter: Santu had become so disgusted with Jezebel that he had delivered his third ultimatum —"Either the *ayah* or I goes today." He was, of course, worth ten of her but we were not pleased with his highhanded style and foolishly let him go. We parted sadly, the best of friends; he went back to Lucknow and, we hoped, to better work with the army. In his stead we hired a very smooth Muslim called Mohammed Hanif who had been in London and spoke remarkably finished English. It was he, I am sure, who took Stanton's gold cuff links out of his suitcase (the ones which had belonged to my father) and the little gold chain and other ornaments. But I doubt if it was he who took the baby's handsome horse, which she had just received from America. No more presents from abroad were to reach us for many years. As I put something in one open trunk, someone was rifling another.

Jezebel, never a favorite as has been made clear, gave herself insufferable airs when Santu went. She considered his fall a proof of her own irreplaceable value and acted the role of Conquering Martyr. So I was delighted to find Aknis waiting on the veranda one morning, well and cheerful, with her new daughter out to nurse. We immediately reinstalled her in the nursery over the head of the outraged Jezebel, who pretended that she had never understood she had come on a temporary basis, as she clutched a month's extra pay in her clawlike fingers and wished everyone all possible bad luck all round. But Aknis did not stay long—she told me she felt the heat and thought she should take the children back to Darjeeling. Whatever her real reasons, I knew she was only acting prudently.

Soon after this, on a hot spring morning, a very fresh and pretty *ayah* in a beautifully draped swirling sari appeared on the veranda, bowing, the tips of her raised fingers poised gracefully together. She was quite the cleanest *ayah* I had ever seen, there were no other applicants as everyone was running away, and I engaged her. It was she who went with us upcountry. She was delighted to leave Bengal though she had never left her *mulk*, her own country, before. She was a true Bengali, a Muslim from Dacca, a fierce little city renowned for its political agitators, once famous for its muslins. In our day a man from Dacca was almost automatically considered a firebrand—and with reason, as this very *ayah* was to show me.

All these shadows combined to make it less difficult to leave our dear little bungalow, where we had been scarcely a year. It is a wrench to walk away from any home and I hated to leave it empty and unloved, the shutters closed, the spiders and scorpions and frogs holding once more their careless court. Someone else would come—soldiers this time—but would they feel for it as I had?

I came out under the portico for the last time, tired and hurried, and paused by the mounting block. We had sold the piano—we had to have some money to get up to Delhi—and aside from losing it, we had been rooked. This was no time for people to invest in baby grands. Even the packing case, which was teak, had been almost filched from us. Everything seemed scattered, it was all part and parcel of this war which had been sweeping me out of my homes for five years, ever since I had had to hasten out of my little bungalow on the Nanking wall in 1937. It was another small personal pang in the desolation and hurricane that was sweeping up the Bay.

IX Delhi

Pleasant things of Hindustan are that it is a large country and has masses of gold and silver. Its air in the rains is very fine. Sometimes it rains ten, fifteen or twenty times a day; torrents pour down all at once and rivers flow where no water has been. While it rains and through the rains, the air is remarkably fine, not to be surpassed for healthiness and charm. The fault is that the air becomes very soft and damp. A bow of those [Transoxanian] countries after going through the rains in Hindustan, may not be drawn even; it is ruined; not only the bow, everything is affected, armour, book, cloth and utensils all: a house even does not last long. Not only in the rains but also in the cold and the hot seasons the airs are excellent; at these times, however, the northwest wind constantly gets up laden with dust and earth.

BABER's *Memoirs*

It was at Delhi that Akbar wrote to Bairam Khan that he had decided to take into his own hands the reigns of government, and, therefore, the latter should retire to Mecca.

MAHAJAN

A HOT APRIL NIGHT found us in Howrah Station in Calcutta, excited and pleased to be going away and having the prospect of seeing Delhi in spite of the miseries of the times. Even dark and wretched Howrah, patterned after the gusty old stations of Victorian England, could not damp our spirits. In fact stations like this, which the English had designed in their most romantic mood when their love of steam and of railroads had captured their imagination and resulted in the erection of these great caverns, were less appalling in India than in England. In both countries they were intolerably congested, but here at least one seldom suffered from the cold. In later years I used sometimes to think that there was nothing to choose between Waterloo Station and Howrah, except that the first was more detestable because nearly always so bitterly cold. And certainly the Eastern crowd was the more pictorial.

On that night the station in Calcutta was even more crowded than usual, scurrying people maneuvering their way past refugees and travelers who were everywhere sitting on their piles of baggage. We made a sufficiently alarming display ourselves, with suitcases, bedrolls, baby gear, and the poor possessions of the servants. The noble old sweeper, Jai Dyal Sifz, was coming with us and *ayah* brought as her entourage her husband and little girl. The husband, a cowed youth and a rickshaw puller, clearly felt it a good opportunity to leave the Presidency—at least he could fare no worse elsewhere. We had no great wish to take these supernumeraries but we could not refuse to bring them. They were all installed in the servants' compartment next to our coupé, everyone settling in with the maximum of confusion and noise. All down the length of the train, which was crowded to capacity with people eager to get away from Bengal, the same scenes were being enacted.

When the train at last drew out of the city, out of the babel of noise and turmoil, to the measured rhythm of its own thunder, it was impossible not to feel a great relief; the packing and moving, the alarm and dismay were behind us for a little season, and we could be alone in our peaceful, dim compartment. Lying on our leather benches under the hot swirl of the fan, we felt in the air a certain finality, different from the usual pause a journey gives; and though we did in fact come back to Bengal, still that night when we left Howrah had in it the elements of a Finale. It was a pleasure to turn our thoughts for a little from the Japanese, and remember the stories of the great region we were to see—to think of the Moguls and the Kashmir Gate, of the Ridge and Nicholson, to hear the wheels chanting "Delhi—Delhi—Delhi."

We had been too busy and harassed to talk much of late except about the war and our own immediate problems; now for the first time I heard some of the recent gossip of the factories. One particularly gratifying story was of the zeal of a superintendent who, determined to burn secret papers before the possible arrival of the enemy but not entrusting the task to any hands but his own, had thrust drawings and maps into one of the largest furnaces. He forgot about the flue, which at once drew them up and scattered them far and wide over the area, to be picked up gleefully by a populace already used to finding leaflets left for them by the

Japanese. Probably they never came into dangerous use but the superintendent's loss of face had cheered up his critical staff.

After this grateful start the journey was in fact something of a nightmare. White dust poured in through the screens, round the doors and windows, and it was almost unbearably hot. When we turned off the fans there seemed to be ńo air at all, but when they were on they only spiraled down gusts of hot air—it was literally like being in an oven. The primitive little shower was a blessing, an entrance to a cool, clean, refreshing world, but its effect had no permanence. But we knew well that it was neither as hard to bear nor as soul-destroying as an unheated train in a northern winter, and that in the West that April many journeys were being made compared to which ours was a paradise.

All the next day we went through sand-colored near-desert country where only occasional short stubby bushes could grow and where the few settlements seemed no more than dreary mud villages. The glare was so great that we kept the shades down but every time we looked out we saw the same harsh landscape. At the infrequent stations we were generally running to the dining car or back to our compartment. But we saw enough, during these stops, of the motley, ragged crowds at the stations to sense that we were coming into a more virile and colorful region where the people had more spirit than in poor Bengal. The stations all had their taps marked "Water for Hindus" and "Water for Mohammedans," and little booths selling *chapattis* and sweets and highly-colored cold drinks. On, on, we went past the old cities of wonderful names: Benares on the holy river, Cawnpore of murderous memory, Lucknow, Mogulserai, till as night fell we ran at last into Old Delhi, the ancient capital of so many vanished kingdoms.

The walls above us were low and slight, compared to those we knew so well in Chinese cities, but they were romantic, as are any crenelated city walls today; and the sight of them was another strong indication of how different this place was from the province we had left behind. The imprint of the capital is strong. When we stepped wearily out of the dirty train onto the dusty station, even though it was late and the platforms were of the most ordinary Western pattern, we recognized instantly that this was a city of richness and grandeur, of memories which were still important.

We hurriedly said goodbye to the dear old sweeper, who was going to his own village a few stations further on. His gratitude for our small parting present put us to shame; we saw him go almost without words. He would have been incredulous had he any idea how much we admired him, but we felt his blessing on us as he salaamed and climbed back into the train, to be lost in the night.

Then we drove away into the dusty darkness, rendered enchanting by the wonderful fragrance of the neem trees which were in flower. As they lined the roads, all that part of the city was pervaded with their sweet, rather heavy scent. The road led under the little pitted Kashmir Gate and, soon enough, to the huge veranda of the Cecil. It was a surprise to find it blazing with light—the war and the blackout seemed then really far away. And for Delhi that was still true.

Only Bengal had really grasped what the Far Eastern struggle might bring to India and Bengal was more prescient solely because of her geographical vulnerability. The capital was still a comfortable place to visit and the Cecil still a luxurious hotel, according to local standards. Soon it would be closed to casual civilians and officers would be sharing the big bedrooms, four to a room, and paying a stiff price for a bed—it was a good war for the hotels. But we had arrived in time to partake of peacetime comforts, though there was, of course, no room service. The *ayah's* husband obligingly turned himself into a bearer.

Stanton was at once busy with appointments in government offices in New Delhi and away all day. The great heat kept the baby and me indoors most of the time, but very early in the morning *ayah* would take the child out into the big hotel gardens where she could play on the lawns, running about beside beds of high red cannas. The hotel was very full. There were commissions of different sorts staying there, as well as the usual complement of officers—there was much in the wind. But in the long, darkened days when the blinds were down and the *punkahs* going, in the active twilights when the tennis courts and the swimming pool were thronged, at night when people in evening dress drove up to the veranda and cars and *tongas* filled the entrance, no one would have dreamed that even in those very hours the Far East was under Japanese rule, that Java and Malaya and Burma had just fallen. In spite of this apparent outward calm and even frivolity, we were all very much aware of it, however. The faces of the Europeans were both anxious and resolute, while among the hosts of Indian bearers who stood everywhere in attendance many looked insolent and moved with a perceptible swagger. The myth of white supremacy was fast fading. It had been taken as axiomatic for too long that a handful of white people could master thousands of dark ones; one could not but understand their pleasure that this could never again be said.

We were so short a time in Delhi that we had to look at it quickly or not at all, and we had to do so either early or late to avoid the sun; in either case one trip had to be made in strong sunlight and it soon became either too hot or too dark to stay wherever we had gone. *Tongas* are probably the most uncomfortable vehicles ever designed, if they were designed and did not spring, just as they are, from the brain of some sadistic genie. The passengers sit facing backwards, one foot braced against a narrow footboard to keep themselves from being pitched into the road; the whole vehicle is always enveloped in a cloud of dust, kicked up by the heels of its own horse; and if the sun is behind you it is full in your face. The little horses caparisoned with plumes, the two high wheels and the canvas awning, suited the background of Old Delhi. But it seems extraordinary that so awkward a carriage should have survived— would a Victorian model have been too daring to introduce? Perhaps four wheels seemed too expensive to make? Still, with the petrol shortage and the advent of so many missions, cars were costly to hire in Delhi and with all their drawbacks *tongas* did at least provide some sort of transport; we were grateful for them.

In these slow, jolting affairs we went out through the clean streets and past the pleasant gardens of the cantonment, straight into the bazaars outside the Kashmir Gate. Here at last we found the Eastern bazaars of legend and romantic fantasy, the open shops full of brilliant silks interwoven with gold, of gaudy leather slippers and bowls of chased brass, of a profusion of striking, bold jewelry. Here were those booths heaped high with mangoes, pumaloes, green and yellow melons, some cut open showing the juicy red pulp and the shining black seeds, with coconuts, with whole branches of bananas. The paths between these bright and glittering objects were crowded with strikingly handsome persons: Sikh ladies in full trousers and long tunics, beautiful women in saris, gypsies in full colored skirts, Muslim gentlemen in miraculously fitting jodhpurs, and great numbers of those ambulatory tents which were actually Mohammedan women in *burqas*. After the drab looks of the usual Bengali assembly it was a captivating procession of endless variety. There were sweepers in huge turbans, clerks in white *dhotis*, swarms of children, beggars, porters with immense bundles on their heads, bullock carts, *tongas*, donkeys, rickshaws—it was glorious. It was no wonder that Chandni Chauk* had such renown.

Not far away is the Jama Masjid, one of the largest and most beautiful mosques in India, foursquare, approached by a high wide flight of steps. At the deep gateway we were given sandals to fasten over our shoes and an attendant carefully bound Stanton's bare knees with strips of linen. My totally bare legs appeared not to matter, presumably because of my inferior spiritual status. Then we were fit to enter.

Before us lay a vast court where space and simplicity engendered immediately a sense of repose and calm. A large pool reflected the cloudless sky. Round the court are great open halls connected by arcades, roofed with superb white domes, and at each corner rises a tall, slender minar. There are never any idols or images in mosques, which are nobly planned with little of any earthly trumpery to distract the mind. A few priests were to be seen, in robes of flowing white, all with hennaed beards. As this mosque is an important one in the Muslim world it contains a few precious objects —an illuminated Koran and some red hairs from the Prophet's beard. Stanton went up one of the minars to gain a view over the city while I waited below in the shade, looking at the Moorish arches of the arcades, reveling in the full curves of the swelling domes, in the space, the proportions, the silence and openness. On one side of the court, behind fine lattices, is a hall for women, keeping them apart, as always in the religion.

We went to the Ridge, which seemed low and oddly unimpressive considering its great role in the Mutiny, and to the Fort, and to Humayun's Tomb, passing on the way sites made famous by one or other of the kingdoms which once held sway here. Several magnificent high gates still stand which belonged to these vanished realms; one of the most beautiful—tall, recessed, and ornate with its little fretted cupolas—was already the entrance to an enemy internment camp and P.O.W. center.

The marble palaces of the Fort have a startling, breathtaking beauty, lying above the river and set off by green lawns—a rare sight in Delhi. Looted and almost destroyed after the fall of Delhi in the Mutiny, they were afterwards partially restored and what is to be seen is surpassingly lovely. The soldiers were not to be blamed, so much, for their vandalism—the British women and children who

* It means the Street of the Silversmiths.

had fled to the Fort for refuge when the rising began were massacred here. But so much has happened in Delhi, its history is one layer after another of conquest and destruction, of fine building and the making of laws, you can't stop at any given place and take it singly. Central India is exciting ground, all of it—Alexander found it so too, and the Indus and the Sutlej had more meaning to the British officers when they crossed them because they had learned of them as children, reading Greek.

Some distance within the walls surrounding the palace precincts is a long, rounded passage above which lies an armory of ancient weapons—lances, swords, and daggers, all very handsome to see. There is, too, a suit of John Nicholson's clothes, a uniform which strikes one as much too small for the tall, striking figure he is always described to have been. It is khaki—the British had finally realized that the color of dust was a protection and had laid aside some of the scarlet coats which made such wonderful targets.

The palaces were only open between seven and ten in the morning and after four in the afternoon, so the beauty of the Diwan-i-Khas and Diwan-i-Am could only be seen in the sweet early light or in the shadowed evening, but any light would have enhanced them. These two halls, of Private and Public Audience, some of the *zenana* quarters, a small mosque, a few pavilions, and the water gardens are all that is left. The buildings are of marble, inlaid with mosaic in Persian design. On the side away from the gardens their lattices overlook the river.

The Diwan-i-Am, the large Hall of Public Audience, has one entire length open to the gardens but is sheltered from too much exposure by an arcade of delicately tapered arches. Here, on a central dais, was once the Peacock Throne. That is long since gone and there is left only the pure white marble of the floor and ceilings, the exquisite floral mosaics on the panels around the hall, and the intricate tracery of the lattices. It must have been to just such a hall as this that Aladdin's mother came with her bowl of jewels to ask for the Sultan's daughter—I could almost see her, standing humbly in a corner, in all this airy spaciousness. Every nuance of light and shade was a delight. I would have liked to have passed my hands over that smooth cold marble, I longed to copy each flowery bouquet in its light and graceful elegance. There was a clarity about the place, no detail detracted from the whole; it was, actually, perfect.

The Diwan-i-Khas, the Hall of Private Audience, is smaller and more intimate—an entrancing chamber. How true it is that the Moguls build like jewelers, every detail tenuous and fine. This hall and the pavilions give the impression of an almost tremulous fragility, an effect produced by the white-shaded rooms, the lacy windows, the slight floral mosaics.

The Persian concept of enhancing the charms of the most precious of elements—water—is carried out here in the most enchanting fantasies. Like the Moors—like any people who live in hot, dry countries—they thought it the most wonderful gift life could offer. So in these living quarters channels were cut through the halls to allow streams to flow in and out, cooling and ornamenting the rooms: channels of marble so carved that the water was braided. Different levels were introduced where small waterfalls made a constant low murmur. There was a deep square tank with the inlet and outlet so chased that the water formed luminous patterns, while in the walls of the tank were little arched niches to hold vases of flowers by day and lights by night. All day the multiple bouquets cast a wavering reflection on the surface of the pool; in the evening these were exchanged for the magic of fire, which carried its light deep into the black, glimmering water.

The marble of the mosque is of a white so absolute that the other buildings seem in contrast almost dun. It has three very small domes and is so perfect that it is almost overdone—a little disorder would really improve it. All these places were set off by the lawns, which were English innovations. There were herbaceous borders and pools—lovely gardens. The Moguls would not have had it like this, they loved formal, geometric, elaborate gardens; but nothing can be better than an English garden, it all blended.

It was the travelers' tales of such wonders and of the rich and varied bazaars which gave rise to the legends of the fabled wealth of the Indies. In the days when London was still a small, cramped city these noble halls were already thronged with the perceptive and able administrators of a great empire, the handsome noblemen we see today in the Mogul prints. When we saw the Fort at Delhi it was only a memorial and many people thought London the greatest city in the world . . .

Delhi, with its highly strategic position standing in the Doab of the Jumna, the mountains on its northern flanks, the plains at its feet, was always an inevitable capital, a rich and glittering prize. Men who live in such a city, whatever comes to it, look upon their vicissitudes with a sort of complacency and inevitable endurance, seldom really shared by their conquerors. The Viennese, with their swift, mocking spirit have expressed this neatly: confronting a catastrophe the citizen of Vienna says, "*Es ist tragisch, aber es ist nicht ernst.*" But the German, they explain, in the same predicament will invert this to "*Es ist ernst, aber es ist nicht tragisch.*"

These two outlooks fairly epitomize the different sentiment felt towards the Mutiny by the people of Delhi and by the English. To the latter it was serious but not tragic, except that they mourned their dead, particularly John Nicholson who fell at the Kashmir Gate. But to the natives of the old imperial city, cynical after centuries of conquest, civil war, and disorder, it was tragic enough—but still not serious. It was just a repetition of a well-worn experience. They probably were not too sure that the new arrangements would last; they had had so many upheavals between the middle of the eighteenth and the middle of the nineteenth century that those who had lived long in the town took them as a way of life.

The old Kingdom of Delhi was, too, somewhat accustomed to a muted type of British rule by 1857. In 1803 the Battle of Delhi, under the command of General Lord Lake, had confirmed an English ascendency, symbolized by Residents and Agents and troops stationed in the area. The Company was always ready to put on a show of force, in addition to its primary functions of trading and collecting taxes, yet it was still handled in a shadowy, imperfectly defined manner. It took the Mutiny, the dissolution of John Company, and the establishment of the British Raj to make the writ run perfectly plain. Those fifty years of partial British control in the Deccan, important and influential as they were, were still not wholly decisive but a part of the century of anarchy and troubles which beset India as the power of the Moguls declined. The house of Timur had been so tremendous for so long and the personalities of Akbar, Jehangir, and Shah Jehan so vivid—let alone Aurangzeb or Baber or Humayun—that their imprint took a long time to fade. Even when the dynasty was played out the Empire lingered on and on.

As long as an Emperor was still living in the Lal Kotla, holding court (to which came the British Resident, nominally as a suitor) with some remnant of display, the country believed that the Mogul Empire still existed. The position of the ruler vis-à-vis the British was anomalous from the start and became more and more untenable as the years passed because each thought himself overlord. The

British, offering a type of homage, were fully aware that this was only a diplomatic gesture which could easily be withdrawn. They really felt the Emperor was a pensioner. But old Shah Alam, whom they had allowed to return to the throne when they took the city, proved to be "very tenacious of royalty" and his successors showed no signs of relinquishing any outward evidence of their supposed high position.

The Emperor afforded the Company a psychological facade, one which men like Wellesley encouraged, aware of its influence and unwilling to slight the monarch personally. Shah Alam had had his eyes put out by Ghulam Qadir, and the British were sorry for him and unwilling to cause him more distress.

As the eighteenth century advanced, however, the Company became increasingly accustomed to its wider powers and a new generation took up the reins of government, men who felt that the Emperor, whoever he was, holding audiences in the Lal Kotla was a sham and a nuisance. It can be seen now that in those decades between the Battle of Delhi and the Mutiny the Court did affect the country in many ways which were of advantage to everyone. They had imposed to a degree a standard of manners. The Mahrattas had none, nor did the Afghans, a rude and savage people, as were the Jats. The very existence of the Moguls, with their love of fine phrases and elegant ceremonies, did something to make their adversaries aware that these amenities existed. They were obliged to admire these manifestations to some extent, even to emulate them. Because of the old dynasty Persian remained the language of diplomacy, and through the interest the Court felt in poetry and the arts these talents could be encouraged. In a time of convulsive change it is not a small thing for these evidences of civilization to continue.

Yet it is not in the nature of a puppet state to endure. Either it becomes strong of itself or it is swept away. The great need of the country was for a strong government to stabilize the kingdoms and impose some rational rule. And lo! here it was, slowly making its way forward, ambitious, but not yet aware of its destiny. The Company continued to grow under the guise of trade, but inevitably plotting and intriguing for position. In a land of adventurers it was the most formidable of them all, but somehow almost unconscious of it. There was a Grand Design but it was not clear to most of the principal actors. The Chinese might have described the situation as that of the silkworm nibbling away at a mulberry leaf.

The whole evolution of the East India Company, which began so simply in a straightforward plan to bring pepper to the English market and finally led to the conquest of the subcontinent, had about it a sort of monstrous innocence. The critics of England could never believe that there was no deep-laid plot, no continuous hypocritical scheme which, ostensibly concerned only with trade, was designed to drive out the other nations and subjugate the Indians. That there was such a design in the end is partly true, but it came about by force of circumstance, coupled with the vigorous and adventurous spirit which animated the British in that century. The Portuguese, the Dutch, the French, were all in a less sanguine mood. Their own troubles at home and the wars of rivalry and succession which wracked the eighteenth-century world had made them, in the final analysis, irresolute on Indian soil. As for the Indians, their own affairs were in such utter confusion with the Moguls, the Mahrattas, the Rajputs, and the peoples of South India all at one another's throats that they were in no fit position to withstand any bold interloper.

From its inception the East India Company found itself obliged to concern itself not only with its primary objective—which was trade and the acquiring of fortunes—but also with political affairs of the most devious description, in the absence of any regular diplomatic body to take care of these matters. The structure of this extraordinary instrument was of necessity highly elastic, as it became through the years more and more deeply and significantly bound up with the whole destiny of India.

In 1570 the Spaniards, having absorbed Portugal, closed the port of Lisbon to the Dutch. Though the Netherlands were then engaged in a life and death struggle with Spain, they yet could not forego their spices, and in spite of their position at home, were able to wrest this trade from the Portuguese and began to send pepper to England. The English found the Dutch prices too high, more expensive than the Portuguese had been, and decided to trade directly with the East Indies through a royal charter. Finding it difficult to compete with the Netherlanders in those waters, they turned instead to India, where the Moguls allowed them to settle at Surat, north of Bombay. This was in the reign of Jehangir. It was nearly a hundred years later, under Aurangzeb, that the first British "factory" was built on the site of what is now Calcutta. In these decades the newcomers had crept round the coast, establishing themselves as traders at Madras and Fort St. George, at Balisore and Hugli. In 1661 the Company began to rent the island of Bombay from Charles II, at the great sum of ten pounds per annum—it had come to the English through the Portuguese wife of Charles II, Catherine of Braganza, as part of her dowry. Little by little, by treaty, by capture, almost by accident, the country began to fall into their hands. From the British point of view the whole process was both haphazard and guileless—it was simply a trading enterprise—but they succeeded where their European rivals failed. The British domination of India is interpreted as the supreme example of economic penetration leading to imperial conquest, and yet for a hundred and fifty years there was no conscious plan, one thing just seemed to lead to another.

It was afterwards sometimes said that the Japanese, studying the patterns of successful imperialism, considered the East India Company a model and wanted to copy it in their attempted absorption of China, not understanding that it could not be duplicated. It hung too much on the period of history in which it developed and on the character of the peoples concerned: it was piratical, swashbuckling, romantic, greedy, mercantile, ambitious—and, as it matured it came to contain a few idealists and scholars who loved the country and genuinely wished to help it.

In London it was gradually realized that there was vastly more to be gained from this mysterious country than trade, than a ground on which to defeat the French, and the ostentatious return of the nabobs with their presents of Kashmir shawls and ivories, their curries, and their accounts of tiger hunts and pig sticking. The pomp and display of the Anglo-Indians added a note of color and amusement to English society. Far deeper than that lay the pride occasioned by battles fought far away, generally easily enough won and little understood at home, but contributing to the confident national consciousness of innate superiority. Some of the successful merchant adventurers on returning from India used part of their fortunes to buy their way into Parliament through rotten boroughs and created a clique in the House ready to further their aims abroad.

Probably the majority of the employees of John Company were only dimly aware of the significance of their acts as they drew up commercial contracts with native states and opened up more and more areas for trade with Europe; they could not have foreseen that they were weakening the whole structure of the country by their steady encroachments into new territory. The crumbling old

Mogul Empire, the quarrels between Mahrattas, Sikhs, and Rajputs, set against the rising imperial power of Britain, are now easily seen as precipitating an inevitable conclusion, but then it was not so obvious. India was without any real central control; the independent or semi-independent kingdoms were warlike and of a certain strength but without direction. It was England's fortune to be there, not exactly waiting to take the reins, but ready to hold them if they came into her hands. Her only serious rival was France, and she was victorious in spite of the ability and vision of Dupleix. He understood very well what was going on in the country and had tremendous territorial and imperial ambitions for France, and for himself. But his country did not support him, he was ill-placed, and, as always, England's sea power turned the scale.

In 1750, the British in India were a company of merchants clinging —not always successfully—to their main trading posts at Bombay, Madras, and Calcutta. By 1850, with the overthrow of the Sikh Kingdom in the Punjab, the Company and the British Government between them were the undisputed masters of India. They had to fight for their position: against the French, against the provincial governors of the dying Mogul empire, against Hyder Ali and Tippoo in the south, and, lastly, against the Sikhs in the northwest. There were wars of aggression, there were punitive wars, there were wars of self-defence: . . . For since . . . 1784 the arrangement had been that the British Government, in effect, appointed the Governor General, nominated a Board of Control in London, and supplied a modicum of regular troops for service in India; while the Company's directors in Leadenhall Street were left in the actual control of their increasingly enormous territories, which they had both to administer and defend. This meant a civil service and armies of their own, apart from trading activities to further what they called their "investment."*

This was the framework of the early Indian Civil Service. It was conceived at a time when the Company was largely unrestrained, often unscrupulous, generally audacious. The territory was so vast, the British involved so few in number, there was so much responsibility to be assumed by anyone willing to take it that the result was a sort of psychological gold rush. The conditions of trade sometimes brought fantastically lucrative rewards for the British merchants. That they might be economically ruining a district does

* Radcliffe, *The Problem of Power*, London, Secker & Warburg, 1952, pp. 67 *et seq.*

not seem to have disturbed most of them. They were emboldened
by every fresh success, while their Indian competitors and contemporaries were debilitated, confused, and divided, seeing their
country despoiled.

The eighteenth century in Europe—and in most other places—
was not a time remarkable for its probity. In fact it is often
remembered for its fantastic profligate corruption—a historical
example from which we may draw encouragement, for it was succeeded by a climate of great honesty. The Company salaries were
so low as to be nominal and a man was expected to maintain himself
by private trading. The servants of the Company, drawing up
regulations to protect its trade and able to enforce their preferences
with arms, soon found that they could create their own monopolies,
sell their own licenses and permits. Corruption reached a towering
scale. One bribe in Madras was said to have attracted much remark
because it was over a million pounds! A man could hope to make a
fortune of at least six figures in a few years. Clive and Warren
Hastings, both great men, both of whom considered themselves
honest, when brought to trial by their enemies in spite of the signal
services they had rendered their country reminded their peers that
in impugning the honor of soldier-administrators they should
relate their judgment to their own actions at home.

But by then the belated conscience of England had been aroused
and the Company was found to be a convenient scapegoat—the
country was jealous of all this flaunting wealth. "Is it not . . . un-
just to throw the exclusive blame of the immense expansion given
to the Anglo-Indian territory during the last twenty years on the
rapacity and ambition of the Company?" asked Valbezen in *The
English in India.** The divided control between the East India Company and Parliament made it easy to avoid responsibility for many
concrete acts—one wonders how it ever worked at all. Yet out of
this maladroit, selfishly-inspired tangle was born the premier civil
service of history, coming so quickly on the heels of total self-
interest. The first great steps of reform were the work of Lord
Cornwallis, who succeeded Warren Hastings as Governor-General,
arriving in India after his misfortunes in the American Revolution.
It was he who created the service which, aside from its integrity,
was to be so remarkable for the capacity and the intellectual acu-

* E. de Valbezen, London, W. H. Allen & Co., 1883, p. 378.

men of its members. This task, begun by Cornwallis, was to be completed by Bentinct, a later Governor-General.

The East India Company, with its immense opportunities, had for long been a coveted employer and the bestowing of its posts was far too often a matter of favor. "By the middle of the eighteenth century the English governing classes had discovered the great possibilities of an Indian appointment in disposing of an embarrassed—or embarrassing—relative. The prospects were more lucrative than anything that could be wrung out of the English or Irish establishments. Besides, the relative was further away. In one year the list of civil servants in Bengal alone included the names of one peer, nineteen sons of peers, and twelve baronets!"*

Such applicants were no longer tempted to enlist. Instead, for many decades, there came some extraordinarily gifted and able men who were of perfect integrity and generally very religious. They came for the opportunity to command, the wide field of action, responsibility, and adventure. Nothing comparable was open to them at home—they were drawn mostly from the ranks of intelligence, not privilege. The intricate examination system, based on the classics, had not yet been instituted; most of them arrived almost as children—in their early teens—and spent their lives in the country. There were no home leaves then, except for illness, so the parting from those at home was almost final. They may have been ordinary youths when they applied, but in this heady climate of command and change they rose above any ordinary capacity. These are the men whom Macauley praises in his lavish way as being of "spotless glory"—men like Elphinstone, Munro, Malcolm, Metcalfe, Outram, and the Lawrences, who counciled, administered, wrote, fought. Some had come in the old, bad, degenerate days but had kept clear of contamination through their own probity and they stayed to form the nucleus of a new and purified service.

But with the passage of time that first fire began to be damped in the heavy toils of administration and the caliber of the service slowly, subtly changed. The country became stabilized, the work was less romantic and imaginative, there was less call to action and independent thought. The service became more of a bureaucratic machine with a core of men of considerable academic achievement but untried in a practical sphere, men who were very much concerned with the interests of the people at home and too

* Lord Radcliffe, *The Problem of Power*, p. 70.

often somewhat undermined by the prestige and flattery of their position.

The obsequiousness of the Oriental—which up to the last twenty-five years was the rule rather than the exception, and which often veiled secret contempt—did much to destroy the clarity of thought of the European everywhere in the East. By virtue of his coloring he was surrounded by fawning dependents from the moment he set foot on Indian soil, by the servile murmur of *"Huzoor,"* by a salaam from every clerk, every coolie. Sycophants were ever near him and it was hard to remember, perhaps, that in some cold northern town, far away over the water, he was only one among millions in a jostling crowd. This was true for all the *sahibs;* doubly true for the Indian civil servants, who had inherited so splendid a mantle.

This attitude is all over now; to the present generation it seems written on old parchment. It crumbled in the end, as though at a touch, but while it was the prevalent mood it was almost paramount, very insidious, very dangerous.

By the time the East India Company Resident was the de facto King of Delhi and known by this sobriquet to the English, the capital had become a rather small, shadowy, and sunken town—there were about one hundred and fifty thousand people living in it, it was partly ruinous, and fields and open country lay within its walls. In the first half of the seventeenth century it had had a population of some two million and was one of the greatest cities of the world, and now it had come to this. Yet it had remained a lodestone, it had never quite lost its aura of significance. To the young men coming out for the Company a post in Delhi was a prize—it meant they were on the road to promotion. Such positions were given to favorites, to those who had powerful relatives on the Board in London, to men like Elphinstone and the Metcalfes.

There was a longish stretch, in the middle of the earlier period of British occupation of the Deccan (after they had established themselves and up to the Mutiny era), which was peaceful and prosperous, when the city revived somewhat and could take pleasure in its own charms. At first there were raids and incursions, but gradually the Company restored order and, assuming practically full command, gave the people of the capital a certain confidence. It was this interval which was to be looked back upon with nostalgia. The university flourished, there was a great interest in mathematics, and there were poets and philosophers. People lived well—the highly placed, magnificently, and even the poor were not hungry. Food was cheap.

The climate, bracing, sunny, and dry for half the year, made for cheerfulness and allowed the Delhi *wallahs* to get out into the country and wander about in those open spaces inside and outside the wall. There was a great deal to explore—ancient tombs, palaces, and forts, the memorials of kingdoms and heroes. As the town began to be built up again, people went further afield and in the hot weather took summer houses outside the wall. Sometimes they took over old tombs for this purpose; no one was squeamish about them, they were vast, cool, and dim, and could easily be made livable for people with a retinue of servants. The British Resident was one of those who used a tomb for his summer home—the English were then much readier to accept a partially Indian style of life than in later years, when as rulers they consciously felt it necessary to emphasize their own ways to a subject people.

In those years when Delhi was a great preserve for the Company, but still nominally under the Mogul King of Delhi, the races mixed rather easily. They met as friends, intellectually, at the university; they were genuinely interested in each other's ideas on abstract subjects. This, of course, went further. Some of the English married Muslim ladies, following Muslim rites, and became a part of the local aristocracy or gentry. More, if they were unmarried, established an Indian lady in a house in a garden. These attachments were often serious, tender, and lasting but the effects were tragic—the children could never hope to find the same niche in society as their fathers. There were then almost no unmarried white women in the country.

Socially Delhi was divided into a number of levels—the civilians, the soldiers, the politicals, the teachers—all within the ranks of the Westerners. The soldiers were divided, again, into those who served the Company and those who had enlisted in the private armies of native princes. Conquest was in the air and the country was full of foreign troops. Many of the French, when their own country left the field, hired themselves out as mercenaries to the different states, serving in company with men of many nationalities, including the British. It was no disgrace to be an officer in the army of an Indian prince, provided he was not attacking your own countrymen, but often the extravagance of these men's lives, their fantastic uniforms, and their self-importance excited a good deal of ridicule and comment from the more conventional Company troops and from the Royal regiments.

Everyone was jealous of everyone else's perquisites and pay. When bribery for the civilian and loot for the soldier were discountenanced, it was only to be expected that everyone was alert to increase his prospects with whatever means he could, provided they fell within the letter of the law. The country was falling apart—it was the ideal moment for the adventurer, the man of imagination and reckless courage, to forge a path for himself before red tape finally enmeshed him. Delhi was three months away by post from Calcutta, the seat of government. What an opportunity was offered then to the ambitious eccentric! Never was there such wild, extravagant living, such opulence, such display! For a short time it was possible for persons of modest background (though not of modest frame of mind) to indulge themselves in the fantastic sort of existence which only persons of great wealth and with high family connections could normally consider in that age— people like Lady Hester Stanhope.

Naturally enough, these swashbucklers were relatively few, but it is they who are remembered—men like David Ochterlony, a sort of white prince who lived in great splendor, with a sphere of influence of his own, traveling with a long train of elephants for himself and his wives; and William Fraser, another flamboyant eccentric, who was finally assassinated.

But the great figures of the time did not succumb to such meretricious attractions—their achievements were real. Certainly, some of them lived splendidly, too. Metcalfe, Elphinstone, Alexander Skinner, Malcolm, and then the next generation, the heroes of the Mutiny—the Lawrences, Nicholson, Hodson, and a score of others —left their imprint on the capital, whether they served, fought or died there, or whether they were only part of the vast general development of the events which led up to the establishment of the Raj. They were men of parts—they could write, command, execute —and they were often scholars too, knowing Persian and delighting in beauty. They were also warm, generous friends.

All this, and much more, makes Delhi a treasure house. We had only a few evenings, a few early mornings, to gaze upon it under the wings of the war, but we saw what we could, jogging about the dusty roads under the scent of the neems. We went out to New Delhi, the British capital, which was full of pride. Here were the palace of the Viceroy, the Secretariat Buildings, the princely residences, all laid out according to plan, and many of them very ugly. How could this town have come about, so near the strong confident lines of the mosques, the powerful Fort, the beauty of the palaces? The round, red sandstone building of the Princes' Chamber we found handsome, but most of the new town gave us, in the Chinese phrase, "a heavy heart and a depressed feeling."

X A Mountain Sanctuary

There is another species of monkey, which is not found in Bajour, Sewad, and these districts, and is much larger than the kinds that are brought into our country. Its tail is very long, its hair whitish, its face entirely black. They call this species of monkey *langur*, and it is met with in the hills and woods of Hindustan.

BABER

OUR HOPES that we might be drawn into the China theatre did not materialize. Disappointed, our short leave nearly over, and almost all our funds swallowed up by the Cecil, we had to make new plans. It had been a sensible decision, we felt, to have tried to serve where we were peculiarly fitted to help, but it had been costly —there were no cheap hotels in Delhi and we had known of no place else to go. Now we had quickly to find a hill station for Rosalind and me, where we would pass the summer, receive the new baby, and wait till it was seen how far the Japanese would advance. Everyone had only the gloomiest counsel—after a winter of such disasters the hills were full of people, the hotels crowded to capacity. Delhi is surrounded by a ring of hill stations: Naini Tal, Mussoorie, Simla, Dalhousie, Kashmir—but we knew nothing of them, except that Kashmir, obviously the best, was also the most expensive. Simla was easy to rule out. Finally, by a process of elimination, we chose Mussoorie, though it was little more than a name to us. A French lady in Barrackpore had once spoken of it to me, likening it to Alpine country and calling it *sauvage*. It was exactly the right one for us.

We arrived at the station one evening at seven, as the train for Dehra Dun, the terminus for Mussoorie, left at eight. Among the many dirty, crowded, confused, noisy stations I have been in all over the world, that hour in Delhi still stands out to me as the epitome of distraction. It was bedlam—ill-lit, jammed with clamorous people, hot and grimy. Desperate travelers shouted and struggled in every square yard. We could not understand why this should be—the capital was calm and there seemed to be little uneasiness over the war among ordinary people—yet in that station everyone was so demented one would have thought the Japanese were only an hour away. Later I realized that this is a condition endemic to Central Indian railway stations, but I don't yet know quite why.

Stanton, always at his best in disaster, typically English, was perfectly unmoved. He found our coupé, put us into it, thrust the servants into theirs, and threw himself back into the boiling pandemonium beyond the platform. He was obliged to fight his way to the baggage room, where with the greatest difficulty he had our pieces weighed and put in the brake. This took an hour, every minute he had. The train was literally moving out of the station, with me anxiously hanging out of the window and wondering if I should pull the communication cord, when he jumped aboard. Our melancholy over the Delhi fiasco was somewhat assuaged by this mild triumph—at least we were withdrawing intact.

We needed some encouragement, too, as an indefinite separation now lay ahead, with Stanton returning to a Presidency which might yet be invaded, while I must await our child among strangers. The dark hours while the train went across the plain were clouded with the anticipation of parting. It was many years before I came to know how many people had approached Mussoorie as refugees in times of stress and uncertainty. Now all the world knows at least the name of this hill town because the Dalai Lama took shelter here; and he is only the best known of its many fugitives. Certainly that summer there were many of us approaching the mountains from afar, bewildered, ill-prepared, taking one clumsy step at a time.

However, in the morning when we woke to find ourselves going through the low hills and pretty wooded country which lead into Dehra Dun, our spirits rose. After the parched and dusty plain we had been seeing for so long, it was wonderfully refreshing to be among fresh, dainty light green birches, growing sweet and uncrowded in that cooler air. Dehra Dun, where we arrived in time for breakfast, lies at a slight elevation and though it was still hot we had begun to discard the heaviness of the plains. In the station dining room we fell into conversation with some American missionaries, also on their way to Mussoorie, who at once began to suggest places where we might stay. In our year and a half in India we had had so much experience of the detached and chilling attitude of officialdom that the warmhearted gentleness of these people seemed doubly comforting and reassuring.

Other travelers assembled and we all waited, patient and resigned, for the Mussoorie bus to appear. The morning grew hotter—even at two thousand feet the sun was very fierce. Stanton and one of the missionaries walked up and down the platform, discussing the news, which could hardly have been worse—it was almost the lowest tide in our fortunes in the war. The Germans were winning in Egypt and near Sebastopol; the Japanese, still gaining ground in Burma, had raided Colombo. India was full of disaffection; the hills received refugees from Singapore, Java, Borneo, Burma, even Assam. I sat next to a kind and motherly lady, feeling how strange it was to be on this remote little station, of which I had never even heard a week ago.

One of the anomalies of India was the great restlessness of its people, whose ideal, theoretically, is one of tranquility. Frequent, long, difficult journeys seemed an essential part of life even for very poor Indians, and ill-paid Europeans had been caught up in this rhythm. It appeared to us to be absolutely necessary to travel hundreds, if not thousands, of miles each year, in spite of the discomfort and expense involved. The trains and buses were always more than full. It was extraordinary to discover when talking to humble Indians—domestic servants, factory workers, clerks—in how many parts of the country they had lived. Most Westerners love travel and pursue it with energy, seeking pleasure or change, and yet with all their enthusiasm probably move about less than these people, most of whom never dream of traveling for pleasure. (Pleasure hardly enters into any aspect of their adult lives.) There was nothing frivolous about their journeys—they were part of the accustomed, inevitable round of living. Were we now falling into this groove ourselves? Thinking of this, I remembered the war. There was surely no groove about that, and that had brought about our present restlessness—and, too, we were paying our way. I wondered if it were possible that most of these poor travelers had actually bought tickets, or did they slip in and out of stations like Delhi, the crush and confusion helping them to get through the gates without passes?

Already the whole atmosphere of these Indian train trips, which at first had so disgusted me, seemed not only entirely familiar but even, with all the drawbacks, rather pleasurable. The dirt was as offensive as ever to me, the unnecessary discomforts as irritating, but neither loomed so large. Even the little station restaurant at Dehra Dun with its stained tablecloths, the black screens which kept out so few of the flies, the tired faces, worn after an uneasy night, surveying without rancor the badly cooked eggs and the butter melting on thick saucers, inspired in me a feeling of affection. Outside on the platform the red-turbaned porters sat on the ground, watching over bedrolls, black tin uniform cases, and felt-covered water bottles. The station was strange but in spite of that I felt in a way that all my life I had been passing in and out of this scene—it was like the first act of a familiar play and I could imagine sitting in a theatre, in the dark, looking at it.

By the time the bus had come and we had arranged ourselves on its narrow wooden benches we were feeling quite lighthearted. Mussoorie was no longer a speck on a map, seven thousand feet up on the edge of Garhwal, and the steep road ahead, with its sharp curves, seemed the prelude to an adventure.

We were now in what was then called the United Provinces, not a hundred miles from Tibet as the crow flies, and going up into the mountains where many great rivers take their rise. The source of the Ganges, the object of devout pilgrimages, is not far away from here, and the Jumna, which we had so lately seen running by the Red Fort, springs only some fifty miles from Mussoorie. The Jumna means a great deal in Central India: one of the Five Rivers of the Punjab, the river of Agra as well as of Delhi, it stirs the heart and the imagination. No one cared deeply about our poor bend of the Hooghly in Bengal, except when they thought of it as "Ganges Bank," but here the Jumna speaks to people. It rouses an emotion, as does the Thames in England; most rivers are beloved— or once were—but some have a particular association with history which gives them an added sentimental significance, people want to see them. The Jumna is one of these.

Next to Garhwal, on the southern side, is Kumaon, famous for its warriors; west and south of Kumaon lies the western boundary of Nepal. Northwards, separated from us by a hundred and fifty miles of tumbled mountains, is Kashmir—it is an evocative terrain, bold and grandiose, on the rim of forbidden heights and vast unknown territories. Now, twenty-five years later, Nepal is open to the world, but much of the rest of this region is more or less closed to most of us. On the northern side of Kashmir is Sinkiang, which seems so old and yet is called new, holding the desert country of Kashgar and Yarkand, the old world of the silk route, of camel caravans. When I was in Mussoorie we wondered if Sinkiang was not part of the new world of the Russian enigma, but today it is quite clearly back within the orbit of Peking. At that time, in the early forties, it was in its last antique stage—Peter Fleming and Ella Kini Maillart had traveled through it only a short time before on their passage through Tartary, going as romantically, as slowly, as painfully, as in the distant past. It was one of the last of those epic journeys.

Up there in those wastes the old Bactrian civilization had flourished and suddenly come to a stop; in those high deserts Sir Aurel Stein had discovered the Buddhistic frescoes of Tun Hwang. Obviously, in that summer nothing of this vast region was to be shown me, nor did I approach it any nearer by story or legend, yet it seemed a great thing to me to be at least on its perimeter, far from the sultry delta of Bengal and the arid plains of Central India.

Stanton could stay only four days, which we spent in an intense effort to find some sort of lodgings. We went first to a rest house which had been suggested by our companions of the bus and where we were so fortunate as to be given a room for a few nights, until the people who had reserved it should arrive. From here we hunted all through Mussoorie, where there seemed to be no vacant rooms at all. Still, we met much kindness as we swung out of the bazaars into the wooded sections and explored the settlement, which extended for miles along a sharp, steep ridge.

By the time he had to go we still had found nothing but we did have the assurance that a number of people were looking out for us and our hostess told us that if nothing else appeared there would always be a couch and a corner for the baby and me in her house. It was a great rambling Victorian establishment, very incongruous in those high hills, owned by an elderly, distinguished lady who was wonderfully kind-hearted and had opened it to missionaries as a sort of holiday home. It had that summer, through her goodness, become a refuge for all sorts of people like myself and round the huge oval dining table sat at least twenty oddly-assorted persons for every meal. We felt ourselves extraordinarily united, so embracing was the atmosphere of the house, and would exchange wide understanding grins when the front door bell rang and we could hear our hostess hastening to it and telling whoever stood there that *of course* there was room and whoever it was was welcome. The housekeeper, who had just lost a son in the war but who never let her sorrow weigh on the rest of us, would get up from the head of the table and continue her task of stretching the house walls. It was a Godsend that we had come here—it was the only place we found for a long time which had any room at all.

Later I learned the story of the lady of the house, Miss Swetenham. Her father had been one of the heroes of the Mutiny and had been awarded a grant of land in Mussoorie when it was all over. That was over eighty years before the summer that we were there and this mansion had been his daughter's home all her life. It was altogether a romantic story. The Major, her father, had been walking on his estate when he was attracted by the sound of a sweet voice singing. Looking for the singer, he discovered that she was a beautiful girl drawing water at a spring. He instantly fell in love. She was an Indian and of low caste; he was a gentleman. He sent her to a mission and had her educated to be a companion to him— if she should so wish, which she did. This marriage resulted in one daughter, who was educated in England and whom we met as an old lady, loved by everyone around her. Any signs of mixed race she may once have had had disappeared under the leveling of age and her beautiful voice and cultivated accent obviated the most usual Anglo-Indian characteristic—the singsong intonation. With such parents she had had a noble start! Yet many of her father's family had disparaged the union and were reluctant to acknowledge their relationship with her, so deeply prejudiced were the English in India.

She herself was perfectly indifferent to such trumpery barriers, far above them. Next to me at the table sat a young English girl, as blond as an angel, well educated, privileged, the daughter of a judge in the Indian Civil Service. But her name was Mehta—she had married an Indian in the same service. I wondered how she had negotiated the perilous sands this entailed—she appeared happy and from what she told me of him it was evident that her husband was very anglicized in his ways. In that house no awkward questions were ever raised.

When Stanton went I was too aware of the number of wives on the hillside who did not even know where their husbands were or whether they were alive, to brood, and I continued, with as much energy as I could muster, to look for some place for us to live. In the next weeks I moved a number of times. Because of this I learned a little of the mountain and its fierce rocky contours—which in easier circumstances I would probably have missed in that period of enforced inactivity. The distances between the different parts of the town were great and the paths steep, so I had to provide myself with transport, though it was expensive and I wished I could have done without it. I moved about either by rickshaw or by dandy, the latter a miserably uncomfortable litter shaped like a shallow Victorian bathtub. In these slow open chairs, pushed or carried up and down the heights, I had plenty of time for observation and reflection—from them I looked out upon the most lively scenes as we went through the narrow lanes of the bazaars.

Mussoorie belongs to the French Romanticists, with its wild irregular outlines, savage glens, and deep, richly wooded precipices. The people, however, were much more complex and not altogether in keeping with this dramatic, but essentially simple, school. Here were a great many schools, mainly for Europeans, together with the poor Indians, the old-style imperialists, the summer visitors, of any hill station—but there were also rich Indians and many missionaries and, that summer, thousands of refugees, mainly European women. These were not the usual complacent but discontented *memsahibs* of the plains, but desperately anxious and unhappy wives, the first displaced persons of the Japanese advance. They were very much in tune with the Berlioz/Delacroix backdrop of the mountains.

The long ragged town lies precariously balanced on steep slopes, overlooking the plain, backed by forest country. At first I found myself always comparing it with Darjeeling—these rugged steeps with those mild and rounded contours, the lean and somber men of these ranges with the cheerful wide-faced Nepalis and Bhutias whom everyone loves. Compared to them the people of Mussoorie seemed violent and unreasonable, particularly the coolies who were mostly Garhwalis and a desperate lot. They were big-featured, dark, handsome, and willful—good Delacroix models for some of those visionary Eastern scenes—and in practical affairs often very unpleasant to deal with, being grasping and unscrupulous. Before I took a dandy the terms were always discussed and agreed upon, but more than once when I was alone on a stretch of pathway, at some dangerous turn round the mountain they would demand a higher rate. With the precipice yawning below me and the dandy swaying it was extremely frightening. In the end I gave up using dandies. It was evidently a rather common tactic; sometimes the men put the dandy down and stood there, arguing and threatening. There were so many newcomers that for a long time they could get away with it. There were no police up in the hills, away from the town.

In Darjeeling everyone was always looking up, enraptured with the snows, but here you looked down, down through the void to the wide and distant plain, blue and enticing, which fell away almost from under your feet. It was a place where a good head for heights was an advantage. Far away, round one corner of the ridge, the snows were visible on clear days. I wanted so much to see Nanda Devi that later, when we were settled, I made a great excursion for this very purpose, but she was veiled in mist and that whole summer I never saw the snows.

Yet even without the snows and the laughing people, I much preferred Mussoorie; it was much richer in interest, larger, more varied than Darjeeling—it had not degenerated into a resort only. It was rather fashionable and even boasted a night life and a social season of sorts, made possible by a large European community with plenty of officers on leave, rich Indians and rajahs. There were good shops, hotels, cinemas, and surprisingly extensive bazaars following the contours of the ridge. It was gay and full of character. Every summer large numbers of missionaries came here from all over India to confer over mutual problems and to be with their children who were attending school in Landour, a suburb at the far end of the ridge. They rented bungalows, reestablished themselves as families, turning their children into day scholars, revived themselves in the cool air, and carried on all sorts of lively pursuits. In September, though most of these people went away, there remained a core of real residents who, with the schools and a skeleton bazaar, held the place together till the next March when the heat would waft the rajahs and *memsahibs* and missionaries up from the plains once more.

Every evening, in the swift hour before sunset, the world walked up and down on the broad mall which overlooked the plain. Lovely Indian matrons in gossamer and glittering saris, elegant Muslim gentlemen, well-dressed European ladies, and officers with shining insignia sauntered to and fro on this high avenue, past a little bandstand. This pleasant European custom was enlivened by the coming and going of spruce rickshaws, with the coolies in livery, adding an eighteenth-century note to the assembly; by the presence of fair-haired children on ponies attended by *ayahs;* and by peddlars crying their wares; everyone passing in the strong light, high above the river-laced plain, which stretched out seven thousand feet below us while the strains of military marches and light opera blew out into the void.

This wide view of the plain was the great charm of the center ridge. At the ends of the town trees obscured it, but from the mall you could gaze over an immense stretch of land, shimmering in heat all the way to the far horizon. Through a light haze rose the Siwaliks, like little artificial mounds on the earth floor, serving to mark the footsteps of Shiva for the pious. From our vantage point high in the blue air, the panorama was predominantly azure and tawny, its contours trembling slightly in the vibrant atmosphere, blurred with sun and distance. The silver curves of the Jumna, winding behind the Siwaliks, were the only strongly definitive lines in that whole expanse of flat and sallow ground. Behind us rose the hills, densely wooded and full of game—panthers and leopards, deer, peacocks, pheasants. *Lungurs,* big black-faced monkeys with blond or russet coats, swung through the trees, wood pigeons cooed and chuckled high in leafy branches. What variety, what riches, the world offers! Alone and homeless in that remote Indian hill station, obliged to turn every rupee in my purse over twice, I never felt more keenly the charm and diversity, the hint of infinite beauty and resource which lie about us.

Beyond the mall lay entwined the steep and narrow streets of the bazaars—some were literally stairways—picturesque and romantic to a degree. Here sat the old men of the mountains, smoking hookahs beside their wares: silver ornaments, heaps of bright fruit and vegetables, piles of soft shawls. After the dull stalls of Bengal, to find myself being carried in a litter past all this rich produce of the Punjab and Kashmir was a sort of enchantment. The glamorous merchants, black-hearted and unscrupulous though they might be, looked the very images of an Eastern ballet. The Kashmiri shops hung flowery woolen rugs at their portals to beguile the passer-by into entering and becoming enamoured of the shining inlaid walnut trays, the delicate papier-mâché coffers, the shawls so finely woven that they would pass through a wedding ring. The cotton shops pinned at their entrances bright bedspreads of purest yellow, deep amber, figured blue, which fluttered in the wind like gaudy sails in that odd twisted setting of old crooked shops clambering up the hillside.

There was hardly a stretch of level ground from one end of the town to the other. Most of the houses were built on *pushtas*, terraces which are dug out of the hillside and project into space and which are not necessarily very secure—whole buildings have been known to slide down the mountain during the monsoon. The paths and roads run along the precipice, with a rock wall on one hand and on the other the *khud*, which may present a sheer drop of a thousand feet. The danger of inadvertently wandering off the path is lessened in the wooded sections, where a falling person might be able to check his descent by catching at a tree, but it is everywhere quite formidable. Going through the bazaars, where the road is lined on each side by shops, you might risk letting go of your child's hand for a moment, but even here the buildings sometimes fell away, leaving an opening which showed the vast distances of the blue and dusty world below.

We are all so absorbed in our accustomed round that it is something of a shock to be precipitated suddenly into a town of which one has never even heard and to find it so sturdy, so self-contained, so rich in interest. I had felt this strongly when I went to Yunnan, a province of enormous fascination, of culture, of involved history, which flourished so long almost entirely apart from the outer world; to a lesser extent I felt it here, during that difficult and tempestuous summer.

I used to think sometimes I would never find a place which was suitable for us but eventually I realized that if such a place existed it would be in Landour, at the end of the Mussoorie Ridge, reached by a long narrow path winding along the precipice, called the Tehri Road. In this part of the town there were a great many American missionaries: here they had a language school, a hospital, a library, and an excellent school, Woodstock, which then had about five hundred students. The pupils came from all over India and even further afield—some were from Burma and Malaya. Among the Americans were a few British children, some Chinese, and some Indians (including Pundit Nehru's nieces). During the long winter holidays they went down to the plains to their homes and in the summers their parents came up to them. At that time there were a great many American missionaries scattered all over India and they were extremely interested in the school, continually trying to better it. That summer they were working on the problem of playing fields, which necessitated the great expense of first building wide terraces to create level ground. The resources of the country were drawn upon as much as possible—there were long scouting trips arranged far back into the beautiful wild hills, a paradise for the botanist and hunter. Landour was full of energy and plans, reunions, homes, studying, piety—it was unique in that setting, quite unlike anything else for thousands of miles.

Here I had only great good fortune. First I stayed with a family from Newfoundland whose field of work lay in Lucknow. Their stories of these two widely dissimilar parts of the world, which they told with a natural dramatic flair, soon made me feel as though I were watching two pageants stream by there on that high mountain. The father would tell of his work as a young padre, years before, in small logging settlements in the cold solitary northern island, with its robust, sad, patient people. He had had a ministry among people of French descent (like his own), whose life was so hard and unrewarding that their only solution seemed to be to emigrate.

Then he would turn to the scene at hand, and the intricate, impassioned city parish where he was working. All the missionaries in India were then faced with a type of nationalist movement within their flocks; many of their converts were eager to have their vicars leave, confident that they would do much better without the Europeans, but, of course, expecting financial support to continue.

This padre had been in India for twenty years and had had many absolutely classical adventures, including being chased by a crocodile in the Ganges and having blackwater fever. That summer of 1942 he was deeply affected by a case which had arisen in Lucknow. Four British soldiers just out from England had gone into a bar one night. All were under twenty, one of them had never had a drink before in his life. When they came out they were drunk. The sidewalk was crowded with coolies, lying asleep in the heat. In front of the door there were some large palms set in earthenware pots; each of the tommies, for no reason, took a pot and brought it down on a sleeper's head. They killed four coolies.

This had aroused a great furor in Lucknow; the Indians, thinking the thing might be hushed up and the soldiers protected, had channeled their grievance into the most active and belligerent part of the Congress Party. The best possible lawyers were engaged on behalf of the victims' families (poor, wretched people, astounded to find themselves the objects of solicitude). The four youths were put in a British jail and were so unaware of how serious had been their crime that when the padre visited them and asked them what he could do for them they replied that they would like a football.

He tried to persuade them that they were in a dreadful situation, but they did not believe him. I never heard the outcome of this case, which made little stir in the European press.

The actual house we were staying in belonged to one of the pretenders to the throne of Nepal—a young man of handsome person and agreeable manner who sometimes came to drink tea with my hosts. It was a large house: the Newfoundland family had the upper part, while downstairs lived a mother and her children whose mission station was on the very borders of Nepal. The father had died and the mother was maintaining the post as best she could, entirely alone most of the year. Only when she came to Landour—her children were in school here—did she see Europeans. Her resolute, solitary stand filled me with something like awe. She was a cheerful person, full of common sense. The loss of her husband, with whom she had been tremendously happy, had not made her lose her faith—she was indomitable—but she did not show it in any aggressive way. To see her with the Nepalese prince was to observe two entirely different conditions of thought—they might have been people of separate planets. The prince had little expectation of succession and lived tranquilly outside his kingdom, administering his properties, one easy day following another.

The house was marvelously placed on the ridge—below us lay the plain, the Siwaliks, and the curves of the river; across the void, the clouds. By the time I came there it was already the end of May. The monsoon was approaching, the mountain was as parched and dusty as the plains, and we longed for the rains almost as fervently as did those who lived far below in the great heat. That June the view over the void was as evocative and tender as any landscape Raphael ever painted behind a placid Madonna—every delineation of the plain was accented by the transmutations in the quality of the air. The gentle Siwaliks glowed like blue jewels, the Jumna meandered through a countryside no longer blurred and hazy but deep in promise, so blue were the folds, so exquisite the lines of the fields. In space, directly before us, swelled the majestic cumulous clouds which would soon engulf the whole mountainside but were first wooing and captivating us by their soft, towering, luscious beauty. How they drew color out of the toneless world of the plain! And how we longed for them to break, that we might hear the delicious music of heavy rain falling on the roof at night, that the hot, brittle air might once more be caressing and muted!

Everything was not always so idyllic. One afternoon while the

family was out and I was writing, I knocked over a bottle of ink—
this was in those prehistoric times when people actually had bottles
of ink about to dip their pens into—and, of course, the contents
missed the floor and fell in a rich stream onto a fawn carpet. I was
aghast but I knew that if I acted quickly I could get it out. I had
to pour milk through it. There was one servant in the house, an
old sweeper. He was very reluctant to let me have any milk, he
thought my story about pouring it over the ink on the carpet very
peculiar. In this sort of catastrophe, every second counts. I wasted
a great many before he finally and begrudgingly brought in a small
bowl of milk and set it on the floor. Instantly a huge white dog
appeared from nowhere and lapped it all up in two great swirls
with his tongue. It was one of the most horrible moments of my
life. I then tried to get more milk but there was apparently none
in the house. It was brought early every morning by a *dudh-wallah*
who went from house to house. We were miles away from any
shops and few sold milk anyway. I had no transport and there was
no telephone. In despair I fell on my knees and tried to scrub away
the stain with water; my poor hostess found me at this dreadful
task. Noble creature that she was, with all the goodwill in the
world, yet how her face fell! But our relationship survived this
supreme test, life went on.

Just before the rains finally broke we had to move again—not on
account of the milk disaster but because my room had been
promised long before to a missionary from Bareilly. This time it
did not prove so hard to find a new home, though every house in
Landour was more than full, and I had only to move a short
distance up the Tehri Road, further round the precipice, to a family
who lived all year round on the mountain, as they were connected
with the school. There were already three families in their house
but they took me in out of the goodness of their hearts. Aside from
solving my own pressing problems of keeping us under shelter, it
was a welcome opportunity to see how people lived who actually
were here as residents, season after season.

The father of the family, a Mr. Fleming, was an ornithologist
who was making a collection of many rare Indian birds, keeping
some specimens and sending others to a museum in America. The
family had long been planning its holidays with certain birds as the
object of their travels and in this way had become familiar with
many distant and little-known parts of the country. This passion
had come upon my new host after he had arrived in India, and it

was while he was here that he had learned, by himself, to stuff and mount his prizes, but he had never had any proper setting for them. At last, this very month, almost on the very day and hour on which I arrived, a little study had been finished for him, resting upon a small terrace and lined with glass cases. The birds which were his treasures had been stowed away in trunks and he was immensely eager to get them out and gloat over them—but, instead, he surrendered his study to a complete stranger and her baby. It was we who reveled in the pristine freshness of that hillside room with its shining paint and wide windows. To give up this immediate realization of a long-cherished dream and be kind was, I realized, entirely characteristic of Mr. Fleming—I have never ceased to be grateful to him for this generous act. We were not to deprive him of it for long, as other transients were to leave in a fortnight and give me their rooms. Then the wide-eyed owls, the pigeons, the orioles and the flycatchers, the pheasants and the hawks were brought in to the shelves which had been holding my books and clothes.

The study was, in fact, not quite finished on the morning I arrived and the workmen were in the very act of fitting in the windows. It was a summer of building alterations to the house and the family was in a state of amused despair over the laziness and imperturbable calm of the mistris. They put the railings on the terrace, worked on the bedroom over the study, and painted woodwork with the same magnificent insouciance and scorn of time which had characterized their brethren in Barrackpore.

In this house we stayed for the rest of our time in Mussoorie; in it the baby was born, and a most happy interlude it was, right in the midst of the darkest hours of the war. India was seething with revolt, everywhere one turned the future seemed dark, yet in that house there was so much sympathy and liveliness, so much courage and humor, that no one ever indulged in gloom or was dull, even during the perpetual rains, which soon came upon us. Never were there so many good-natured persons under one roof, even though we were all together four families in not much space and one family was in the act of selling their building to the Flemings that very summer.

Everyone was good-natured, that is, except the servants. There was an excellent bearer who had, alas, a strong antipathy for the cook, who returned his animosity. I remember the cook as an artist in the making of feathery dumplings, dumplings lighter than clouds, with which he adorned the generous stews he put together for the hungry people who gathered round the table—never less than eight, often more. The cold war between the cook and the bearer did not much disturb us as there was always far too much else going on for that to distract us—we only fervently hoped neither would resign. There was always a great deal of conversation, about irrigation, the caste system, civil disobedience, Burma, Africa, India's future, drowning out the mutterings in the kitchen. It was here that I first heard of a pressure cooker—there could have been few in India at that time, but Dr. Fleming, the lady of the house, had brought one from America. It was sometimes a topic of conversation because at seven thousand feet it had become a rather different proposition from its mild and orthodox self at sea level. It was used in preserving beans and tomatoes and added a final note of interest and incongruity to a kitchen which was to become more and more complex and unusual as the season advanced.

My *ayah* had of course also joined the household, with her little girl—her husband had stayed behind with the Newfoundland family as their cook. Servants were hard to come by that summer on the mountain and he was evidently a versatile character. *Ayah* had a good godown and a bathroom for herself but her quarters were too far from the house to please her—a ten-minute walk. She was the best-paid servant on the estate, which included The Ferns (our house), but she was not satisfied, as she knew that *ayahs* were scarce on the mountain and that she could earn more from a rich *memsahib* who was staying in a hotel than from someone like myself. She had become aware of this almost as soon as we arrived in Mussoorie and soon forgot everything in demanding More! More! More! till at last, to her astonishment, I took her at her word and told her that I would not stand in the way of her prosperity. Then, very angry, she vanished like a djin in a swirl of dust.

There then arose the question of a successor. A buxom young woman came to offer her services but only on the condition that she should never be asked to push a pram, which she seemed to think would lower her prestige in the eyes of her friends. We had no pram, and though we had as yet no baby to put in any we might acquire, I felt this not a proper approach to *ayah's* work. A stout old lady, impressively dressed in a silk blouse and much heavy jewelry, her sari draped like a Roman toga, came in as stern and commanding as Volumnia and gave me to understand that if she became my *ayah* I could leave everything to her—she had cared for more babies than I had ever seen. No one else appeared and I thought she could at least take Rosalind for walks, something which was daily more arduous for me on that precipitous mountain. So she came for half a day, during which time I discovered that her secret of solving the washing and ironing problem was simply to hang unwashed garments in the sun and then put them away. When I suggested soap and water she left in great style, being above anything so common.

These storms were only preludes to a great calm. Before long a lovely woman, a peasant, came to the door unsought. She was so completely the reverse of the old tyrant who had just left that she did not care to discuss terms—whatever I gave her, she said, would be all right. She wanted to help us and to learn to be an *ayah*. We found her as endearing a character as the old Barrackpore sweeper, like him of the lowest status and the highest nature. How she had ever maintained, let alone acquired, this frame of mind in Mussoorie, which was full of carrion crows like the recently-departed Volumnia, was a constant wonder to me. Not only the *ayahs*, but the *dhobis*, the dandy *wallahs*, and most of the servants on the mountain, were exploiting their position to the full—understandably enough. More and more terrified passengers were telling stories of being held out over the *khud* while the coolies altered the terms agreed upon at the beginning of a trip. Even Dr. Fleming, who had lived so long in Landour and was constantly helping the sick and the poor, decided to walk everywhere that summer rather than take a dandy.

The new *ayah* was not austere and had a pretty taste in dress in spite of her poverty and lack of vanity. She arrayed herself in her best to work for us. I loved to see her coming through the trees, wearing light pastel colors, her mild and gentle countenance set off by a silver nose ring, anklets lying on her little brown feet. She always pleased the eye as well as giving balm to the spirit with her soft radiance, as expectant of kindness as a happy child.

But the best was yet to come. There was then yet another couple in the house, people from the Central Provinces. In their station they maintained the usual trio of establishments—a church, a school, a hospital, in the last of which many orphan girls were trained to become nurses. Many of these had been abandoned children found in wretched circumstances whom the mission sheltered and educated and who generally became teachers or nurses. Whatever the end result of the missionary effort in the Orient, let none of these girls be forgotten—if they are the only justification (and indeed they are not) it would be enough. It occurred to this couple, who were friendly and helpful, that I might like to have one of their graduates as a nanny, which would not only give me the rare boon of having a trained nurse to take care of the children but would also provide a change and a sort of holiday for one of "their girls," who had spent her life within the walls of institutions. They wired and in a few days Romela, dark, pretty, and competent, was at the door. She came alone, a long journey on the train and her first to the hills, in itself an indication of what her education had done for her. What a wonder it was to me to have a real nurse, not just a poor native woman who, however delightful, had constantly to be supervised and taught!

Romela was very pretty, with beautiful long hair, big shining eyes, and a graceful figure—slender and elastic, without the languid stance of most young Indian women. Many in her walk of life would have lacked vivacity partly because they had seldom had enough to eat. She had been found, a forsaken child, on a railway station and had been adopted by one of the missionaries, so that she had a European surname. Her adopted mother had sometimes had her in her home for holidays but she had really lived in the mission school and orphanage for some twenty years, until now she possessed a nurse's certificate. She wore an Indian version of a nursing sister's uniform—a white sari fastened over one shoulder and bound in tightly at her small waist, with a starched linen square over her head, a very becoming costume for her, very trim, very modest. Gradually she told me what she had done and I found that she could sew and cook. Besides, she sang charmingly, long Indian lyrics and hymns. She became a great friend and was with us for over a year. Her foster-father had had the misfortune to have been killed by a tiger—though a missionary, he had had no scruples about hunting and had met his end in this sad but dramatic manner. But her own life had been even and rather monotonous until she came to us, as must be the fate of institution children till they go out into the world. It was even more so in India than in the West, as the mission was most careful to shelter the girls it had in charge. And where could they go when they grew up? Unless they married, there was no place for them to work in a proper social environment in that country, without protection.

The day after she arrived the rains broke, tension easing in more ways than one, as generally happens. Great clouds moved in upon the mountain, wrapping it in soft, cool, exquisite mist. We heard with unbounded relief the wondrous sound of heavy rain beating on the roof. At once, almost overnight, everywhere on the mountain ferns sprang into life. They gushed up like little green fountains, with their curling fronds, from every crack in the rocks, from the trees, from the paths. The Mussoorie Ridge, I found, was one of the most prolific regions of the world for ferns—over two hundred species are to be found there, if I remember correctly—and they only show themselves during the brief weeks of the monsoon. Now, having lost the outer world, which lay unseen below us, being quite isolated in our high aerie, almost like a fogbound ship, the mountaintop became doubly vivid and absorbing. We forgot the great void in which we were suspended and became more aware of the peculiar beauties near at hand, delighting especially in the tender fronds which leapt out of the rocks, in the intricate, varied perfection of every plant. Being myself one of those persons ignorant of botany, but deriving constant pleasure from nature, I was then "much given to exclamations of wonder," as I believe Linnaeus described himself.

The Landour community, also, seemed to glow more brightly during the rains. People came in from the dripping woods and burst into talk. Ideas seemed to play and flicker round the drawing room, much as did the lightning which attended the summer storms, though much more agreeably. Many people were there who had come recently from territory now in Japanese hands, who could give firsthand reports of what had gone on. One padre, who was no longer young, was asked how he had made his way out of Burma—we knew he had come by land. He dismissed it lightly, saying it had been "a very easy trip"—no one was making capital out of these experiences. The fall of Burma was so appalling to us in its implications, such a shock, that it was hard to discuss it. We had been unprepared for its collapse. General Wavell and General Alexander had both issued firm and encouraging statements as to its holding out—apparently as it was falling. The persons who came out in the air lifts were nearly all white—members of the government or of foreign firms. What of the Indians, of the Burmans? The long line of refugees making for the frontier, decimated by exhaustion, hunger, and disease, reflected no credit on an administration we had thought able and wise. The Governor himself, Dorman-Smith, had flown out, reluctantly it was said, yet he had not stayed with the mass of people who had no transport. It was to be many years before the events in Burma could be assessed. Meanwhile, in Mussoorie, the missionaries explained what they had done: Some had felt it better to stay with their converts, risking capture by the Japanese. Others thought this would be an additional burden for their Christian flock, who might be made to suffer by the new conquerors if they were in any way associated with Europeans. There were families here who had left with great reluctance, as the fathers had waited behind—now what were the wives and children to do in India? Their missions, certainly, were behind them, but the outlook was somber. One could not but admire their courage and faith—I never heard one complain.

The community was very busy; no one wasted time in wringing his hands or trying to apportion blame. Mission affairs were discussed and ordered; plans were made for the school; there were lectures, concerts, theatrical performances. One lady, a refugee from Malaya, gave memorable readings, after the style of Ruth Draper—if anyone could be compared with that genius. The missionaries had many problems in common, whatever their church. A great proportion of their converts, obviously, had been untouchables—these were the people who were the most unfortunate and unhappy, who had nothing to lose in trying another way of life. The missionaries were eager to help them, rightly feeling that they were the poor and downtrodden for whom they had come. Yet they did not wish their Christian churches to become known as centers of untouchables. Once these persons became Christians, caste should have been forgotten, but man being what he is, that did not happen. People of supposedly better caste would not associate with a religion which invited outcastes inside the doors. This was a hard problem. Then there was a peculiar issue in the Native States. Some of the rajahs were friendly, some hostile. In these territories they were autocrats—the missionaries had no rights, only privileges. There was no security as to what policy might endure. The general political atmosphere all over India that summer was full of unrest and discontent over the conduct of the war. The British reverses, which to us were so plainly only temporary, did not look that way to Indian eyes. There were threatening speeches, unfriendly gestures, even our own mountain bazaars were not necessarily welcoming, and there were frequent threats of *hartals* or boycotts.

Our household, though serious, was also gay. The cook continued to fight with the bearer but, happily, also to create his perfect dumplings, which contributed to the success of our dinners. The ferns, which the monsoon had brought to life, were collected by Mr. Fleming and brought into the house in plumy sheaves. Trembling and vibrant they were cut and laid between huge leaves of blotting paper and then sent to the kitchen, the only dry place in the house. As it was the only place free from the plagues of mildew and of mold, the cases of stuffed birds had already been piled about the stove, leaving only narrow channels for the tall and morose chef who, fortunately, was thin and able to maneuver past these hazards. Though always bellicose with the bearer, he was complacent as to the orthodoxy of his kitchen and bore cheerfully with the immense albums of ferns, the large and dappled birds, and, very soon, the garments of the new baby. A line for the diapers had to be rigged up in the ktichen as there was no possibility of their drying anywhere else. Over two hundred inches of rain in under six weeks demanded these Draconian measures.

During the whole of that monsoon period there was one unexpected afternoon of bright sun and in it, weeks ahead of schedule, the baby arrived. The hospitals were full, but no mother on the hillside was so fortunate as I, with a doctor and two nurses in the house and an extra *ayah* for Posy. Sukhiya took care of the baby at night and for a few weeks I had the great pleasure of doing nothing, lying in bed and listening to the rain drumming on the roof while I read everything I could get hold of. The papers were horrifying. Conditions in the country below had gone from bad to worse. The campaign for civil disobedience, accelerated by the scorn felt over the management of the war, which, the leaders claimed, was ruining the country, had intensified, and both Gandhi and Nehru had been put in jail. An unpopular government, an unwanted war, gave the Indians every opportunity to make threatening speeches everywhere on every occasion, a boycott was proclaimed, riots took place. Post offices were burnt by the hundred and the railways were only kept running by constant patrolling and aerial surveillance. Even in Mussoorie there were repercussions of these affairs—I myself had no mail for many days after the baby arrived and no letters from abroad for over six months. It was not important in comparison with the great troubles of the times. A number of Europeans were murdered in scenes of mob violence. Further afield, all the news was disastrous—Tobruk fell, and though Stalingrad was being defended street by street, every day seemed to bring it inevitably nearer surrender. The U-boats were sinking thousands of tons of Allied shipping. The Indians openly exulted over these blows to the Allied cause. When the Viceroy, Lord Linlithgow, finally arrested the leaders within the country, the Europeans were greatly relieved, as were many more sober Indians—there seemed no other way to avoid the possibility of another mutiny.

All these events took place to the accompaniment in our hills of extravagant and theatrical weather—tremendous storms broke over the mountain, rain poured down in mad cataracts, thunder reverberated from the ridges, lightning flashed through the trees. We lived in a constant deluge, the waters seemed of Biblical proportions. The rain and the wind dislodged huge boulders, sending them hurtling down the mountainside. One, weighing several tons, came to rest a few yards from our front door; I alone wasted a second thought upon it. Everyone assured me, with the most admirable aplomb, that though these enormous stones were always dislodged from the ridge during the monsoon, they invariably played the game and only came down certain courses—following the beds of streams and the gullies. There were hundreds of possible tracks for them to follow within these Hague conventions and there was no time limit, but the conservatism and basic sense of fair play of the boulders seemed to set everyone's mind at rest—except mine.

During the storms fire balls of lightning sometimes danced around the rooms, settling on bureaus and bookcases for a few dazzling, apocryphal seconds, moments of brilliant illumination. At night I would lie in my little room (for then we were living in small chambers in an outside cottage), and listen to the boulders being torn loose and catapulting down the mountainside, while the wind screamed through the trees and the rain pelted down, and wonder if the big house were still there. The people in it would be having the same thoughts about the little house but no one ever went outside to investigate. One house near us—a big one—had actually gone bodily down the mountain three summers earlier in a storm, but this catastrophe was always laid firmly on the builders, who had not allowed sufficient time for the newly cut terrace to settle before the house went up, it was said. After a *pushta* was made nothing should be built on it for at least two years, but this rule had been ignored because everyone was in a hurry. One person in the house had been killed and the others had been very fortunate to escape.

A rainy season in a high altitude is supposed to be excessively depressing—one rest camp for soldiers laid out thoughtlessly in a very rainy area had had to be abandoned, so many of the troops had become almost suicidal in their gloom—but I found the gales too exhilarating, too exciting and awesome to be depressing. All I wanted was proper behavior from the boulders and firmness in the foundations of the cottage.

It was not cold enough for fires and life was sufficiently costly without buying wood to burn. But it was superlatively, incredibly damp. Everything was penetrated with water. To sit on a sofa was like settling into a bog. Everything you touched was wet—tables, clothes, toys. The trees, the bushes, the ferns, dripped incessantly, the gutters of the wide roofs overflowed upon ground too supersaturated to absorb any more moisture, while thousands of rivulets tore down the mountain. People came in with wet shoes and streaming raincoats and their umbrellas dripped pools onto a vestibule already beaded with humidity. I was glad to be in bed.

The problem of laundry assumed gargantuan proportions as nothing would dry and we were a household of eight persons, not counting the servants. It was a problem in any weather, in any case, for everyone. The *dhobis*, confronted that summer with unlimited patronage and lending an attentive ear to the persuasive agitators in the bazaars, had taken full advantage of their powerful position. It is difficult to recapture their importance in a time of ubiquitous washing machines and dryers and in cities with laundry services. But none of these were to be had then. The *dhobis were* the laundry service. They were, understandably, a surly lot, full of resentment at their misfortunes, which though neither directly nor solely the fault of the European were laid easily at his door. On the mountain there had long been an arrangement whereby the *dhobis* washed at a certain stream, rather far down the hill so they would not pollute the drinking water of the settlement. It was a mean plan, as it gave them a great deal of unnecessary labor in carrying the clothes to and from their customers, always up or down hill, on their backs. This had been long endured but now they suddenly discovered that they had been subjected to a flaming wrong.

Heedless of their customers' dismay they now kept sheets and shirts for weeks, ignoring any pleas for their return. Most people, living in cramped quarters (and before the rains water was short in some places), found it difficult to do much of their own washing and there was not much linen to go on with. The *dhobis* took their things away and did not return. During the rains they had an excellent excuse—the charcoal shortage made it impossible to heat their long drying sheds adequately. The nearer the Japanese and the Germans pressed on either side of the vast triangle that is India, the more insolent and contemptuous grew the *dhobis*, the dandy *wallahs*, the rickshaw men, the merchants. Most of them had no idea where Japan or Germany was or what lay behind the war but they recognized certain results. It was uncomfortable for everyone—even dear Dr. Fleming was not free from insult when she went out.

The household at The Ferns managed to keep itself free from most disagreeable entanglements—they went everywhere on foot, and when the *dhobis* tried to intimidate them, they washed at home where there was an ancient, very contrary, washing machine, which was almost more work than washing by hand. The boycotts never seemed to affect us either, stores appeared in surprising ways. We lacked our mail, which became involved in disasters at sea and on the plains, but that could not be helped.

In spite of turbulent times life has to go on. The additions to the house were finished; all summer we seemed to be wandering into buckets of whitewash and meeting odd coolies in corridors. The rains went on and on, till we forgot how we had longed for them and only wished that the fountains would cease to play. Sometimes the mist and clouds parted long enough for us to glimpse, far below, the little mounds which were the Siwaliks on the plains, plains now green as grass, with the curving river full and swollen, running beside them. The new terrace, the little *pushta* outside the study, had at last been finished and was already set about with a whole nursery of potted plants. These were tended and cherished by the lady from Lahore who, with botanical cunning and great enthusiasm, had selected many rare flowers from the treasury of the slopes and brought them home to bloom. Surrounded by lilies and curling ferns we had an aerie at once secluded and bold from which to look down upon the unfamiliar verdant plains.

The mountain abounded in large monkeys, langurs, blond creatures with black faces and long tails. They leaped about the treetops, often in sight, always noisy, so you knew they were there even if you couldn't see them, and sometimes they landed on a roof with a heavy thump. They were fully four feet tall, large-boned, quite formidable. Posy loved them and would look up with eager wonder, crying out "monkey on tree," and then at once "gone now"—regretting already the evanescent quality of life, accepting it in the touching way children have. She was two that summer, yet these langurs made such an impression on her that she never forgot them—one evening long afterwards she remarked to me, "Now it is as dark as a black-monkey's face." All the children used to shout after them, "*Kala mou! kala mou!*" It was one of the familiar cries among the gardens.

After the baby was born I was uneasy when I heard the Valkyrie sounds of the langurs plunging through branches or banging down on a roof, I was afraid they would pluck the sleeping infant from her cot and dash away into the treetops with her, so idiotic are the fears of mothers.

This was particularly foolish because we never could take the baby out, it was always too wet. She throve, however, the pet of the household, after the manner of her kind. The young people who were friends of the one Woodstock pupil in the house would come in begging to be allowed to give her her bottle, a service seldom denied them. It was something of a surprise—and a welcome one—to have so many teenagers about of our own race. At that time there were few white girls and boys to be met with generally in India—they had almost all been sent home.

When the baby was six weeks old the Lahore contingent decided to return to the plains and invited me to go with them. Mussoorie had clearly now fulfilled its purpose in our lives, we were ready to go, though I knew that I would always look back upon this hilltop with an especial awareness—it had been so wonderful a refuge in a time of trouble. Our departure had its comic moments: I tried to telegraph Stanton that we were leaving. The telegraph clerk pleaded with me not to telephone him the message (I had no way to get to the telegraph office), insisting that he could never write down what I said, but I persevered. We became quite friendly during an agonized half-hour of his despair and my encouragement, but in the end he proved right—the message Stanton received was gibberish and he could make nothing of it.

XI A Glimpse of the Punjab

Since the days of Alexander, a period to which the first certain information about the Punjab goes back, to the reign of Ranjit Singh, their (i.e., the Pünjabis') history presents nothing but a long series of wars and revolutions. Lying on the route of all the adventurers who have been periodically attracted from the depths of Asia to the soil of India by the thirst for pillage and conquest, it has witnessed the passage of Greeks, Parthians, Scythians, Tartars, Moguls, and English, all of whom in turn it has accepted as masters.

VALBEZEN, *The English and India*

As the Lahore family were to leave the Landour house finally during the year (all their children would have gone through the school by then), they took with them on every journey back to the plains such household goods as they wished to keep. On this trip Sally Stunz had with her a large number of tin trunks as well as a couple of bedrolls, several suitcases, a long white duffle bag, and a number of well-filled baskets. My own luggage was not beyond reproach from the point of view of the dream-traveler whom we see advertised on every hand, as he jauntily approaches the station or airport with his fresh, gleaming bags and his glamorous but quiet clothes, debonair and confident. Though I left my trunk and heavy boxes in the hills, it being still uncertain what we would do after the Lahore visit had ended, I still had a horrifying amount of baggage: a great many suitcases, the baby's big basket in which she would sleep during the journey, and a whole swarm of lesser baskets—one for dry diapers, one for wet, one for bottles (this contained a large saucepan full of boiled water in which the bottles floated), and one for baby food. We also had Celia's wicker cot, which she would use in Lahore, and the playpen and pushcart, which we could not forward, as they would certainly have been smashed in transit if they were not watched over. All these horrors, covering the floor of a good-sized room, seemed an impossible array, but they had to come, all of them. As a final *coup de grâce*, though the journey would begin on a chill wet afternoon high in the mists, by nightfall we would have reached the plains and be in extreme heat, so we had to have a change of thin clothes ready, as well as allot sufficient space in the bags for the raincoats, sweaters, and thick shoes which we would then shed. Packing is always torment but this time it surpassed even its usual good average. I reflected gloomily as I wedged bottles of baby oil into a high square basket that my idea of hell was one Dante had not drawn. Mine is cold and I am always packing in it.

Coolies were hired to carry all these bundles to the bus stand, the point of departure for the plains. A trusted man from the estate on which The Ferns stood accompanied them, promising to watch over the bundles like a hawk till we appeared. This first party set off early, a long file of Garhwali ruffians balancing trunks and baskets on their heads as they followed the narrow trail of the Tehri Road down to the bazaars. At the last moment Sally decided to take with her a large tin bath, which became the imposing burden of the last coolie of the procession, overshadowing his thin frame fore and aft.

At four o'clock, after a hasty tea and many fond farewells to the Flemings, Sukhiya, and our dear *ayah*, we set off ourselves in the streaming rain, all wrapped in mackintoshes. The baby and I shared one dandy and Romela and Rosalind another, umbrellas over our heads and tarpaulins over our legs, for this most uncomfortable and impractical litter ever devised has no arrangements for rain or hot sun in a country which offers no other type of weather. I suppose that when dandies first appeared, anyone of sufficient status to use one would automatically have had a slave to run beside him, carrying a large red parasol finished off with gold tassels. (The dandy and the *tonga* are, of course, the only type of transport available in my hell.)

Sally Stunz, being an energetic person (happily, for the future survival of this expedition), walked the three miles. As we went along the Tehri Road for the last time the rain stopped and the clouds lifted for a few moments, so that we could have one last glimpse of the steep descent to the plains and see the little blue Siwaliks resting lightly on the checkered carpet which led to the river. Then came the fantasies of the bazaar; I was loath to see them disappear, so enchanting did they seem as we went down the steep, narrow lane, our dandies almost on top of each other, the men shouting constantly to keep the way clear.

Once at the terminal we were confronted by our immense pile of luggage, which was topped by a pathetic little suitcase belonging to Romela. This was a shiny gray tin model with a large red rose painted on it—it was absolutely new and she was burstingly proud of it. Each package was solemnly weighed and then lashed to the top of the old lumbering bus—only a minimum was allowed inside. There was indeed very little room inside even for the passengers. The first-class victims were assigned two narrow wooden benches, with scarcely enough room for their knees to be wedged in sidewise, then came the slightly narrower second-class section, behind that the proletariat was jammed together.

The competent Sally took charge of everything. While Romela and I watched the children and the baggage, she supervised the weighing, directed the coolies where to stow the pieces, and paid the complicated charges. It was all done slowly, noisily, and with great inefficiency on the part of the bus *log*, and it was soon apparent that we were going to be at least an hour late in starting. This necessitated feeding the baby before we left. There being no waiting rooms, we had to do this in the open, carefully and precariously mixing a bottle, shooing away flies and interested but extremely dirty onlookers (mostly beggars and children), while we tried to keep the contents clean and warm. Soon afterwards the passengers were told to enter the bus. This, too, took a long time, as more people than appeared humanly possible were squeezed into the vehicle, already heavily loaded with mountains of luggage on the roof, but we were all so tired of waiting and too glad to get in to be concerned at the prospect of hurtling down seven thousand feet in two hours in the hands of an insouciant slapdash Indian driver. (It must be added that he did drive skillfully—I never heard of an accident on this road.) Romela was crushed into the first-class with us so that she could take charge of the baby while I occupied myself with the two-year-old, who was acutely aware of what was going on. It seemed to me that if Romela had entire charge of the infant that would leave me freer for the other one—there never seemed to be any end to my innocent illusions. With shouts, yells, howls, and screams of excitement and farewell, we started at last to lurch down towards the plains by an interminable series of hairpin bends, all negotiated at high speed and in a jocular style by our dark and hairy driver.

It was then that we discovered that Romela was no traveler. We had not gone a quarter of a mile before her usually dusky countenance turned almost pitch black and she thrust her shapely head out of the nearest window. From then on, as Sally said, "She gave up her whole soul to being sick."

Time passed slowly. Even for good sailors it was an uncomfortable experience, as the springless bus tore round corners, bumping on the bad road, forcing the already crowded passengers closer to one another. Sally held the baby, I had Rosalind in my lap, and we braced our feet on the floor. Slowly the plain came up to meet us and we went down under the clouds. Then the heat began.

At dusk we drew up for a few minutes on level ground before starting through the Siwaliks, which had neatly transformed themselves from stepping stones into great heights. Everyone, even Romela, got out of the bus and took the air—except myself. I lay down on one of the wooden benches and stretched out flat, luxuriating in the pleasure of being alone. With the quick twilight it was night before we started off again, a quarter of an hour later. It had become very warm and close and the mountains seemed already far behind, in time as well as space, though indeed in a less spectacular neighborhood the Siwaliks themselves would have been credited as mountains. Passing through them in the dark, we could see almost nothing of them—only the road, winding ahead in the light of our headlights. Romela, still in misery, was at least quiet and the children fell asleep.

This passage through the Siwaliks was enveloped in the strange, dreamlike quality some journeys assume of being part of a small world hurtling through space, unconnected with any other place or time or people, like a sort of lesser comet. One is free, if bemused, actively participating in one of Eddington's time triangles. Whether the people of the journey are getting much older or much younger than the persons in the Absolute Elsewhere through which the travelers are hastening is unsure—the only certainty lies in the conviction that the traveler's Here Now is of some different dimension from theirs.

The meandering road and the dark hillside, heavy with trees, shadowed with bushes, became to my enchanted gaze the background for little, ancient scenes. Round the curves and into the arc of our bright lights came wooden carts, small covered wagons, bullock-drawn. Sharply flood-lit, these night travelers huddled half-asleep under the matting roofs of the wagons, lulled by the pace of their beautiful slow-moving oxen. They were hardly seen before they had vanished, though to use any word suggesting speed seems an anomaly, as nothing could have given a stronger impression of drowsy, unconcerned placidity than these old carts, laden with sleeping families. A father, wrapped in a shawl, nodding over the reins, would be half-roused by the horrid apparition of the bus, his shoulders would straighten against the strong, simple lines of his dark cart—then he would be gone to us, and we to him. At odd, frequent intervals in the heart of the Siwaliks we met more and more of these phantasms, sometimes singly, sometimes in a long file. They seemed as old as time, the same time we were flashing through, but utterly untouched by it. Studies in black and brown among the shadows and sudden lights, they gave no impression of color, they were made of the very stuff of night.

About ten in the evening, more dead than alive, we arrived in Saharanpur. All the Delius vanished from the atmosphere and withdrew to the Siwaliks and we, now outside the enchantment, the strange, wainscot music, drew up before the station a very ordinary, very dirty bus, full of very ordinary dirty tired people. The Lahore Mail, they told us, was due to leave in an hour but had not yet come in. After the dreamy visions of the dark roadway, the station seemed a madhouse of noise, light, and confusion, with quiet Mussoorie a world away. That we had left Landour only six hours earlier seemed a nonsensical reckoning.

Sally the intrepid, Sally the heroine, plunged into a boiling mass of porters and, choosing several by some strange instinct of her own, started to locate our gear and have it brought down from the roof of the bus. But before dealing with it further she escorted the babies, the wretched Romela, and myself to a waiting room. She knew the station well, having gone back and forth between Lahore and Mussoorie scores of times, and as soon as she had installed us in a suitable apartment she dashed back to the luggage.

It was a hideous hour. The waiting rooms were dark, dirty, ill-equipped, and generally loathsome. Romela, in her own estimation clearly at death's door, cast herself at once upon a bench, oblivious to everything. She put up her feet, shut her eyes, and wallowed in self-pity. I brought her some tea and urged her to pull herself together, but she was like a victim of seasickness, to whom the call of duty is not only unheard but is quite out of the question.

I might have been insane as far as she was concerned when I begged her to at least watch the baby while I tended Rosalind. Supine on the only couch in the room she floated, indifferent, in some other sphere.

Though the waiting rooms were small, crowded with heavy black furniture, and noisy from the cries of the people on the platform outside, they were still something of a haven. I washed the children's faces and hands, mixed a bottle for the baby, and gave Rosalind something to eat. An English lady who had been in the bus was also here, waiting for the Frontier Mail, and seeing my plight most kindly took the baby from me so that I could go out into the darkness and get boiling water for the next feed, which would have to be given on the train. "Why had I had so many children?" I asked her, groaning, to which she replied, "It's a little late to think of that now." The sluttish old *ayah* who was the waiting room attendant offered to fill the thermoses for me but I was sure that she would put in the first hot water she could get hold of on the platform whether clean or dirty, boiled or unboiled, and swear to me by all she held holy that she had seen it boiling with her own eyes. Father of my Fathers! So I went myself, thermoses under one arm, Rosalind by the hand.

The station kitchen was a foul place, occupied by dirty cooks, flies, cockroaches, and a large stove which burned charcoal. No one was pleased to see us. The cooks noted my critical and horrified Western eyes taking in the insects and the unwashed saucepans and my paltry rupee did not satisfy them. (I had been told by other mothers that this technique of seeing the water boil yourself was quite often done and a tip made the operation palatable to the kitchen staff.) The Japanese had shown them that the days of obsequious politeness—indeed any politeness at all—to Europeans was past, and in any event I was only a woman. So my kettle stood by the side of the range while they made toast and fried sausages and I waited. The minutes ticked by, I realized that the water would never boil in time, and I filled the thermoses with hot water, thus being suitably rewarded for wantonly transgressing a prime maxim of the East: "Never do anything yourself that you can get anyone else to do for you." We went back to the waiting room, gathered up our dilapidated party, and staggered out onto the platform to meet Sally.

During this interval she had secured a compartment for us and a berth for Romela in "inter" class, which was a step below second but much better than third. Our coupé was practically saturated with all the baggage she could persuade the porters to cram into it as, quite rightly, she mistrusted the train brakes. Another passenger, a very angel in disguise, had already installed herself on a top bunk. This was a young girl from the Kalimpong Homes, a Protestant school originally founded for Anglo-Indian orphans, who was on her way to Kashmir to take up a post as a nanny. These Kalimpong girls were the best nannies in India, which her new mistress must have known, for she was spending quite a considerable sum in transporting this young woman, whom she had never seen, all the way from North Bengal to Kashmir and I am sure she never regretted an anna of that money. The maiden sized us up at once, took the baby in her arms, soothed her expertly, got her to sleep, and then repeated the process with Rosalind, all without a whisper from me. It seemed almost too good to be true. The narrow, dim, overflowing little room seemed heavenly to us as we all fell asleep.

Too soon it was morning, but the Anglo-Indian fairy lightened it by immediately dealing with the children, long before we were able to buy breakfast trays through the window. Soon afterwards we were joined by two Muslim ladies. They were young and elegant, wearing *burqas* of very fine soft black crepe made in two sections, which gave them some freedom of movement. A little servant attended them, as gaudily dressed as it was possible for any human being to be, an absolute contrast to her mistresses. Her costume consisted of brilliant peacock blue trousers, immensely full, and an orange tunic; she made music wherever she went by the tinkling of great numbers of silver and glass bangles and anklets; her hair was long, her eyes were roguish. Smiling joyously she followed the two somber, concealed black figures into the carriage, carrying straight in front of her a large brass spitoon, which she placed between her two mistresses. This object was quite two feet high, and very wide at the top, tapering to an ornate base, and took up every inch of space left in the compartment. It was, of course, necessary on the trip to facilitate the chewing of *pan*, the mixture of spices wrapped in leaves. Having thus installed her ladies, the little servant withdrew smiling merrily—much to my regret, as she was a pleasure to have with us in spite of the congested space, she was as gay as a butterfly. All this time two pairs of captive eyes, ringed with black paint, framed in black draperies, watched us intently and in silence.

Then they threw back their head veils and chewed *pan*, spitting out the red juice into their splendid spitoon. They seemed amiable but were not disposed to conversation. In their dark bovine manner (enhanced by their habit) they were quite beautiful.

We were several hours late in reaching Lahore, where the Reverend Mr. Stunz was waiting for us on the platform. He at once put the children and me into a *tonga* and then turned back to deal with the luggage, which Sally was already collecting, and to find Romela. The kindness of these people was almost overwhelming, I could never have made the journey without them. Sally had even left the carriage in the dead of night at some station when I was sound asleep and had the thermos filled with fresh water. The last stage of the journey, in the *tonga* during the greatest heat of the day, trying to hold both children at once lest they slip out of the wretchedly balanced vehicle, was something of an ordeal, but at last, covered with dust, we turned into the lane that led to the big quiet mission bungalow, to be met by Gindo Bhai, the placid old family *ayah*, and her solicitous ministrations.

This dear old woman, swathed in fine white shawls, led us out of the sun, through a darkened sitting room, into a large dim room on the lower floor which had been prepared for us. It was the same room I was to see many times in the years to come—every time we passed a night in a mission bungalow—and every time I loved it. It was protected from the sun by a wide and shady veranda. The high ceiling, the fans, the whitewashed walls, the stone floors, and the few pieces of plain furniture made such chambers cool and austere— which meant comfortable. The bedsteads were of hard wood and draped above them were snowy mosquito nets. From this room opened a long narrow dressing room and beyond that was our bathroom. Here, instead of the usual tin baths of the missions, the Stunzes had installed a "throw bath" after the Hindu model where, fenced in by low walls on which stand basins and pitchers of water, one gives oneself refreshing showers. Light filtered in through a high lattice. Altogether it would have been impossible to have imagined anything more cool and clean, bare and Spartan, and after the heat, the noise, the glare and the dust, the crowding and confusion of the past hours, it was a blessing to enter this tranquil haven. Old Gindo, the epitome of serenity, took the baby in her arms and directed the servants who were bringing in the bags. She then went off to fetch a small bath—there had been many babies in that house—and soon had the little creature in cool water, giving rapturous six-weeks-old smiles. Not once on the tumultuous journey had either child cried—they had not found it hard.

Eventually everyone arrived from the station and we all bathed and dressed and had lunch. Romela, installed in the dressing room, was soon in her right mind, but as rapidly lost it when we discovered that her beflowered suitcase had been rifled on the journey and all her best saris carefully abstracted by some light, ruthless hand. It was a cruel blow to the poor girl, who had almost nothing of her own in the world, but it was not long before we had replaced everything from the tempting bazaars of Lahore. Anarkally was a treasury of saris, as well as other, less innocent delights—Anarkally, which in the years since that time has so often figured in the world press for its riots and disasters, but which was then a shopper's paradise. Gindo comforted Romela with motherly sympathy, establishing an easy and pleasant relationship which worked out well in the care of the children. The Stunzes had to go away out of the city to a conference, leaving me alone, and I occupied myself in falling in love with Lahore.

Neither large nor small, neither sophisticated nor countrified, it had then great charm and a quality of grace not often found in cities. There was a pleasant cantonment—but not an exceptional one for British India—and a fine "old city," walled and colorful, with splendid mosques, a fort, Mogul tombs and gardens, rich bazaars, a fine park (the Lawrence Gardens), a museum rejoicing in first-rate Mogul and Rajput prints, and a handsome population. It had been made famous in the West by Kipling, and was in every way a far cry from poor, dreary Bengal—how I wished that our lines might have been cast here.

In those days, before Partition, when the city was highly cosmopolitan and had large communities of persons from far parts of the subcontinent, there were many racial types to be seen on the streets. Besides the good-looking native Punjabis, there were Sikhs, Rajputs, Pathans, men from Kathiawar and from South India—drawn here for trade nine times out of ten. Rajputs and Pathans are tall, strong-featured people with a physique like our own and sometimes quite fair-skinned. Occasionally one sees a Pathan of an almost ruddy complexion with reddish hair and blue eyes. Looking at such a man, I would wonder if he were in truth a European in disguise; so like us, except that they were darker and generally better-looking, were they really Orientals? Their dress helped their appearance—even an insignificant figure was set off by a big turban and an embroidered waistcoat, full trousers and fanciful leather slippers. The Pathans, though not neat, dressed in this romantic style. The Punjabis were much better groomed, often real dandies, in their tight jodhpurs and long coats.

Indian babies, so they say, are born white; their mothers hasten to anoint them with oil and put them in the sun where they quickly acquire that skin which marks the race. But all over India fairness is prized and many of the women who have passed their lives in purdah are not at all dark. Indians filling out forms used to describe themselves very often as "light black" or "pale black"—why? As you go on towards the northeast you feel more and more among people of your own race till in Afghanistan and Persia the inhabitants are Caucasians with fair hair, blue eyes, and white skins. But their mentality is much more akin to the peoples living east of them. Clearly it is all nonsense, this elaborate structure of race and color which we found so demanding, so difficult to live with. The inconsistency implicit in it became more and more obvious. An Indian, bristling with resentment against the white peoples, should certainly not want to stress the light shade of his color. In India it seemed obvious that the races had grown apart mentally rather than physically; the mysteries and the silences of the Valley of the Euphrates, the puzzle of the Lost Tribes, were not to be pushed out of the mind in Lahore.

But, at first, I was most struck by the fact that it seemed to be still Kipling's beloved city. The *Civil and Military Gazette*, which first published so many of his tales, was still running. "Kim" began his wanderings with the old teacher from Lahore, and the gun, "Zam Zama," on which he is sitting as the story opens was still there at the portals of the museum. "Whoever holds Zam Zama holds the Punjab," runs the legend. I put Rosalind astride it, hoping that she might remember it.

She and I used to go together to the Lawrence Gardens, which were not far from the museum, in the late hours of the afternoon, there to wander under the huge trees and admire the flaunting flowers of the heat. Beyond this lay the zoo, where there were mongeese and tigers and a very fine aviary, with cockatoos and peacocks, parrots, pheasants, ducks, and cranes. The curator was a White Russian who was disheartened over the meager wartime allowance allotted him for upkeep and repairs. Pointing to a broken water dish in the bear's cage he once cried out, "You see that dish? And when will he have a new one? When Jesus Christ He rise again!"

But it was lonely for me in Lahore, with no one to talk to except the infants and the servants, and I was overjoyed when the Stunzes came back from the country and Stanton arrived from Bengal. He had had a memorable journey: without knowing either Brigadier Wingate or Major Short he had found himself sharing the compartment of the first as far as Delhi, and of the second to Lahore.

Orde Wingate was startlingly unconventional in his habits and arresting in his mental processes, which made him a stimulating companion. All the way to Delhi they had discussed the Japanese invasion, the arts of war and weaponry, the counteroffensives which must come about. He was already training his Chindits for raiding Burma but it was still a secret; his ideas were never congenial to Headquarters, where he had made many enemies, but he was fortunate enough to have gained the attention of Churchill, who let him have what he needed. He had brilliant light blue eyes which held his listeners like the Ancient Mariner; he would buy *chapattis* from a station vendor and eat them without a qualm, something few officers of his time would do, and in the compartment he liked to throw off all his clothes.

Major Short also was of an unorthodox character but he was never able to attract the favor which had smoothed Wingate's path—in so far as one could think it had been smoothed. Short had spent his career in the Punjab and was particularly knowledgeable about the Sikhs; he was an officer much loved by his men. But he seldom agreed with Authority and had not had the advancement due him. He was still only a major, though considerably older than Wingate—this did not in itself disturb him but it meant that he had little real freedom of movement. The establishment was conservative to a degree and Major Short was so far out of step with it that he had even worked closely with Sir Stafford Cripps when the latter came to India with his doomed offer. Major Short was on his way at that moment to stay with the Chief Secretary to the Government of the Punjab, and because of this we soon afterwards found ourselves dining with him in a great house among V.I.P.'s.

The setting was delightful—servants in livery, immense high-ceilinged rooms, the quiet and the calm—but all this did nothing to hide the extreme contrast in points of view held by the persons there that evening. The Chief Secretary was of the old school in every way, an out-and-out imperialist, entirely unimpressed by the realistic outlook of Major Short. It was one of those evenings one knew would soon disappear forever—the necessary background supporting it was crumbling away. In a way it was to be regretted, it was so pleasant for the few, so rooted in a past which had many merits, but to some of us it was as evident that this sort of society could not exist much longer as if we had seen a hand come out and write on the wall. Major Short remained our friend till the end of his life; many of his assessments were admitted to be justified when it was too late to do anything about them.

The gardener at the mission bungalow was a small and earnest man with a deep passion for chrysanthemums; in the autumnal season he was always absorbed in the art of setting out and tending hundreds of these in pots, assisted by a little disciple as serious as himself. The paths were lined with flowerpots; here and there he had created miniature forests with them, each green stem supported by its slender bamboo mast. The dull green plants with their strong branches and leaves like little delicate suede hands made visible daily progress. As the first hint of color began to appear in the tight buds, we all took pleasure in the sight. The training of every plant was of ardent interest to the old man; he knew each individually as a true gardener must.

I was particularly delighted by the chrysanthemums because of their Chinese associations. The Chinese have all sorts of fancies about them—that they should be about when people are eating crabs in the autumn, that they should be tended by "remarkable persons who love the ancients." They are given many romantic names and are associated by poetic tradition with rusticity. Seeing them here was like meeting old friends again—we had had none in Bengal.

As the shadows began to encroach upon the lawn Gindo would bring the baby out and pace up and down the grass with her in her arms, while the gardener stooped over his charges and the little boy devoutly followed him with a watering can. From this engaging background we then set out, on the few days that Stanton was there, to see the beauties of Lahore.

Jehangir's tomb lies outside the city. Though the tombs of the Great Moguls are so large a part of the heritage, in fact only Shah Jehan's and Jehangir's are truly beautiful—appropriately enough, as only these two were real connoisseurs. Humayun's Tomb at Delhi is amusing in a bizarre, geometric way, Akbar's near Fatehpur Sikri has something about it that is almost grotesque. Aurangzeb, the last of the giants of his family, wanted no tomb at all—it was almost two centuries before Curzon made his grave a site to visit. But Jehangir's and Shah Jehan's—and the Taj—were enough. Everything pales beside the Taj; but even with that as a comparison Jehangir's is still wonderfully beautiful and splendid.

One hot evening we traveled for some miles in a *tonga,* crossing the Ravi and entering a wide and silent plain far beyond the city (as it was then). The distance and the slow old carriage were an advantage, helping us to forget the present and reenter ancient times, once more to be amazed at the dynasty established by the first Moguls. Those bold horsemen and conquerors of Central Asia seizing upon the plains and, for a time, exhibiting so great a talent for governing, for statesmanship! Akbar outshone them all in his versatility, a person of startling dimensions—but not of taste. Jehangir developed this quality somewhat in himself—he encouraged the court artists, especially Ustad Mansur, "the Wonder of the Age," and he built lavishly, as had his father. Jehangir loved music, painting, flowers, gardens, the chase, and a number of earthly pleasures; he followed the classic pattern of rude conquering dynasties who in time become patrons of art. His tomb reflects this sensibility. But it was Shah Jehan who was to bring to the highest point a true feeling for artistic achievement; and with him the immense capacity once latent in the family was already declining. Compared to his grandfather he was a slight man, but he was richly housed, the facade was overpowering; the forts, the palaces, the tombs, continued to astonish and awe the multitude.

There is seldom much variation in the basic design of these Mogul masterpieces—Jehangir's tomb is no exception. Within fine gardens, laid out when we saw them in an English manner, with lawns and massed trees, stands the four-square building of pure marble, executed with precision and grace. It is so perfect the mind rests in it, just as it is. Here are the domes and minars, the gleaming marble, the mosaics and screens, the space, the restraint, the exquisite finish.

After our long and dusty ride, when we had passed under the gate and entered the silent, empty gardens—which at that sunset hour were quite deserted—we came into an atmosphere eloquent, poetical, discriminating; I well remember how happy and at ease we felt, strolling over the grass and sitting on the marble terrace admiring the floral mosaics, which are particularly lovely. From the minars you could see far out over the flat countryside beyond the park. At last we had to go back to the *tonga;* the driver lit the bobbing lanterns above the wheels, roused his slumbering pony, and in the dusky haze of early night we passed again over the Ravi, back into the roads of the city noisy with the cries of street vendors and came again to the star-lit mission garden.

Lahore has a splendid though much ruined fort, red and massive, with gates and ramps which seem even deeper and more impressive than those at Delhi. Within the gates the land rises steeply, and the inner section, once devoted to palaces, halls of audience, and gardens, was in our time almost entirely wasteland, desolate and scarred. It had been destroyed by the Sikhs in the nineteenth century, fighting against the Muslim rulers of the Punjab. There still stood a little pavilion with a fantastic roof—a swelling, mushroom curve of white marble resting lightly on white lattices, with an effect so graceful, humorous, poetic, so captivating that it is almost startling to find it here on this old battlefield, once the scene of the most violent and cruel passions. There must have been here an exquisite series of reception rooms and inner chambers, set among the broken terraces and pools of the gardens, but nothing is left, one can only wander about among the ruins and cleared spaces where tall thin grasses blow over the stones.

The Shalimar Gardens are the loveliest of all the treasures of Lahore. Ancient, silent, tender, they breathe a mood at once poetic and philosophical; they are beyond a doubt the very sort of garden which charmed the melancholy of Omar Khayyám. "And still a garden by the water blows" became for him a reason for hope and immortality—the rose, the hyacinth, and "this delightful herb" were as dear to him as that red wine in which he sought forgetfulness. And a lover of gardens cannot fail to find here in the heart of this old dusty city one of the most perfect achievements of that art of which Bacon says, "It is the purest of human pleasures; it is the greatest refreshment to the spirit of man. And a man shall ever see that when ages grow to civility and elegancy men come to build stately sooner than to garden finely, as if gardening were the greater perfection."

The entrance to this gentle paradise is humble; the treasure is, at first, veiled. A low dull wall and a small archway usher you into those green courts where long pools, as still as the heavens, stretch out between lanes of cypresses and roses, where you may wander and muse. But at a touch the mood of the gardens changes—the guardians of the gate have caused the slight graceful fountains which inhabit the pools to come alive and toss their benediction into the grateful air, disturbing the profound reflections of dark, reserved trees, the lower images of the roseate flowers. A series of these entrancing waterways, whose lips are fledged with tender green, leads you to a small marble palace which has on its far side four square pools, divers little pavilions, rose gardens and lawns, all of a quiet, simple perfection.

These gardens, like all of their kind, were intended for sitting rather than wandering in—they were designed to induce a mood of revery and reflection. You are only able to go a little distance at a time before you must sit down and gaze from a new angle at the panorama before you.

At certain symmetrical points are little marble kiosks of an airy and fragile delicacy. Everything is so arranged that the water plays the major role in every scene, by its reflections, its sound, its coolness, its very being. The large buildings provide banqueting halls, open to the winds, set off by flights of graceful stairs, with special vantage points lightly accented where particularly clear and delightful views may be obtained. All the charms and delights of Eastern gardens seem to have been gathered here in one exquisite fantasy.

During our autumnal visits the chief flowers in bloom were little mauve-blue summer chrysanthemums, offset by low pink asters, which were planted before white marble banks and reflected in the waters throughout the whole of the gardens. There could be nothing anywhere more lovely—the great royal gardens of the West are garish beside this chaste delicacy. The pale sky of evening would begin to deepen and gather the first delicious blue of the night, which would glow for a brief moment before the somber shadows took command of that "wide, inverted bowl." The little moon, which all day had been struggling to keep her white torch alight, grew silver against the cerulean curtain till, when the colors fled, she came—first modestly, then grandly—into her own, and rode supreme over the Shalimar.

> The Moon of Heav'n is rising once again:
>   How oft hereafter rising shall she look
> Through this same Garden after me.

Too soon it was time to go back to Bengal. We decided that as it was the only home we had, and as the Japanese showed no immediate signs of advancing further, we would all return. So another journey lay before us, with all its rigors and its unexpected

charms. The veranda of the mission bungalow was heaped with
our appalling luggage on the boiling afternoon of the appointed
day. We had not only all the gear we had brought from Mussoorie, but Stanton's bags as well and the baggage of his bearer, old
Eniat. We had also acquired in Lahore a very large flat basket which
we had filled with tins of milk, some instinct having warned us
that we might not be able to buy any more baby food soon—a
surmise which turned out to be perfectly correct. In the rich
Anarkally district we had found the fascinations of the bazaar
irresistible, to the extent of buying some brightly painted little
stools with short knobly legs and gaudily braided seats, combining
red, orange, royal blue, and white in a wild but successful medley.
In an inspired moment, and with the aid of an enamel basin,
Stanton turned two of these into a hat box for a precious straw hat
which I did not wish to expose to the dust of the train. It could
not have been a more practical container but it did not increase the
respectability of our luggage and he shuddered from head to foot
when he surveyed the pile of bundles which had to start its way to
the station on two overloaded *tongas*. I was so hardened after the
trip from Landour that it in no way fazed me—I even thought it
was funny. Romela took the baby, I had Rosalind firmly by the
hand, the water bottles were full, the hour struck. We left our kind
hosts and the charms of Lahore with true regret. Sally came to the
station with us, once more exerting her magnetic sway over porters
and impedimenta. Coolies pushed our pieces into the compartment
and, in the irrevocable way of partings, the doors banged; in a
flash Sally's little figure was lost to us among the milling crowd on
the platform and then the whole was metamorphosed into the
dusty plain of the Punjab.

We found we were to share the compartment with two *babus*,
who were already unobtrusively occupying the upper berths, and
an English petty officer from the Burmese Navy, a cheerful and
companionable man. The train had no restaurant car and we descended at Amritsar, the city which holds the Golden Temple of
the Sikhs, to dine in the station. Romela stayed on the train with the
baby, Eniat bringing her meal to her—a couple of large *chapattis*
and a wide green leaf which held a little mound of henna-colored
paste and a dab of saffron. She bought herself some tea from a
passing vendor and looked very happy and excited, Youth Seeing
Life. Eniat was bent and wan under his immense turban, an aged
man beyond any feelings except scorn. For his dinner he took a sip

from the tap labeled "Water for Mohammedans" and ate an unadorned *chapatti* in a sparing manner. Then the Punjab Mail moved
out of Amritsar and we disposed ourselves on the long and slippery
benches. No one undressed, but nonetheless we felt the blessing of
the "gentle . . . loving, black-browed night," we were still and
stretched out, alone with our thoughts.

Soon after it was light we stopped at a station where hosts of
bearers ran down the side of the train like gulls meeting a ship—
in an inverted sense, as these swift, restless beings, dressed in white,
were bringing trays of *chota hazri*, not swooping them away.
Everyone sat up and started to drink the strong rank tea and eat
the thick sour toast with its indifferent butter with great gusto.
We had to swallow the tea while it was still almost boiling hot,
as the gulls insisted that the trays, with the necessary rupees, be
passed out of the windows very quickly and not be left at the next
station. This cruelty at once bound the passengers into a sort of
league but we complied, meek as lambs, bowing before officialdom.
Somehow, in our crowded second-class compartment, we all felt
that this was going to be a wonderfully satisfactory day.

In Shen Fu's *Six Chapters of a Floating Life* the author tells of
the great happiness which came into his life at a time when he was
living in a setting of absolute simplicity, even poverty. In the
chapter called "The Little Pleasures of Life" he describes a period
when he met with congenial friends—"the whole day long, we were
occupied in discussing poetry or painting only" and "these friends
came and went as they pleased, like swallows by the eaves." He
explained that, "There were four things of which we all approved—
generosity, romantic charm, free and easy ways, and quietness."

Nothing, outwardly, could have been more unlike these scenes
in old Chinese gardens, where they drank "warm wine in the
presence of flowers," than our grimy carriage and our oddly-
assorted company of strangers, who had no wish to discuss either
poetry or painting in the midst of a terrible war. And yet in some
mysterious way we achieved that feeling of companionship, ease,
happiness, and even—in spite of the roar of the train—quietness. The
gentle, tactful *babus* frequently withdrew to their high perches,
like a pair of discreet birds. They each had neat little suitcases and
frilled, colorfully embroidered pillows. Their shoes they placed
tidily at the ends of their beds and there they lounged, read, and
conversed with each other. Romela, still excited, still feeling this
an adventure, bathed the baby, washed everything she saw, and

made the compartment shipshape. The washing dried almost instantly—one advantage of the heat. Then she settled down to playing long, leisurely Indian games with Rosalind. Mr. Paul Jones, the
naval gentleman, had a seamanlike neatness. He had with him a
white naval dufflebag (white as snow, too) near the top of which
he had laid a bright tight-woven frontier basket in which were all
his necessities for the journey. His part of the carriage he had
arranged with almost mathematical precision and he disposed of
his possessions with the greatest dispatch, being always very economical as to space. Being extremely neat by nature myself, this
manifestation of order was delightful to me.

We began to talk when we got off the train at Mogulserai for
our breakfast (of more rank tea and thick toast) and we never
stopped all the rest of the day. Burma lay unfurled before us in the
perceptive, humorous, dispassionate survey of this petty officer.
It was true that little he told us was creditable to the British administration at the time of the disaster—most of the ugly stories we
had heard rumored were vividly substantiated in his account. But
he was without rancor and able to take a long view. His choice of
words smacked of the sea and the quarter deck, and though his tale
was sad, his outlook was resilient. The plain went by, I found I
had learned to love these journeys. We had tiffin in Lucknow,
crossed the Ganges at dusk (in the blue haze of the evening it
looked a perfect Whistler nocturne), and dined in Benares.

In the afternoon we ran out of boiled water for the baby, but
Mr. Stunz had told us what to do in such an emergency. Stanton
hopped out during a short stop at a siding, ran up to the engine,
and asked the engine driver if he had any hot water. "About two
hundred gallons," replied a blue-eyed Scot from his inferno. "Want
it for tea?" "No, for a baby." "Ah, that's important. Get in, will
you?" A small aluminum kettle was produced and held out on a
pole over the roaring fire by two stokers. "But look here," said
Stanton, more mindful of the train than of his child, "shouldn't this
train be moving on?" (It was, of course, the mail train.) "Won't
hurt it to wait," replied the engineer calmly. "I've been on this run
for thirty years and I can spare a few minutes. And," he added,
"send someone up here with an empty thermos at the next stop and
I'll fill it for you." "Do you like this job?" "Love it, wouldn't do
anything else." He, too, was under the spell.

XII Palta

Now turn we again.

Morte d'Arthur

THE NEXT TWO YEARS we were to spend in Palta, a tiny station on a bend of the Hooghly between Barrackpore and Ishapore. As for so many others during the war, those years, which were of tremendous moment for the world and hourly teeming with great events, were for us restricted and monotonous. Yet the months were never dull for me in that lonely and restricted little place, which caught and reflected in its own way the tremendous storms raging over so much of the earth.

The mental climate of Bengal had changed very noticeably in the months between the fall of Rangoon and that October of 1942. The panic of the first months of the year had gone; there was now, if not resolution, at least something approaching composure in the air, coupled with a marked sense of relief that though war on Indian soil remained a possibility, so far invasion had not come. We had not been engulfed in the first terrible post–Pearl Harbor tide, and whatever the Bengalis might think of the relative merits of the British and the Japanese, they did not want to be swept up into a fighting war.

There were terrible times to come. Though most of us were quite unaware of it, the first causes of the Bengal famine, which was to hold the Presidency in its deathly clasp for over a year, were already beginning to operate. We were to be raided and the people of the district terrified to a degree quite out of proportion to the dangers involved—these poor Bengalis were astounded by the swift, machine-borne disasters which came upon them and could not reconcile themselves to these perils as had the harder, more knowledgeable Occidentals. Compared with the raids on Rotterdam, London, or Berlin, ours were trifling—but what comfort could that be to people who had never heard of these places? And an inflation so severe as to push millions to the wall was to confront us all in the course of the next months.

I look back with some sentimentality on the entry of our little family into Palta, carrying the babies into the bungalow with relief and pleasure that the journey from Lahore was over, all unconscious of the heavy clouds looming ahead. I think that it was in this extraordinary nonentity of a place that Stanton and I finally grew up and relinquished forever the blithe expectancies of our salad days. There was something in that scene reminiscent of Breughel's quiet world of peaceful men in the fields, unaware that Icarus is falling in flames from the sky into the sea behind them.

The Europeans in India were now gathering themselves together and assessing the military problems, much as had England immediately after Dunkirk. The Indians, in the main, were out of this dilemma—many would be deeply affected by the decisions made but were much less involved in the assessment of causes and remedies. As in the West, the solution was hard to find, slow to achieve.

Nearly six months before—in May—the Generals Alexander, Slim, and Stilwell had come out of Burma with what was left of their forces, fighting a rearguard action from Rangoon. Now twenty-five thousand square miles of lost territory had to be recaptured. Once it had gone, the terrain was against us—the Japanese had been imaginative enough to turn it to their advantage in their attack but they would not be caught napping in its defense as we had been. They were to hold this area fiercely to the end of the war, as it formed a great defensive ring around their new conquests and through its possession they could control a vast network of rivers, roads, and railways. Burma was always a rich country for rice, here they had no difficulty in living off the land. How quickly had these vital areas been swept away! It seemed incredible that they could have slipped out of our fingers so fast and be so hard to regain! Of course, in the end, Burma was never really regained—she was recaptured only to shake herself free of the old ties.

This Far Eastern front implied reconquering a territory of high mountains and deep jungle-choked valleys which had literally no lines of communication. There were not even paths cut through the thorny scrub and the thickets of bamboo and elephant grass. Before 1943 there were no roads at all running into Burma from the north and after the fall of the country one of the first and most obvious tasks was to plan and build highways. During the rains the flooded paddy fields were almost the only open ground over a huge area. Geologically the country was against us. The rivers and mountains of that strip of coast, from the Himalayas inward and southward, follow a north-south line. Entering from the west, as the Allies must needs do, meant that they were going against the natural contours of the land. The lower reaches of the great, wonderful Brahmaputra are unbridgeable—they were of no use to us. The whole problem of our return centered on logistics and it took the better part of two years before any attack could be delivered in force. Wingate's jungle spearhead reentered the country somewhat earlier in a daring thrust, but that was more valuable for psychological than strategic reasons.

Early in 1942 General Stilwell had been in China, as Chief of Staff to Chiang Kai-shek, training Chinese divisions. Some of these men were hurried into Burma that spring to try and halt the debacle (in a halfhearted way, as history was to relate) and came out of India with escaping British forces. In India General Stilwell began then to rebuild a Chinese Army with his evacuated men; at the same time he was given the task of creating a chain of airfields in northeast India which could supply the Chinese Army in China, thus helping to keep China active in the war now that the whole seascoast and the Burma Road were lost to her. This venture involved a wide field of cooperation between the British and Indian armies and civilians in India and Assam—tea planters and Nepalese, Naga and Kachin hill people. These diverse elements were drawn into the work of creating an air transport line which was to lead over the "Hump" (the Himalayas between India and China) and which eventually carried more military tonnage than was ever sent in along the Burma Road. During this period General Stilwell also began the building of the Ledo Road, which started from the railhead of the Bengal-Assam Railway at Ledo, and led down into the terrible Hukuang Valley, the scene of the flight from Burma of our armies and refugees, the grave of so many pitiful and unprotected families.

In 1942 the position at sea was no less black. After sinking the *Repulse* and the *Prince of Wales* the Japanese had swept on, taking Singapore, Java, and Sumatra, and had occupied the Andaman

Islands and the Nicobars as forward air bases. They had raided Columbo and Trincomalee, sinking the aircraft carrier *Hermes* and the cruisers *Cornwall* and *Dorsetshire*. Our Eastern Fleet, badly damaged and now unable to find refuge in the docks of Singapore and Columbo, was obliged to steam to East Africa for repairs—a place not prepared to meet such an emergency and obliged to use every expedient to cope with the situation. Madagascar was then in the hands of the Vichy French; it was unknown how they might regard the Japanese.

Why did the Japanese not press on with their advantages that year? As Hitler halted at the Channel, so they did here, for a long pause; and though, nearly two years later, they did invade India by land, it was too late for them and the attack was soon frustrated. Meanwhile our plans had matured; South East Asia Command had been formed under Lord Mountbatten, while General Slim had rendered his Fourteenth Army a magnificent fighting force.

By amphibious assault Madagascar was first secured and the navies and merchantmen of the Allied world began slowly to return to Far Eastern waters. It was imperative to supply the enormous needs of our fighting forces and hamper the Japanese, whose logistic problem was also great, with their armies flung far and wide over so many Eastern islands and ports. But for many, many months the Japanese were paramount in these seas. Calcutta as a port was paralyzed for the better part of a year. No shipping was able to come or go without almost prohibitive risk.

Through all these great events the ordinary minutiae of our lives persisted. We endured the long languor of the heat and reveled in the fierce storms of the monsoon, Stanton went on inspecting metals and war potential, the baby cut her teeth and took her first steps. We chafed at the slow passage of time and longed for a second front to open in Europe. More and more soldiers poured into the area, camps were set up. We made a few friends among them and had long evenings of conversation about India and the war; we would all wonder how long we would be in Palta and feel that it was so strange to be there at all that we half-doubted the existence of the little station.

Our big government bungalow here, though not of the romantic elegance of No. 1 Riverside, was far more comfortable. This house was ringed with wide verandas, upstairs and down, had roomy teak cupboards built into its thick walls (teak is practically insect-proof), and, better than everything else, had proper sanitation. It stood in a large though neglected garden in which an earlier tenant had planted many rose bushes, which now bloomed sweetly under the benign guardianship of four great oleanders. We were separated from the river by one house and garden—on the other side was a wide *maidan*, and then came the Grand Trunk Road.

Our boxes of household goods had been stored in the garage of this house ever since we had left Barrackpore some months earlier. Palta had an evil reputation in the matter of white ants, but the cases were tin-lined and had been placed high on bricks, so we had not worried about them. When we opened them the morning after we arrived, everything was unscathed save for one of the book boxes, which was not only lined with zinc but had even been soldered all around the edges. Evidently some minute opening had been discovered by the voracious little horrors and half the precious contents had been devoured. Here in the light dust lay only a few torn scraps of bindings to mark the *Vanity Fair* which had belonged to my grandfather and the *Jane Eyre* which had been his father's. A handful of loose notes were all that was left of a volume of Mozart's violin sonatas. The hoard had only been discovered a few hours earlier, else nothing would have remained. Books, ever a prime necessity, were so important there then that this was almost a major tragedy.

White ants were the real inhabitants of Palta—we were literally living on an immense ant heap and were every day conscious of the active, silent, subterranean colony, which no doubt considered us trespassers on their territory. The one crack in the stone floor of the drawing room had to have boiling water and kerosene poured down it every day to keep the ants from coming up and eating the rugs. Once this was neglected for a few days and holes appeared. (Calcutta, though it had no pesticide firms, had an amenity the West does not offer—the rug merchants would not only mend your rugs free, but while they were in their workshops they would lend you others to replace them.) Everyone had his own desperate and ineffectual remedies; the government bulletin issued us in this respect really sided with the white ants by counseling patience. The only victory I ever heard of was won by two bachelors who lived next to us who became so exasperated by the creatures that they blew up a cupboard with cordite (there were advantages to working in ammunition factories). This appeared to have been a cure.

Above ground Palta was, to put it mildly, a station of severe limitations. The Grand Trunk Road ran through it, dividing the half a dozen bungalows on the riverside from the dozen that lay between the road and the encroaching jungle. Beyond the bungalows on the riverside lay the great enclosure which harbored the waterworks and tanks that supplied Calcutta with all its water. This was a place we loved to visit, with its still pools, but which was a source of great anxiety to the authorities as the system was old and outmoded and the laborers dissatisfied. Behind the houses across the road was a thick and dusty jungle, cut only by a few lanes, holding occasional small clearings in which were dingy and wretched huts. It was not an interesting jungle, being airless and monotone, of thin, sad, brownish, wispy trees. From it the jackals came out at night to give vent to their mysterious howls.

Yet, as Bengal was becoming a military stronghold, Palta, even obscure, sultry Palta, became involved in the new activities. One hot evening, out for our usual stroll, we sensed movement behind the trees across the Grand Trunk Road, and turning in to look, found to our surprise and excitement that the whole jungle had been suddenly and secretly transmuted into a scene of intense industry. Thousands of little dark aborigines were felling trees under the direction of earnest *babus* who, dressed in white *dhotis*, with spectacles on their thin faces, were holding plans, studying charts.

An airfield was being constructed on our very threshold and through all that mild winter we watched it come to life, springing out of the jungle as though centuries were being thrown aside with the tree trunks. It was our great good fortune to be able to see here with our own eyes this concrete part of the plans for the defense of India and the recapture of Burma; we no longer felt so remote, so far from the vital theatres of the world.

Constructing the field reminded us of the pictures in old childish geography books of the building of the pyramids. It was done almost entirely by manual labor, but there were so many thousands of workers that it progressed rapidly. The coolies (many of them were actually pygmies) came from Bihar and were small and poorly built—"jungly," with bent shoulders and bowed legs—and worse, they seemed quite without spirit or hope. Beside them the Bengalis seemed very impressive beings. The *babus*, in their full white garments, looked opulent too next to the Biharis who wore only loincloths. The little women, who labored beside their men, wore dull saris wound tightly round their narrow hips, and dark bodices. They never smiled.

They worked steadily, if slowly. They must have had extraordinary enterprise to accept this task, allowing themselves to be
transported hundreds of miles, to work for months on the site of a
field, of whose use and purpose they could have no possible conception. Until it went into action, by which time most of these
people had been sent back to Bihar, the great majority of them had
never seen a plane, and from first to last they understood nothing
of the war, nor even of the countries involved in it. They built
themselves small huts of palm leaves under the trees on the edges of
the field, and in the dusk kindled little fires over which they boiled
their rice in vessels of red clay. As we went away down the lane
that led from the rough patches of cleared ground we would smell
the smoke which curled round these cooking pots and rose softly
above the palms, gracing their piteous effort at homemaking. The
Biharis were not cheerful, but neither did they give an impression
of sorrow. Nor did we see any ill-temper or impatience on the part
of their overseers.

After the trees had been felled and hauled away, leaving only a
few copses to shelter the little huts before they were supplanted by
hangars and workshops, which would need, not the benediction of
shade, but that of camouflage, the great task of leveling the acres of
uneven, muddy ground began. The plain was marked off in sections
by string and the whole scene, as far as the eye could reach, was
dotted with thousands of small dark figures laboriously pushing
earth into baskets. These they heaved onto their heads and, swinging off to the nearest jungle pool, emptied the mud into its stagnant
depths. There had been many of these black pools, magnificent
breeding grounds for mosquitoes, and we were delighted to see
them disappear. Till it was thus annihilated each pond had its complement of palm leaf huts beside it, providing the settlers with
plenty of dirty water for every purpose. The little clusters of
homes under the trees, beside the somber waters, when the women
were cooking rice, their naked black babies about them, were (from
a distance) of a certain charm. Gradually as the pools were
rendered extinct the hutted settlements grew larger, as they formed
and reformed themselves round the last waters. Certainly these
strange people were able to adapt themselves to changing conditions, up to a point.

In the jungle there had been, hidden away, a few fairly substantial brick houses; long negotiations took place before the reluctant landlords made way before the advancing tide. Even one Hindu

shrine was induced to change its ground, though another held its ground and a runway went past it. The taboo here did not seem absolute. In our Metal and Steel Factory there was an old shrine which its priest had refused ever to abandon; the RAF, whose aegis was over the field at the beginning, were sure no shrine could be moved for the planes. The Americans, whose field it chiefly became, were equally sure that enough money and the offer of a better building would persuade the priest to find another site. He proved in fact quite eager to do so, being discouraged with his unvisited little temple.

When a part of the field was sufficiently flat files of bullock carts began to arrive laden with bricks, which were sent down to Palta by the river from kilns further upstream and were unloaded from country boats at the *ghat* below our house. At this time it was quite impossible for ordinary people to buy bricks or to engage a cart—they were all fully absorbed by the field. When I was buying manure for the garden I was told that it could not be delivered till the runways were finished. The precious bricks, having arrived at the snail's pace which is all the bullock cart affords, had then all to be laid by hand, equally slowly, before they were tarred over and the whole immense expanse covered with enormous tarpaulins. Yet even with these conditions the number of workers was so great and the organization so good that each evening we could see an appreciable gain. How we loved that field! Like doting parents we pointed out its virtues and progress to each other; we could not see too much of it, and we thought with gloom of the time when it would be finished and no doubt closed to us. When the light began to fail, we would turn away from it towards the remaining stretch of jungle with regret.

A milestone in the history of the field was the debut of the bulldozers. Most of their public had never even heard of such machines and their appearance caused a sensation. With them came American soldiers, crashing them lightheartedly into the surviving jungle. In that setting the bulldozers seemed like prehistoric monsters, knocking down palms, filling in craters, to the accompaniment of their characteristic loud whirring sound. Crowds followed them everywhere with amazement and joy. The Biharis were stupefied by the sight of these great creatures, which appeared even more antediluvian than they. The sound of the engines brought the whole world out to see the marvel—the villagers from Ishapore, peons on their way to Barrackpore, Europeans from Palta. Together we would watch smiling, healthy, well-dressed, well-built G.I.'s hand-ling their prodigious tools with something very close to affection and doing in a few hours what would have taken as many days in the hands of the miserable half-starved illiterates they were sup-planting. They were paid so much more because they could do so much more—the lesson was obvious. The bulldozers did more than complete the hewing out of the field—they opened another vista there on the flat ground, which, however dimly understood, was nonetheless arresting.

A camp was now built with startling speed: neat huts, equipped with screens! showers! sanitation! By this time none needed to be told what country was behind this field. Workshops and hangars went up, the project accelerated, everything happened faster and faster—the Bihari period was disappearing. G.I.'s began to stroll in and out of the narrow strip of jungle, never apparently hurrying but, from the local angle, accomplishing wonders.

Then the first planes arrived, gargantuan cocoons, with narrow, cylindrical, wingless olive-green bodies. They were Mustangs and came out from Calcutta by the river, the last stage in their long journey to activity. By this time a pier had been built out into the Hooghly only a few yards above our house, the bank had been paved, and a crane erected. The planes began to come before the site was ready, so a crew of Americans settled themselves in two tents on the riverbank and quickly put up a temporary pontoon. It would be difficult to overestimate the effect of these white men—*sahibs*—working with their hands, quite unconcerned with, and apparently unaware of, the great unseen dominating force known as "prestige." The workmen among the Indians who observed them were surprised and pleased—their own status was somehow raised by this. The British private was much worse paid and lived infinitely more meanly than his American counterpart but it was official policy that Indians did the manual labor, so the American impact was quite new. The Americans had, in fact, been offered local labor but had refused, knowing that they themselves were far more efficient—they worked so smoothly in their teams, hardly needing an order. The British would have felt this work inconsistent with their position and dignity, but this illusion did not burden a more practical people accustomed to a more genuine social democracy.

The Americans' better pay, at all levels, was already occasioning jealousy among their British counterparts—an American sergeant compared financially with a British brigadier, who traditionally had to have private means to eke out the pay which merely kept his stables going. There were even some British officers who proclaimed that the Americans should receive no more than they did while in the country, for the sake of justice. Yet these same men never thought it an injustice that the Anglo-Indian officers received less than they did, nor men in other services. I felt the disparity keenly, on other grounds. The inflation and the famine conditions were beginning—I longed to be hospitable but had not the means. The first evening the tents were up we went down to see how the men were faring, only to meet an English couple, neighbors, who had already visited them and told us their menu, which included tinned turkey—something we had not tasted for years. Before long the soldiers were offering us luxuries from their rations. The military personnel among the British and, of course, the rich did not feel the famine as did the rest of us and ignored our plight. Just as the field was opening, however, the famine had not assumed its later terrible proportions and we were ignorantly going on from bad to worse without much concern.

The proximity of an active field in wartime is seldom an asset for civilians but any possible danger was to us a bagatelle compared to the charms of the site. Our position next to the river was in any case so clearly defined, with the waterworks and two munition factories as our neighbors, that one hazard more or less made little difference compared with the pleasure of watching Kitty Hawks, Mustangs, and P. 38's lifted lightly ashore by the little Eiffel Tower, our crane, or seeing Lightnings dart over the house on their trial flights, their ungainly bodies transformed once the cocoons had gained their wings. Rosalind would ask me to sing her "the aeroplane song," which contained the magic words, "He shall loose the fateful lightning."

Before this galaxy took to the air the whole experience was epitomized when we saw the first plane go up from the field—a big Catalina, pale blue and fabulous. She took off one cool wintry evening before a wildly excited, incredulous, albeit quiet, crowd of Indians. It still seemed too extraordinary and incongruous to be true. The patches of dark jungle, the odd ungainly palms still thrusting their rough, feathery crowns in the air, the new and untried runway, the fat white-clad merchants from Ishapore village, the Biharis in their poor tatters, a few pallid Europeans, were the audience for this great floundering blue bird with its double wings, scooting about the runway with loud roars, tearing past us in clouds of noise and speed as it began to feel its strength, till at last it flew up, full of joy, into the light, hazy air. A new sensation of liberation, of release from the narrow confines of our earthbound paths, enveloped us all as we saw our gallant Catalina soaring away above us.

The field (which was claimed by Barrackpore as of that name) became a base for aerial photography over Burma, Siam, and Malaya, from which findings future offensives were mapped. From here planes loaded with steel ingots started their perilous journeys to China over the Hump; from here the wide-winged Catalinas went out over the Bay of Bengal on their air-sea rescue work.

For a time this was the busiest field in India. It maintained a pool of fighters, sent a stream of transports over the Hump, and launched Wingate's Chindits. It would be rumored that this or that shining plane had brought Wavell or Mountbatten to Bengal—in our little world it was the heart of all the great affairs. We heard tales of the poor Indians who were doctored in the field dispensary, of the daring escapes of pilots, and of the great machines they guided into the high, pale, burning air.

The Maidan

Palta's *maidan* was next to our garden and a great pleasure to us, being wide and green, with a few fine great acacias. Slow-moving, big-eyed cattle fed on it and at the "hour of cow-dust" a procession of them crossed it. At the end where it most nearly approached the river a beautiful lane of trees lined the *ghat*, supposedly planted by Kitchener. Passing Muslims said their prayers on the grass if they chanced to be there at a time proper for devotion. Rosalind, observing this from the shade of the nursery veranda, studied their every gesture and would prostrate her little person in the direction of Mecca in the most faithful of imitations.

All this was traditional. It was the jeeps and the baseball games which brought it up to the present. Surprised children came up from Ishapore village and gazed in wonder at this marvelous performance. Undisturbed, the cows searched for fresh blades; unconcerned, the faithful unrolled their prayer mats in the direct line of the flying balls.

At the time of the Muslim festival of Moharram the *maidan* was bedecked with poles and banners and all the world came to watch the dancing—then the baseball players had to withdraw. Moharram is concerned with the sequence of the Muslim hierarchy and the troubles which arose after the death of the Prophet. There was then a sharp divergence of opinion as to who should be Mohammed's successor, which resulted in a schism and the formation of the two sects—the Shias and the Sunnis. The Shias are faithful to the memory of Ali, son-in-law of the Holy Prophet, and to his sons, Hasan and Husain, sure that they and their descendants are the true "Imams," temporal and spiritual leaders of the religion. These three were (according to their supporters) martyred. Ali was assassinated, Hasan wounded so severely that he later died, while Husein, the other son, fled Medina, making his way into the Arabian desert where he hoped to find help which would enable him to return and establish his claim. He was cut off and surrounded, meeting his end while he was mounted, a sword in one hand and a Koran in the other.

The opposing sect, the Sunnis, then appointed the Imams they held legitimate. The Shias have, however, never ceased these thousand years to revere the memory of Ali and his sons; at Moharram they still display their sorrow and indignation. Today they are often joined by the cheerful Sunnis, who enjoy the excitement of the festival as much as anyone. Then, when the subcontinent was one country, Hindus came out to see the sights and Moharram presented an excellent opportunity for the fanatical or for political troublemakers to start communal riots. The police were always very alert at that season.

Stanton, having lived in the Middle East, was familiar with the Moharram, and explained it all to me. I asked him if he was for the Sunnis or the Shias. "For the Sunnis." "Why?" "Because it is the True Faith," he answered gravely.

The classic rites involved the parading of *tazias*—tall painted structures representing the mausoleums of the martyrs, but in little Palta the chief feature of the holiday, aside from the general drunkenness of all concerned (this was not necessarily confined to the Moharram), was a sort of combination maypole dance and stabbing party. Fifty-foot poles were erected on the *maidan*, with banners waving from their summits. Outwardly they were very much like maypoles, as brilliant ribbons depended from them, but they were far more interesting and virile, almost heraldic, calling to mind the Crusades. The long banners were of splendid concept, many of them Muslim green and bearing the wonderfully decorative emblem of the star and crescent; others were of scarlet or saffron or magenta—most were ornamented with gold. The ribbons which floated from the poles were of equally positive colors and were wide and shining.

As the evening drew on an excited crowd of men danced round these poles, pretending, when the height of their frenzied dance was reached, to stab their partners and sometimes doing so in real earnest. The air resounded to shouts of "Hasan, Husain!" and a good deal of palm toddy was enthusiastically consumed by both onlookers and participants, though of course an orthodox Muslim should never touch strong waters. Moharram was very dashingly celebrated on our *maidan* with three poles and three sets of Corybantic performers. It seemed incongruous that all this was set afoot by the austere men who came out onto the grass with little prayer mats all the other evenings of the year.

That first Moharram we spent in Palta our sweeper, though a Hindu, joined the dancers. No one seemed to notice or to care that he was not of the True Faith as he cavorted round the poles, but he was himself so overcome with his exertions that he later retired to his godown without saying a word to anyone and by the afternoon of the next day had still not emerged. The other servants simply said that he was ill and seemed amused. I sent Romela out to see if he needed any attention, but she returned calmly, saying in the mixture of Hindustani and English which we used together: "*Jemidar bilkul* [absolutely] unconscious *hai*."

While the *jemidar* was in this condition I missed a spoon: when he returned I asked him, as I had asked everyone else, if he had seen it. He said no, but there was a strange look about him . . . when Stanton came home I suggested that he go out to the man's quarter and look in his box, the first and last time we ever did such a thing. Stanton did so, and found not only the spoon but a dozen other articles, even the baby's shawl. So that was the last of the sweeper as far as we were concerned, except that after a little time we found that our bringals were all bearing profusely. I was delighted, but mystified till the servants told me that our former incumbent had had a vegetable stall in the bazaar, noted for its excellent bringals.

The War

During these months every day notices like these appeared in the papers:

IN MEMORIAM

Browne—In 1942, while on the trek from Burma, Malcolm, late of
B.O.C., Syriam, his wife Una (née Wales), and five children, Hazel,
June, Carlyle, Gerald and Charmaine.
"Thy will be done."
(Inserted by their aunt Agnes and brothers, Frank and Garnet.)

Cooper—In 1942, while on the trek from Burma, Edward (Ted), late
of Rangoon Corporation, his wife Constance (née Wales) and their
four children, Ivan, Neil, Patsy and Noel.
"Thy will be done."
(Inserted by their aunt Agnes and brothers, Frank and Garnet.)

Mrs. Phyllis Barnard, wife of Cpl. O. Barnard, 1st Bn. The Gloucestershire Regt. Original residence 245 Barr St. Rangoon. Left Rangoon on or about 31st January, 1942. Heard of in Maymyo in February,
1942, and later reached Myitkyina in April, 1942. Seen in Myitkyina on
7th May, 1942, making for India by the Hukuang Valley, carrying her
child and in company with another woman believed to be the wife of
a soldier in K.O.Y.L.I. Description:—28 years old, height 5 ft. 8 in.,
dark hair, dark complexion. Any information as to fate or present
whereabouts gratefully received by O.C., The Gloucestershire Regt.,
No. 6 A.B.P.O."

Raids

The Japanese hesitated before bombing India—they did not wish
to endanger the valuable support they were enjoying from the
anti-British section of the population and it would have been difficult to have kept this sentiment intact had they hurt their own par-
tisans. Yet they wanted to hinder the growing strength of the war
industries and to strike terror and inspire respect after the model
of their 1937 and 1941 attacks. Their raids had therefore to be
accompanied by artful propaganda, explaining to the poor victims
of white aggression that they were suffering only because of the
wicked British imperialist who was still in their midst. The soil was
fertile for this sort of suggestion and people like Subhas Chandra
Bose were very adept at phrasing such ideas. The average Indian
had as yet no idea of what was actually going on in the countries
now enjoying the blessings of Japanese imperialism. However, once
the raids began, no propaganda made much difference one way or
the other. To these poor Bengalis they meant the very end of the
world and their interest was solely in effects, not causes. As one

of the *babus* in the office said to Stanton when he heard his first siren, "Oh Sir, we are in the jaws of death!"

The attacks began in December, 1942, a little before Christmas. The planes always came at night and in small numbers, staying only a short while. All in all there were not many raids and very little actual physical damage was caused either to life or to material. But for the Bengalis it was a catastrophic experience, particularly since the first raiders were given virtually a free hand. We had no suitable planes available to meet them, even though the attack had long been considered inevitable. The area from Calcutta for forty miles up the river was a perfect target for the enemy—the river showed up like a broad ribbon in the moonlight, which would be clear and fine every night at that season. Objectives were packed into the countryside, almost like the Ruhr—war industries, war personnel, camps, dumps of material, airfields at Dum Dum and Barrackpore. Both Cossipore and Ishapore had ordnance factories, Eastern Command Headquarters was at Barrackpore, aside from power stations, waterworks, railway lines—one wondered how any bomb could miss something of importance. Yet in point of fact they hit very few targets and the success they achieved was chiefly psychological.

The Viceroy, Lord Linlithgow, had paid an official visit to the Presidency that winter and had left Calcutta a few hours before its first raid. He was told that the situation was in hand and therefore sent messages to the city immediately afterwards congratulating the population and saying proudly, "Calcutta can take it." A few days later, after a million people had fled in panic and essential services were disrupted, those of us who stayed behind wondered a little wryly what matters would have been like in a city that could not take it.

A few small bombs fell in the city near Dalhousie Square and in some bazaar areas, causing almost no casualties, miraculously, considering the density of the city, but rumor multiplied every accident a thousandfold. For the next month the stations were choked with people trying to board trains and the roads leading out of the city were black with refugees trudging out with their bundles. There was no pride, no wish to endure, to see matters go on "as usual." Yet the Bengali was basically not so different from the man who proved a hero in Spain, Holland, England, Russia, China—the difference lay in the fact that in those other countries the people felt they were fighting their own war, in their own interest, no matter how dreaded and terrible the consequences. The Civil Defense forces made a very poor showing but it was all part of the same picture.

In our own Inspectorate, staffed with six hundred Indians and four Europeans, a call was made for volunteers who would be prepared to come to the factory at night as fire fighters in the event of raids. Only two of the Indians responded, a small boy and an old man, neither of whom seemed to know why they had had this gallant impulse. It was decided that should there be raids, the Europeans must deal with whatever conditions might arise by themselves, so when the sirens went off the *sahibs* had to hurry to their posts, leaving their families alone with panicky servants. After the first attacks this was changed so that the men took turns in going and it was our good fortune that on the night of our raid (which did no damage) Stanton was at home.

We ticked off the major objectives as the raiders came and it seemed evident that we would be next on the list. We were in fact visited on Christmas Eve: we heard the sirens, the planes coming down the Hooghly, leaving the river, and attracting a great burst of AA fire from a battery on the bank. The house shook and the shutters banged, a few bombs landed in the jungle, and it was all over—except for the tremendous effect on the Indians.

Palta was part of the famous district called Twenty-four Parganas, the area surrounding Calcutta which had been the East India Company's first territory, ceded to them by the Nawab of Bengal in 1757 (pargana being the name of an administrative unit of land ever since Akbar's day). In 1757 Clive was granted the tax income from Twenty-four Parganas (882 square miles) for himself—it was called Clive's *jaghir*, or fief, and it was a lucrative possession which he held till 1774, when it reverted to the Company. This was the historic ground which the Japanese were now bombing.

There had been some ten people hurt in our raid but the next morning, which was Christmas day, the whole area seemed totally disorganized. We went down to the waterfront and watched hundreds of distracted Indians being ferried across the water—at profiteering rates—to any destination, just to get away. This exodus continued for many days, thousands and thousands starting off with their cattle, urging the beasts onto the wide, flat boats, while desperate arguments with the ferrymen over fares rang out. Of course, Christmas was no festival for the majority, but it seemed a strange day that year. Our thoughts were very much with the prisoners in Japanese hands, all down the China Coast and in Burma—and now here we heard the lowing of the cows as they were urged down the *ghats* and saw the terrified, impoverished people of Twenty-four Parganas senselessly rushing away from their homes and work, very often to even worse disaster.

On the day after the raid no bread, butter, milk, or meat could be had—a minor difficulty, but sufficiently felt in the heat. Most of us did not have refrigeration (we never had a Frigidaire after Barrackpore) and these things had to be purchased fresh every day. Most of us had small children and we were already feeling the effects of the blockade; no one had much of a reserve in the way of tinned food.

The poor who did not go reacted in other alarming ways. After the raid many of the Bengalis went into the jungle to sleep rather than remain at home. It was the cold season and very damp and chill under the trees after the sun went down—especially so to people accustomed to passing the night shut up in airless godowns. Our own sweeper took his family into the open in this wise and attributed the subsequent loss of his baby son to the cold of the woods. It was impossible for us to advise these people with any conviction—if we urged them to stay where they were and they were the losers thereby they would never have ceased to hold us responsible for their misfortunes. We did, in fact, never have another raid on our part of Twenty-four Parganas in spite of the airfield and the waterworks. The Japanese probably gained as much as they wanted in the dislocation of industry through labor troubles and demands for higher wages, and in the collapse of morale—at little cost to themselves.

In a few days Beaufighters were sent in from Egypt and when they were in the air over us the Japanese began to lose planes and stopped coming. Australian pilots flew these ships, one of them bringing down three of the enemy planes within a very few nights. We were happy enough to meet this hero and were delighted by his cheerful and insouciant manner. On one expedition he had had to bail himself out of his burning Beaufighter, landing on one of the Sunderabunds, the islands at the mouth of the Hooghly. He was unhurt but had lost his clothes and the villagers were horrified by the sight of this apparition, whom they took to be either a demon or a Japanese. They tried to get him to give them money and he escaped from them with difficulty, sighing for the simplicities of the air.

In our household our cook became a problem. This man was a young Mugh, a refugee from Rangoon, apparently as mild and gentle as his race implied. However, after the raid, while the servants were all drinking tea together—the alarm seemed to have made caste unimportant for a short time and we had immediately given them tea and sugar—he took the floor and told them in hair-raising style of the awful days in Rangoon before it fell and of his terrible journey to India. He described the dead he had seen lying in the streets of the city and on the road through the Hukuang Valley, telling of the hunger, fatigue, and sickness which had overwhelmed Europeans and Indians alike. It was true and tragic, and in a few minutes he had weakened the fiber of the household. The servants had little enough courage to fall back upon in any case. Even Romela, who had been as brave as a young lion as she sat with us in the drawing room when the bombs fell, holding a baby in her arms and saying she would like to be at the guns, in the presence of the cook and his tales became infected with fear and cowardice like the others.

Romela

Romela was a delightful girl and seemed satisfied with the simplicities of her life—she had little with which to contrast them. In the mornings she would walk by the river with Rosalind, bright and graceful figures. Rosalind was by now a fountain of bilingual conversation and fantasy. The small blond child was a foil to the maiden beside her, tall, dark, pliant, in her white and gauzy garments, now often with a peacock-blue shawl over her shoulders. She was happy to have her own room and here with the children she would sing long Bengali ballades, accompanying herself on her harmonium. She painted, she sewed, sitting cross-legged on the floor and glowing like a dark rose. Late in the afternoons she took the baby out in a large high-handled basket; (the carpet *wallah* had the pram). Sitting on the grass under the shade of a huge mango tree by the river she would wave a great leaf slowly to and fro before her enraptured charge, both seemingly perfectly amused by this ceremonious entertainment. Then she would sing to the *baba*, especially a long refrain which went *"Sundar Daria, Sundar Daria, gai se tu, baiti hai"* and which praises the beautiful river.

But of course it was not enough for her. I could not find any circle for her. The servants were uneducated, and in any case the missionaries responsible for her had warned me to keep her away from the men in the household and to rustle the chaperon's petticoat frequently. This I did, but to no avail. They all fell in love with her, and with thoroughly dishonorable intentions. She was a Christian, an untouchable (that they knew because she washed the diapers), and she was old—probably twenty-four—and unmarried! Only the cook, our same urbane Mugh, was of a different turn of mind, and it was even more difficult to deal with him. He was determined to marry her, magnanimously overlooking her being an outcaste, Christian and educated. I protested vigorously with him. "Cook, you cannot marry her, she is a Christian! She is an educated girl!" "I don't mind," he shouted, beside himself, "I don't mind any of these things!" We had to stay home to take care of her more than the children. We sent her back to her mission for a holiday and the cook followed her. It was all terribly tiresome.

She did many things with us which she enjoyed, such as going to the theatre in Calcutta. We once saw there a Bengali play about Tippoo Sultan, admirably acted, so vital and so impassioned that we could follow it though it was not even in Hindustani but in Bengali. The Frenchmen in the play, acted of course by Indians, wore red wigs and were voluble and excitable; an Englishman was paraded as a prisoner, bound (probably David Baird); Tippoo was magnificently costumed, and most striking; his widow calm and courageous as well as beautiful. It was all interpreted to make marvelous anti-British propaganda. The theatre was small, without any cooling devices save a couple of old *punkahs;* in the intervals we paced in a courtyard where there were oleanders. The audience, all Indian except ourselves, was perfectly civil to us, propaganda or no.

We told Romela the classic story about David Baird's old mother who, when told in Scotland that her son was a prisoner and chained to his captor, remarked, "De'il help the cheel that's chained tae oor Davy!" It would probably not matter, for most Indian theatre, in what war David Baird was a prisoner; he has become the type.

Finally we decided that the best thing would be to have Romela go into the army. This cost us many pangs, she was dear to us, and besides, her care of the children had smoothed away so many difficulties, and she was happy with us. But she was restless. Yet she did not want to return to the mission—she was grateful to it but she wanted to spread her wings. India was in need of trained nurses and in that organization she would be protected—our conscience urged us on, this would be a contribution to the war effort. We wrote to the recruitment center in Delhi, which advertised fairly often beseeching women to apply, stressing the urgent need of the army for trained nurses.

After a very long delay we received a sheaf of forms so complicated and detailed that it took months before they were completed and she was finally admitted to the service. The forms were drawn up in English and had to be answered in the same language, though it was hoped to recruit *Indian* nurses; the Europeans in the service were nearly all trained and recruited in Britain. Romela could not possibly have filled out these papers with her school English, nor had all her interviews and examinations, nor even have ordered her uniforms without such willing patrons as ourselves. Yet the army constantly complained of the great difficulty it had in recruiting nurses—there were few enough women willing to apply in any case, due to the prejudice against the profession. Paradoxically it was (in the eyes of the orthodox) only possible for outcastes, and yet few outcastes were sufficiently educated to enter it. Most reasonable, trained, young Indian nurses simply could not have tackled the paperwork which preceded appointment: these women had in nearly all cases been trained by the missions, which were naturally loath to lose them once they were useful, and could hardly be blamed for not filling in forms which would take them away. They needed nurses too. The army offered many times the pay a mission could afford, as well as a degree of liberty the missionaries often thought dangerous for Indian girls. Both of these factors were attractive to the girls, who were only human. Romela, however, did not wish to enter the service for either reason—not that she was averse to good pay or freedom, commodities of which she had little experience—but from good motives. We had tried to inculate her with the idea that the war was worth winning and we should all help. And then there was a normal measure of enlightened self-interest—she had little chance to develop further where she was. None of us knew then what good pay the army offered, we were all very innocent.

The military hospital in Barrackpore, an ancient institution, was now greatly enlarged and very busy; we sometimes visited patients there and had become acquainted with its commanding officer, a lively and energetic Irishman who had no love of red tape. Renting our furniture from Mr. Nundy, which I now did without a qualm, I still felt a little squeamish about his mattresses and asked Colonel Austin one day for his advice. "Delouse them!" he cried at once. "We'll do it for you, a pleasure, we do it every day, just send them over." It evidently was the most natural thing in the world to him; I felt I ought to be horrified at sending my babies' mattresses to be deloused; on the other hand I was glad the facility was there and it evidently was quite usual in Indian Army circles—not surprisingly. After this happy encounter I took a number of problems to the helpful doctor, including that of Romela's forms. He agreed with me that they were ridiculous and urged me to write Delhi in full, describing our experiences and recommending that the applicants should certainly be able to use either Hindi or Urdu, at the very least. I did write and six months later had a reply, which consisted of forms which would allow *me* to join the auxiliary training branch for nursing sisters, if I could meet the standards. It seemed useless to continue this type of correspondence, so I gave up. To-day I would persevere, but I doubt if I would get any further in like circumstances.

The first thing Romela needed was a birth certificate, the sine qua non of our times. She of course did not have one, so we went to Barrackpore to apply for one in the Treasury Building, the local office of the Indian Civil Service. We took rickshaws to the canton-ment from Palta; Romela was very excited and full of anticipation, it was all an eager adventure to her as she went down the Grand Trunk Road with Rosalind sitting beside her. It took two hours to procure the birth certificate though there was no one else waiting for attention—the simple document seemed to need the concerted efforts of eight *babus*. After they had asked Romela about herself —she had little enough to tell;—I sent her and Rosalind into the garden while I waited in the silent little courtroom under the high desk of justice. There was no one else there.

Except for the small central courtroom, the whole building was so overcrowded with clerks, cabinets, desks, baskets, papers, files, that it was difficult to move about in it at all and every place, every article, every inch of everything was dirty. On the walls under rich garlands of cobwebs hung large heavily-framed photographs of former Indian Civil magistrates who had served in Barrackpore—

their terms of office together covered almost a century. Sitting gingerly on the edge of a grimy bench and looking up at their candid open brows, I wondered if they, too, had tolerated this dirt and disorder. The British are not famous for cleanliness or tidiness; they have relied on their servants to keep their surroundings pleasantly fresh—without servants or with sluttish servants they have often lived in squalor. The horrid condition of the building was in no way to be laid only at the door of the present magistrate —Stanton (no stickler for daintiness himself) had often commented to me on the disgusting state of the Treasury Building when he had visited it to draw funds for the office. It would have taken years, even in India, to have achieved such a complete squalor and disarray as this office presented.

All business seemed to be conducted in an amiable, desultory, confused manner, with much searching for papers; but I believe that in the end most things were found and that this little headquarters handled great sums of money with perfect honesty, locking up *lakhs* of rupees in old rickety cupboards. As an administrative unit this office must more often than not have been a brake, rather than a help, to persons in the field who needed quick action to follow their findings and decisions. The filthy, crumbling bazaars of Barrackpore seemed a natural accompaniment, an inevitable consequence, of a governmental headquarters such as this —the same lethargy, the same complacency in the face of uncleanness and disorder, the same absence of vigor. One longed to be able to seize a great broom and sweep the cobwebs out of them both.

In the room where I waited there had been many trials held under English law, that noble instrument of justice. These would have been scrupulously fair and unbiased, as far as the letter of the law went and as far as an honest judge could conduct them. Yet it was often patent to everyone, the judge included, that justice miscarried because the law could not here be upheld according to its intent. An innocent man was often penalized with the full knowledge of the court through the fact that English law is to such an extent dependent on the honest witness. In many countries such a code is practical—when a man swears on the Bible, even an irreligious man, he is very loath to lie. Perjury is not a light thing, even to an immoral person. In India this check did not exist and the dishonest witness could be, and was, put on the stand to flout justice in the full light of day. No oath mattered to him. Baber found that "the people of Hindustan . . . are a strangely foolish and senseless race, possessed of little reflection and less foresight."

For certain short periods the Service was a wonderful instrument of government, holding within its ranks many giants. But there were too few persons in it to cope with the vast size and population of the country and its diversity, all of which led to enormous problems. Particularly after the country was stabilized, the Service was allowed to become enmeshed in administrative detail and paperwork—and that resulted in little places like this Treasury. The officers prided themselves on their fewness of number and the huge territory each one called his own, but in point of fact this could continue only as long as a great deal was left undone. In the course of time the magistrates became isolated from their districts by paper, forms, and endless petty regulations. There was also the canker inherent in the very eminence of the Service—"*the* Service," as they called it—jealously excluding all other branches of government. In their hearts the Twice-Born* believed their sobriquet deserved. Yet at its best there was never a better record of devotion, intelligence, and imagination on the part of a small ruling cadre in an alien country than this body which developed gradually, through force of circumstance, out of the first formations of the East India Company. It is true that it was, in relation to the country and the times and English salaries at home, highly paid and highly pensioned. This was later held against it by the Indians, who maintained that it was a drain on the finances of the country and that its pay scales were disproportionately weighted in favor of Europeans.

It was also severely criticized, and with justice, over this matter of introducing English law. The old village *panchayat*, or council of five, had previously, since Akbar's day and before that, governed each village community. Here in a small circle of men known to one another, judged by their peers, trials were undoubtedly fairer than they became under the British system. Mountstuart Elphinstone, Metcalfe, and Sir Thomas Munro all contended that the old Indian council should be retained but they were not able to stem the tide of centralization and control from above.

Indian Theatre

We used sometimes to see Indian dancing in Calcutta, performed by the students of the Timar Baran School, the institution inspired

---

* Brahmins, according to the Hindu religion, are twice-born.

by Rabindranath Tagore, whose poetical works they often interpreted on the stage. The influence of Tagore on the modern arts of Bengal was marked, and the Bengalis' pride in him evident. The director of the school was Timar Baran himself—he was also the producer and chief male dancer.

One of the dances of this troop was so remarkable that it stands out in my memory as an epitome of the magic of their art. It was the story of a poet, a type of Eastern Keats, and danced by Timar Baran. Inspired, exhausted, desperate, he was to pass a night alone in a deserted palace. An extremely romantic character—Byron and Liszt had their counterparts in him too—melancholy, thin, dark, he roved about a great marble hall, restless and searching. Timar Baran's mime was so subtle, he was so absorbed in his problems, that one forgot he was dancing, almost. He was dressed in the long *sherwani* and tight jodhpurs of a gentleman; neither his costume nor the scenery could have been more simple, or more elegant. Finally he falls asleep on a sofa.

Then his dreams come before us. Some of these are happy, when exquisitely beautiful girls come down the long spiral of the marble stairway to charm him with their soft, haunting ways. Others are of ghastly import; wicked and vengeful figures, emaciated and worn, come to threaten him for having rendered them desolate. The poet, lying long and wan on his sofa, never moves. Each dancer has the stage to herself and her own fantasies.

It was a long dance, handled with lightest, surest, touches, bringing with it a sense of universality and perfect art. The accompaniment consisted of the usual group of musicians, sitting on the stage with their lutes and drums.

The drummers of Bengal were particularly versatile and gifted, and it was a pleasure not only to hear them but also to watch their hands, their thin brown wrists as flexible as vines, and the whole palm of the hand being brought into play, the thumb giving the beat, the fingers the melody.

Every year in Ishapore the apprentices studying and working at our factories used to put on a show, engaging Indian dancers. I looked forward eagerly to seeing them; these affairs would coincide with a sort of local *puja*, when the workmen would decorate the machines with chains of marigolds and serve refreshments, turning the shops into an open house. It was amusing to sit beside the lathes eating sweets and seeing petals scattered about, it humanized for a few brief hours the dreary industrialism of Twenty-four Parganas.

Sometimes these hours did not seem so brief—I remember one of these celebrations on a hot spring afternoon which seemed absolutely interminable.

When we arrived on the scene, the long hall of the apprentices' school was already quite filled with Indian families, dressed in their best. It was still very light, and no one had had time for a siesta (since it was a Saturday we expected this), as the entertainment was to begin at what seemed to us a fiendishly early hour. The windows were open, and the fans going hard, but it was so intensely hot that they made little difference. Parties of any kind were rare in wartime India, and it was touching to see what efforts the apprentices had gone to to make a success of their day, and give everyone a good time. They were all in snowy *dhotis* and shining clean shirts, showing everyone in, anxious to show themselves attentive hosts. I felt ashamed that so few of the Europeans had taken the trouble to come, as we were ushered, with many bow, into the best seats—that is, into the front rows of the hard wooden benches. We had a long wait before anything happened. The setting was that of a school, but not an ordinary school—it inevitably partook too much of the prevalent atmosphere of the country to seem primarily academic.

At last a thin young man came out on the stage, wearing a white *dhoti* and a long blue shirt, and carrying that favorite Bengali instrument—the harmonium. Sitting down on the floor, he at once began a long, mournful, high-pitched song, rather like a weird operatic recitative to our ears. This was well received; after a quarter of an hour he withdrew, and his place was at once taken by another young man who took his turn at the harmonium, singing another equally long, equally mournful, equally high-pitched recitative, presumably a different tune. This appeared to give pleasure to the public also. Then a third youth appeared, stood before a microphone, and sang what seemed to us an interminable Bengali ballad. After an hour of this type of music we were bad-mannered enough to ask when the dancing would begin . . . "Soon," replied an usher, soothingly. After several more soloists had come and gone, we asked again about the dancers, and had the same reply. No one else seemed to mind. The Indian public fanned themselves, chewed *pan*, dandled babies, and gazed into space with perfect content. This went on for another hour and a half, when we went out for some tea.

While sipping hot tea and refusing bright pink cakes, I asked the agreeable apprentice who was our host at the table why they did not bring on the dancers earlier, or have them appear between the musical selections. "Oh no, Madame," he said, "that would be tedious and boring."

We hung on through several more renditions on the harmonium, doggedly determined to see the dancers if it was our last act. The hall began to smell strongly of *pan*, and the last rays of the sun slanted fiercely through the windows, but at last, just as darkness began to fall, they arrived. There were only two of them, but they proved more than worth the long hours of expectation, which, it appeared, were due to the performers' lighthearted unpunctuality. Artists in the Far East then felt no obligation to be on time. Why should their audiences not wait? No one minds waiting! What else has an audience to do? I once heard of a huge audience being kept waiting for some dancers from 7 till 9:30, the delay caused because the cast had decided to go to a party before the show. Only the Europeans felt this behavior remiss.

We had hardly grasped the glad news that our trial by harmonium was over when a radiant, slight girl ran out on the stage, literally shining with joy. She was to dance the part of a boy, and after a few preliminary turns, she was joined by her partner, a short, plump, moon-faced maiden, who was also delightfully happy. These two young persons were clearly enchanted with their art, their engagement, that evening, each other, and the whole world besides. There is so little joy on the plains of India that it brings the rarest pleasure to see it expressed—particularly by girls.

Mrs. Beveridge wrote at the end of the nineteenth century that over the greater part of India there were no girls—only children and married women. That, at least, had altered, and largely through Western influence. These young dancers, we learned, were amateurs, dancing just because they loved to do it, and for a few bright moments everyone in the hall was able to enter their charmed circle of pure gladness.

The shorter girl, who was perhaps fourteen, wore a full skirt and a tight blouse, and they had bedecked her with bangles, necklaces, anklets, earrings. She had large, rolling, mischievous black eyes, and was particularly good at jerking her neck and head from side to side, a favorite movement in Indian dancing. Her companion was in jodhpurs with a fitted jacket and a Gandhi cap. Like two bright birds they winged their way through a few swift dances, and then the program reverted to the mournful Bengali musicians. We hurried away, not to blur the images of the dancers in our minds.

The Bengal Famine

In 1943 the Bengal Famine came upon us. There have been great and terrible famines in Indian history—no period has escaped them, no traveler but has told stories of their horrors. China had them too, on a vast scale. British India, however, it was assumed, was now almost free of these disasters; the railways, better planning, the marshaling of relief if a province were threatened, had obviated the worst of the problem. Whenever the blessings brought the country by Britain were related, the fact that there were no more famines was always stressed. After a time within the country I began to realize that this was not strictly true—famine was endemic (not vast famines; it was a question of degree). In a land where nearly everyone was so bitterly poor, with no reserves, very little —a crop failure, a bad storm—could mean the difference between subsistence and starvation. Now the war was blamed, but to say that was to oversimplify the issue.

When the worst was over, in 1945, the Famine Commission published its report in which it said that the Bengal Famine of 1943 "stands out as a great calamity even in an age all too familiar with human suffering and death on a tragic scale." It was conservatively estimated that a million and a half died, but probably the figure was twice that. Officially the reasons for it were the drastic fall in the supply of rice and the great rise in prices, as the famine was accompanied by a mounting inflation—some items went up as high as one thousand percent. By the time the government at last bestirred itself to take steps it was too late to save millions of people from death and many more millions from near ruin.

There was a very severe and destructive hurricane upcountry that monsoon, which destroyed the crops of a rich rice-growing area. The imports of Burmese rice were now entirely cut off, and that was in itself serious, as Bengal had depended upon that crop also. Transport and manpower were dislocated because of the war and the authorities had been most improvident—the allocation of grains to the army had ignored the needs of the civilian population. The government appeared to be both blind and incapable of rational action. The greed and corruption of the profiteers, the stupidity and general helplessness of the people, did the rest. The famine need not have developed as it did—to a large extent it was man-made. As the government was still in British hands, theirs was the blame, but they blamed the Indians.

Much was later made of the superstition and reluctance of the people to eat unfamiliar foods when their familiar staple failed, but this was, I think, overemphasized as an easy excuse, just as was the loss of Burma. Burma had never supplied more than a small percentage of the total rice consumed in Bengal, but its capture was constantly given as a major reason for the famine. Thus no one was obliged to assume the responsibility or take the onus for what had happened, and for many months that seemed the chief interest of the authorities—to wash their hands of the affair after attributing the disaster to some cause beyond their control. It was like the great Irish Famine; the men who were ultimately responsible and those in high office lived comfortably and shut their eyes. As with that disaster a lethargy seemed to come upon the English, and though normally humane and quick to aid the suffering, they remained, as individuals, largely aloof. Perhaps this is the background of all great famines—otherwise they would not occur.

During the first six months the government, admittedly beset with many other great and pressing problems, attempted to push this issue where they knew it would be neglected—into the hands of Indians who could not cope with it. The Indians did not have the positions which would have enabled them to take the drastic steps that were essential, they did not have sufficient authority even on the city level. The Calcutta Municipality was not an admirable organ but many Indians were good-hearted, though weak. Many, also, were only too ready to profiteer in food. It was lamentable. Before most of us were aware of the magnitude and horror of the catastrophe, the whole situation had got out of hand and thousands were dying in the streets of the cities and towns of Bengal. It was primarily a human tragedy but it was also an administrative breakdown of the most appalling dimensions.

The Governor of Bengal, Sir John Herbert, was ill at the beginning of the famine and did not survive it. The Viceroy, Lord Linlithgow, had had his office for seven years and seemed to many of us to have lost interest in his task; he did not even visit the Presidency during the crisis. Between them they did nothing. It was obvious for months that only the strongest and most rigorous emergency measures, perhaps even martial law, could deal with the situation, but these steps were not taken until the famine had claimed most of its victims. The courageous Calcutta daily, the *Statesman*, did its best with vigorous and truthful reporting to awaken the dormant conscience of those in authority and resisted the efforts made to silence its columns. For a long time it printed every day the number of persons picked up on the streets who were so near to death that their plight was acknowledged and they were sent to the hospitals. The government insisted that these unfortunates must not be designated as "famine victims"—as the paper quite rightly had called them—substituting instead the misnomer of "sick destitutes." To conceal conditions seemed more important than to heal them.

It was a wonderful opportunity for Japanese propaganda and our enemies were not slow to capitalize on it. It was true that in that year the Bengalis could hardly have been worse off under any flag. With three million dead and millions more weakened and even incapacitated, and most of them financially ruined, selling everything they had to keep alive from day to day, the people in the famine districts could hardly be expected to be pro-British. The farmers even had to cut down their splendid old mango trees and sell them for firewood; it would take twenty years to replace them. Hundreds of thousands of people from the country swarmed into Calcutta, hoping for relief, work, food—but there was absolutely nothing for most of them. There seemed to be an almost total paralysis on every hand. After our experiences in seeing great multitudes of destitutes on the move in China in the wake of floods, famine, or war, and the efforts made in some places to receive and help them, we were appalled by the lack of action here. Private charity stood aghast at the magnitude of the suffering—one did not know where to begin. A few helped a few, but it must be said that the vast majority did nothing at all. The Red Cross, the Salvation Army, the missions, did what they could and that little was good, but they could not assume the leadership which belonged rightly to the government. One of the most horrifying aspects of the disaster was the fear, greed, corruption, and heartless indifference of much of the public. There was a meteoric rise in prices, enormous profits were made by speculators. Hundreds of thousands literally starved in Calcutta; others lived in comfort. There were almost no controls, indeed no effort to ration or plan. It was, as the Famine Commission was afterwards to admit, "a moral and social breakdown, as well as an administrative breakdown."

The report on the Inquiry, which was published in the Calcutta *Statesman* of May 8th, 1945—a very considerable time after the impact of the famine—read in part:

The Commission declares that the arrangements for the receipt, storage, and distribution of food supplies despatched to Bengal during the autumn of 1943 were thoroughly inadequate, and that between the Government in office and the various political parties and, in the early part of the year, between the Governor and his Ministry and between the administrative organization of the Government and the public, there was lack of co-operation which stood in the way of a united and vigorous effort to prevent and relieve famine.

The Government of India . . . failed to recognize at a sufficiently early date the need for a system of planned movement of foodstuffs, including rice as well as wheat, from the surplus to the deficit provinces . . . ; in other words, the basic plan should have come into operation much earlier that it did. . . .

Yet the government had had over a century of experience in these matters in India. To continue:

We have criticized the Government of Bengal for their failure to control the famine. It is the responsibility of the Government to lead the people and take effective steps to prevent avoidable catastrophe. But the public in Bengal, or at least certain sections of it, have also their share of blame. We have referred to the atmosphere of fear and greed which, in the absence of control, was one of the causes of the rapid rise in the price level. Enormous profits were made out of the calamity, and in the circumstances, profits for some meant death for others. A large part of the community lived in plenty while others starved, and there was much indifference in the face of suffering. Corruption was widespread throughout the province and in many classes of society. . . .

The Bengal famine resulted in high mortality, the basic cause of which was lack of food. . . . The health situation which arose in 1943 was beyond the control of any health and medical service. The health and medical services in Bengal were, however, unfitted to meet the emergency because of defects in organization and inadequacy and insufficiency of staff and some of the mortality which occurred could have been prevented by more vigorous and timely measures.

During the famine period, up to November 1943, there was almost a complete breakdown in the health services. . . .

The inanition was not confined to Calcutta and Bengal; Delhi showed equal indifference and in Westminster the issue was constantly played down and evaded. The war was still in a critical stage and Churchill always had a blind spot about India—he saw it as existing to complement the interests of the mother country. He despised the Indian leaders, and he would never further independence. He foresaw what a loss that would mean for the English in terms of jobs and prestige. His Secretary of State for India was Leopold Amery, a man whose whole political career was devoted to championing Churchill. The Opposition did finally begin to raise the question of the famine in the House, questions were asked, and with reluctance a few admitted that it was indeed a catastrophe, but still there was no aid to Bengal. There were many resemblances to the attitude of Whitehall during the Irish famine.

However, at last changes were made in key personnel. Much had been made by the imperial press of the heroism of the Governor of Bengal for refusing to quit his post, though he was so ill. He was indeed very ill and in fact did not survive, and it would have been a thousand times better if he had stepped down earlier and let someone with energy take over. Lord Linlithgow left India and Lord Wavell was made Viceroy. He came at once to Bengal and called upon the army to distribute grain. The entire community was inspired with hope, the atmosphere of defeatism was lifted, and at last the famine came to an end. But scars remained. This Bengal Famine of 1943 was of such proportions that it would for long be remembered. Under British rule the frequency of such diasters had greatly lessened and the British were proud that freeing the country from this fear had been one of the blessings of their rule (Churchill often made such a claim). After 1943 no informed person could ever feel that this statement could be strongly upheld. Many minor triumphs were forgotten in such a fearful failure.

In our small way we suffered too in this time. The inflation made it impossible for us to get enough to eat and I myself weighed under a hundred pounds at the end of 1943 (I am five-feet-eight). Salaries had been fixed many years before and no consideration was given to any plea that the war made life difficult—the war made life difficult for everyone and it was unpatriotic to complain. This noble official stand was facilitated by the old British axiom that a gentleman does not expect to live off his salary. He either has private means or marries them. If not, he is no gentleman and should be quite content to live like a workman. An officer's salary covered his stable and his family provided the rest. Government servants, if officers, should be considered in the same category, though on a lesser plane. So we had scant success in pleading that we could not manage as prices soared. Delegations were formed and went to see senior officers in Calcutta and Delhi and were generally insulted. After some years our pay went up ten percent; by then prices had risen one thousand percent. The whole story of the men in Indian government service, particularly those on temporary war contract like ourselves, is a shameful one of exploitation. Be that as it may, we found ourselves in serious difficulties as the year went on. It was an old story, really. Early in the nineteenth century Metcalfe wrote of "the determined spirit of penury which is evident in this administration"; he felt keenly then, at that stage of his career, that honest work should be decently rewarded and throughout his time in India he insisted that the natives of the country were cruelly overtaxed and that the government was callous in its treatment of them. As he grew older and was knighted, his tone changed and he became mean himself, begrudging all expenditure. The outlook on salaries was influenced by such early governors as Cornwallis, who looked upon the country as a landowner and wished to see it in the hands of great landowners who would administer it as England was administered, for their own benefit, with a quiet and docile peasantry. The English dislike change and this attitude, which was very congenial to the ruling clique, took fast root, though Bengal never was literally owned by British landlords. Financially and economically the country was run in such a way that only a few could derive profit and the underlings were supposed to be contented with a very little.

In our part of Twenty-four Parganas we were not beset with refugees, as most people pressed on to Calcutta, the Mecca of their poor hope. One evening, however, going through Ishapore on our bicycles, we noticed a woman crouched by the door of the village dispensary, with two children beside her. Something in her attitude arrested our attention, though it is common enough in India to see a poor woman by a doorway, watching her sons sleep on the stones beside her. We got off our bicycles and walked back to them; then we saw that they were famine victims. The boys were lying on the floor of the veranda almost insensible, their mother was the very image of despair. Dozens of people were passing but no one took any interest in their distress till we went to them; then a crowd gathered at once.

The woman told us that she had hoped to find a doctor in the dispensary who would help the children, but that he was out and the assistant ignored her. She was too tired and dispirited to say more. We went through into the little office and chivied the assistant who gave us some glucose water for the boys and then we sent out for tea. A woman in the crowd quickly brought some from her home and refused payment—the people were not basically hardhearted, at least not the poor. But the children could not swallow.

The doctor arrived at last, a Bengali who was obviously loath to concern himself in any way with these poor folk. Several persons in the crowd volunteered the information that a rich family in the village was feeding the poor every day at their gates; we decided to turn to them for advice. They lived nearby on the river in a large house behind high gates. After we had passed through these and gone up to a terrace on which strutted peacocks (this house could not have been more incongruous, situated as it was in a village of straw huts), we saw Mr. Das, the owner, a fat man in a fine white *dhoti*, coming out to meet us from his entrance halls which were lined with enormous mirrors. The house was the oddest anomaly— almost a palace with its marble floors and huge mirrors, its profusion of lights, yet the overabundant sofas and couches and divans were one and all so decrepit and grimy that one shuddered at the thought of sitting on them. Mr. Das evidently did not see the dirt, in this he was like Mr. Nundy. He was most unsympathetic about the little family and I wondered why he went in for good works at all—perhaps it was some sort of protection to him, as his wealth was almost dangerous in the midst of Ishapore's poverty. (Why should it have been poor? Why did the factories not pay their men decently?) "What can I do?" asked Mr. Das. "It is the government's business."

We felt that the famine children were too far gone to be taken to our house as they were—should anything have gone wrong it might have raised an outcry. Leaving them in a sheltered arcade in the village, we cycled off to a small Indian-owned, Indian-managed hospital some distance up the Barrackpore Road. The doctor in charge was a man with an apparently pleasant manner, who agreed to receive them and care for them till they were able to come to us. Before we left we saw the little boys comfortably installed in clean beds in a small private room and had every assurance from the staff that they would be well attended. The poor mother was quite bewildered by this miraculous turn of events and was by this time attempting to kiss my feet every time I came near her. We could hardly exchange any words, as she knew almost no Hindustani, but we did not need them.

The next week I found great pleasure in making a godown ready for her. She had clearly sold all she had before reaching such straits and needed everything. But it was so hard to find even the simplest necessities unless one had a great deal of money—in the last months the bazaars had been denuded. The price of the cheapest sari was now twelve times what it had been when we arrived in India two years before, and cheap ordinary saris, such as I used to buy for Aknis, were quite unobtainable. The poor were almost as badly off for their few garments as they were for food. The mills were devoting themselves to khaki for the soldiers and towels and sheets for the army; they had no interest in the civilian demand. According to the papers some women had committed suicide because they literally had not a scrap of cloth to wrap around themselves. In the end I got hold of a length of coarse white material, without a border, and paid the better part of a pound sterling for it—a poor man hardly made that much in a month. I could have bought her luxurious clothes without any difficulty save for payment—the bazaars in Calcutta had plenty of gold-embroidered chiffon and gauze saris, the rich lacked for nothing. It was still possible to buy earthen cooking pots though, and I remember buying a comb, which was later laid aside when the mother showed me, laughing, her round, dark, clean-shaven head, which had been concealed in the folds of her shabby old sari.

Several of the servants helped by contributing little things to the new home—the bearer gave me an old mat for the stone floor—but some of them evidently resented a newcomer receiving such attention and made it clear that she would not be welcome. An old gardener who had once worked for us and for whom we had later found a job in the factory at his own request had been allowed to keep a godown. He was very angry to learn that we were to receive strangers. It transpired that he had been using two godowns, one for himself and one for a grandson, a lout of sixteen who was as disagreeable as possible about doubling up with his relative. He had never turned a hand since his arrival, but when he found he had to vacate the godown, the boy not only objected but finally went out of it leaving it unswept.

It was the question of the newcomers' food which needed most thought. The factories had long since been obliged to provide staples for their workers, else all production would have stopped. They had laid in stores through government channels and sold us a certain ration at a fair, prefamine price—for although grain was available at profiteering prices that meant nothing to most of us, whatever the color of our skin. We received a weekly issue of enough rice, *ata*, and *dal* to feed the servants, with a little over for ourselves—we needed it too. That year we were ten months without either flour or potatoes; there was a little flour to be had in some of the big European stores, but only for old customers or for the new, all-powerful customer, the army officer.

In 1940 potatoes had cost two annas a seer and this winter the same amount were three rupees (sixteen annas to a rupee). When we arrived in India a chicken cost a rupee, now two pounds of potatoes cost three times that! Chickens disappeared as far as we were concerned. After the raids the people who left Bengal took their fowls with them or slaughtered them; the remaining ones could be sold for whatever the owners liked.

Rationing of a sort was introduced in Bengal but it was so iniquitous that the Japanese themselves could not have improved upon it. The army had what they wanted, the ordinary European came next, and there was very little left over for the Indians. Our family of four (and we actually were five, as Romela ate bread as we did) was allowed two pounds of bread a day and each European was rationed to eight ounces of sugar a week, the same amount he would have had in England. It was liberal, but the Indians had very much less, only a few spoonfuls, and they could not believe that we were actually limited to this amount. I had always given the servants tea, milk, and sugar as a perquisite and they could not imagine that the Europeans could really be so short. I found I had to lock up our small store very carefully. We ate meagerly but there was enough for the children always, which was my chief anxiety. Dried milk disappeared very early and there were no more prepared baby foods to be had, but luckily the two *babas* drank boiled buffalo milk without complaint and thrived on the local fine wheat, called *suji*. There were plenty of oranges to be had too.

When our weekly quota of grain arrived from the factory the servants with Romela and Rosalind and myself would all go out on the front veranda downstairs and weigh it out in council, with an old hand balance. Very often it did not come till the evening and we would do this by lantern light. We would empty the grain into heaps on the stone floor—a pile of rice, a pile of the coarse golden wheat called *ata*, a smaller pile of *dal*, the green split peas that are so essential a part of the Indian diet. The hard grayish little grains of our poor rice would catch a few gleams of light, the *ata* was only a soft brownish mound, the *dal* a dull Nile green, a small cloud on the terrazzo. The lantern we put on the floor, where it could light only a small discreet circle, not disturbing the blackout. Within this orb the Indians squatted, their dark faces shining in its soft glow, their eyes intent on the trembling needle of the scale. The night would close in around us, gathered low against the light, while moths and other flimsy winged creatures would appear wildly out of the void and rush in upon us, beating their poor silly breasts against the glass chimney. The veranda was still half-shaded by its jilmils and the night was young. No blackout precautions ever hindered our earnest consultations. I sat on a low chair and looked down upon the little circle. The most visible feature of the grave faces was their eyes—in the dim grayish and brown tones the whites of their eyes were startlingly distinct.

We always agreed most amicably upon our several ratios, the Hindus taking the larger share of the rice, and the Muslims of the *ata*. We all wanted the lentils. The quality of all three was poor and the rice shamefully adulterated with stones, but we were so glad and grateful to have it at all that no one complained. Now we had to stretch this to provide for the mother and her children and I began to lay aside our own share for her.

Many Europeans seemed unaware of what was passing. During that summer we were invited to a big RAF party in Barrackpore and the nurses, who had not long been out from England, could not stop exclaiming over the buffet supper, saying it would cause a sensation at home. It was equally sensational to us. The services had plenty and did not realize that civilians were not in the same position. Big military lorries were at this time driving up to the markets early in the morning and buying literally everything in the stalls. At long last the authorities took note and General Auchinleck put the army on field rations.

The hotels were always full and there people ate luxuriously; the immense contrast between rich and poor could hardly have been more marked. People went into the city to elaborate dinners, passing at the very doors of hotels and restaurants (like Firpo's and the Great Eastern) the unconscious forms of persons lying on the sidewalks in the last extremities of hunger and despair. The diners were not brutes or sadists but somehow the whole tragedy seemed to be outside them; they could go in and eat and drink and be merry, forgetting the scene outside the windows. We could not do anything about Stalingrad or Tobruk—and this problem, actually so near, seemed also very far away to the average European. It was a strange and terrible phenomenon.

I kept expecting to hear from the little hospital about my famine family or, I thought, the mother would just appear in a rickshaw— I had asked the doctor to arrange this if it were convenient. We had no telephone. Therefore I was proportionately dismayed to see the poor woman stagger into the garden early one afternoon, exhausted, dirty, and hot, having walked all the way (some four miles) carrying the boys in turn. Once we had left the hospital after our first visit, the staff had lost all interest in her, she said. They had been almost entirely neglected, till they were finally turned out. The hospital was not crowded and was to be paid for their care—one despaired of these cruel people! However, at least she had now reached a haven and appeared enormously cheered by her Palta reception, delighted with her godown and stores and the thought that someone actually cared about her.

This mother had a sweet nature but she was almost unbelievably incompetent—she seemed to have no idea at all of how to care for her children, or to cook, or to arrange the simplest affair. For some days I went out myself every few hours and fed the boys, mixing canned milk with water and pouring it down their thin little black necks. She did not seem able to do this herself—if I did not come, it was not done. Yet she clearly loved them. The older boy was about eight and had been in much worse condition than his little brother. Now he was at least able to lift his head and drink eagerly, the hospital had presumably done something to help him. After a few days I was overjoyed to find him sitting on their veranda one morning, waiting for me, and after that he could soon eat his rice and *dal* like any normal child and began to be lively and happy.

Somewhat to my alarm the woman's husband then appeared from across the river, with three other sons. The poor fellow was a whitewasher by profession but in his district there was no more demand for this service—everyone had left there and in other places people did not want anything whitewashed, not for the duration of the war. I appealed to our RAF friends, who were just starting an immense garden upcountry where vegetables were to be grown for the troops. They instantly responded and agreed to take the whole family. They went off by air—what a change for these poor people, who had hardly ever been in a wheeled vehicle in their lives! We parted with strong, though unspoken feelings— the mother and I, when our eyes met, had always felt in the deepest harmony.

During the famine Stanton had occasion to go up to the copper area of Ghatsila, a short distance from Calcutta. In his compartment on the train was an Indian merchant from Agra, a man too full of his grievances to keep silence; he told Stanton what had happened to him in the city. He was a dealer in *ghur*, the unrefined, molasses-like sugar of the poor, and had in store 200,000 pounds of it, which he wanted to send to Bengal. He wrote the food authorities in the Presidency several times about it, but not receiving any replies whatsoever, finally came down to Calcutta himself to try and sell it. He was astonished that he should have to do this, hearing, as we did on every side, of the acute shortage of all basic foods. Once in the city he was directed to an office full of young men who were the relatives and friends of ministers in the local government, who told him that the only way he could import his *ghur* was to form a company with them as partners, which they would agree to do if he promised them fifty-five percent of the profits. There seemed to him no way out of this dilemma except to accept their terms. Now he was on his way home with this shameful contract and very, very angry.

All the way up and down the railway line refugees and the poor of the district waited and watched for trains which might be carrying food to Calcutta. When one loaded with rice wagons pulled up on a siding these wretches would poke sticks into every aperture, trying to break the grain bags and cause a little rice to fall on the tracks. Everywhere men were searching the ground, hoping to espy even a few grains that might have fallen, a treasure which would be eagerly seized and hidden away in the ragged folds of their *dhotis*.

It was terrible to see that England, so bravely and splendidly resisting the evil of Nazism, should at the same time treat her poor companion in arms in so scurvy a fashion. There were Indian troops in Tobruk, the Indians did well in Burma and would excel in Italy and in the northern passes of their own country. And yet the government at Whitehall would not help them, even by word or gesture, till it was almost too late.

Imphal and Kohima

The next year in Palta seemed very long. It was a time of waiting —waiting for D-Day, waiting for the Japanese to attack, waiting for news of our forces in Imphal and Kohima once the fighting had begun. On the local scene everyone was worn out, worn out with long hours in the factory, with the intense pressure put on the inspectorates, with the political troubles of the country, and with the inflation. The famine was petering out but it left exhaustion in its wake. The Congress leaders were still in jail, relatively silenced, but the rank and file and the Muslims had plenty to say. The redoubtable Mr. Jinnah of the Muslim League was free to make what political capital he could while Nehru and Gandhi and the rest were shut up, and he made the most of his opportunity. He was able to talk right through the war; the British had always had an affinity for the Muslim *zamindars*, the landowners who like to fight and to shoot and were not very interested in education. Mr. Jinnah had had plenty of education and was a brilliant lawyer, but most of his peers were Punjabis of comfortable means who got along with the British officers in the regiments. They constituted a sort of squir-archy which had no parallel further south. Here in miserable Bengal the average man was not cast in a martial mold—all he wanted to do was to read law and rail at the government.

Many of the Europeans in India had now spent seven or eight consecutive years in the country without a single home leave and very little time in the hills and they were becoming increasingly tense and unreasonable, quick to anger. The inflation showed no signs of abating. We felt so poor and so irritated that the government would not help us that we began to act irrationally. For instance, we had then a neighbor, a woman who came from some English town, amiable and pleasant enough and in her own setting probably perfectly sensible, who could no longer behave reasonably in India. She had told her gardener that he was not to run away after the raids. He did, of course—he was an Uriya and terrified. After about three weeks he came back and went to his former *memsahib*, asking for the wages due him up to the time he left, a matter of perhaps ten rupees. Her husband was a foreman in the factory and no doubt keeping their small bungalow going at all was a strain, but they could afford to lose ten rupees much more easily than the *mali*—who had, after all, earned them. But the lady refused to pay her debt; she insisted that this poor man had forfeited his pay through disloyalty and disobedience. The *mali* had no redress but he did what he could, which she found absolutely unbearable. He stood outside the garden all day, watching the house, and whenever she appeared at a window or door, watching her. He also came to see me and asked me to help him. I was very sorry. I told him that I would certainly advise his *memsahib* to pay him and I hoped they could come to terms. It was a delicate matter. Before I could call on her, she rushed in to see me, demented that anyone, particularly the wife of an officer in the Service, might take another point of view from her own. Her arguments were not uncommon at that time, though there was no defense for what she said. Now, she contended, was the time for all the white people to stick together and uphold the honor of their country. I agreed and said that in that case she obviously should pay this poor and ignorant servant what he had earned. There was no question in anyone's mind that he should be reimbursed for the time he was away, but merely be given what he was owed for work done. But she could never see it—I had "let the side down," and she neither paid him nor ever spoke to us again. Under normal conditions she would never have behaved like this, I believe.

We could now no longer visit the field and were driven back into the narrow confines of our strip on the river. Sometimes we took a country boat over to Chandernagor but it seemed a weary, dingy travesty of a place and only turned our minds more insistently to France, which was still under the Nazi yoke. Small local happenings impressed themselves strongly upon us in the monotony of those months.

When we were in Barrackpore I had been lucky enough to find a very good house tailor, called Cassim, who would come and sew all day on the veranda—a very clean, honest old man, clever and deft. He came to Palta and turned old clothes into things for the children. I remember with regret a shirt I once had him cut up into a little dress—it was quite a good blue cotton shirt, but for some reason Stanton could not wear it. Cassim fingered the material and looked at the pattern and asked if I really wanted this done. I said "yes" with reluctance, and I am still sorry—I should have given it to him outright, he needed it more. But the children needed clothes so much and I could scarcely buy anything.

Then there was the terrible affair of the horse. A couple of riders dropped in to see our young bachelor neighbors on a hot Sunday morning, leaving their mounts in the garden, where one suddenly and dramatically expired—it had probably been ridden too long and hard in the heat. Its rider, a soldier, had to get back on duty and left our friends with the almost insoluble problem of what to do with the body. No sanitary office was open; they could not dig a grave large and deep enough to be jackal-proof, and anyway it was illegal even to bury a dog in your garden. Not a servant would help because of caste. It was extremely hot; the problem had to be solved. In the end this was possible only because of the gallant aid of the AA batteries on the riverbank, manned by Madrassis who are not so caste-ridden as most Indians. They behaved most heroically and the river received the dismembered horse, where, no doubt, the crocodiles soon disposed of it. A macabre event, in keeping with one aspect of the country.

Still, it was a great year. The tide of the war turned. The Japanese invasion was quickly repulsed and in June there was the joy of the landings on the Continent. Normandy seemed very close to us then, nearer than Calcutta. Europeans feel the East is far away, but the Westerner in the Orient does not feel that of his home countries; the measurement of distance is variable.

After the Teheran Conference some of Lord Mountbatten's landing craft were withdrawn from the Eastern theatre and diverted to the Mediterranean, delaying his plans—there was no help for it. The Japanese no doubt soon knew this and felt their moment for action had come—they were not having an easy time with their conquests and were eager to press on to fresh fields which would be less disappointing, perhaps. On St. Patrick's day they crossed the Chindwin (this was in March of 1944) and struck out for Imphal. It was the Allies' main advance base, the key point of the defense of the frontier, and if they could capture it and secure the line of the Imphal-Kohima supply road they wanted to go down into the Assam plain and cut the Bengal-Assam Railway. This, they hoped, would stop General Stilwell from coming up from Ledo. At the same time they could overrun the Allied airfields in Assam which were so necessary to the air lift over the Hump. This service was responsible for a constant flow of munitions to Chiang Kai-shek's

army and the petrol which enabled General Chennault to keep his
air force bombing from the China side. None of these aims was
achieved, though there were initial successes.

In spite of censorship and the silences imposed by the war, we
knew that the munitions going to China were very often not used
against the Japanese but put aside for civil war exigencies, later. It
caused a good deal of skepticism, particularly as the losses over the
Hump were great, but in wartime there is no argument. Stories
were also told of the Wingate thrust*—some of us had seen him in
Calcutta, wearing his battered and theatrical *topi*, his brilliant light
blue magnetic eyes fixing the beholder. His men had taken off from
our field and the plane that finally took him to his last rendezvous
also came from Barrackpore. The crew told of his anger when the
pilot refused to wait for him, as he had no orders from his own
command to do so—on the contrary, he was obliged to come
straight back. This controversial, strange genius had given us all
much hope and encouragement, even though we knew the cost was
tremendous. Now there was a front, there was an understandable
battle going on, and it seemed as though there might be decisive
action which would bring the end of the war markedly nearer.

The fighting went on right through the monsoon, to the end of
August, when the invaders withdrew—they had suffered heavily,
they knew they could go no further. The Fourteenth Army and
General Slim, with the help of Eastern Air Command, were responsible for this campaign; we felt great pride in them, as they had
annihilated five Japanese divisions and severely hurt many others,
besides taking a great number of prisoners (the Japanese lessened
this figure by their own suicides). A few years before we would
have taken such a victory for granted—but not anymore! Few of us
knew then that in this theatre there was an Indian division which
fought against the Allies—turncoats from among the Indian prisoners the Japanese had taken earlier in Malaya and further east. These
were members of the Indian National Army, which drew its inspiration from Subhas Chandra Bose, whom they called Netaji and
who was in Burma, and they felt themselves fighting for the libera-

---

* Brigadier Orde Wingate led a "Special Force" known as the 77th Independent Indian Infantry Brigade across the Chindwin and stayed behind the
enemy's lines several weeks. He caused much havoc before he returned,
leaving many of his own men, killed and wounded, behind. This first expedition in 1943 was on foot, but air-supplied; his second and larger operation,
in early 1944, was airborne and air-landed. Wingate was killed during this
second operation.

tion of India. It was all hushed up at the time, but tremendous repercussions were to come.

The two decisive battles were at Kohima and Imphal but it was not a front which could be lightly summarized by two victories of a more or less orthodox kind. The area involved was vast and fantastically difficult to control and maintain. There was fighting in the jungles and on the roads, by troops of so many different nationalities and in such strange circumstances that it must have been one of the most intricate and confused of all the campaigns of that incredibly complicated war. The Central Front covered twenty-five thousand square miles; the whole front some one hundred thousand, in country rising up to ten thousand feet in altitude, the mountainous sections intercepted by deep valleys almost impassable with vegetation. The Allies had here over five hundred thousand soldiers and three hundred thousand coolies of many nations—among them Indians, Chinese, Gurkhas, Africans, Canadians, English, Scottish, Australians, and Americans, who flew most of the planes. With the enemy were Koreans, Burmans, even Malayans, and possibly, men from the Shan States—but we had Shan people with us, too.

Most of the Westerners were incapable of telling people from a number of these countries apart by their looks or language, and there were always tall stories being told of the confusion resulting from vain efforts to disentangle Koreans from Burmans or even Gurkhas from Japanese. The West Africans, who were going up to this front with the greatest enthusiasm, constituted something of a problem for their officers, we were told, as they were extremely puzzled as to who the enemy was and what he looked like. They were very quick with their knives and their officers were anxious lest they carve up some Allied platoons before they could be stopped. The Africans did not believe many of the stories which were told them of the enemy and one particular detachment thought that the instructions to be quiet and careful in jungle warfare must be utter nonsense. To move stealthily behind trees, to keep apart from each other, to half-expect a gun in every bush, struck them as absurd and they did not take their orders very seriously. However, their first trip to the front surprised them. After it they assured their officers that now they understood what they had been taught; thereafter they could hardly have been more formidable. It had even been difficult to convince them of the identity of the enemy. "Those are the Japanese." "Who? Where?"

"Those men." "Oh, no," with shouts of laughter. "*Those* aren't Japanese."

Lighthearted and jolly they were very popular with everyone with whom they came in contact (except the enemy). These West Africans had never been out of their own country before and were, despite their smart British uniforms, entirely unsophisticated —they were in a sense only exchanging one jungle for another. They had been brought from the villages and jungles of the Gold Coast and Nigeria by all the swift devices of modern transport over the unknown sea, where they were attended by the appalling dangers of the U-boats. Once in India they were plunged into a melée of different nationalities and people, culminating in this fantastic mountain war and the escort of planes. They were illiterate, honest, curious, friendly, and brave. Considering that they might well have felt themselves suddenly on another planet, they were also possessed of both poise and aplomb. Had the war come later, or had its political effects on Africa been felt sooner, they would have approached the scene very differently.

It was not only the inexperienced soldier who was confused by this campaign and its motley personnel. An officer whom we knew and who was serving with the Seventh Division in the Arakan was awakened one night by the noise of a patrol passing through his area, attended by mule-drawn ammunition carts. He could hear voices, the jangling of bits, and the creak of carts. Furious and horrified by such an indiscretion, he sprang up, threw a bush shirt over his pajamas, grasped his hat, and rushed out of his tent. In a few moments, driving his jeep down the dark road, he ran right into the column. It occurred to him, even in the blackness, that the company was rather oddly dressed—as he told us later, they looked like Gurkhas in American helmets—but he felt that it was not the time to bother about trifles. As soon as he saw a man whom he took to be a sergeant he seized him by the shoulders, shook him, and told him to keep his column quiet because the woods were full of Japanese. Repeating this operation with another noncommissioned officer, he then backed off and drove away.

Back in his tent, he went over the incident in his mind and became more and more confused. The men's dress . . . the look of the column . . . and no one had answered a word. . . . Finally he telephoned a detachment a little further down the road and told them that if they wanted to capture a large party of Japs they could have them in about a quarter of an hour. This was duly done.

To keep the vehicles moving through the jungle, climbing the heights, to keep the men fed, were great feats. Farms had already been planted in some forward areas (to one of these our famine family had gone) and rations were sent on in every possible way, from planes to elephants. The elephants were too intelligent to be much used as porters, they were more needed in the building of bridges and roads. Mules and donkeys came from as far away as Africa and America to transport food and ammunition through the hills.

Then there were the extreme difficulties the hospitals had to overcome, not only to care for the wounded but also to cope with the prevalence of malaria, almost a greater foe than the Japanese. In some of the battles there were as many as twenty-seven thousand wounded; ten times that many were down with disease. As soon as possible the sick and hurt were flown back to safe areas—our Barrackpore hospital was full to overflowing, with great numbers lying in tents. They came out by stretcher, mule, sampan, jeep, flying boats (landing on Indawgi Lake in Japanese-held Burma), and had hardly a mishap. Throughout were the attendant trials of leeches, ticks, the rains, the sun. Romela, who was now in a hospital in the Arakan and very busy, told us stories about them. She was in her element, as we realized when she came to spend her leaves with us, an affluent young lady who traveled with a military pass, first class, wearing khaki slacks, but whose head had not been turned at all.

The wounded were a cheerful lot of young men, most of whom found their lives very amusing—they were young enough for that. A great part of them had never been in the East before and many had come straight from school. One lad, just out of public school, had hardly got into his trench in Imphal before he received an injury sufficient to send him back to Bengal for a few weeks. Sitting on our veranda one afternoon he heard me complaining about the price of bully beef, an unattractive but more or less constant part of our diet. "What," he cried, genuinely astonished. "You don't mean to say that you *buy* bully beef! Why, we line our trenches with tins of the stuff!"

Slowly South East Asia Command, under Lord Mountbatten, with headquarters in Ceylon, was regaining the control of the sea. The air was no longer in dispute and the Fourteenth Army was immensely superior to the invading forces. By the end of 1944 it was evident to everyone that India would not again be in danger from Japan. She could, instead, turn her thoughts the more passionately towards her own struggle, the triangle of British Rule and its uneasy quasi-partners, the Muslim League and the Congress Party.

But for us, the Europeans, the war was far from over and we deplored the necessity of having to deal with so much trouble and resentment within the country while the struggle in Europe was still so severe. Germany was not to surrender for nearly a year—the Allies were yet far from the Rhine. It seemed to us then that it might be years before the Japanese were finally defeated, though they were now checked. The Indians were not so interested in all this, but the country must still be the base of a great army, in training and in transit. Nevertheless we all rejoiced that this campaign had ended so well. It seemed to pass over with the rains. There were many nights of conversation on the verandas with convalescents who had been wounded at Kohima or Imphal who gave us sharp vignettes of their strange journeys and encounters. Then, suddenly, they had all gone back to Europe—our part of the world had ceased to be a front. Bengal became again a jealous and angry nation in itself.

Husseina

After Romela left we had a succession of *ayahs*, each one with a history of complicated family entanglements and problems, and for one reason or another none stayed very long. There was, as an example, Husseina, the widow of Nebu.

After Abdul left, Nebu had been the Stoddards' bearer. He was a good-looking, vigorous young man and everyone was astonished when he suddenly died. He had been with them about two years and though, according to local rates he had been reasonably paid, it was found that he had not left an anna behind him. In spite of the warnings of the Prophet he had been, alas, unable to resist the charms of wine. His widow, the comely Husseina, had lived in proper Mohammedan seclusion in the one-room godown allotted to Nebu and was recognized only as a very fat woman, swathed in flowing garments and saying nothing. She proved to be the perfect specimen, the logical result, of sheltered womanhood, as the Stoddards, disposed to help her, discovered.

There had been no children of the marriage, which had endured for fourteen years. When she lost her husband Husseina was only twenty-eight. She shed not one tear for him. The other servants were startled by her determined, almost spectacular, destruction of all possible mementos of Nebu after his untimely end. He had been handsome and a reasonably intelligent and agreeable domestic but, it would seem, not a beloved husband. Still, she was his widow and the Stoddards felt a certain responsibility towards her—they proposed to give her a sum of money and send her back to her village. The godown was needed for the next incumbent and there was no reason for Husseina to stay on. But they reckoned without the lady.

In reply to their offer she told them that she did not know the name of her village or where it was, nor the name of Nebu's village nor where that was. She did, she said, know that they had come to Ishapore on a train. To their further discomfiture she added that she did not know her name (other than Husseina) or her father's name or Nebu's family name. Whether this was true or not they had no means of discovering. As for the future, she knew nothing of money, she explained, and had no plans whatever. The Stoddards were her father and mother and she intended to stay on, relying on their boundless mercy, which would, at the proper time, be recompensed by Allah the Most Merciful. Husseina definitely won the first round. The Stoddards withdrew, appalled, while she sat in her godown, lamenting in a cowlike fashion not for Nebu but for things in general. She was as fat as possible but in spite of that good-looking, young—and unworn—and in outlining this design for living she was perfectly calm and easy in her mind.

At this strategic moment the Stoddards' old *ayah* was obliged to visit one of her married daughters, so the exasperated couple decided to call Husseina into the ring and make her earn her keep until her memory could be induced to return to her. She must be the substitute *ayah*. Husseina complied—she was, in most matters, of an amiable and complacent disposition and she slouched into the house the next morning with her eyes cast down but her wits about her.

The old *ayah* was a lively creature and quick in her movements— she said of herself that she was "*howah ke-mafik*" or like the wind, which made the leisurely pace of the young widow more deliberate than ever by contrast. She had, naturally, to be instructed in every least detail, but *ayahs* were hard to come by, the old one would be back in a month, and at least Husseina was earning her curries. At the end of the time she was able to bathe the baby, make up the cots, do some washing, and even take the children walking in the park. She had lost fifteen pounds and began to show signs of real beauty. Some animation came into a face which was of the proportions of the full moon in Arabian Nights style, and her natural amiability had survived the strain of her initiation into the working world.

Then the old *ayah* came back and lo! at that very moment we lost our *ayah*, a slovenly maiden called Tara who had had an unfortunate affair with a neighbor's bearer. It was unfortunate in that her family discovered it and objected on the grounds that the man in question belonged to the sweetmeat-makers caste, which was inferior to that of Tara's. He was married, also, but that was not important. They forced her to leave at once. When they heard on the local grapevine that we were *ayah*-less, the Stoddards with undisguised relief realized that Allah really was merciful and had picked out another father and mother for Husseina.

I liked her—she was good with the children, teachable, honest, and clean. Not unnaturally she was lacking in self-confidence and needed a good deal of reassurance. She would protest that she *could not* learn to iron, not because she was lazy or stupid but simply because she really did mistrust her own ability to do almost everything. Had Nebu destroyed what little self-esteem she had? A Mohammedan woman has a bad start in any case. When I persuaded her that she not only could learn to iron but that she could do it beautifully and even enjoy it (not that I ever had!), she quickly became something of an artist with the implement and was quite excited at discovering her capability. (Most *ayahs* iron rather badly; indeed it was not a national gift, to put it mildly. Mr. Jinnah was famous for refusing to have his shirts done in India and used to post them to Paris, rather an extreme gesture perhaps, but he could well afford it and liked to be well-groomed. I wish I could have told Husseina about this, but as events turned out there was not time for me to give her a course on world geography and French skill.) There was something very pathetic about her first attempts to use her wings; I hoped that she would take pleasure in her independence and develop herself. Husseina's difficulty in a world which militated against women making their way alone was not caste, as she was a Mohammedan. It was her good looks.

While she was with us, though she got on well with everyone in the household, she insisted that she could not leave the Stoddards' godown. This was inconvenient for us; like Aknis in a similar case, she came late and left early, not wishing to pass alone through the dark bazaar, but she protested that she would be afraid in a strange godown. She continued to lose weight and became prettier every day, enhancing her charms with new clothes. The two walks every day between Ishapore and Palta and her activity in following the two little girls about, after the absolute sluggishness of her previous life, made her drop another ten pounds and she was so young that this did not add a line to her face, now no longer a full moon but beautifully shaped with cheeks like dark petals. When she had her pay in her hands, unrestrained by any ties, she joyfully invested it all in red blouses, gauzy scarves, and a white sari with a wide scarlet border. After her years of inanition, the years spent in a tiny dark room doing nothing, hope, life, interest, awoke in her. She played with the children, catching up the baby in her arms with true affection—it was a great pleasure to see her unfolding from day to day.

I knew that I was not the only one who admired her curves and her rich coloring, set off so bewitchingly by the new finery, but I did think that some decent interval would elapse before she allowed herself once more to enter that state of slavery which she knew only too well by experience, and bury her gentle gaiety in the harsh monotony of a Muslim marriage. Yet, evidently, it disturbed her to be alone. Though she had always been poor she apparently felt that she had lowered herself by taking employment and used to murmur apologetically, when asking if she might go home early, that she was not used to working or moving about unescorted, as though she were a gentlewoman fallen on hard times.

Six weeks after she began to work for us, just when she was beginning to be really useful and dependable, she came to me, gave me an embarrassed but satisfied smile, cast down her great eyes, and announced that she was going to get married. "*Kab?*" I asked. "The day after tomorrow," she replied, smiling gently. And I had thought she was enjoying her freedom! No one, I felt, could be so stupid about Indians as I. Why do I bother with them? I might just as well run a training school for *ayahs* and be done with it . . . Husseina told me modestly that since losing Nebu she had had three offers of marriage. One from the Stoddards' new bearer, one from someone in the bazaar, and one from a cook who worked next door—and this last suitor she had accepted.

Hope sprang into my bosom. "Then, Husseina, will you go on working for us, as he has no children here [he was a widower] and is away most of the day working in the Smiths' kitchen?" But oh no, she said, when she was married she would certainly stop working. At this time poor Indians—among whom domestic servants must certainly be included—were feeling the inflation cruelly in the rise in the price of food and textiles, though they had no rent to pay. Their jobs had no security and they found themselves without a roof if they lost them. An *ayah* was paid as well as a cook, and if her earnings had been added to his, this new alliance would have been relatively comfortably off. But it could not be considered, she asserted, though she sighed at the thought of leaving the *babas* and hoped that they might come often to visit her. I wished her joy and she slipped out into the night, trailing her red-bordered sari with real grace.

Two days later she was married and disappeared into her new husband's godown, whose little roof was clearly visible from our back garden. Though she was so near, we saw her rarely and then for brief moments only, when she would hug the children and go back at once to her dark purdah, the cage she had deliberately reentered. What effect had those few weeks of life in the open had upon her, when she had, like a bemused, dark, nebulous body, swung into our livelier orbit and then had been carried away on some other course? What memory had all this left with her? Had it been only like the patterns of light cast into shadow by a chance wind lifting a vine—would she, in the gloom of her purdah, think of those gleams of sunshine and try to understand them? I would never know.

Uniforms

I sat waiting one day in the small hot shop of Purham Singh, the Sikh tailor, and considering, without rancor, how dirty and disgusting it was. I remembered, as in a dream, Western counterparts— the charm, the chic, the daintiness and elegance, a Louis XV chair there, the pier glass here, the half-finished gauzy dresses tossed negligently over a screen. Where I waited there was one wooden kitchen chair and a sort of counter in front of a broken-down wardrobe. Why was it that so many Sikhs had become tailors, I wondered—they seemed to have no ideas at all about cutting, styles, or sewing women's clothes, though they could make superb jodhpurs and riding jackets. But they were available and cheap and it was too hot to sew, the needle slipped from the wet hand. I couldn't sew anyway—the wonderful Chinese tailors to whose perfect work I had been accustomed most of my life had seen to that. Who would waste time learning to sew in China in the old days?

Purham Singh had gone off to find my dresses from the back of his loathsome shop and was taking a long time about it, but I remember distinctly that I wasn't feeling irritated, I was in a rather exalted mood of patient calm. Suddenly a tall, fresh American girl came briskly through the door, very smart indeed in a thin beautifully cut khaki uniform. I had never seen so fine a tropical weave in India, where khaki originated, where it had been worn by soldiers far longer than in the West (in fact we got it from them and used their word for it). The young lady's shoes gleamed with a military shine, her whole person was efficient and also elegant. I immediately felt unspeakably jungly, but as quickly forgot to sorrow over this as she plunged the little atelier into a summer storm.

She had come, she told Purham Singh, to collect the uniforms her friend had ordered, and the other dresses. She explained carefully how the bills were to be made out—the dresses she would pay for privately but the uniforms were to be charged to the U.S. Government and there must be separate bills. Evidently she was one of a troop of girls who had just flown out and who had immediately realized that they had to have more thin clothes and then, in their innocence, had come to Purham Singh. His shop was right in front of the big Crawford Market which everyone visited—presumably they had gone into his spider's web exactly as the poor fly makes his fatal error. Purham Singh was very competent with money and with the few words they had in common they soon agreed on the prices. This was made surprisingly easy and quick because she accepted all his figures and did not even ask to see the clothes first. The tailor then went off to fetch the garments, hardly able to disguise his amazement and joy. He ignored me, my order was of no importance compared to this wonderful killing.

In a few minutes he returned with his arms full of uniforms and light dresses. He was a very fine-looking man, tall and strong ("God never made an ugly Sikh"), dressed in jodhpurs with a large, well-wound turban, and of course sporting the beard which every Sikh must wear. It seemed absurd that so martial a figure should be a ladies' tailor. He probably thought so too, as he handed everything over to Miss Des Moines and stood complacently waiting for her to go.

The young lady took the dresses calmly, little realizing what a bombshell she was accepting. She began to count and examine. Her face fell. Dismay, horror, incredulity, were mirrored one after the other on her pretty features. Then rage, black, black, rage. She didn't know enough to guard herself against the choler of Bengal—we all had to learn that, and generally the hard way. It seemed that everything was wrong—everything, everything. The sample uniform had been copied only approximately. Detail by detail, her voice mounting, she pointed out one horrible mistake after another, ending with "Couldn't you even have used matching thread?" Purham Singh paid not the least attention to these vapors. He had been paid, which had shown him that she had no sense at all, and in any case it made no difference one way or the other what women said.

The poor girl then broke down. She could not bear it. "Do you know who these dresses are for?" she screamed. "Miss Schiaparelli! *Miss Schiaparelli!* Her mother is the *best dressmaker* in the *world!*" But he had never heard of Schiaparelli and remained perfectly unmoved. He had stopped listening. Miss Des Moines rushed, trembling, out into the heat of the sun.

Purham Singh then brought my clothes. I discussed the affair with him and explained who Madame Schiaparelli was. It had never occurred to him that there was such a thing as a great industry for women's fashions and he knew none of these big names. He thought the whole thing beneath contempt. I picked up one or two dingy fashion magazines (prewar) from his shelves and tried to illustrate my point. But he could not read English and he saw no necessity for styles altering anyway. In the Punjab styles had not changed for centuries and he could not see that that made things any the worse.

He had won. He had been enormously overpaid. I felt proud too. None of the thread used on my dresses matched either but I had managed to remain perfectly calm. Beside that fresh daffodil of a girl I looked like something dragged out of a duffle bag, but my years in Bengal had given me something else: sometimes I could reject the almost overwhelming temptation to explode. And Miss Schiaparelli? How did she receive her uniforms, I wondered.

XIII Sikkim

Adieu! adieu! thy plaintive anthem fades
Past the near meadows, over the still stream,
Up the hill-side; and now 'tis buried deep
In the next valley-glades:
Was it a vision, or a waking dream?
Fled is that music:—Do I wake or sleep?

KEATS

IN NOVEMBER OF 1943, when the famine was waning, we took a short leave and went trekking in the hills. The baby we left with a friend on the plains but Rosalind came with us. She was past three and well able to sit in the saddle all day.

We went to Sikkim, then a little-known rustic native state chiefly noted for its devotion to Buddhism and its abundant oranges. It had been sometimes crossed by mountaineers on their way to the northern peaks and it was on one of the main routes to Tibet—if such a term could be used when speaking of that closed, forbidden land. Sikkim had, in fact, once belonged to Tibet, like much of this mountain country. Most of the population were Nepalis and Bhutias but there were, too, the original settlers, who were Lepchas. Buddhism was the state religion—this and the lineage of their rulers had come to them from Tibet—but the majority of the people were Hindus.

The Maharajah, being unwilling to have his people marred by industrialism, would not consent to Europeans settling in the country or even entering it except for brief holidays and with special permits. Few availed themselves of the privilege, and unless something very particular was going on, like a Kanchenjunga expedition, there might be not more than a score of travelers a year to break

213

the rural quiet of the state. A notable exception had been John Morris, who lived for six months in a remote valley, afterwards recording his experience in his *Living with Lepchas*. The area was, however, closely watched by the British Raj through the eyes of the Resident who lived at Gangtok, and the Government of India had built *dak* bungalows through the hills for the convenience of people passing through. There were no hotels.

It offered the charms of riding past terraced fields and looking down on hillsides planted to orange trees—seeing the golden fruit ripening in a genial sun which also warmed one's back and the pony's mane, which made the giant poinsettias even more brilliant, which glinted on the eddies of the streams. The sound of the water mingled with the slight jangling of the bells round the ponies' necks; on such a journey you could partake of the mood of *Eothen* or *The Bible in Spain*, the leisurely, personal pace of the traveler who came into the world before the engine.

We started from Kalimpong, a blithe little settlement on a ridge two thousand feet below Darjeeling—a fine place with a good bazaar and many schools, which had somehow escaped the ghastly Westernization of the better-known town. Kalimpong had some mercantile significance and occasionally was politically important, but what struck you about it was its gaiety, its lightheartedness. It was then the Indian terminus of the Tibetan wool route; to its marketplace came long files of gallant, sagacious mules who had found their way up and down the fierce defiles which led from those high and secret plateaus. With these caravans and their laughing, stalwart muleteers came sometimes great men of the East, seeking a political haven. To the embarrassed statesman or rejected religious leader of those regions, Kalimpong was like London to the harassed refugee of the Western world in the days of Nazi tyranny —when he had achieved this modest town he also had crossed a channel.

Once in Kalimpong, we were told, we should seek out a Tibetan named Tsering who lived in the bazaar and who would tell us all we needed to know. The authentic Eastern quality of this advice was delightful to us.

The train left from Sealdah Station in Calcutta. We shared our large and dusty second-class compartment with two Bengali *babus* who were so unobtrusive that they seemed almost nonexistent. Installing themselves quickly in the upper berths, they rested their well-oiled heads on their frilled pillows, their shoes placed neatly on their small suitcases. One of the pillow cases was embroidered, in red, with the English words "Good Morning." Groaning with fatigue after the labors of our "last day," we unstrapped a bedroll and pulled out some blankets and a couple of wholly unadorned pillows to fall asleep on the narrow benches.

At dawn we awoke to see the snows, rose-red, high above the plain, seemingly unconnected with the earth, a miracle of beauty. Soon the sun passed over them and they turned to crystal. The paddy fields, the flat, muddy country of the plain, broken by occasional clumps of bamboo or by wavering lines of uneven palms, seemed in this light to extend directly to the mountains without the intervention of the foothills, an illusion which heightened the astonishing contrast of planes and of color.

At Siliguri, amidst the usual bedlam of changing from one train to another, the confusion was intensified by the lack of places on the minute narrow-gauge train which was going to Gila Kola—it was filled to the saturation point by soldiers on leave. A sympathetic Anglo-Indian guard finally installed us in a fairly roomy purdah carriage, the windows shrouded with deep blue curtains, which we unwisely pushed back. Two American G.I.'s had been trying to appropriate it, and the guard had only restrained them by saying that it was for "two ladies in trouble." We made it obvious that these two ladies were Posy and myself, in the best of health and spirits. Looking down at her yellow curls and infantile glee, they seemed nonplussed, consoling themselves only by remarking scathingly to Stanton, *"You're* no lady!" We then started off across dank, jungly country with bamboo, palm, banana, and paddy on either hand. The train was so tiny, its appointments so fragile, that we felt at one with the passing scene. Lumbering across a clearing, four people on its back, was an elephant, the perfect complement to such a background.

After a few miles we entered the valley of the Teesta and began to climb. It is a beautiful journey, far lovelier than the road to Darjeeling, rather like a pass of the Canadian Rockies, except that it begins in semi-tropical vegetation and provides an occasional glimpse of Nepalis driving their covered-wagon bullock carts, their women wrapped in short, brilliant shawls—cerise, emerald, ochre. The Teesta flew over the rocks in deep, cloudy blue eddies, or wound in wide and placid bends, edged with fine white sand— we longed to get out and dip our hands into it. The train puffed, panted, and moaned. Firemen lounged on top of it, strolling from carriage roof to carriage roof as we went; at the frequent stops several would descend and tie up the machinery here and there with bits of string. We were making perhaps fifteen miles an hour. Tipsy soldiers blew the whistle and monkeyed with the tiny engine, which delighted their mechanical sense. Everyone was gay and exhilarated in the freshness of the morning. Laughing Nepali girls stood beside the track selling oranges in the early sunlight. We were by now truly in the Terai, we had left the world of large, heavy, shiny leaves for the crisp moderation of oak and pine, the jungle for open hillsides, set off as if for a gala by immense bushes of scarlet poinsettias, brilliant under the brilliant sky, and clumps of equally tall greenish-white lilies. It was like a fantastic ballet. "Oh boy!" cried an enraptured G.I. "The leaves are getting smaller!" The languor of the plains had vanished.

A car took us from the railhead to the town where we went directly to the *dak* bungalow, which was very well appointed, boasting such rare luxuries as electric light and even plumbing. It was set in the usual pleasant garden, where flowers were in bloom in the borders, and seemed to have only one drawback—the personality of the cross and disobliging old *chokidar*. This functionary, accustomed to officials traveling with large retinues, was disgusted to have to accommodate people who came alone and who would probably not be in a position to tip well. He was dressed in a well-cut pepper-and-salt tweed jacket (clearly made long ago for some gentleman by a London tailor), shabby white jodhpurs, and an immense dust-colored turban, and for all his irascibility presented such a picturesque figure that it almost made up for his disposition. At four thousand feet, in sparkling air, a bad servant was easier to endure than he would have been on the plains.

Soon we went off to find our counselor, whom, we discovered, everyone knew, so that we had no difficulty in making our way to his house. Tsering lived on the far side of the bazaar in a house perched on a huge black rock, beside the main road leading up the hillside—he could see from his own windows the travelers arriving from Tibet. To reach his fence we had to climb some forty steep steps leading over the curving side of the boulder, beyond which lay his very small garden, bright with nasturtiums and enlivened by a goat. Skeins of yak wool were drying on the wooden palings of the fence. Mrs. Tsering, beaming and radiating hospitality, opened the front door, admitting us to a tiny square hall which was flanked on either side by a small room, with two slightly larger rooms at the back. It was a Dickensian scene, translated to the Terai. Every inch of space was crammed with furniture, bedding, pictures, boxes, and above all wool and instruments to deal with wool. Our hostess, tall and comely in her Tibetan dress—a horizontally striped apron over a long black robe, her long plaits wound round her head—at once showed us, complete strangers though we were, all over the house. There was a churn in the kitchen, used for making buttered tea, and in every corner were shelves and bookcases holding tracts, maps, and books in English, Tibetan, Hindi, Urdu, and a few other languages we did not recognize.

In the hall, beside a desk littered with papers, an old woman sat on the floor, deftly spinning thread on a small wheel, looking like the witch in "Sleeping Beauty"—except that she was benevolent. In the room beyond two more women were spinning and combing masses of fluffy wool, which was of a natural color, rather darker than a sheep's; sitting on the floor they were surrounded by enormous chunks of the fresh light material, which had only lately arrived from Tibet. Though I had never seen anything like this before, it all seemed perfectly natural, perfectly right. Mrs. Tsering, the perfect hostess, then took Posy by the hand, leading her into another room where there was an immense goldfish in a bowl and encouraging her to put her hand in the water and agitate the surface, thus exciting the mammoth occupant and making him more fun to watch. I reflected that most Westerners would have cautioned the child not to touch it rather than enticing her with this pleasure. The room of the goldfish held three couches, with their bedding rolled up on the pillow space, a desk, several small bookcases full of books in English, a small table, a dressing table, chests, curtains, pictures, calendars, strings of beads, and vases of marigolds, all arranged with great neatness and total indifference to dust. There remained room on the floor for a couple of small Chinese rugs—the workmanship was coarse but the design was so un-Indian, so un-Persian, that one realized instantly that this part of the world looked to the East, over the Himalayas, not down into India.

So small was the space involved that all this took only a moment; meanwhile Tsering himself, a small man in an old shiny blue serge suit, appeared, welcoming us with most friendly enthusiasm though he had never seen us before in his life. Leading us into his study, he desired his secretary to bring tea. This person was a tall and splendidly handsome young Tibetan, dressed in a shining black robe, his coronet of hair so twisted round his head as to display to its best advantage one huge bright turquoise earring.

This apartment also had three of its walls lined by three couches, spread with rugs, and with the bedding rolled up as in the other room. A small table between the three beds filled up the space so completely that one could hardly get one's feet on the floor—but then, one was intended to sit cross-legged. On the walls hung pictures of the Dalai Lama, King George, and Queen Mary, several large photographs of British battleships, a study of the great Potala, and a bewildering number of extremely large calendars. Stacks of newspapers, English and Indian, had been piled in the corners, having overflowed from the bookcases which contained chiefly Bibles and tracts. Tsering quickly told us that he was a Christian.

The glamorous secretary returned with the tea and then we knew that we were indeed within the sphere of Tibetan influence, for it was the famous brew of tea, rancid butter, and salt, well churned together, of travelers' tales. It seemed to me, as I struggled with mine for the sake of manners, that all I had ever read of its flavor had been a gross understatement. Stanton, who suffers from a Tibetan complex, claimed he liked it and had three cups. It looked like cocoa.

There was another guest in the study, a gentle ancient scholar from Tibet, garbed in a flowing russet robe and of a spiritual, benign appearance. When we entered he was reading from a thin paper volume covered with Tibetan script, while he turned the beads of a rosary; he gave us a reserved yet most kindly bow and smile, and later, encouraged by Tsering, spoke to us in hesitant Chinese. He had in his time, he said, ventured so far into China as West Szechwan and he was happy to speak of what he had seen. Tibet was the center of the world in which we now found ourselves, every subject seemed oriented from the angle of how it might appear in Lhasa. Tsering, we discovered, was the editor of the only paper printed in Tibetan in the world. This was a carefree periodical whose contents he described as "general" and which, though theoretically a monthly, sometimes appeared every three months and occasionally missed whole years. This disconcerted none of its subscribers, few of whom ever paid for it. The circulation, though not large, was far-flung, copies being sent all over India. At the beginning of his enterprise Tsering had sent free copies to Tibetan notables and to *gompas;* gradually their interest was awakening, sometimes someone would even pay for it. He had himself been to Lhasa several times, though he was not a Tibetan but a Bhutia.

While we were in the hills it was known that a mission had been dispatched by the British Army to Tibet to study the terrain in the hope that the Allies might be allowed to start a mule route through the country to China, so great was the need of a land route now that the sea was closed to us. However, the Tibetans did not wish this to be developed—they were afraid of being bombed by the Japanese and they desired to be entirely free of any entanglements with China, always stressing their own independence from that country. They recognized that China desperately needed this lifeline but they would not grant the permission. "Trouble is," said Tsering, "Tibetans are Buddhists, Japanese also Buddhists, Tibetans think Japanese must be all right. Very difficult."

From this engaging setting came all the details for our trek. Tsering sketched the route, told us of the porters we might engage, promised to hire our ponies himself, gave us letters to friends of his whom we might meet on the way, and told us what to see in Gangtok. Nothing, he insisted, was any trouble—and indeed, in his world, this was the normal way of travel. In entering Tsering's small home we had left the mechanical and hurried perplexities of the modern world behind and had gained a lodestone which was to regulate every stage of our idyllic mountain journey. His solicitude for two strangers of another race, whom he would probably never see again and to whom he was under no obligation, was the happiest of auguries.

After this we set off to explore Kalimpong. The sweet air and the company of the Tserings had so invigorated us that we felt ready for anything.

This delightful town had been built on a fairly sheltered ridge; on clear days one could see Kanchenjunga towering up over the settlement and on every hand there were forested and terraced hillsides. It was a busy place because of the wool trade. Mule caravans took three weeks to bring bales of raw wool from Lhasa, returning with more sophisticated products such as matches and Gramophone records. In 1943, when any road leading towards China was important, there was a greatly increased traffic and mules were much in demand. Now trekkers had to pay eight rupees a day for a mule—before the war one rupee was the price (the inflation also played a part in this figure). There was a Tibetan colony in Kalimpong, ministering to the wants of the robust and jolly muleteers, and there were caravanserais for the mules, godowns for wool, factories for carding and spinning. There was evidence of considerable fortunes having been made in the trade. Every woman in Kalimpong seemed to be either spinning, washing skeins of wool, or knitting the coarse gray-brown thread into sweaters or stockings—producing very handsome garments which were wonderfully warm, due partly to the oil which remained still in the wool. (It made one think of Shetland Island sweaters, though those are made of a softer, finer wool.) The bazaar, with wool as its chief merchandise, is a trade center for the surrounding districts and many hill people congregate there: Nepalis, Bhutias, Sherpas, Lepchas and Sikkimese, besides Indians and Chinese. Owing to the war a great many Chinese had come to the town.

There was also a European colony, chiefly missionary, of whom the greater part were Scots, and there were a number of schools. The Kalimpong Homes, founded long ago for the children of tea planters and native women, was an immensely respected institution whose pupils had a name for doing well. The conditions which had brought about these unions no longer existed, the tea companies now paid their young men enough to enable them to marry and bring their wives to India with them, but the Homes had gone on for the descendants of the first generation of the children of mixed blood. Often the white men living on the tea estates had loved the native women with whom they had become familiar and they loved their children, but they could see no way to bring them up or educate them. Marriage with the mothers seemed out of the question. That this evil was put right and so many children made happy was due to the vision and efforts of one Scotsman. It was a school rich in legends of the gifts of fathers who had done everything but acknowledge their children, of the babies who had been left there secretly, accompanied by fabulous gifts of gold and jewels. The boys and girls lived in cottages scattered over a hillside and never wore a shoe till they were seventeen, on principle.

The bazaar lay in the central hollow of the ridge; down the hill from the chief shopping street twisted a strand of narrow lanes with open-fronted shops leading to the marketplace and from that to the wide *maidans* where the mules were loaded and unloaded. The only transport was by pony, except for a few very expensive taxis, so equestrians were everywhere to be seen, suiting the medieval aspect of the town. Ponies were offered for hire, congregating near the bakery, where they were lined up, looking very alluring, their saddle cloths made of bright strips of carpet. There were Chinese restaurants, and shops selling solid silver spoons made of Tibetan silver, shops which sold Nepali rope-soled shoes made of felt or velvet in every brilliant color, and a place where you could buy yak-tail fly brushes, very useful when riding. The proprietors sat on their big platforms, smoking hookahs like the Caterpillar's, and everyone seemed to take pleasure in observing everyone else, we were such a motley crew. The streets seemed full of soldiers on leave—it was an easy place to reach and not expensive and the climate was never very hot, never very cold, so whenever one had a few days free Kalimpong was always good for a holiday.

Twice a week there was a *maila* in the marketplace down the hill where the country people brought vegetables in the large conical baskets which rested on their backs and were strapped to their foreheads. It was colorful, with pyramids of oranges and tomatoes, which here seemed to be a particularly small species, looking like carnelians. We were struck by the rice, which was white and of even grain, so unlike the poor reddish kernels we had been glad to get on the plains as our famine ration. It was the new crop and expensive, over a rupee a seer. Kalimpong rice is well known in the area for being of very good quality. An old man in the market was selling turquoises from his booth which was about a foot wide. We bought two fine stones from him for two rupees, eight annas; a pound of bread cost eight annas. The Hindus were selling saris and Kashmir shawls, adding more color to the scene. One could hardly have imagined a more brilliant bazaar, it was like a setting for a fairy story.

Big sunburned muleteers strode about, hand in hand, laughing uproariously, delighted to be here after their arduous journey with the wool. Their high black felt boots were decorated up the back with highly colored patterns, their loose robe was more often than not of black but sometimes of a royal purple or a priestly tangerine, belted at the hips with a wide sash. Some wore their hair in a long pigtail, swinging freely or wound into a coronet like a Du Maurier lady, but a number had chosen to simply let the whole thing degenerate into a wild, uncombed mat. Their hats were superb, high and fur-lined, and a large turquoise in the left ear was *de rigueur*. Their good nature, their evident happiness, was most marked—at no time, anywhere in the world, have I seen so many happy adults.

The Tibetan women wore the same sort of robe as did the men, except that it came to the ankle instead of just below the knee—the men's shorter gown served not only for more mobility but allowed them to display their magnificent boots. The women were much neater and their sashes were deftly tied; they wore also the long, narrow, horizontally striped apron which we had seen on Mrs. Tsering. Their braids fell below the waist or were in a beautifully oiled, smooth coronet, in contrast to the Nepali girls who affected great disorder in their dress. The teachers in the Kalimpong Homes told us that their Tibetan pupils were very clean, contrary to the usual criticism that these people were dirty even by hill standards. The Tibetan belles were bewitching, one we saw had the charm of a Lynn Fontanne. Her high stovepipe hat was trimmed with a wide pale green ribbon, interwoven with strands of silver and gold, the fur-lined brim curled up above her roguish eyes, rouged cheeks, and scarlet lips—she was painted to the eyes. Her satin blouse of the same pale green, her robe black and without an apron, she was perfectly groomed, very elegant, and at the same time merry, youthful, gay. The impression these Tibetans made upon us in those few hours was strong—such vitality, such self-command!

Lithe and free in their full skirts and bright shawls, erect as arrows, strong, graceful, finely developed, the Nepali women moved through the *maila*. They were so poor! And yet they did not seem to find that depressing. One shawl was enough and no one minds bare feet! The only sad faces were those of the ever-melancholy Indian merchants who brooded behind their bolts of stuff, suspicious, dark, mournful. There was a bejeweled old woman presiding over one booth who looked like a gypsy from Turkestan. Her features were strongly Semitic, her glance arrogant; the kerchief on her dark curly hair and her wide-hipped, big-bosomed figure put her in another category from the small-boned women of the hills. One could have watched the people milling about that little country fair for hours—ordinary Orientals are much more vibrant than ordinary Occidentals, more interesting in feature and gesture.

By the next day Tsering had collected our porters and ponies and we had our stores ready. We knew the route we were to follow to and from Gangtok, we had only to mount.

The native state of Sikkim is only some three thousand miles square. A rectangle to the north of Bengal, bounded by Bhutan,

Nepal, and Tibet, it is a position of incalculable strategic interest. The Indian Army officers spoke of it as "a dagger pointing at the heart of India." Wholly mountainous, it then raised only rice, oranges, vegetables. The people were friendly, simple, and backward; racially a mixture of the hill tribes round about, except for the Lepchas, who were native to the state. The standard of life was low, but apparently happy. There were no towns save for the mock-metropolis of Gangtok, with its marketplace, Maharajah's palace, the *gompa,* and the British Residency. The only trade with the outer world was with India in the export of oranges and the importation of cloth. There was just one modern road, which led from Gangtok to Gila Kola, the railhead below Kalimpong; transportation was almost wholly by mule or porter. The only serious traffic was that of the mule teams from Tibet which entered the state from the northeastern side, descending eight miles of steep stone steps from the Jalep La, the route that led on to Kalimpong. These eight miles of steps had quite a formidable reputation in the district, particularly when slippery with ice. They seemed always to be accomplished in one day: once you started you had to go on, whether up or down.

Our route took us first to Pedong on the border, ten or twelve miles from Kalimpong, most of them uphill. The wide and dusty road—still in India—followed the mountainside as we climbed under the brow of the ridge, Kanchenjunga hanging in the air above us while we went by bamboos, poinsettias, and waxen greeny-white trumpeting lilies. Far down on our right fell terraced slopes where rice was being harvested, the husks drifting down in a light stream from high-held baskets. On the hills across the valley blue shadows outlined the curved shell-like lines of still more terraces. Mule team after mule team met or passed us, raising clouds of dust, full of animation.

The leading mules, unled and even unaccompanied, so clever were they, were very handsomely adorned with necklaces of large bells, bright bits of carpet fastened to the headpiece, and, as a badge of office, an enormous yak-tail tassel dyed vermilion or scarlet and worn under the muzzle. The following mules were less conspicuously got up, but all were belled. If they were an incoming team they all carried heavy packs of wool. At the end of each string, sometimes on foot, more often perched on a bale of wool, came the laughing muleteers, perfect subjects for Frans Hals.

At about three in the afternoon we came to the cobblestone

street of Algorah at the top of the rise and, accompanied by mist, entered a forest. Tall, thin trees were silhouetted through the light and milky air, as delicate and lovely as a vision. The damp rich scent of humus and fern rose from the earth, the boulders were green with moss, and after the parching and dusty day we felt we could not have too much of this cooling and fragrant atmosphere. The road was paved with huge, worn stones about a foot square, very pictorial but extremely hard going, as there were more stone hollows than level places—it seemed to have been laid down shortly after the Flood. It was a typical Sikkimese road, as we were to learn to our cost. The model seemed to have suited the public in the distant past and no one had thought of any better way of doing things. My pony, irritable after his long plod uphill and anxious to get his day over with, especially as he was carrying not only me but also Posy (though together we constituted no great weight), with great deliberation put his foot square into a hole and came down. As we had not much further to go, we decided to send him back to Kalimpong forthwith with his *syce*. He had artfully made such a show of fatigue that we were considerably annoyed to see the spirited way he turned his head homewards, dancing lightly over the cobbles. Nothing so deceitful as the noble animal.

By this time we had reached the beautiful Pedong district, where there were fields of brilliantly green paddy and cherry trees in full bloom shadowing thatched cottages. Beside a green pond set about with the blossoming trees was a *gompa*, beyond that a meadow, and on the other side of it, the *dak* bungalow. A *chokidar*, all smiles and welcoming bows, came to meet us, apologizing for a huge hole in the roof caused by a summer storm and not repaired. The little house was on the border and neither Bengal nor Sikkim wished to foot the bill. The damaged roof caused us no uneasiness that night and we slept soundly in the lovely valley, though we had some trouble with our porters. These men did not compare with the ones who undertook the work at higher altitudes—but perhaps the progress of the war had already drained off the better type of porter, who were being enlisted to make roads through Manipur. These carriers had rested for some time at Algorah and become rather tipsy; they arrived late at Pedong, in a truculent mood. We never were on such terms with them as we had been with the porters who went with us to Sandakphu —Djalgen and Ajeeba and the others.

The garden of the *dak* bungalow was sweet with roses and heliotrope, sparkling in the early sunshine, as we made ready to start off the next morning. Tsering had arranged for us to pick up ponies as we went along, thinking this would be more economical than to hire them for the whole journey in sophisticated, worldly Kalimpong. The arrangement was thus rather tentative—for instance, on this first morning we discovered that there were no ponies to be hired in Pedong and we could only hope for better luck in Rennock, the first town we would reach in Sikkim itself. A smiling Nepali was engaged to carry Posy down the five miles of pitted stones called the road (and in which she would have sunk to her knees at every step) which led to the river marking the boundary between Bengal and Sikkim. He tied her on his back with a white shawl, and taking the tiffin bag in the other hand, flitted off on his bare feet as lightly as a butterfly. Leaving the village of Pedong we had to pass the post of the frontier police, who inspected our pass and in whose book we inscribed our names. Then we staggered down the execrable road, which was like a long, narrow honeycomb conceived on a gigantic scale. There was never one level spot on which to place a trembling foot, a bending ankle. The hillside which bordered it was as slippery as soap, or else terraced, and there one might not tread, so one could only hobble from knife-edge to deep hollow. The hill people ran past without a downward glance, their bare brown feet bounding off the flints. They knew of no other roads, so they did not question it.

At noon, much the worse for wear, we reached the Reesa River where, to our amazed joy, a pony had been sent for the lady at the telegraphic request of the angelic Tsering, who must have had second thoughts about the availability of mounts en route. The pony was a fine sturdy white creature, twice as lively as the one I had had from Kalimpong and entirely contemptuous of the stones. Posy and I were in the saddle in a moment. The path now led upwards, between huge clumps of yellow daisies—the exaggerated type of flower which seemed natural to Sikkim—and before long, in high spirits, we entered the village of Rennock which was enjoying its weekly *maila*.

As we approached the village square, we passed on our left an enclosure in which a dozen mules were drinking. The path was so steep that in a moment we were looking down on them from a higher level to see them crowded together as though in a lofty, roofless room above which water was pouring through six or seven channeled openings. The eager, jostling animals were lifting their heads to these crystal streams, rearing and pawing each other's backs in an effort to reach the waters. Outside the pen lay their harnesses. Any water they did not secure ran down over their shining backs and out under their hoofs, to be guided back into the main water supply for the village so that nothing would be wasted. Tsering had told us that in Rennock we should seek out the local dignitaries, a Rai Sahib Bahadur and his brother, eminent horticulturalists; we found them in a little building overlooking the square in which the *maila* was in progress, and very near the mules. It was arranged that we should call upon them and see their gardens on our way back to Bengal.

We were to spend that night in Pakiang, so we did not delay further but pressed on beyond Rennock. No one seemed to have a very clear idea how much further Pakiang was—we found that the Sikkimese had a fine scorn of time and space. Stanton had found a pony awaiting him in the village square (and it was the Rai Sahib Bahadur who had sent mine down to the bridge), so both being mounted and the sun shining, the path now of good mountain earth, we soon lost all care in the perfections of the hour, riding past bamboos, orange orchards, rice terraces where the peasants were at work with sickles, past rushing streams and masses of honeysuckle. Both the horses were belled, a slight plangent tinkle further enhancing the idyllic nature of the early afternoon. We recrossed the Reesa on a long and swaying suspension bridge, which ran over a wide stretch of dry sandy riverbed and a narrow strip of wild water of a delicious jade green color. Then a fine tree-lined causeway rose like a dike between some low, alluvial rice fields and we had once more to cross the Reesa and begin a long uphill journey.

My excellent pony had been with us only from the first crossing of the Reesa till we reached the Rennock bazaar—it belonged to the Rai Sahib and I had been given another mount in the village square. This new one was not in the same class and as the hours began to pass we realized that we had, in fact, a pair of very sorry nags indeed.

Early in the afternoon, when we had finished our picnic lunch, a lean and aged villain, complete with fez, had suddenly appeared from behind a boulder to remark that we had astonishingly poor ponies and would certainly never reach Pakiang *that* day. He further volunteered that the *memsahib's* pony was unsafe and frightened of slopes—he would undoubtedly fall down some hillside. We could see that behind him, partially hidden in a clump of feathery bamboos, he had two ponies tethered. Though we did not like his tone and thoroughly appreciated that he was biased, we finally yielded to his blandishments. There was clearly little to choose between his ponies, whose points he praised, and our own—all four were ill-fed, long-maned hill creatures; but Stanton's mount was faltering under his unaccustomed weight, most of the hillmen being small and light, so in the end we went over to the tempter. It was a mistake.

On good ponies, or had we been less footsore, we ourselves, could have finished the day's trek in good time but, not realizing how far off Pakiang still was (the horse dealer had at least told the truth on that score), we dreamed and dozed while the beasts dragged slowly on, our way lying through lovely forest country. Sun and shadow marked deep ridges in the slopes and folds across the valley, emphasized the lines of the terraces, and carved a cliff into a macabre face. The sound of the stream died away, the sun dropped behind the hills, and we woke to the fact that it was late and that as we could see our path leading over at least three ridges ahead, without a sign of a village, the bungalow must indeed be a great distance away. The *syces* were indifference itself. The ponies stumbled in the growing dusk, shadows fell, the air grew silent. We dismounted and walked. It seemed years since we had left Pedong, and as for Kalimpong, that was another life. Only Posy retained her buoyant morale, convinced that at any moment the *dak* bungalow would appear—"only lickle furder now." Finally we could not see the path and hugged the hillside lest a false step might start our descent to the Reesa. I was sure that if I fell I would just go on rolling over and over, I would never have the energy to stop myself.

At last, far off in the blackness of the hills, a wavering light showed itself. It came nearer and to our relief proved to be guiding the porters who, despite their low caliber, had grown anxious and had started back to look for us. One took Posy on his back and with the heartening swaying circle of lamplight before us we hastened over the last mile, our shadows immense against a muddy cliffside. Many little streams ran across the path, their ripples almost phosphorescent. Everyone talked and laughed, explaining the difficulties of the day, till we gained the village and dismounted, the better to pass through a vast assemblage of mules, and came finally to the lily-lined entrance of the bungalow. Here it was light with many kerosene lamps and warm with a wood fire roaring in the deep hearth. After boiling baths and supper we fell into bed and knew no more.

The next morning we found that on the brow of the hill near us were two *stupas*, both of a considerable size with a face painted on all four sides of the squares under the spire. The faces were identical—Buddhas with large eyes, full flat nose, curving and benevolent lips. Next to the *stupas* a *mendong* with prayer flags. Even more than in the countryside of southern Europe, with its plethora of humble wayside shrines, do these large *stupas* and *mendongs* seem to dominate a region, to insinuate into the mind the idea of a Presence. This atmosphere, engendered in Tibet, has extended outwards into these lower hill kingdoms, into Sikkim and Nepal, into Bhutia.

The Pakiang *babu*, to whom we had another Tsering open sesame letter, sent over a pony, so we were happy to be able to return one of the Rennock hacks. The new steed seemed to have just walked off a Chinese scroll—he was yellow with a henna mane, big-bellied, black-nostriled. At the sight of him and his strong and prancing gait, his assured style, my long-locked, bebelled, languishing palfrey braced up and went well for the whole stage, which took us to Gangtok.

We first rode down to the Pul River through Sherwood Forest country—with a difference. The open spaces between the glades were terraced and the mammoth lilies and yellow daisies were not what the Merry Men were used to seeing, but there was a romantic flavor about it, a beauty which was not controlled by man but, equally, was not that of the jungle. There were immense trees, many of them oaks, again reminiscent of Elizabethan England. The lilies never seemed to me quite of this earth—they were too big, too improbable, with their long trumpets giving out that theatrical green glow. Sometimes there is a real bliss in ignorance. My appalling lack of botanical knowledge did not disturb me as much as it should have—I could not have been more delighted with the lilies if I had known their true name and pedigree; all that would have been folly to me, compared with the legend I constructed about them.

As seemed to be the way in Sikkim with travelers and rivers, we found that we were obliged to cross and recross the Pul several times during the morning. We were joined in the forest by two puckish little boys who were, surprisingly, on stilts. They were also on the way to Gangtok and stayed with us for the rest of the day, which gave us great pleasure as they were well-mannered, helpful, cheerful, and full of admiration for our quaint ways.

Early in the afternoon we came to Gangtok and our idyll was abruptly shattered. As we climbed for the last time above the clear and rushing waters of the Pul, we suddenly found ourselves upon a wide, incongruous macadam road. The ponies' hooves rang on the hard surface, and though it was an infinitely better road than the cobbled paths, which had been particularly horrible that morning, we instantly resented it. There was no traffic whatsoever besides ourselves. The Maharajah was out of town and at such times Gangtok slipped back into its old ways as far as possible.

It was extraordinarily discouraging to approach this little capital, which we had eagerly wished to visit, of which we knew little more than its fine, ringing name. Yet its banal atmosphere extended out along the road and we sensed that we would find it disappointing. Built on the side of a hill, with splendid views far out over the valleys, overhung by Kanchenjunga, so near the snows of Tibet, how could Gangtok have become so commonplace? Western influence, which the Maharajah had succeeded in keeping away from the rest of the state, had had its vengeance here and the ruler's residence had been made vulgar, dull, and bourgeois. Wishing to keep the countryside bucolic, the government apparently had thought that the capital might be allowed a deliberate mixture of Eastern and Western culture. This is something the world has found very difficult to achieve with any harmonious results. The experiment in Gangtok only resulted in a type of prefabricated capital.

At the near end of the ridge, approaching by the new road, was the ugly pseudo-Chinese palace of the ruler. Next to it was his *gompa*, astonishingly new and clean, topped with corrugated iron, alas, though the style of building demanded the magnificent Tibetan roof. At the far end of the ridge, deep in woods, was the British Residency. Between these two paramount sites ran the macadam road, bordered by cherry trees, a park, a fountain, a kiosk, a statue of Queen Victoria, and a bust of King Edward VII. Perhaps by now time and the sturdy character of the hill people have softened the outlines of Gangtok, and the hospital, the concrete high school, the playing fields, and the Western-style homes of the Maharajah's secretaries do not look so grim and gray. The institutions were needed. But seeing them through the fine drizzle which enveloped the town as we entered it induced in us a mood of gloom, *Weltschmerz*, and boredom.

There were three *dak* bungalows, one given over for the duration of the war to an English wireless operator, Robert Ford of *Captured in Tibet*. The little houses were substantially built and much more modern than the simple country bungalows, but they were very cold—they were following British standards. They were equipped with fireplaces, but though the state was half forest, wood was exorbitantly expensive and what one could buy was green and damp. We were cold all the time we were in Gangtok, which was only to be expected, considering the nature of the town and those statues down the road.

Only one feature of the past had survived—the old irregular marketplace under the lee of the hill. Its uneven rectangle supported, on sandy soil, three lovely blossoming cherry trees and the next day, when there was a *maila*, we found that the country people who came in with their vegetables and saris and turquoises were as gay and vivid as the Rennock folk, though in this town they seemed utterly out of place.

Our letter of introduction here was addressed to one Rai Sahib Rennock Kazi, the manager of the Maharajah's estates, an intelligent and capable Tibetan. He dressed in Chinese style in a long gown with a black satin overjacket, in which he looked well and no doubt kept warm. He welcomed us very hospitably to his home, which was fragrant with Chinese lilies growing from bulbs in pebble-filled bowls, and presented us with apples and white scarves. All gifts in these parts must be accompanied by white scarves. Apples are rare in India, they were a delicacy we had not tasted for a very long time.

With the Rai Sahib was his sad, weedy secretary, a young man of religious bent, shivering in a gray cotton robe and wearing a dull knitted cap crowned with a small pompom. He spoke quite good English, made faint by his own excessive melancholy, which was, I assumed, brought about by living in Gangtok. He was clearly weary of this world. Conversation was not easy and I understood then as never before what Solomon meant by being comforted with apples. It was arranged that we were to be shown over the *gompa* the next morning and might see the Rai Sahib's carpet factory on the following day, as tomorrow it would be closed. On asking why, we found it was a Buddhist holiday and, as we gathered its significance, we exclaimed together, "Of course! It's Buddha's birthday!" The secretary winced and corrected us. "His *descent*. Our Lord was never born, he *descended!*" We apologized. He then told us how fortunate we were to have come just at this moment, as the *gompa* was giving continual services and one hundred and eight lamas were about to recite the *sutras* in three days, a very considerable feat. They had come in from many different temples in the state.

The Rai Sahib sent servants to us that evening bringing presents of vegetables and fruit, with white scarves, and we replied as best we could with a tin of butter and some guava jelly. The vegetables were very welcome, especially some delicious *knol khol,* a type of dream turnip. The nearer you get to Tibet the fewer vegetables there are, and those tend to be either turnips or radishes.

The next morning at ten o'clock our dejected religious guide was waiting for us on the terrace outside the *dak* bungalow. He led us along some sandy paths under an ugly and inferior *pailow,* (an imitation of the striking Chinese arches) in the direction of the palace. As neither the Maharajah nor his family was in residence it was closed up—a large wooden edifice with a multiplicity of gables and many-paned windows, suggesting an unhappy combination of Swiss villa and Chinese temple. His highness had three wives, but only the first ever lived here, the others had houses of their own. One was French.

The distances in Gangtok were not great and very soon we came to a wide lawn, screened on the far side by prayer flags. Here stood the *gompa,* a fine building except for the unfortunate roof, the outer walls white with the usual broad dark-red border under the widely projecting eaves. We began to encounter lamas on their way to the services and were immediately struck by their cleanliness, not a usual attribute in their calling, and their open countenances—the lama monks we had seen in Peking and elsewhere had so often looked degenerate. Barefoot in spite of the raw air, they were otherwise splendidly attired in full regalia: long full robes and wide sashes in opulent Venetian colors—purple, scarlet, orange, tangerine, saffron, yellow, gold. As in all religions where there are many priests and a great organization, no theatre can rival them for display when they are celebrating some significant event in their calendar. The majority of these persons going towards the *gompa* were young—some only children.

The *gompa* likewise astonished us because it was spotlessly clean

—the eaves freshly painted, the tapestries new, not a speck of dust anywhere. We had seen hundreds of Buddhist temples in the East and a fair number of the lama persuasion, but never one in this condition before—clearly great religious zeal was abroad in Gangtok. Music was being played before the altars in the main hall: a drum, two nine-foot horns, and four shorter ones were wailing away, and a few lamas intoning. These long horns, which are not coiled up as are ours but extended to their full length, give an excessively weird and ghostly note, designed to "strike terror and inspire respect." Our guides showed us other halls, other altars, rooms where devil masks (for the dances) were stored, a library, and the kitchens with their vast churns, making enough buttered tea for hundreds of monks. Near these outbuildings a friendly monkey was chained. Beyond lay a small nunnery, another surprise. We saw no nuns, however.

Finally, following the booming of a gong, we came to the building where the services were being held. The monks sat on the floor before low stands which held the *sutras*. As they intoned, an old monk went round with incense, blowing it into the nostrils of each person in turn. The chanting continued without any halt, while newcomers came in and settled themselves with apparent casualness. The monks seemed to represent every type of individual—aristocrats, peasants, the devout, the base, the indifferent, old men, and children not more than five or six years old. Some were clearly spiritually involved, some in a half-trance. The atmosphere tended to become mesmeric; the scene was so arresting and varied that it was difficult to leave it.

After we had left Gangtok and entered again the valley of the Pul the charm of Sikkim once more enveloped us. Well-mounted, thanks to the Rai Sahib, we retraced the mountain paths, coming again to Rennock where we waited upon the two brothers whom we had met on the outward journey, surprising figures to meet in that rustic setting. Neither had ever been abroad, yet they were in touch with the great gardens of the world and had introduced into their own nurseries many rare plants. The older brother had received his titles (Rai Sahib Bahadur) from the Raj, showing that his work had been recognized—probably by the Forestry Department which was so active in the Himalayas.

The Rai Sahib had a particular love for orchids and had then under cultivation over four hundred varieties. Many of these grew on terraces which overhung a hillside—at that season brilliant with cascades of chrysanthemums. Down their land streams flowed, which the brothers had had guided into little channels artfully made to form waterfalls, lily ponds, and brooks, and which were edged with rare grasses. So few educated Orientals, in those days, ever cared to return to their villages and enrich the local scene, so few seemed aware of the potentialities of their own environment, that these two rather lonely figures were the more admirable, the more surprising.

After we had seen the terraces and the flowers they gave us a festive meal, conversing but not eating with us, as they were strict Brahmins. Their ladies being in purdah, we met no one else. The cuisine was appropriate for a Hindu household: fried cauliflower made into delicious patties, snowflake rice, and unlimited quantities of fresh orange juice from fruit which had just been picked from the trees.

With them we deplored the conditions of the Sikkim orange harvest; so abundant that within the state a hundred oranges were sold for six annas (about half an American cent). Oranges lay under the trees, anyone could have them for the asking. With no roads and no carts, the only way to export them was in the porters' baskets on their backs. Outside the state the price of the fruit soared, naturally, and the army contractors were making fortunes out of them. In Darjeeling they cost forty to a rupee, on the plains you might get only twelve oranges for a rupee. The Ratna brothers, elegant in their tweed jackets and white jodhpurs, sighed. Without proper communications the state was terribly hampered. The Maharajah had his own road and cars which carried him between Gangtok and the frontier, but men like our friends had to employ the same combination of stone pathway and coolies which had been in operation in these hills since they were first inhabited.

A few days later we were in the little train going back to Siliguri. In the compartment with us was a charming young lady from Assam who had just escorted her little sister to school in Kalimpong. Pale, slender, and elegant, with beautiful manners, she was a pleasure to be with and she was intelligent. Her home, she told us, was in a district in the Khasi Hills near Shillong where, evidently, her family had a prominent position. Her English was absolutely perfect. One of her brothers was in a training ship of the Royal Indian Navy. He had longed to go to sea ever since he was a small boy, though he had never once seen the ocean. She explained that this passion had come upon him after he met an English sea captain who was on holiday in Shillong and had told the child of his life on the waters. The Khasis, she told us, felt akin to the Polynesian peoples, as do the Burmans: many of them had a strong bond with the sea, perhaps because of this kinship. "We are Mongols," she said, with great simplicity.

As we talked it grew dark. Below the narrow road bed the white and rushing waters of the Teesta foamed and shone. Once more time was invested with an atmosphere of fantasy, so improbable seemed everything we heard and saw.

XIV Ambernath and Bombay

There are landscapes on earth, landscapes in painting, landscapes in dreams, and landscapes in one's breast. The beauty of landscapes on earth lies in depth and irregularity of outline; . . . the beauty of landscapes in dreams lies in their strangely changing views: . . .

FROM THE Epigrams OF CHANG CH'AO

Ambernath

BY 1944 a new armament factory in the small station of Ambernath, near Bombay, began to go into production and we were sent there, as they were ready for an inspectorate. The factory made cartridge cases and, in common with most of the new ordnance ventures, was rumored to provide very uncomfortable living conditions. The bazaar rumors frightened the servants and in the end we went away without any of them. We were sent across the country in comfort, being allowed to take the rare air-cooled carriages, but having to care for our lively children, now two and four, it was not a particularly restful journey. Stanton told me afterwards that he had been as unconscious of the scenery as though he had been in the underground.

The line runs across the dry flat wastes of the Deccan, the old Mahratta country, till it reaches the Ghats; here one comes to a rude, savage, wooded landscape, very vital and romantic, plunging down to the coastal plain. It was delightful to come to this colorful stretch after the days in the desert. After passing through the Ghats there is another strip of sere plain before the coast is reached and it was in this arid patch that we left the train, at a horrible little town called Kalyan. It was half-past two in the afternoon and 115 degrees in the shade. Someone had come to meet us with a lorry— the factory was so short of transport that they could send nothing else and Kalyan had nothing but wretched shabby *tongas*. We sat on our suitcases in the lorry, broiling under the thin canvas covering. Our air-cooled days vanished like a dream.

Ambernath lay four miles away from Kalyan across a plain which was traversed by a small stream, too small to temper the sterility around it, crossed by a low and perilous bridge. We traveled like the Great Djin in a cloud of thick yellowish dust, bumping over the mud road till we came to a small settlement of military huts scattered on a burnt-out section of rolling land. I could hardly believe this could be our destination. The little huts were so solitary, the whole panorama so unaccented, that compared to this Palta was the very flower of civilization and variety. I understood now the bazaar gossip and realized why the servants did not even want to consider the move. My first impression was that it was uninhabitable.

The lorry drew up beside a high latticed fence, through which we could see a large bare compound—the earth so scorched and bare that literally not one blade of grass adorned it. In it was the wooden hut which, our companion assured us, was ours. I still felt there must be some mistake—we *couldn't* live *here*. We all climbed down docilely from the lorry and, the sun striking our shoulders, went through the compound and up onto the very narrow veranda, where the stone was hot under our feet. A *chokidar* stood by the door, and a clerk from the factory, fumbling with keys. They seemed to find nothing extraordinary in our coming and cast a sort of spell upon me to that end; we all went together into the house, where the clerk took upon himself the qualities of the Sheep in Alice's dream. I could almost see him knitting and looking at me through a great pair of spectacles.

The Sheep had been dispatched to see us into our quarter and to provide us with such furniture as we needed. This had to be decided immediately, as there was not so much as a bed in the house and we were to sleep there that very night—there was no place else to go. He had with him a long list which I looked over in a dazed way while the rooms were being opened up. They were as harsh and unadorned as the settlement itself, with rough, colorwashed brick walls and unpolished gray stone floors. Everyone was theoretically entitled to a certain minimum of furniture, it seemed, but we, being among the last to arrive (because of the nature of inspection work), found that almost nothing was left in the stores. At least there were beds, but no, sighed the Sheep, there were no more wardrobes, no more couches, only one tin tub, and no basins at all. The house contained three bathrooms, each of which boasted a tap and a toilet—nothing else—but at least there were these essentials and I was so pleased to have plumbing that I was not worried about the rest. With the rest of the furniture I felt like Alice in that shop—I could lay hold on nothing.

Out of the earth at this moment arose a *dhobi*, sensing, in the uncanny way of his kind, the arrival of travelers from afar as the vulture finds his prey in the wilderness. I turned from the Sheep and his phantom wares with some relief to prepare more realistic lists for the *dhobi*, who soon disappeared with a great bundle of our clothes on his back. The fans were swirling in every room of our new home but it was still as hot as an oven. There were no blinds on the verandas and the sun had taken possession long before. Our suitcases and bedrolls, half-unpacked so that the *dhobi* could take what was soiled, lay on the floors in the glare from the windows. Then a message came that we were expected to tea in the superintendent's bungalow, two hundred yards away; it was already after four and we set off at once, dusty as we were, glad enough to hasten away and see what evidences of life there might be in this sear and Spartan setting. Going up the rise of ground which led from our compound to the next (the superintendent's), the light and heat seemed to dance round our feet. It was not the heavy damp air of Bengal, but as dry as tinder, the stuff mirages are made of.

The superintendent had already been six months on the site and his hut, which was only slightly larger than ours, had been made quite reasonably comfortable, which encouraged us. They were kind to us and had already performed something of a miracle on our behalf—they had found us a cook. Hardly any servants would consider coming to Ambernath, we learned, unless they were virtually unemployable—labor was one of the great local problems. This was true for the factory as well and was a factor that had been dismissed far too lightly when it had been decided to build here. The planning commission had thought only of dispersing the factories and making them less vulnerable from the air, forgetting that they were vulnerable in other ways.

That first evening our furniture began to come in from the stores with our own boxes, which had been brought over by rail with some metal ingots which the factory needed. The government, which had posted us across, was too mean to pay for shipping our household goods but they did allow us to use wagons which were not entirely full. The night held an unexpected gift for us, suddenly we found our first great recompense for the trials of the move. We could turn on our lights freely! We had even forgotten that this could ever be done. As we came down the hillside from the superintendent's bungalow we saw the bright lines of the windows of the new settlement, placed here and there over the wide and treeless expanse of darkness where the obscurity was absolute, harboring no deeper shadows from monuments or trees. There was no blackout on the Bombay side.

There was still another surprise in store for us before we could fall asleep. We had gone to bed and were lying listening to the whirr of the fan, a pleasant small sound after the roar of the train, when we heard loud grunting noises and realized that some sizable animal was charging about the bedroom. Stanton hurried out from under the mosquito net and put on the light, grasping his *kukeri*, to find himself confronting an angry, frightened, aggressive bandicoot, who was just as surprised as he was. The bandicoot was outraged because we were trespassing on his bungalow. Stanton and he rushed about through the rooms, shouting and grunting at each other till the poor rat finally located one of the many French doors and tore out into the night. Then we became one with the deep silence which enveloped the station under the myriad pricking stars.

Behind Bombay the land stretches from the sea to the Ghats in a wide dry plain, slightly relieved by occasional low rolling patches and by certain abrupt, fiercely eroded hills which jut out of the earth as though they were giant pieces of sculpture thrust up through the topsoil by some gargantuan hand. These hills give the landscape interest and character. Brown, sere, and rocky as their surroundings for nine months of the year, early in June they glow with deep color—purple, azure, garnet—as they begin to draw the high cumulous clouds towards them, making the whole field of vision teem with light and color while the world waits, panting, for the promised rain. A fortnight passes, while the clouds grow fuller, taller, more majestic and the wild hills lovelier, but the sun is as fierce as ever, the earth as parched. The romantic craggy heights seem to come nearer the plainsman, as their every detail of deep ravine and weathered summit is sharply etched in the blazing air. Then at last the rains break, the hills disappear behind a cloud of mist, reappearing for brief intervals to reveal themselves newly clothed in freshest green. Then—tender, gentle, and alluring—they look upon a plain equally vivid and transformed, rejoicing in its brief span of fertility and growth. By October the sky is hard and blue again, the green has withered from plain and cliff, the streams are dry, and the sharp rock faces of the twisted hills command once more a monotonous, bleak, brown expanse, shimmering in heat. This uniformity is broken, at first, by the autumnal fires which sweep over the low ranges, burning the grass—that grass which grew long during the monsoon, prospering only for its own inevitable destruction—and chasing out the snakes and scorpions which have made their homes under its winding canopies. Above, hawks hang in the hot air, expectant, vibrant, scarcely moving, ready to swoop down in an instant upon any living thing which has escaped the initial peril.

From Ambernath we had in view two hills, one of which was known as "Cathedral Rock" because of its Gothic lines. The other was larger and more formidable. Their outlines wavered and altered under the sun during the long days but became always more familiar, so that today if I shut my eyes I can see with great distinctness every turret of rock, every black slanting shadow. They made our scene, the eyes turned to them in the absence of other landmarks. Purple Mountain outside Nanking draws the eye in much the same way and becomes curiously identified with the city itself.

There was one other important natural feature in this desert. Appropriately enough, that was the water, which was its greatest blessing, as it was as soft as silk. One flick of your finger and a basin would be foaming with soap suds (none of us then had heard of a soap powder and we used native products, scented with neem). The pipes for the bungalows had been laid too near the surface, for cheapness, and often the water ran out so hot that we had to let quantities flow away before it was cool enough to use. So few places have good water—most cities indeed have water which is positively bad, hard and harsh—that it seemed a strange boon that this poor little desert settlement, whipped by the hot and dusty winds, should have been granted such a rare favor. The irritable *memsahibs* and the weird *ayahs* were at least a little soothed in their difficult domestic round to find that everything they washed could be so fair and fine.

We needed the consolation of the sweet water, also, because of our bathroom problems. When we arrived we were issued, as I have said, with one tin tub, a very uninviting object and, in any case, inadequate. The children had a little bath which, perforce, was good enough for them, and which could stand under their bathroom tap and then be turned over to empty out on the stone floor. The contents ran out of a small hole in a corner of the room and watered that part of the garden, in theory. An enamel basin on a shelf was also soon installed. But that was no solution for Stanton and myself and the factory admitted that they did not have any intention of supplying any more tubs. Wasn't there a war on? Were we not capable of making sacrifices? I knew just what I wanted to do; ever since I had seen the bathrooms at the Lahore Mission I had thought that type of Hindu bath ideally suitable for the country. We hired a mason, who built a low wall with steps of different heights in the little room. I painted them and we bought pitchers and basins, which were filled for us, and we enjoyed our throw baths to the full. When we left the station the garrison engineer sent us a bill for "defacing government property" which we indignantly refused to pay.

This desert countryside, where there were only a few bazaars, railway junctions, and military outposts, continued till the Ghats were reached, the wild cliffs that lead up to the Deccan. Such an area had been thought very suitable for an armament factory, being not far from Bombay and the sea but well situated from the security angle. The chief drawback, that of attracting sufficient labor, was now being felt. There were too few local people and outsiders did not want to come. The factory, which was built in wartime, was one of the most modern of its kind in the world, it was a very model of cartridge case production. It was of British construction—the engineers, the plans, the machinery, all came from that besieged, hard-pressed island, all the way through dangerous seas to India, where, on the west coast, there had hardly been a shot fired in anger. The factory was a true anomaly. It was run wholly by electricity, streamlined, with wide, light shops and splendid machine tools, while the workers who brought it to life were drawn from the most primitive human category. The Indian laborers were, of course, illiterate, but they were much more ig-norant than that word suggests. The Chinese workman was often

—indeed generally—illiterate but he had every instinct of the trained artisan, and he had great intelligence. These Ambernath coolies were like something out of the Stone Age. But they could, with little direction, run that great factory. The natural setting of the buildings in our burnt-out wilderness was like something out of a surrealist dream, the factory was a mechanic's joy, the labor was troglodytic, and the majority of the Europeans who were supervisors and managers were unhappy, ignorant, quarrelsome, and given to strong waters.

The war had brought to the plain under Cathedral Rock more than our incongruous factory—it had brought also a huge transit camp.

As the war continued, increasing numbers of troops of all nationalities found their way in and out of India, most often through the port of Bombay; eventually it was decided to build a transit camp for these men between Kalyan and Ambernath. The camp and the factory were established almost simultaneously, transforming the wide and silent plain into two centers of life wholly connected with the business of war. Hundreds of temporary buildings were erected, military lorries and dispatch riders thundered by on the bad roads, and troops poured in—Negroes, Chinese, Indians, Scots, Americans. There were hospitals, canteens, cinemas, Indian quarters, European quarters, administrative centers, and thousands of huts—whatever purpose, nearly everything looked more or less the same. In the dust and heat, the aggravation attendant on trying to make everything functional at once, the authorities strove to organize a way of living for this great transitory population, all waiting for postings, bored, restless, privately absorbed in the complexities of their own existence.

The camp was a boon to the factory. It meant that we saw people who had other horizons than ours; and they helped us also materially as they had relatively so many more comforts and pleasures than we did. We had the immense advantage of being able to draw military rations—we had plenty of sugar and flour and rice again. We used their cinemas and opened our club to them; they dined with us and the wives of the factory personnel were welcome at the military dances, where they were always short of women. We helped run their canteen, and in the long-drawn-out weariness of the war, in the uncertainties and dangers of our residence in India, which was every day becoming more restive under British rule, we found a certain camaraderie with these young men, though in normal times most of us would have remained strangers. The Ambernath posting also afforded us one other diversity—Bombay itself.

Bombay

In the eighteenth century Bombay was the Cinderella of the English settlements in India, the unhealthiest, the poorest, and the most despised.

PERCIVAL SPEAR

. . . Bombay, an isolated and fragmentary property overshadowed by the power of the Marathas.

EDWARD THOMPSON, *The Making of the Indian Princes*

Bombay seemed to us a happy city compared with poor, moldy Calcutta which, Stanton always said, exemplified Splendor sinking into Slime. Architecturally disastrous, a horrid mixture of Victorian Gothic and the worst elements of Indian building, its situation put it beyond the reach of superficial criticism—the sparkling blue of the harbor, the long white beaches, the constant breath of the sea, and its own magnificent flowering trees made it almost a debonair city. In spite of its slums, profiteers, riots, explosions, inflation, and heat, it retained an air of gaiety and bravado.

After the dank and languid despair of once-elegant Calcutta, we found Bombay invigorating and hopeful, in spite of the heat and the fantastic cost of everything we thought we needed. The inflation in India had now risen to staggering heights and a great many items were cheaper in the West End of London than they were in this city where millions were so poor. We had to catch a very early train from Ambernath to go into Bombay and return on a late one, so it was rather an exhausting affair to go at all, but we always felt on these excursions that we had reentered the stream of life. The people of the town were quick to riot and anger was a commonplace, but they still seemed more agreeable and less calculating than the Bengalis. All the main roads were enriched by cassias, magnolias, acacias, and the astonishing Flame of the Forest, their branches laden with brilliant flowers. It seemed to us that no city in the world could boast so many beautiful trees—we were constantly arrested by their luxuriance and color.

The famous Breech Kandy, one of the most beautiful of bathing

pools, gave us immense pleasure. It was open to all the Europeans
—one did not have to be a member, pay a subscription, or know
anyone in particular, so that to people like ourselves it was a godsend, and we looked forward eagerly to having a couple of carefree, prewar hours there whenever we were in the town. Calcutta
had offered nothing like this. The more nationalistically inclined
Indians fiercely resented this pleasure ground to which they were
not admitted—it was reserved exclusively for Europeans. This was
really not so unfair; there was nothing to prevent the Indians from
building their own pools—Breech Kandy consisted only of walls
enclosing part of the sea, which protected the bathers from sharks.
There were a number of pools and they were large, but they were
only enough to accommodate the European population and the
great numbers of visiting troops—they could not have begun to
include the Indians as well. On the landward side the enclosure was
surrounded by a garden always full of flowers—bougainvillea,
phlox, stock, and roses—which displayed their brilliant petals
against the luminous sea and sky, the turquoise water of the baths,
and the deep blue of the harbor.

The city has another treasure—a splendid old library, a branch of
the Royal Asiatic Society founded by the joint efforts of the English and certain prominent Indians, chiefly Parsees. It is housed in
a large yellow Georgian building, with many enormous statues of
famous and learned men in the halls and on the stairways. It
asked a modest subscription and as far as we were concerned was
worth its weight in gold. It had an outstanding collection of books
and was doubly valuable because it had no rivals. It was open to
both Indians and Europeans; the founders had hoped that it would
further friendship between the two races. Certainly it was used by
both peoples in that genial freemasonry which scholarship creates,
if it is genuine.

One of the most grievous mistakes the British made in their long
period of dominance was that they never started any free lending
libraries. Many educated Indians (and of course it is granted that
their education was due to the British primarily or secondarily)
were extremely poor—their talents could only command the small-
est salaries—and even the few pounds it cost to join the Royal
Asiatic Library were enough to bar its doors to them. For a great
number of students it was an impossible luxury. The first free
public lending library in India was not to be founded till 1952
when one was established in Delhi as a part of a UNESCO proj-

ect. The *Manchester Guardian* of October 4, 1952, makes melancholy reading indeed:

. . . In existing public libraries in India there has never been general access to the shelves and the librarian's job has been to stop people taking books away rather than to encourage them to do so.

There were some fears . . . that book losses would be very heavy, especially until people got used to the idea of a lending library. But in the first nine months forty-five thousand books were lent, twenty-five lost, and twelve not returned. The average loss in English public libraries is about four times this. There is a system of reminder postcards and small fines, but the good results are regarded as the outcome of completely trusting people.

About two thousand people go to the library every day. There is room in the adult library for fifty-six people to sit, but usually about five hundred are there. A children's library was started with four thousand books but after the first ten days the shelves were empty. Books and catalogues are in three languages, Hindu, Urdu, and English. About sixty per cent of the demand is for fiction and the rest mainly for "How to do it" books. A hall is kept for film shows, lectures, and for helping illiterates.

How much had been spent in Delhi alone during the imperial years for pomp, when there were so many Indians hungry for this honest fare? The *durbars*, whether Mogul or British, were justified by the Raj as creating and reinforcing a sense of unity, as well as giving pleasure to the poor. The British love of pageantry and show is so great that they feel it an essential element of government and cannot believe that this sentiment is not shared by all the peoples they have ruled.

However, though it was not absolutely free, the Royal Asiatic Library in Bombay did reach many people who considered it almost their greatest pleasure and luxury—that included ourselves. The Victorian founders were men of scholarly tastes and we found there many a curious volume we might have had great difficulty in unearthing in more favored centers in the West. It was surprisingly strong in astronomy and mathematics: there was a first edition of Newton's *Principia,* and an early Leibnitz, *Méchanique Celeste* by La Place, and an excellent reprint of Southey's edition of the *Morte d'Arthur* with wide margins and splendid type. This we read through in its entirety—I shall always associate it with the desert airs, as though it were a series of romantic mirages. In the library there were old-fashioned black leather sofas, very wide and slippery, under ceiling fans, and *babus* passed back and forth with their arms full of books about which they were often very knowledgeable.

Bombay has had a strange and varied history. It is actually an island, though no one would ever suspect that today, so entirely has the land been reclaimed from the sea. The first town, built on the old island, was called Mahim and was sometimes under Mogul, sometimes under Mahratta, rule. Whatever sovereignty nominally held sway, it was always subject to fierce attacks from the pirates of the coast and from marauding tribesmen from the hinterland; this went on till the middle of the sixteenth century. Then it was absorbed by the Portuguese in one of their great waves of conquest. They were cruel masters to the poor islanders; their whole record in India makes savage reading. But they maintained their position in Bombay till, a hundred years later, by one of those seemingly fortuitous twists in the strand of history, the unhappy and impoverished colony came into the possession of England as part of the dowry of the Infanta Catherine of Portugal on her marriage to Charles II. Seven years later—in 1668—the East India Company leased it for ten pounds a year. There came then a period of development and prosperity due to the talents and character of one man, the father of the city, the brilliant governor Gerald Angier.

This name should be better known. Angier was an administrative genius and, in spite of that, an idealist, remarkably democratic for his age. He was so far in advance of his times that he had an understanding of and love for the principles underlying the liberty of the individual and devoted himself to making the city a place where such freedom might be realized. In order to develop, the colony had to have peace; he raised a militia strong enough to ward off the raiding Mahrattas and the Malabar pirates, and as he built the new town, he fortified it. He drained the marshes surrounding the settlement, established courts of justice, started a constabulary, and even called a representative assembly. The Portuguese had levied oppressive taxes—these he reduced so that the merchants, who had been very nearly ruined, were able to get trade going. The pirates and bandits were first kept at bay and then driven further off (the Mahrattas were not finally reduced until long after Angier's time), and the town began to have a name for security and order. Drawn by the wonder of a just government and the blessings of freedom of worship and of trade, men flocked to the new city which was now beginning to fulfill its destiny—it would become, it was clear, a great port. In ten years the population increased from ten thousand to sixty thousand, chiefly Hindus, Parsees, and Armenians.

This was long remembered as its Golden Age. But it rested too heavily upon the virtues of Angier; when he was gone, no one of his stature appeared. Bombay suffered from the competition of Surat, then far larger and more important, and from the enmity of the Portuguese further south and from the Mahrattas. It seems also to have been peculiarly unhealthy, something difficult to understand today, when Bengal's climate has so much the worse reputation. It was corrupt and suffered from remarkably difficult and choleric governors, it was parochial, it was socially undesirable, as everyone preferred to be in Bengal or Madras where the important English officials and officers were and the native princes of significance made visits—Bombay was considered only fit for traders and even so was not prosperous. However, gradually all these conditions began to improve; in the long run the city was bound to thrive—its situation was so good that when better government prevailed at last and when the external enemies slackened, it had to go forward. It was more cosmopolitan than other cities in India and among all the peoples who came to it the Parsees played a major role in determining its character and its development. A shipbuilder called Lowji came to Bombay in 1736 at the urgent wish of the British, who had much to do to persuade him to leave Surat, and it has been said that it was the people of this highly intelligent and forward-looking community, rather than the British, who were the builders of the city. The Parsees have been called the Jews of India—meaning that they have embodied those qualities of industry, cleverness, perspicacity in trade, and a free and genial social sense which have distinguished those other exiles who have settled in great cities and almost made them their own. The Parsees considered Bombay their home; they never intended to leave it and they have benefited it in a hundred ways, with their philanthropy and good sense, their freedom from bigotry and their outstanding looks.

In 1853 the city was joined to the mainland by rail and in that era its industrialization began. Today these early struggles and triumphs seem entirely overlaid by the rather prosaic life of the port—one is quite ignorant of the past. Neither the Mahratta Wars nor the Mutiny seem to have left any somber traces, and for long Bombay remained in a sense divorced from the hinterland, drawing her prosperity from the sea. However, as India developed as a great possession of the Raj and was continually more unified, it was inevitable that the city should begin to play an important role; as the Indian struggle for freedom became intensified, Bombay took her place in that strife. The greatness of the center made it imperative that significant speeches and gestures, plans, intrigues, should take place here, at the gateway to the subcontinent.

In the fall of 1943 the city suffered a great disaster. A convoy of vessels, some carrying ammunition, came into the harbor, but not before a message had been sent to the port authorities with the grave news that one of the ships, carrying a cargo of cotton and powder, was on fire. Through a negligence which is almost incomprehensible the ship was allowed to enter the harbor where, still on fire, she tied up at the docks. The fire services were summoned at once but it became evident almost immediately that the blaze could neither be controlled nor extinguished and that she constituted the greatest possible menace to the ships alongside, as well as to the wharves and the adjoining district of the town. The fire burned on, gaining in strength, for some hours of daylight after this fact was well established. There was ample time for her to have been towed out to the middle of the harbor, or even to the sea, and sunk, but, caught in some paralyzing web of official forms, no one would take the responsibility for giving the necessary orders—the vital signature of some senior official was unobtainable.

Early in the afternoon the doomed ship blew up, killing thousands of persons—firemen, stevedores, policemen, sailors, and a vast crowd of spectators who had been allowed to come near and watch the fire; the persons who were then nominally in charge had not even cleared the docks. This catastrophe was far more destructive than any but the greatest air raids. There was enormous damage to property over a vast area, thousands of people were injured, great numbers simply disappeared—nothing was ever found of them again. A sense of terrible calamity hovered for months over the port. Other places were experiencing explosions of like magnitude but here it was not only totally unexpected but also totally unnecessary.

In the months of inquiry which followed it was agreed that the cause was not sabotage but rather that the port and city authorities (all British) had somehow been so drained of initiative and common sense that in the temporary absence of the man who should technically have signed a certain form no one else would step forward and do the obvious and necessary thing, lest he endanger his job. What an outcry there would have been if the city had already been in the hands of Indians! How everyone would have blamed this on the faults of native character! It was perhaps time that we should be shown the fatuity of our boast of supremacy, in so unmistakable a way.

This extraordinary inertia manifested itself in other places and in different circumstances many times in the East during the war. One example was the development of the Bengal famine. This symptom was again manifest early in the war, when an Allied passenger ship was permitted to run into a mine in Singapore Roads in broad daylight, in the sight of many spectators. Those watching her were aware of her peril but were unwilling to take the responsibility of signalling to her. She touched a mine, blew up, and went down. It was as though the European, clinging to his proud attitude of superiority over the Oriental, vaunting his own ability to take responsibility, his own trustworthiness, had to suffer these falls to expose a fantasy. In each case the officials acted as though they were mesmerized. But in any event, it was too late now—the white man was passing from the scene of his former significance.

The Myriad Things

The universe is a lodging house for the myriad things and time itself is a travelling guest of the centuries. This floating life is like a dream.

Li Po

The Ambernath bungalows followed the same design as the officers' huts which had been put up by the hundred thousand all over India during the war years and were reasonably well suited to the needs of single officers who were out all day. They were supposed to cost very little to construct but were sold on a basis that made them very profitable for the builders. These flimsy little houses had laid the foundations of vast fortunes, it was said, and if the figures we were given were correct they were certainly a racket. The plan had been worked out on the idea that each officer should have a bedroom and bathroom and that there should be a veranda in front of the living rooms and the bedrooms. As they were only intended to be of temporary use, the workmanship was of the shoddiest possible quality. This was the only type of building for the whole of the factory personnel, as well as for the camp. For the camp such a plan was justifiable but the factory wives felt that they had been hardly used.

The superintendent had the most commanding house of any allotted to the factory people—boasting six rooms, each narrow and of regimental exactitude, behind them small dressing rooms and bathrooms, and with a separate cookhouse. We ourselves had five rooms, being just under the superintendent in privilege (each man down the hierarchy either had fewer rooms or they were smaller—in other details they corresponded exactly). Every single room had five wooden pegs hung high in a corner to take the officers' caps, and we all had garages though there were only two private cars in the whole colony. If we opened a window carelessly the sash came out in our hands, just as it did for an assistant foreman, and no one had screens or other newfangled, decadent improvements. Most of us had little glass—it had run out—so that half the panes were filled in with a sort of strong paper.

During the rains all our roofs leaked with equal enthusiasm. The rooms were very high and had canvas ceilings which went up to the ridgepole like tents. During the monsoon the ill-laid tiles let in streams of water which were caught in the canvas, causing it to fall in large balloonlike bulges till the flood finally worked its way through into the room below, where we put out pails to enhance the elegance of our drawing rooms. No one really minded this very much and we were well aware that it was a wartime factory, but it was exasperating to be exploited by contractors in this way and given such "amenities" as garages which the authorities well knew we did not need while denied even the comfort of a sound roof.

The floors were of rough putty-colored stone, laid in large blocks; the walls were unplastered colorwashed brick—both features in keeping with our desert and pleasingly cool and austere. Later on a plot was consummated to plaster the walls of our main rooms which, presumably, would be very profitable for someone but was probably of all household features the one we needed least. I for one did not even want it and resisted ferociously. We should, for instance, have had some protection from the sun that struck so fiercely across the pitiful verandas—none were fitted with jilmils and there were no blinds.

The first necessity was to find servants; everyone gleefully assured us that was next to impossible. Any intelligent domestic went to the camp and became a bearer, where the work was light and he could draw rations as part of his pay. We had no rations for our servants here—the famine subsidy had pertained only to Bengal. The cook was a treasure; but he would only cook. Dust poured in like air and a sweeper was imperative.

The morning after we arrived in Ambernath a sweeper came onto the veranda and salaamed—a young man, clean and strong, dressed in spotless white and with a Gandhi cap on his head. I was pleased to see such a presentable candidate after hearing that there were literally no unemployed sweepers in the whole area, so we soon came to terms. He told me that he must have thirty rupees a month but that he did not need a godown. That should have made me suspicious—how did he have a godown?—but I was a simpleton. The figure was high but wages were steadily rising and, as always, lagging far behind prices. While I considered, the aspirant sealed the bargain by rapidly darting over the house with a twig broom, throwing water on the bathroom floors and sweeping floods out of back doors—he was irresistible. I felt elated. Already a cook and a sweeper!

That evening, however, we met some of our new colleagues, who enlightened us about the sweeper. He was also their servant, they assured us, and worked for a number of other families on the estate as well, skirmishing about their bungalows in a hasty fashion and then moving on to other clients. This was actually a very good system but not common in the country—it seems absurd now that any of us should have minded. The price everyone else paid for this service was eight rupees a month, we were told; he generally came late and left almost at once, and sometimes omitted his errand entirely. He had a monopoly on sweeping in the station, farming out the sweeping of some of the bungalows to coolie women, whom he paid very little. His pride in his position was mounting; he was full of self-importance, we were told, and he must not be paid more than the usual rate. Looking back on this, I admire his enterprise—he was freeing himself from the downtrodden role of his kind. Before we had left Palta we had had such a good sweeper for a time that we had promoted him to be our bearer. He had proved himself perfectly able to do a bearer's work, being intelligent, clean, and civil. But the experiment had failed because none of the other bearers nor the vendors nor the other servants would accord him the authority and status of his new post—in the end we found him work in the army where there was more possibility of his being judged on his own merits. This man in Ambernath, whose character was very inferior to our Jharia's, was yet trying to solve his problem by working within his own sphere—he became a super-sweeper with a host of employees and had to be accorded some recognition. The trouble was that he was not only intelligent, he was also a good deal of a rogue.

The next morning we told him that we now understood the position and would only pay the local tariff. He was angry but still preferred half a loaf to no bread—and he had, besides, other ways of raising money. He collected from each of his victims enough to cover brooms and poles, if they did not have the equipment he liked—which was fair enough. I had been particularly careful to include in the wagon which brought our boxes from Bengal an extremely long bamboo pole, used for sweeping the high ceilings to discourage the active and enormous spiders. This was unloaded at the Ambernath bungalow, and immediately vanished from the veranda. The new sweeper said he had to have such a a long bamboo, and as ours could not be found, he collected two rupees from me, disappeared, and came back almost instantly with our own bamboo. We were all convinced of this crime but we could not prove it, as everyone had been inside doing something at that strategic moment and the precious reed had been imprudently left unguarded.

We saw less and less of the sweeper every day and soon engaged in his stead a comely young Mahratta woman. Tall and strongly built, she dressed herself in a careless and lavish way—a very full orange skirt to her ankles, a colorful scrap of veiling over her head, so adjusted that it revealed more of her large brown eyes and thick curling hair, her full, curving throat, than it concealed. Immense earrings gleamed through its transparent folds, her nose-ring was of silvergilt filagree, bangles tinkled round her shapely arms, heavy silver anklets banged against her small brown feet. She was fond of vivid colors—large red beads adorned her neck, a tight green bodice partially confined her swelling bosom. She was, withal, a perfect sloven, bringing in more dirt than she ever took out; she smelled of *pan* and garlic and she had a troop of naked children who ran after her up to the gate of the compound. But still, she did sweep, she was wonderfully good-natured and happy —and she was scrupulously honest. I never missed any of our possessions while she was there and I looked forward to her daily call because of her beauty and cheer—it was like having a gorgeous bird swoop about the house.

A "friend" often accompanied her, a neat, good-looking youth wearing a fez. She explained that he was her brother—he was most helpful for a brother, I thought. The arrangement did not last long; the irate husband appeared and exposed the other relationship. It had all been too good to last and the bright bird flew in no more.

We became enamoured of our desert home. I bought roses in the Bombay market and set them out in a round bed, and we went to Poona to buy lilies. We even sowed a strip of grass, four feet wide, all along the front of the house and created a rockery at one end. We built a low and curving brick wall to give some shape to our wasteland. When the monsoon came we put in oleanders and hibiscus, alamanders and morning glory—these clear and heavenly blue flowers were incongruously beautiful against the sandy and rocky confines of our world—I have never loved them so much.

In Bombay rationing of all sorts was in force and had been well maintained, so that it was possible to buy cloth at a reasonable figure. For the first time in India we were able to supply ourselves with curtains—and never had it been so necessary as in that slight house, so exposed to the sun. The five long windows opening onto the front veranda were soon shielded, and when in the late after-noon a breeze sprang up, looking down the house where the line of doorways formed a sort of passage, we could see the vari-colored curtains—white and Persian blue, the brown of the Indian prints—billowing and swelling in the wind like so many gaudy sails. I looked forward to this little ballet as the light airs of the evening arose and the worst heat of the day was spent—the spirits of the household revived and the banners seemed to partake of our gaiety.

On this side of the country winter brought no coolness. In the extreme and arid heat when fires broke out on the hills, low lines of flames ran over the plain, advancing, often, towards the station. None of our huts ever caught fire but the summer grasses burned right up to the edge of the compound, where lizards, snakes, beetles, and all manner of insects had already taken refuge. Then the landscape would be black and surrealist right up the rise of Cathedral Rock and its companion height, till the strong hot winds and swirling little whirlwinds had blown all the charred dust away, leaving the earth brown and muted, cracked with heat.

This was the winter of 1944, when the Allies went across Germany and the enemy began to experience the invasion which they had so often inflicted upon their neighbors. The retribution was just but it was nonetheless terrible to read of the flight of the people, already exhausted by the repeated raids on the cities—raids so much heavier and longer than England and Holland had endured. It was in the heart of this winter, in snow and sleet, not knowing which way to turn, that so many Germans fled their devastated homes; then I did not suspect how soon I would be hearing the stories of some of these refugees from their own lips. After the war, we were sent to Kiel and met people who had walked from Berlin and Magdeburg, from Dresden and Halle. Cruel and unrepentant though the Nazis were, the role of the avenger is one that a humane country is reluctant to assume. When the papers came in from Bombay on the early train and we read them on the veranda, looking out on that sere plain, their content seemed hardly credible.

We had planted fast-growing vines which made natural blinds for the verandas, so that we could sit out there early in the day and in the evening, watching the swelling-throated chameleons which had come to live and play among the leaves under the little pinkish flowers. These small creatures did not have the sweet and graceful ways of their cousins the lizards—they were of warlike, Prussian mien, suspicious, fierce, and aggressive. When they left the intricacies of the world of the vines and came down onto the veranda itself they would scuttle about, swishing their brittle metallic tails. Their backs were gray-green, their throats yellow, and their eyes stuck out of froglike heads. They were unfriendly but I had pleasure in them, they were such quaint characters to have sharing the bungalow with us. We got up early, the beds were hot and the rooms airless. After the mosquito curtains were looped up we went out onto the veranda hoping there might be a little freshness in the morning—and the first thing we saw were these chameleons. They took the place of the conventional robin that spring; weird as they were they were suited to the background of blackened fields.

Still that year spring was less of a travesty to us than it was to the people in Europe, where under the trees bedecked with delicate blossoms, through the green meadows where once you waited to hear the cuckoo call from the neighboring wood, now passed the spectacle of war.

It was evident that the war with Germany would soon be over; then how long would it take to deal with Japan? The politically-conscious Indians were looking at the world in another way—how soon would they be free from foreign control? Indian nationalism flourished. They had almost forgotten the Japanese; the wish to be rid of the Raj was always stronger and more desperate.

This feeling was intensified by economic distress. The value of the rupee had so declined that every person in the country was affected by it. Though profiteers had made fortunes out of the war, they were numerically so few that the general reaction was one of hard times, and hard times are excruciating in a country where conditions are always terribly hard. And this was in the train of a war which the vast majority never understood at all. The enlisted men of the Indian Army had had a good war. Very few had been sent to Burma and Italy or even up to Assam—they had drilled and trained and had enough to eat and enough to wear and something to send their families. Most of these men were really mercenaries, as the regiments with an old martial tradition were relatively few compared to the huge new army, and they were very susceptible to nationalistic indoctrination. It was now realized that once the hostilities were over there would be a great unemployment problem. Where would these millions of men in the army and in the ordnance factories find work? The war years began to look as though they had been both comfortable and safe for many people.

The agitators seized upon these problems and Britain's sins of omission and commission were magnified by constant propaganda. It was widely broadcast that poor suffering India was England's creditor and that that nation was not in a position to pay her debts —the money, they said, had simply been whisked away. There was no gratitude that Britain had saved India from the Japanese—it was felt that this menace had existed only because Britain was there. Certain shortsighted and tactless governmental policies aggravated these sentiments: little was done to encourage those Indians who were friendly towards Britain and trade was manipulated to the advantage of the United Kingdom. The Home Government in the hands of Churchill and Amery was naturally unpopular in India because these two men were so imperialistic and old-fashioned in their view of the country. Many individuals did little to pour oil on these troubled waters in their day-to-day relations with the other race. One incident after another, involving harshness and violence, exasperated the whole country.

The impasse between Congress and the Muslim League seemed hopeless—most vocal Indians felt that without recourse to arms they would never get hold of their own country. Every conference failed. The Muslims appeared always to be the favorites, but even they could not achieve the partition upon which they had set their hearts; the Home Government and Lord Wavell, the Viceroy, could not bring themselves to grant it. Mr. Jinnah had never been more arbitrary, more difficult, and more humored than in these months, but there was still no progress—the only visible result was the increased pressure within the country, where the days grew hotter as the monsoon drew near and the temper of the nation became increasingly exacerbated and dangerous.

In the midst of these troubles we escaped from our own particular framework, where little Ambernath was fairly smoking in its own heat, for a brief but glorious leave. We were able to fulfill one of Stanton's great ambitions—that of visiting the caves of Ellora and Ajanta in Hyderabad.

XV Hyderabad and the Caves

A brother, who lived in Chi-nan, hearing how I passed my time, wrote me some verses on the subject, and named my tower the Tower of Contentment, in reference to my knack of enjoying myself under all conditions. This, because I could roam beyond the limits of an external world.

Su Tung-po

Antiquity is unrolled before us.

P'u Sung-ling

AS THE FIRST STAGE of our pilgrimage to the caves, we went to the small and ancient station of Jalna in Hyderabad State where we had relatives who most kindly offered to keep the children while we went on south. Jalna lies a hundred and fifty miles east of Bombay and could then be reached only in a circuitous manner. It was necessary to go north to Manmad, on the border of Hyderabad, and there make a connection with a state train running on the narrow-gauge line of the Nizam. The passage from Bombay to Manmad took five hours—all one hot afternoon and evening. There were twenty-two of us crammed into our second-class carriage—seven of them children, all, fortunately, very well behaved. At Manmad we dined and at midnight caught a very tiny train which got us to Jalna at dawn. It was an exhausting trip, though fascinating, as all these railway journeys in India were, with their great range of passengers. However, we decided that if it were humanly possible we would avoid a return journey via Manmad, which had a particularly loathsome railway station and where every connection seemed to entail intolerable waiting.

The state train had no water and was bitterly cold—to our

astonishment, as it was already March and we were unprepared for anything but heat—so we were more than glad to reach Jalna where we were met by a fine *tonga* with a dashing horse, well bedecked with plumes and bells, who went through the dim bazaars in great style and finally turned into the drive of an old mission bungalow. Stanton's cousin was the doctor of the hospital here and knew all the area round about.

Before we set off on our adventures we explored the town which, though of small consequence in itself, yet gave some hint of Anglo-Indian history and maneuvers over a long period of time. Parts of the old wall and its round towers still stood in the bazaar, beyond the confines of the small, dusty cantonment where, set about with neems and oleanders, a mission and a garrison had been maintained by the British for over a century. A mission and a garrison! An epitome, a paradox of Western rule. The British Raj was, however, far more benevolent than any government the Indians had evolved for themselves. The garrison had been vastly increased during the war and a huge camp had gone up outside the town. Everywhere we went in this poor and obscure little town we met soldiers and lorries. The size of the new barracks seemed disproportionate to the significance of Jalna and its environs; in the constant discussions of Indian affairs which went on at the hospitable mission dining table we sometimes heard army officers wonder if the Raj might not be hoping to hold this great native state even if most of the country had to be given up. They thought the Nizam might welcome such a proposal—that he might countenance the great cantonment at Secunderabad and the lesser ones scattered about the state in return for the preservation of his own titular sovereignty.

We walked through some part of the new camp on our way to see the old cemetery on the outskirts of the cantonment. Though all the military equipment was modern and the huts exactly like ours at Ambernath, they were still using the same methods for obtaining water as had been in effect for hundreds of years. We stood for a long time beside a great deep well from which two oxen were slowly drawing up skinfuls of water, the precious cold water of the parched Deccan. The scene was entirely Biblical—the straining, great-horned beasts walking up a ramp as they turned the waterwheel, whose ropes brought up the black and glistening skins almost bursting with water, while round about were the dark, thin figures of the soldiers, who were seizing the dripping skins as they rose above the huge stones of the well coping, and shouting at the oxen.

The camp had swallowed up a great part of the *maidan* which had once separated the town and the graveyard, so that it was not far past the well when we came upon the small enclosure, which was surrounded by a low wall. There were almost no trees in it. From the short, dry grass rose only the unshaded tombstones of the young men who fell long ago in the Mahratta wars in the Deccan. Their wives and their infant children lay beside them. The memorials were simpler than those of elegant Barrackpore, as befitted this remote and lonely country district, but the tale they told was the same.

Here lay the Persian Interpreter to the Poona Subsidiary Force, killed in a Deccan War of 1818, when he was twenty-four. Here was an officer of the Madras Light Cavalry, "prematurely cut off by the Hand of an Assassin"; here a "surgeon," aged eighteen, poor child! The oldest person of the company was Alexander Speirs:

> Here lie the Mortal Remains of
> Alexander Speirs Esquire of Elderslie
> Arrived in India in 1805
> And serving his Honourable Masters
> with unwearied industry
> Acknowledged ability and eminent success
> Rose through successive distinguished posts
> in the political Dept
> To the High Station of
> Representative of the British Government
> at the Court of Nagpore.
>
> Died at JALNA on the 19th of March 1847
> in the 60th Year of his age and the 43rd of an
> Unbroken residence in India.

He had arrived in India when he was seventeen and had seen its entry into the British sphere firmly established though, happily, he missed the Mutiny.

In 1850, at the age of forty-three, a Major Horatio Nelson Noble had been buried here beside his baby daughter, Fanny Charlotte Emily, who had passed away the day before her father—they were not long separated. With what pride had his parents, in 1807, named him after the brilliant captain who was proving invincible at sea! It was all melancholy enough, in spite of the stalwart record of Alexander Speirs Esquire. There was one tall obelisk marked only "Carissima"—it seemed almost the most eloquent there. A Muslim gentleman who was wandering in the cemetery at the same time as ourselves, with equal curiosity but with less sentiment, remarked to Stanton that he found it strange that we should write so much on our stones, for, as he said, "There are no words for grief."

Aurangabad

Our cousins told us that we had best start our expeditions to the caves from the old city of Aurangabad, from which Ellora is twenty miles and Ajanta sixty. To visit the caves we would have to have passes for the adjacent *dak* bungalows, and would of course have to take our food and bedding with us, besides a servant. To make these arrangements we made a preliminary trip to Aurangabad and then came back to Jalna for our stores. We were given a letter of introduction to the Church of England Mission in Aurangabad and could not have been more kindly and hospitably received in it. The lady in charge of the mission school took us under her wing and made everything easy for us.

The Aurangabad train left Jalna very early in the morning and to have caught it from our cousins' bungalow would have raised difficulties. There were few *tongas* about at dawn and if one was ordered the night before it was doubtful whether it would come or not—the driver would certainly *agree* to come but his actual arrival depended on an elastic factor called Fate. While we were discussing this a friend of the family happened to be there, an official of the railways, who at once came forward and invited us to spend the night before our departure in his bungalow, which was very near the station. He did not know just when the Aurangabad train left but he agreed that it would be perfectly useless to telephone the station about it. It was ten to one that if we did no one would bother to pick up the instrument, and if this miracle did occur, whatever clerk answered would never find out what we wanted to know. The station staff, we were given to understand, were monuments to idleness and stupidity. However, Mr. Howard, our cousins' guest, was himself going to Aurangabad the day before we were and he promised to inform his servants about the train and they would tell us the exact time.

Mr. Howard had long been an employee of the state railways

and had a deep interest in the historical relics of Hyderabad; he was most knowledgeable about the caves and gave us much good advice about seeing them. After his decades in the country, spending long days under the sun inspecting the railway lines, he was burned almost black, but on these lonely expeditions he had developed very original and independent habits of thought. A patriotic character, he had joined up early in the First World War and gone to fight in Mesopotamia. The railways had made it a policy that none of their staff were to join the forces, taking the stand that they were needed where they were. When Mr. Howard returned he had had to pay the penalty for defying them and lost years of seniority towards his pension. He had married and lived with his family in this lonely station without any chance of promotion because of his youthful gallantry. His wife had found Jalna unbearable and had solaced herself with the forgetfulness found in the bottle. Finally she went back to England, taking the children with her. Mr. Howard was lonelier than ever, but not embittered; he blamed neither the railways nor his wife for their acts but undertook his minor duties with a philosophic zeal and an unflagging interest in the world around him. The offer to lend his bungalow to strangers was typical of him.

One evening in high spirits Stanton and I set off at dusk in a *tonga,* bound for Mr. Howard's bungalow, lulled by the driver's assurance that he knew just where Howard Sahib lived. As Mr. Howard had been in the town for thirty years and there were so very few European residents—almost none who were permanent except the mission and railway personnel—it seemed reasonable to believe the *tonga wallah*'s words, so we permitted him to drive us about in wide circles for quite some time before we realized that he had not the remotest idea of where he was going. The narrow, unlit lanes were difficult to negotiate and we were a long time stumbling about in the darkness before we finally found the house. Then a little *ayah* admitted us to an interior which Kipling would have found familiar. Like most of Jalna it was lit only by oil lamps. It had still pull *punkahs,* their wide surfaces spanning the little rooms. The sideboards, beds, and tables were of massive design in heavy wood but the chairs and small tables were of very beautiful, elaborate, slender cane-work, of a sort not seen today. There were many ornaments of figured brass and the walls were covered with photographs of the Howard children, who had left India when they were small. They were now grown men and women and had scarcely seen their father for many years. It was all very touching and I found myself becoming quite distressed on our host's behalf, so that I was rather glad when the obtuseness of the little *ayah* called our attention to other matters. Like so many Hyderabadis, as we were coming to realize, she seemed to have no sense at all.

We asked her at what hour the train would leave in the morning. "Howard Sahib told me to tell you that it leaves at five, so that I must call you at six bringing tea," she replied with perfect calm. To prove that this was so, she showed us the alarm clock which had been set at 4:30. She herself could see nothing incongruous in this and we decided that the safest thing was to assume that the train left at five, so we hastened to get under the enormous, old-fashioned mosquito net. It was all a mistake, as Mr. Howard afterwards told us, but we were not to know that as we hurried to the station before five the next morning, only to find that the wretched train left at six. The next hour passed quickly, as we paced back and forth in the darkness in the quiet that precedes a town's awakening. We had to step carefully to avoid the many poor travelers who were sleeping on the ground, wrapped in thin shawls. When at last the train came in it was so full that we were obliged to enter a small compartment holding two English officers in pajamas, who had only waked up enough to receive the trays of *chota hazri* which were being handed in. The one who was lucky enough to have the upper berth resumed his slumbers but the other, poor fellow, got up and dressed so that we could share his bench. In another two hours, when the sun was already hot, we came into Aurangabad, that almost forgotten city, with its Mogul heritage, its somnolent charm.

Aurangzeb's old capital is like a Chinese painting, in that the empty spaces are at least as important as those which are filled. The color of the city, too, is reminiscent of an old scroll painted on brownish silk. It still covered a wide area, partly confined by the old wall with its high and splendid gates. At wide intervals there were bazaars, mosques, public buildings, and the cantonment; but the greater part of the town consisted only of open uncultivated fields, where cattle wandered browsing beside the relics of the past—here a fallen cupola, there a trembling archway, mute evidence of former loveliness. The whole life of Aurangabad lay in the past, the faint memories of old splendors, the monuments of empire. Perhaps today it is quite different, but at that time in the deserted and almost forsaken former capital the dead seemed more evident and of more consequence than the living. The Moguls had made a strong, enduring imprint, interlopers though they were. After them who had concerned himself with this little city?

Through Aurangabad, skirting the wall, goes a river, almost dry for the greater part of the year, where *dhobis* standing in the stream bed beat clothes and spread the red and saffron saris to dry on huge black boulders which in summer are covered with rushing water. The very aridity of the present is another contrast with the halcyon days of old when, they say, the plain was plenteously watered by nine famous springs. Then no one needed to depend, as now, on the wells. One family had had the charge of caring for these sources, and when that clan died out five of the nine ceased to flow and are considered lost.

Huge old banyans shade the fields and ruins, lining the dusty roads with their deep cool shadows. Everywhere ranged herds of cattle. All Indian cities have cattle in the streets, even Calcutta and Bombay must play host to the sacred bulls, but nowhere, it seemed to me, were they so numerous as in Aurangabad. Buffaloes, cows, goats, even sheep (which are not so common) fed meagerly on the brown fields which separated one bazaar from another. To see this sleepy, stagnant Deccan town was to understand how cities come to be buried and lost. Here the past seemed to be slowly eating the city away, till it could be ready for the eager vitality of the archeologist.

The low rocky hills which encircle the town in a wide arc are now little more than windbreaks, though once they were of strategic consequence as outer defenses against the Pathan and the Mahratta. Twice dictators came here from Delhi, uprooting the nobles from the old capital, forcing them to leave their homes and the luxuries which were dear to them, in an attempt to break up the cabals of that ancient center of intrigue. In the fourteenth century Muhammad Tughlaq, "learned, merciless, and mad," made two attempts to bring his people away from Delhi to Devagiri (now called Daulatabad, a few miles outside Aurangabad), and in the seventeenth century Aurangzeb actually succeeded in doing so. The journey from Delhi over the Deccan was in the highest degree difficult and unhappy and many failed to survive it. In the new capital the courtiers felt themselves in exile; uncomfortable, resentful, wretched, many lacked the courage to resume the burden of life and the whole tomb-studded plain is a witness to the years that followed.

Aurangzeb, a Sunni Mohammedan, as zealous and bigoted as a fanatical Puritan, broke up the great Mogul Empire over which Shah Jehan had ruled, rather than share any of it with his brothers. Ambitious and treacherous, cruel and unstable, he had still enough qualities to be the last "great" Mogul. After Akbar the line had degenerated—both Jehangir and Shah Jehan were despots and steeped in pleasures, but the influence and power of the family were great enough to carry them on. Aurangzeb reacted fiercely to the atmosphere in which he was brought up and in which he found little favor. Most of his reign was spent on the battlefield. Harsh and ruthless as he was, his farewell letter to his son cannot but disarm the reader: ". . . I know not why I am or wherefore I came into the world. I have not done well for the country or its people. God has been in my heart; yet my darkened eyes have not recognized His light. . . . The army is confounded and without heart or help, even as I am. Nothing brought I into this world, and I carry out of it the burden of my sins. Though my trust is in the mercy and goodness of God, I deplore my sins. Come what will, I have launched my bark upon the waters. Farewell! Farewell! Farewell!" In the course of his career this emperor had showed none of this humility, but the dictators of the twentieth century have left no such message behind them.

He was revolted by the luxury and extravagance of his family and, as they were great builders, he wished to build nothing. The tomb of his first wife, who was buried in Aurangabad, is thus not due to her husband but to her son. The Bibi-ke-Maqbara is a small replica of the Taj Mahal, which does not mean that it is small in itself. Though of humbler materials than the marvelous tomb in Agra and lacking the jewels, it is a beautiful memorial, with the lovely mosaics and flower panels which distinguish Mogul architecture. It is faced with fine old plaster which has become as hard as stone, yet has a soft and gleaming surface. Because it was built by a son for his mother it contains the symbols indicative of that relationship, in accordance with Mohammedan tradition. On the pall lie peacock feather brooms and at the doorway hangs that strange mortuary offering of the bereaved son—strings of green glass bangles. The long and tranquil pool which led up to the building was lined at the season we visited it with phlox, stock, and other temperate blossoms which were reflected in the water.

Going out through the deep cool gateway, we were surprised to find nearby, in the shelter of the wall, two very small European cemeteries—one French, where the monuments have been so eroded that the names are no longer decipherable, and the other English. Here there were a score of graves, the usual testaments of youth: a girl-wife, the "pride and ornament" of her husband's life, a doctor called Eben Young of the Bombay Establishment, who had been laid here in 1816—part of this dusty corner's mute evidence of an alien culture which had struggled to preserve itself among the Moguls and the Mahrattas. What were they doing here on this remote plateau? They must have often asked themselves that question. Were they happy here? What a mystery it all seems! Though it was a land of remembrance these were the only graves we found saddening, our countrymen not scrupling to inscribe their deep despair. For the Muslim courtiers lying in the open fields, unconfined by the orthodox gloom of the graveyard, any shady kiosk seemed a haven, a refuge under the honest earth from a tyrannical and unhappy court.

The treasure of the town is its superlatively lovely water garden, a gentle masterpiece. It far outranks the Bibi-ke-Maqbara—it transcends artistry and achieves grace. The place is called the Panchakki and, according to legend, began long before either Tughlaq or the Moguls came to trouble the area. There lived then by the river a holy man who cared for the sorrows of the poor; being of a practical nature, he diverted a stream above its banks so that it turned a mill wheel, where he ground corn for the poor without charge. Beside the waterway he taught his disciples. From this beginning the limpid gardens were gradually created, the name deriving from *panch*, water, and *chakkhi*, wheel.

To visit the gardens we had to drive through the checkerboard of fields and bazaars which made up the city, till the *tonga* came to a dazzlingly white mosque lying on the river bank, its minars and whitewashed domes just beside a high gate of the old city wall. Passing under the gate and crossing a bridge, we were then directly before the first large tank of the Panchakki—an immense pool of clear green water which lies high above the river. At the roadside end of the pool was the noble mill wheel, with its vast sweep and high narrow tower, down whose side water fell in a light cascade; at the other end, well within the gardens, was an enormous and venerable banyan. Under the wide shade of this hospitable tree sat a few passersby who had turned from the glare of the sun to this open, quiet refuge where they could fill their water skins without toiling down to the riverbed and its scanty pools and then back up to the level of the road. Between the gardens and the road there was no barrier, it was as free and open as the old holy man had desired it to be and anyone was welcome to receive the peace which permeated the very air in this long strip above the river.

Stanton and I sat for a time on the terrace above the first pool, watching with pleasure the swift movements of some large and translucent gray fish which sported in it and turning from their play to see the fantasies of light which spangled the water falling from the tower. We could hear its showery sound above the soft gurgle of the water going into skins at the edge of the tank and the murmur of the old men talking under the banyan. It was noon, the hour when all who can hasten to some shuttered stillness, but here by this shaded expanse of green water we could not have been more soothed and at rest. The easy, unhurried presence of these old men, who had come with their water skins, accentuated the solitude of the Panchakki—they were so unobtrusive, so content to be there; for all their poverty they had access to these riches.

Behind this serene vestibule is a small mosque from which cool arcades, shadowy and silent, lead to a series of pools of quiet water, overhung by heavy trees and connected by small artful channels where streams of braided water may flow, with slight waterfalls breaking their passage. Long ago a vast hall had been dug out of the low rock cliffs above this river and over this stone chamber a long oblong tank built, rendering the study hall virtually an air-cooled apartment. The pool itself lies just above the river, parallel with the bank, and is enriched with many fountains, set in simple bases placed in ranks across its length, interlaced across its breadth. These provide little more than a discreet spray, almost like dew, which descends lightly upon schools of goldfish which sport in the clear depths of the pool. The water here was made the focal point of every scene, whether it appeared in the charms of falling crystals or as the glassy profundity of little seas. Where there is no dew, where for most of the year there is never rain, where the wells can fail, man has learned to cherish water, to rejoice in its every bubble, in every spray which catches the colors of the rainbow as it passes through the hard, dry air.

An enthusiastic curator had lately had all the little kiosks and arcades freshly whitewashed, bringing their curves into sharper relief against the intensity of the sky. He was planting roses and hibiscus, caring indulgently for the gray and gold fish, and looking after some beautifully illuminated Korans and other sacred Muslim writings. He himself lived in a walled-in corner of the arcade and told us that on moonlit nights he sat under his archway and fancied himself a Mogul emperor.

Hyderabad was a native state then, eighty percent of the population were Hindus, most of these Mahrattas and desperately poor. The ruling minority were Mohammedans and the ruler was the Nizam. It was everywhere evident that within the confines of the state anyone of any consequence was a Muslim—they rested in their privileged position and wore their authority with easy assurance.

Before we could visit the caves we had first to obtain passes from the Public Works Department in Aurangabad—these would enable us to stay in the *dak* bungalows near Ellora and Ajanta. To this end we called on the appropriate official in the city, an agreeable Muslim gentleman of a hospitable disposition who spoke good English. He invited us to drink tea with him while the passes were prepared, and to our surprise and pleasure sent a message to his wife asking her to join us.

We waited for the lady in her husband's office, a little room which contained a splendid chalk copy of the "Black Princess," one of the most beautiful of the Ajanta frescoes. The reproduction was done on vermilion paper, the color da Vinci used in his sketches, almost a brick tone, and was supported on an easel pushed well forward into a commanding position in the study. How often afterwards did I remember this picture! We were unable to find a copy of it anywhere for ourselves, but it was unforgettable. It represents a dark, devout girl who, her eyes shining with spiritual awakening, leans against a pillar apart from the crowd thronging the Buddha. Her pose is unique—she stands on one leg; the other, bent at the knee, rests on the slender pillar which also supports her head. The pose, odd as it sounds, is anything but ungainly—on the contrary, she is a figure of consummate grace. The fresco conveys the idea that her thoughts are wholly absorbed in the message of the teacher.

Our host was an enthusiast of the caves and seemed to us unlike the average Aurangabadi in that he was living in the present. So was his wife, who soon rustled in wearing the crispest of primrose yellow saris—no purdah trappings for her! This tall hook-nosed lady, handsome and strong, might well have walked off a Mogul print—I felt in her presence some hint of what those grandees who had occupied this plateau for so many generations were like. While she poured out the tea and gave us all little packages of *pan* to chew, she talked to us in fair English. Her outlook was a provocative blend of modernity and medievalism, typical of many Orientals today trying to bridge the immense gap that has opened before them and their children—that gap of the mêlée of the past and present, of East and West, this ideology and that ideology. The old paths were disappearing, and bemoan it as he may, the Easterner was driven to take note of the fact.

Mrs. Khan was not bemoaning anything, she was too practical for such vaporings. As the mother of six children, ranging in age from thirteen to one, she was much concerned over the problem of education in Aurangabad. She was reluctant to send the older ones as far as Hyderabad City for their schooling—she had herself studied there—and yet there was no place for them to go in Aurangabad. I asked her if she would not consider the girls' school run by the Church of England Mission, whose lady principal I knew to be both experienced and charming, as we were staying with her. Mrs. Khan replied with disarming candor that she had no objections to the children's attending a Christian institution, provided no attempt was made to tamper with their religious convictions, but that it was quite impossible for them to attend the mission school, as most of pupils there were Mahrattas and all the teaching was in that language. She and her family spoke only Urdu and English and could never stoop to the medium of these poor Hindus. There is a parallel to this situation nearly everywhere and I felt for her.

We went on to speak of food. I asked her if she had any difficulty in managing with the meager rations of sugar, oil and *ata* allotted (on paper) to all Hyderabadis. When she answered I understood that as far as she was concerned there was no rationing, though all she said was, "Of course we are lords here." The Mahrattas had driven the Moguls from the Deccan in the eighteenth century but the Nizam's forebears had managed to live on in a quiet way, avoiding both pomp and poverty, till, after Wellesley had defeated their old enemies at Assaye, they could openly regain their local power. The Muslims never abandoned the region and certainly never felt, man for man, a conquered people. The

Mahratta victories did not seem to have made the race feel sure of itself—they were too divided among themselves, too quarrelsome and disorganized. Certainly at this time in Hyderabad State they appeared to be wholly subservient, without even a tradition of dominance, whereas any idea of belonging to a conquered dynasty was incongruous in connection with the lady beside me, whose bold carriage, confident eyes, and assured manner all contributed to an air of calm security. A few of the children came in, handsome girls in saris, little boys in jodhpurs, delightful young people.

Our hostess, passing easily from the topics of *Kinder* and *Kuche*, then went on to literature. She had, she told me, just read her first "political book" in English and had enjoyed it very much. It was Wendell Willkie's *One World*. Mrs. Khan declared that she agreed with it absolutely, but I could see that in her acceptance of the necessity of One World there was the tacit condition that people like the Mahrattas remain as subject races. No question as to the propriety of this stand could be raised—it had not crossed her mind that her position was contradictory, and I did not enlighten her. We are all the same.

After obtaining the passes and arranging that the mission should find us a cook, we went back to Jalna to collect our clothes and some stores for the trips into the hinterland.

Ellora

When we came back to Aurangabad we were met at the station by our new servant, Soble, who had been recommended to us by the mission. He was a stout and placid person who had endured many journeys to the caves; he proved to be indispensable. He had with him the fresh provisions we would need—vegetables, fruit, and a leg of the delicious Aurangabad mutton. We had the dry stores—sugar, flour, and tea. The only flaw was that neither Soble nor we had been able to buy any bread. It was rationed both in Jalna and in Aurangabad, transients could only get it with special permits, which were troublesome, and we had hoped we could somehow get round this, perhaps by baking bread. But we had no oven, nor could we buy yeast. So we fell back on *chapattis*, which were tolerable. With mutton they were even quite good, but I could never rise to the heights which Stanton achieved by eating them with marmalade for breakfast.

We just had time for breakfast in the station before the Ellora bus started, so we hurried through an indifferent meal and then boarded our vehicle, which filled up fast and was well over-crowded before we left, long after scheduled time. A few seats were partitioned off from the rest by a curtain and here the first women passengers hid themselves, but soon this area overflowed and, pulling parts of their saris over their heads till their faces were concealed in a sort of poke, they had to find places among the men. It was past nine when we at last started and by then we were al-ready very hot, as the sun beat down on the thin metal roof of the bus and baked the victims wedged together underneath. An inspec-tor struggled in and slowly went through the list of passengers, checking us off on an immense complicated form, but he did not object to the fact that we had more people on board than any country interested in the safety of its citizens would permit. At long last we lurched off, to the accompaniment of much shouting from the occupants to their friends who were seeing them off and loud anxious inquiries as to the safety of this or that bundle lashed on the roof.

We then wound our way through the devious lanes of the bazaars, delightful to the eye but distressing slums. Many of the high old tenements with their fretted wooden lattices and frail long verandas were poems in line, the intricate balustrades accented by long lengths of brilliant saris hung over them to dry. There were many mosques and occasionally we saw the heavy arched gateways of the old city, with their wide benches lining the entrances, those stone benches for the gatekeepers and the messengers, and the enormous studded doors. The roads were crowded: men in large turbans, carrying huge flat baskets heaped with vegetables on their heads, and women with shining brass water jugs, borne in the same grand style, which gives the porter such a wonderful grace of carriage and gait. *Bhistis* went by with huge skins of water weigh-ing down their thin, stooping black shoulders. The shops were opening and the merchants already sitting cross-legged beside their wares on large white mattresses.

The bus stopped frequently and more and more people crammed themselves in, to the despair of the overworked conductor, a lean fellow in a khaki uniform and a red fez topped with a slight black tassel. But he did nothing to stop their entry. We had been given what were evidently considered the best places—near the front, with only a narrow bench before us, at right angles to our own seat. Opposite this hung the curtain of the purdah *log*. We soon felt that this was not at all the best position, as we were directly exposed to all the incoming hordes and the area within the right angle became an absolute Dark Hole, but it had been offered us in all courtesy and good faith, so we could not have tried to change. On this Hyderabad visit a great measure of civility and deference was shown us simply because we were Europeans—much more than we had received in British India. The attitude was, I suppose, indefensible per se, but it was pleasant after the hostility of so much of the country and the indifference of the rest.

A woman perched herself on the bench directly in front of us, her dirty sari squeezed against Stanton's bare knees—I felt thankful to be wearing jodhpurs. She had a baby in her lap and a tiny girl jammed in beside her. In her hand was a very small ornamented brass cup and she smilingly explained to us that the baby would probably be sick any minute now. As she was sitting crosswise to us we were not very advantageously located in the event of this horror—however, she was soon elbowed out by a man asserting his natural rights to a seat. Should a man stand while a woman sits? She retired to sit on the dirty and dusty floor down the small center aisle, where she suckled the baby with perfect calm, ignoring the throngs standing above her and the other unfortunates sitting with her in the aisle.

Meanwhile we had come to open country and were passing through wide brown fields, bounded on every horizon by sere ranges. The arches and domes of Muslim tombs were everywhere to be seen, the little white cupolas standing out against the dun backdrop: I constantly turned round to catch another glimpse of each graceful little edifice, till a hill began to arise in the distance and in a few minutes the whole scene was dominated by the fortress of Daulatabad.

This famous ancient fortress is built on a rocky height, commanding the plain for many miles around, with the garrison town lying at its feet. It is now deserted, its fascination unmarred by travesties of the present day. We were ourselves soon to explore it but on that day we went straight past and were almost at once ascending rising ground, scored with deep ravines. After a gradual climb of a few hundred feet we came to the walled town of Khuldabad, passed under its recessed gate and quickly left the little city behind us. Then we arrived at a fork in the road, where the bus stopped, and we disentangled ourselves, rejoicing, from its cramped quarters. It then lurched on its way while, as though out of the dust, some Khuldabad coolies appeared whom we engaged to carry our gear to the travelers' bungalow which, Soble told us, lay on the other side of the hill. It was by then almost noon and exceedingly hot.

The coolies hoisted our suitcases and boxes of food onto their heads and went rapidly up the unshaded road, past a number of *durgas* and *macqbaras*, till they disappeared from sight under a freshly whitewashed arch on the brow of the hill. We followed more slowly, feasting our eyes upon one remarkable mosque of very great beauty, dazzlingly white against the brilliant blue sky, which fronted the road with a pair of splendid green bronze doors—the dark, metallic Muslim green. Passing this building, which was surprising to us because we had not realized what riches were to be found near the caves of Ellora—riches quite apart from the tradition of the hillside—we came upon a plethora of guest houses scattered over the putty-colored hillside between the white tombs, which were as frequent here as they had been on the plain behind us. On the summit of the highest hill was a very small, very exquisite minaret and mosque, giving the impression of pure fantasy, something right out of a tale of the Djin. The hill we were climbing (which was actually very low) culminated in a bluff and here, overlooking a wide expanse of parklike country, was the Nizam's guest house, where the coolies had preceded us. There were so many isolated buildings to be seen, yet against the vast emptiness of the landscape they seemed no more than a feeble outcropping, the small efforts of man striving to make himself a place to lay his head in this hostile land where the sun burnt everything it could to dust and rock.

The Travelers' Guest House turned out to be a long, comfortable building but it seemed that we must take our choice between this rather ordinary accommodation and another place, called the Inspectors' Bungalow, which lay a few hundred yards further on. Having been on our way since five in the morning, when we had left Jalna, and after our culminating struggle up the hill in the full sun, we felt then that it was immaterial where we stayed so long as it was tolerably clean and cool. We cast ourselves down in long wicker chairs on the deep veranda and dismissed any idea of stirring an inch. This, alas! was a very great mistake as we afterwards discovered, for the Inspectors' Bungalow, despite its name, is the most poetic and romantic of resting places. Even today, nearly thirty years later, I cannot reconcile myself to the lamentable inertia which deprived us of savoring the pleasure of living under its domed roof and seeing the light filter through its filigreed lattices.

Soble, who had borne the heat and burden of the day with philosophic calm, went to work at once and produced some tiffin, after which we fell into a deep sleep till four o'clock. We had been given two bedrooms with Hindu baths, opening onto the immensely large veranda which overlooked the plain. If other travelers came, it was possible to divide it into several compartments by drawing curtains, but as we were alone we could rest in the echoing tranquility of an apartment some sixty feet long.

Fortified by tea, we set off on the half-mile walk which led to the caves, though the sun was still terribly fierce. We could not wait for darkness—the caves had to be seen in daylight or not at all. The path led downhill towards the plain, which had an inviting charm, like an estate, due to its wealth of large and beautiful trees. We were eagerly anticipating what lay ahead of us, though we were uncertain as to what it would be like—there were then almost no guidebooks or reproductions of the treasuries. We were the only living creatures in sight in all that great expanse of dry countryside, as we walked down the sere hill following a narrow path which led, apparently, towards nothing at all. Soble had simply indicated the direction we must follow with one vague wave of a brown hand. There was not a building to be seen, not a goat, not a cricket, not even a vulture, not one sound to be heard save our own footfalls.

The ground fell away from the path on our left hand—we were descending the bluff. Suddenly, when we had almost reached the plain, we saw on our right a very low stone roof rising from the hillside, supported by short pillars. The stone, which was almost black, was simply carved and the little shrine (as we imagined it to be) surrounded by a small ruined terrace. The roof was far too low to admit a person under it and, peering inside, we saw to our immense excitement and mystification that below it was apparently only a great black hole. Turning away from it, we walked a few steps across to the enclosing balustrade of the terrace and, quite unprepared for what we saw, started back in astonishment and wonder.

Directly below us, sunk in a deep chasm, stood the great Kailasa, its highest point rising to the level of our feet. From our little balcony we looked down upon its vast proportions, its crowning ornamentations almost straight before us—the oddest way to look upon a huge building for the first time. The base was too distant to see properly, and besides, we were too close to it to have a proper perspective—it was like discovering Notre Dame by walking towards it on the upper branches of tall trees. And indeed to come upon the Kailasa in this way was almost as startling as finding a cathedral hidden in the folds of these barren hills. I was glad I had not known what to expect, this time ignorance really was bliss. For a long time, forgetting the sun, we stood on the edge of the hill marveling. Then we returned to the little path and followed it down to level ground where we saw the entrance to the temple.

This lofty richly-carved stone edifice had been cut out of the living rock by sculptors and stone-cutters who had worked their way *downwards* from the top of the cliff: the apex of the building is at the summit of the bluff and our "shrine" is the roof of a clerestory which illuminates a hall below. A deep cleft, one hundred fifty feet deep by seventy feet wide, had been cut out of the stone face of the hillside; in this stands the main part of the temple —the central building and the great single columns of the courtyard, while in the surrounding rock sides are galleries and halls. In the whole temple there is not one piece of wood, not one joint or seam.

There are thirty-four rock temples at Ellora, excavated and carved between the second century B.C. and the fourth A.D., and extending for a mile and a half along the side of the hill. The first twelve are Buddhistic, from number thirteen to twenty-nine they are Brahminical, and the last five are of the Jain sect. (This order does not imply historical age.) By far the most imposing and elaborate is number sixteen, the Kailasa. If we had followed the motor road we would have seen the Buddhistic caves first, but by coming down the cliff path and almost falling into the Kailasa, we had inadvertently entered the sequence in the most effective way.

The cliff is of trap, in some parts gray, in others weathered to a velvety black. Here and there the paint with which the temples were once lavishly and brilliantly adorned has left faint traces of scarlet, ochre, or silver, but the general effect is now sober—gray and black against the dun hillside. All the caves are well lit by windows, clerestories, and archways, so that it is easy to study every detail, though exploring cave after cave is arduous because most of them consist of several stories which are reached by high flights of stone steps. The Brahminical caves are chiefly concerned with Shiva and most of their statues and bas-reliefs center about the various legends of his miraculous career. The Buddhistic caves are, of course, devoted to the life of Gautama Buddha and the rites and practices which have been appended to his teaching. The Jain caves are most intricate and elaborate, heavy with carving. This religion is an offshoot of Hinduism and to the outsider as involved and complicated as are these temples—the central themes never became clear to us. They suffer also from their location, for after seeing twenty-nine rock temples the visitor, however ardent and curious, is apt to falter before ascending the last five.

That first afternoon we gave to the Kailasa, which is named from "Kailas," the symbol of the earth, the mountain of Brahminical imagery. There is no temple among the thirty-four to compare with it for sheer magnificence and earthly pride or for its extraordinary quality of surprise. On the right facade of the entrance is a famous yet startling bas-relief which depicts Shiva dancing on the earth, a conventional pose for this god, who treads carefully lest he slip from his narrow pedestal. The head is in profile—it is one of the representations best known to Westerners, one recognizes it at once. It is full of motion, grace, and power. The unknown sculptor, the dark artist working here at the base of the cliff in strong sunlight centuries ago, caught every suggestion of free yet controlled and strong action—one feels that in another moment the pose will change to another of equal grace before one's eyes.

The main body of the temple is adorned with the usual images of the Brahminical legends: huge friezes of Shiva meeting Brahma, of Shiva alone, of Shiva with his wife Parvati, of Vishnu, and of Kali, the terrible goddess of destruction. Aside from its basic construction, the interest of the place lies in these studies—the rooms themselves are entirely subordinated to the ornamentation. All parts of the temple are open to the air with wide, generous windows and frequent open doorways—it is a comfortable place to be during the heat of the day. The rock surfaces are somewhat weathered and there has been some vandalism, but the effect must still be much as it was in the first centuries of our era. In that dry air little has crumbled away; though the priests and the pious throngs, the flower petals and the stir of life have gone, though the caves seem now entirely secular, yet the Hindu religion retains its hold on the mind of the country, as enduring, apparently, as the rock itself.

The other tourists we encountered here were all Indians, but as far as we could see they did not visit the caves in the spirit of reverence—they were interested in them only artistically and as historical sites, since they were not in use as temples.

Around the main building of the Kailasa runs a high dramatic frieze of elephants. Each is in a significant pose, or holding an object of symbolic importance, such as the lotus. Flanking the temple are two lofty columns, each resting on a colossal elephant, majestic and calm. This splendid beast, so pleasant, helpful, and sagacious in life, lends itself admirably to statuary and design—one felt that the artists must have thoroughly enjoyed working on the frieze.

The mythological themes are constantly repeated in great scenes and small—the poses of the gods are conventional but often very graceful. Each part and every inch of the main building is encrusted with ornamentation up through the three stories, each smaller than the last, and terminating at the top, on the level of the hillside, with a Shiva *lingam*.

On an exterior wall of the building is a large bas-relief of Shiva and Parvati experiencing an earthquake—an admirable study. The phenomenon is very exactly depicted: they are sitting on the earth, while under it is the notoriously tough and disagreeable demonking Ravana, who is shaking it with all his might. Parvati, frightened and agitated, clings to a perfectly calm and undisturbed Shiva while a small maidservant dashes off in a panic. (The earthquake is drastic enough to alarm most *ayahs*, Ravana exhibiting great strength and brute force as he humps the earth about.) The figures are beautifully grouped and their flying draperies accentuate the wild movement of the scene. The stone is rough, the strokes of the chisel apparently crude and careless, but the effect is masterly.

After seeing all this, we turned to the vast hollowed chambers which lie in the cliffs that embrace the central building on three sides. For a moment we hesitated to leave the open air and the wide blue sky to go into the gloom and silence of the galleries, with their immense tableaux of alien gods: there was something a little repellent about them, until familiarity rendered the sinister less obtrusive. The cold, rough stone of the walls, ceilings, and floors has been so simply hewn that there are almost no smooth, flat surfaces—there is everywhere a Rodin type of background. Only the thresholds and the floor before certain favorite friezes have been worn smooth and black by the passage of bare feet over the centuries. On the ground floor, which is only a little above the level of the outer courtyard, are three long connecting galleries with windows which look out upon the elephant frieze and the columns; above these are large halls reached by outer or inner stairways—the latter very dark and damp after the heat without.

These galleries contain, in my opinion, the most interesting and splendid bas-reliefs of the whole Kailasa. There are in them panels of great size devoted to Shiva, depicting the important moments of his earthly sojourn. He is always shown as a tall and slender god of Praxitelean proportions and of great grace and strength, supporting his many arms in such an easy and natural manner that eventually they seem no longer superfluous. No one could have portrayed the arms in that way who did not feel that they were an enviable physical attribute. Parvati is always made on a much smaller scale than Shiva, as befits the consort. She is the epitome of feminine grace for the time, with the tiny waist, minute feet and hands, and the beautiful round swelling bosom which is *de rigueur* for the beauties of Ellora and Ajanta.

The themes are limited: the marriage of Shiva and Parvati, their affection for one another, a quarrel, a game, Shiva's dance, and Ravana up to his old tricks with the mountain. A few are not so purely trivial and domestic—we see Shiva spearing different demons and saving his devotees from Yama, the god of death. The appeal of this god seems here to be on an entirely earthly plane—the temple, though a wonder of art and curiosity, carries for the outsider no spiritual message whatsoever. Shiva, with his greater size, his beauty and strength, dominates every tableau. Beside him is always the graceful Parvati and grouped about them the attendant figures the story demands—fairies, servants, worshippers, demons. Both Shiva and Parvati wear elaborate high headdresses, a girdle, and a wispy bit of drapery for a skirt. Every one of the carvings is remarkable for its vivacity and grace, its air of suspended animation, quite unlike the repose of a Greek stele. The great panels are perfectly balanced and planned. What artists designed this structure? Who executed it? One is full of wonder—it is like the building of the medieval cathedrals in Europe in the anonymity and the exuberance of the execution and the success of the edifice.

The pearl of the collection is at the extreme end of the north gallery, where it has a commanding position as the eye falls upon it from a far distance. In this lovely scene, which tells no story and is of the most absolute simplicity, Shiva is shown standing beside Parvati. Both figures are in easy and natural poses, expressing in their gentle manner the most beguiling, sweet affection and calm. In this last study the limbs of Shiva and Parvati are lightly chiseled in the rough gray trap, showing scarcely any delineation of muscle or drapery, but the slight cuts of the sculptor's tool have suggested just enough. Though the work is done without any apparent perfection of detail or finesse of line, and in this respect cannot be likened to Greek sculpture, yet the effect is superlative. It appears as light as air, though wrought in the roughest of freckled stone, and the facial features, blunt and crude, assume aquiline elegance and majesty, linked with the bliss of delighted affection.

On the other side of the court in an upper chamber devoted to the Five Goddesses (and lit by that same clerestory down which we had first peered) are two remarkable seated figures of Parvati. Her hair is here dressed in Grecian curls and worn high on her head; and in her manner she suggests that once away from Shiva she is herself something of an independent character. She sits cross-legged on a lotus, slender, supple, royal, and on her face a truly heroic expression of freedom. Here she is a lovely woman and much less earthy than most of the figures of the Hindu caves.

The next day we began at the beginning and went through the Buddhistic caves. These seemed to us morally superior to the Brahminical in that they appeal to thought and spiritual ideas, however imperfectly understood, rather than to the violent and sensuous conceptions of the other faith.

Of the Buddhistic caves only two—number ten and number twelve—are considered "important" but most of them, even the least pretentious, have a certain quality of sincerity, of dignity, of earnestness. I felt that monks who lived here so long ago must very often have been both gentle and inspired and have genuinely longed for enlightenment. These caves have not the rich ornamentation of the Brahminical shrines, being as a rule more remarkable for their simplicity and use of space than for any particular bas-reliefs or sculpture. The columns left by the stone-cutters to support the ceilings are here not the elaborate, encrusted pillars of the Kailasa and its satellites, but generally only squarish supports with plain capitals, everything showing the marks of the chisel. Sometimes they are slightly carved, in a way that suggests the old temples of the Nile. A number of these caves were intended to be used only for study and contemplation and are quite bare save for low stone tables, elevations in the stone floor left to hold the sacred writings. In some, small cells had been dug into the walls as dormitories—

extremely uninviting bedrooms almost without light or air, as they have no windows except for tiny openings into dark corners of the main hall. Stuffy in summer, freezing in winter, they were presumably well suited to the monastic temperament.

There is only one important figure represented—the Buddha. He appears with his few attendants in almost every cave, as a rule in a recessed alcove at the back. Roughly cut, but with a very considerable beauty and an indication of spiritual force in the sweetness and repose of his expression, he casts a benign influence over his temples, in marked contrast to the other caves of the cliff. The images of the Buddha are much larger than any of the Shivas—like the enormous ones to be found in the temples of China. These at Ellora date from the early and purer days of the faith and it is evident from these monuments that at that time the religion was not degenerate.

Buddha is usually attended by Padmapani, standing on his right holding a lotus, and Vajrapani on his left with the *vagra* or thunderbolt. There are occasional *vedas,* or plump, pleasant little fairies rather on the order of the *apsarases*, with lovely feminine contours and swirling if scanty draperies, and sometimes disciples. There are several portrayals of the deer sermon, the St. Francis story, showing the animals running to Buddha. In a few caves Buddha is represented in multiple panels, in the various attitudes with which he experimented in his efforts to find the positions most favorable for contemplation, according to some legends. He is shown with one hand lifted—the teaching position; with his eyes closed—when he is being tempted; and with the thumb and index finger of the right hand holding the little finger of the upturned left, the legs crossed and the soles of the feet turned upward—the most familiar of all his postures. Generally he is seated on a lotus. He is almost always of heroic size, his expression mild, and his thoughts apparently above the earth, though benevolent towards men.

But to the two "important" caves. Number ten was a great artistic surprise. After the simplicities of the first nine we found ourselves in the nave of the first cathedral in history! The long, narrow roof is arched and ribbed—we almost felt within a whale, looking up at the ribs. A narrow aisle surrounds the nave, separated from it by pillars, while at the end, instead of an altar, is a large round support in the form of a lotus holding a huge Buddha. This form of hall is known there as a *chaitya*. Where the ribs terminate above runs a wide frieze of bas-reliefs and at the end, above and facing the Buddha, is a gallery for a choir. The acoustics of this little hall are remarkable—every whisper resounds and reechoes. It seemed so like a church after the temples we had been observing that we could not resist singing while we were in the gallery. Every note boomed and thrilled against the arches, the Doxology and "Oh Come All Ye Faithful" seemed at once to reduce the image of the Buddha to a poor heathenish idol instead of a work of art, and our guide was perfectly astonished at our behavior. He did not expect his victims to react so strongly to *his* important cave. (There were few guides then at the caves and they were unsophisticated creatures, knowing little of the treasures to which they led us.) In the well of the rocky courtyard outside the *chaitya* there is a spring of pure cold water which seemed to us in keeping with the grand old hymns.

Number twelve is a superb temple—the best of the thirty-five, we thought. It consists of three stories built above a front court, with small chambers on the side. One of these rooms is a perfectly charming little study, lit only on the courtyard side, the walls and low ceiling much blackened with lamp smoke—how long ago did those lamps flicker here! One wall is chiefly occupied by a most graceful group: the two attendants of Buddha and one of their wives. Padrapani is in the center with his wife beside him and Vajrapani on his other side, all easily seated, in a smiling, contented, harmonious mood, beautifully balanced. The central figure is considerably larger than the others and has one leg swinging down, the other tucked up. The carving, as usual here, is not remarkable for any particular detail, but as a unit not one stroke of the chisel is wanting or is false. A small Buddha faces this trio and a fine lotus is set into the ceiling.

Going up the stairs you pass a small bas-relief—perhaps a foot square—of Buddha setting forth from the paternal palace on his horse with two attendants—a little masterpiece.

The hall above is divided by massive, plain, square pillars into five wide corridors, running parallel to the courtyard. At each end of the aisles so formed—that is, at the far sides of the room—heroic seated Buddhas face each other, each pair identical, but each pair in a different pose. They are, as usual, abutting from the rock, roughly done as Rodin would have had them, all expressive of dignity, goodwill, and thought. At the end of the room, facing the courtyard but separated from it by the width of the five aisles, is an alcove for the main Buddha. Before him are many figures, chiefly disciples, of whom there are fourteen men and twelve beautiful women whose lovely forms and swelling bosoms suggest the goddesses of the Hindu caves, but their faces are modest and devout. This temple seemed to us the most worthy of study and praise of the whole series—the magnificence of the Kailasa pales before its austere grandeur and simplicity.

Then we turned again to the Brahminical series. The Kailasa has no rival among them; some, indeed, are quite insignificant, hardly more than a single room to be reached only after scrambling up the cliff face. A few of them have rather interesting *nundies* (the figure of the sacred bull) in the forepart of the cave. Every single one works up to and terminates in the final object of worship, the phallic symbol of the Shiva *lingam*. After the calm piety of the first caves they were a depressing contrast, always reiterating the lamentable step India took in yielding to the domination of the Brahmins, rejecting the faith relatively so much more enlightened. In the fifth and sixth centuries A.D. Buddhism was growing so rapidly in India that it seemed as though it might well become the major religion of the country: this so alarmed the priestly caste among the Hindus that they mustered what power they had and succeeded in stamping out their gentle rivals. They did this by persecution and ruthless aggression and the Indians chose the "worse rather than the better reason," paving the way for centuries of avoidable miseries.

The thirteenth cave has no features worthy of note and the fourteenth emphasized this prevalent feeling of degradation, following, as it does, so soon after the dignity and worth of the great Buddhistic cave known only as number twelve. Number fourteen is a poor little temple of crude carvings, the Shiva figures particularly base. At the back of this simple one-storied cave, at the right, is a large wall space depicting the Five Goddesses and near them the figures of Yama (death) and Kali (destruction). These two surpassed anything I have ever seen in the way of imagery of evil. Their cadaverous, stooping forms and avaricious sadistic faces were, considered as sheer art, of the most astonishing power and perfection of execution and have surely never been bettered in their sphere. Bosch, the Breughels, some of the Spanish representations of hell, Gustave Doré in his more fantastic moods, were yet incapable of such representations of pure evil. These reliefs must have struck terror and dismay in many a simple heart.

Then came again the Kailasa. After that the most interesting temple is number twenty-nine, a truly delightful and original cave. It was dug out of a curve in the cliff, down which, during the rains, a waterfall plunges. Even during the dry months its situation is impressive, as a vast amount of light streams in through the wide doorway built to look out upon the water. The cave is on one level only, hollowed out high and deep into the cliff. Its immense hall is supported by the usual strong, ornate pillars common to all the Hindu caves (differing in this from the simpler type in the Buddhist caves) and is devoted to deities and legends not honored in the other temples. A gorge was artificially excavated on the other side of the hall from the course of the waterfall, so that daylight pours in from both sides. Though the shadowy coolness of the temples is welcome and pleasant in the fierce heat, yet it was a cheerful and surprising thing to enter one cave which was not dark.

Here the theme of the "guardians of the gate" is treated with great elaboration. These *dvarpala* are common to Hindu temples: the Jiya and Vijaya. Here there are four pairs, each set identical, all of heroic size. In the center of the hall is a square shrine with eight guardians flanking it, the strong light beating in upon them. When the rains bring a river over the cliff, how this cave must reecho to the thunder of the falling water! On the walls are a few odd Shivas and *apsarases* but the most interesting statue is of Sita— the only representation of this goddess in the whole of Ellora. She is on the side of the great window where the waterfall finds its way, with light air wafting about her, illuminating her lovely and grace-ful person—she is sensitively wrought, an idealized gentle maiden. Near the water, too, is an enormous mill wheel and two huge sac-rificial hearths.

The last five caves along the cliff came far too late for our enthusiasm. We were too tired to study them, too sated with what we had seen, and, as always, too baffled by the ideas of the Jains. Two of these temples are somewhat like small Kailasas, in that they have a main building rising from a central courtyard with carved surrounding galleries and halls. The work is intricate and elaborate but between our exhaustion and ignorance we were uninspired by it. As we went through they were being visited by a score of Indian soldiers, big, strapping fellows in Rajput turbans who leaped and clattered up the stone stairways while I drooped at the thresholds. We had given the caves three days. Tourists staying in the luxuri-ous hotel which Aurangabad boasted (to everyone's surprise, as there seemed little demand in wartime for a really good hotel in that small city) would motor out from the town and give the caves an hour. To see them well would demand a long stay.

On the day we took our cursory glimpse at the Jain treasures we walked back on the road till at the Kailasa we met Soble, whom we had told to be there with lunch. He had brought us our rough black goat's-hair blanket and some delicious cold mutton with *chapattis* and beans. We stretched the blanket out on the floor of the Shiva gallery, looking down towards the wonderful scene at the end, and in the coolness and quiet of the stone hall ate our meal, rested, and talked in that endless conversation which is the mainspring of a happy companionship. Near this cave is a fine spring of icy water, so we lacked nothing. Afterwards Stanton went away to pore over some of the carvings again, but I lay still in the galleria, in the shadows of that ancient rough hall, content to gaze only at what met my eye and to ponder upon the dramas that lay behind the creation of these caverns.

The Charms of the Hillside

That night we slept soundly and woke refreshed, ready to explore the delights of our immediate neighborhood—the mosques and the tombs, and the Inspectors' Bungalow of the prosaic name and the bewitching interior. The character of the Nizam's rest house had changed while I was lying prone on the floor of the Kailasa—a large Indian family had at that hour arrived to share it with us. When we came back in the evening we found a vast curtain dividing the veranda into two parts and small black-eyed children roving the gardens, like little flowers in their gaudy silks. They were attended by several *ayahs* and bearers. Soble told us that a *taluqdar* (a state official) was the father of these young visitors; for the place and the time this was a News Feature, and our cook was pleased to be the first to break it to us as he served dinner on our diminished veranda. Our share of this apartment was still a large room and perfectly adequate to our needs, but it takes no great while to feel that a veranda *must* be sixty feet long or else one is cramped. In a few hours man adapts himself easily to a higher standard of living, whereas he is never really reconciled to a lower one. We were at the same time rather amused than otherwise at the turn of events, while the consciousness of having a person of importance under the roof infected our erstwhile somnolent and quiet home with the bustle of affairs and of sycophancy. The low cries of the babies and the murmur of conversation had no effect upon us after our great days at the Caves and could not have kept us awake had they been ten times louder. We had no encounters with our neighbors in the morning, before we strolled out to enjoy ourselves in a far less strenuous manner than the temples had demanded as we rapidly stepped up the centuries into our beloved Mogul architecture.

The Inspectors' Bungalow lay at the back of a garden which contained a number of fine Muslim tombs, so much an ornament to their surroundings that they did not depress the spirits—on the contrary. Our only depression arose from our deep regret that we had not stayed here—I could not reconcile myself to having missed the pleasure of seeing it by lamplight.

It was a long, low, whitewashed building surmounted by three domes, another example of the Persians' comprehension of the type of architecture best suited to this dry and sunbaked climate. Here again we saw the repetition of arches, domes, and colonnades, the lines broken by the fretwork of lattices. Under each of the three vast arches which commanded the front of the bungalow was an enormous double door, all leading into the one very large long room which almost comprised the house. This hall was divided lengthwise by having the back portion a step higher than the part near the doors, the dais being separated from the lower floor by three heavy square pillars which rose in a series of diamond buttresses in order to support from within the three domes which had been enclosed by flat ceilings. The three entrance arches had lattices above the doors and all the windows were latticed so that no light could enter which was not soft and subtly shaded.

The walls were recessed at intervals by little arched niches designed to hold a lamp or a book. There was no furniture—had we used it, a few deep cane chairs and a table would have been fetched for us. Properly furnished, the room should have had only carpets and low tables. The stone floors, the white walls, the height of the irregular ceiling, fortified by the diamond buttresses, the unbroken simplicity, and the great size of the room, all made for quietness and reflection. By night, when the oil lamps were brought in, they must have cast entrancing shadows.

Four very small rooms opened off this chamber, bedrooms and bathrooms; the persons using the house were intended to spend their time in the poetic elegance of the hall. I felt there a great happiness and have always been able to recapture every line of it in memory.

Coming out of the garden, we had only to choose where we would wander on our hillside and which tombs we would visit. They are here in great numbers and, incongruous as it sounds, are of great charm. There was something here of the peaceful unidentified little Chinese mausoleums which used to lie at the base of the hills in the Yangtze Valley country—nothing ornate or voluble. If there must be a "grave culture" this is a much better sort than that of the crowded cemetery. The more pretentious of these Ellora Mogul tombs were set in little gardens, hidden from the world by high walls and heavy domed gates. Within these portals were benches offering rest and shade to the weary pilgrim—the gate itself is a room. Beyond it are arcades and, in the larger tombs, recessed verandas with deep arches where it is possible to spend the night. In the sun-baked courtyards roses and oleanders had been planted; beneath them were generally a few minor graves, little more than stone slabs. Within a separate building, of a single white dome, was the burial chamber. Sometimes there were two or three of these single domes in a biggish garden, everything whitewashed and still, the bright flowers in bloom and a feeling of solicitude and shelter about it, in happy contrast to the barren heat without the walls. The enclosures are small but never cramped—they have a singularly peaceful and easy atmosphere.

One particular garden which we visited that morning was full of a covey of Mohammedan women, completely swallowed up in their *burqas*, chattering to each other and apparently thoroughly enjoying their outing. They were surrounded by their children, who were brilliantly clad. When we entered they were clustered— the women looking like big, bunchy fowl—at the small porch door of the main grave, waiting to go in. As soon as he had espied us, however, in spite of our protests, the old, old, older-than-old caretaker, who seemed to have some priestly standing, at once shooed the ladies away, giving us precedence. Waving two peacock-feather brooms over us he blessed us and then bade us remove our shoes. We were then allowed to go into the tiny circular room which was almost entirely taken up by the sepulcher. The grave itself was covered with a very handsome saffron-colored pall on which marble weights, flower petals, and peacock brooms had been carelessly disposed. Around the circular wall were little recessed niches holding a few old books and from the high lattices came a dim light.

The large mosque just below the hill, which we had seen in passing when we first came to Ellora, was probably the most interesting building on the hillside and we soon left the little gardens behind us and made our way toward it. This mosque—that of Zahkir Baksh—we found to be one of the most captivating places in that whole enchanting, and enchanted, countryside. As soon as we stood before its wonderful green doors we felt as though we had somehow entered a romantic dream, as though we were entering the *mise-en-scène* of a Moorish legend.

At the top of a flight of wide steps we took off our shoes, still standing in strong sunlight before the heavy, studded, azurite-colored bronze doors, which make such a note of surprising color against the white of the building, the dun of the earth, and the blue of the sky, all of which we accepted without conscious thought. Then we went lightly in under the cool, deep gateway where watchmen and servants were reclining against the stone, dreamily passing away the hours undisturbed by any rumors of a war which was convulsing half the world, by the struggles of their own tormented country, by inflation, by the heat, or by any local problems. They roused themselves just enough to salaam and look mildly affable as we went past them, collecting one lotus eater as a guide.

There are two courtyards in this mosque, the first, directly before the entrance, of very wide proportions and shaded by two immense trees. Thence the way leads up a very high, wide flight of stairs and through a second gateway of three wide arches. In the second and smaller courtyard, which lies above the first (being further up the hillside), are the small tombs of Zahkir Baksh and his mother. The paving stones at their entrances are copiously bespattered with tiny fragments of bright tiles and semiprecious stones set haphazardly into a neutral background—an unexpected little carpet of childish decor here among these noble, silent courts, the soaring minarets, and the grandeur of the gates. Such was the apparent sanctity of the tomb itself that we were not allowed to enter it but could only peer into the dim interior. Here had been arranged a tentlike canopy of old brocaded draperies, which, fastened to the center of the inner dome, fell in pale, musty, golden folds around the sepulcher. This was, as usual, weighted with little marble blocks, whose solidity made the rose petals and bright feathers which had been tossed beside them seem even more transient and reminiscent of the theme of "dust to dust"—though I do not know if the Muslim would interpret these symbols in such a way.

The doors of the tomb are of repoussé silver, finely wrought into an ornate floral design, and exceedingly handsome in a lavish rococo style. The artists and architects of this mosque had evidently been particularly interested in doors. Could they, possibly have known of the beauties of Florence, of the work of Ghiberti? We could not find out from any of the languid servitors when the place had been built, but it did not seem very old and might well have been constructed after the glories of the Renaissance had been related to the Indian courts by the rare travelers of the sixteenth and seventeenth centuries.

The maternal tomb had at its low doorway the symbolic, strangely frivolous green glass bracelets sanctioned by custom, fastened here in shining bunches which, catching the strong light, shimmered and sparkled. In the courtyard itself was the memorial of a humble retainer, his stone slab supporting a grotesque scaffolding of a few sticks lightly tied together and bedecked with faded garlands of marigolds. In many of these rich *durgas* the servants of the departed lie under such extraordinary monuments, presenting the same sort of contrast that one finds in a Shakespearean tragedy— the subtle eloquence of Hamlet beside the earthly profundities of the gravedigger, the sweet lyrics of Juliet and the vulgarities of the Nurse.

One of the great beauties of this building lay in its arcades with their slender, swelling arches, cherishing the precious shade which lined part of both courts. One of them concealed in its dim length a long line of hanging lamps whose intricate chains had been carved from stone; when lit the effect must have been entrancing. Crossing this arcade we went down a flight of steps to a pool which ministered to the needs of the community who lived in the mosque, though the main water supply was outside. Without the high crenelated walls (in certain ways the place resembled a small fortress) was a large and very deep pool, carefully bricked in and covered with a canopy. When we saw it, in the arid spring, the treasured water was quite twenty feet below the surface, but later in the year one might have had the pleasure of seeing it brimming over.

Above the great gateway of the main entrance the most delightful part of the mosque is to be found. Here, just under the three main domes, is an airy enclosure called the Howah Mahal or "Hall of the Winds." Lined with stone benches, it has at its four corners very small domed cupolas and minute fretted balconies, whence, fanned by the shaded breezes which come through the open arches on each side, one may look out upon the charms of the mosque or on the wide vistas of the countryside. From here, too, one can stroll directly out onto the flat roofs of the arcades. We climbed up here by a narrow, steep stairway which runs up inside the wall; having arrived, we were so entirely captivated with it that we decided to go no further but to spend the rest of our day within its arches—we knew there could be nothing lovelier in the whole treasury of the district. True to its name, it seemed almost to float above the world and it was perfectly private—no one could look into it, though in proper oriental style we could here see out without being seen. We stretched ourselves out on the long stone couches and decided that we had found our earthly paradise. Between the heat and our own thinness and our becoming so accustomed to Indian ways, we felt it now no hardship to lie upon smooth stone. There were a few slight niches in the walls; we put the two little books we had with us in two of them and felt at home. It was all so airy and light that the years had brought with them no mustiness; by its own sweetness the Howah Mahal maintained a foothold in the present. A mosque is a much more intimate and practical building than most churches, certainly than most churches used to be. It provides, in its own fashion, both for this world and for the next, for the past and for the future, for the devout and for the worldly, and does not trouble the traveler for his reflections on these scores. We were assured by our guide that we were perfectly welcome to stay here as long as we liked and only wished that we were able to do so. Stanton handsomely went back to the Nizam's bungalow to fetch a rug or two (we did not want to test our reaction to cold stone too long) and to tell Soble to bring our lunch when it was ready. Then we gave ourselves up to the charms of the place.

We were directly opposite (across the larger courtyard) several brilliant white domes which rose into the intense pale blue of the sky, a combination which never fails to please; below lay the deep shadows of the arcades and the lacy shade of the trees. Before this dramatic stage setting we saw a number of pilgrims sweep by on their way to visit the tombs. Why Zahkir Baksh merited this honor we did not discover, but the mosque itself, we felt, was sufficient justification for any pilgrimage. The visitors, however, seemed interested only in the sepulcher.

A party of ladies, in flowing *burqas* of brown, of pink, and of black, rustled across the paving stones accompanied by their little boys, who were attired for the occasion in garish and glittering fezzes. With their immense skirts and their pervasive femininity, their color, they brought with them a great feeling of vitality and movement, enhanced by the sweeping draperies and the sprightly grace of the lads. The charms of the setting were enriched by this party, so unlike the usual groups of Muslim women we had seen in the cities. There was about this little company an air of fashion and of mobility which surprised us after the sad and depressed air which the animated *burqa* generally expressed. Perhaps that hillside pilgrimage had some special note of festivity for Muslim ladies —those whom we had encountered in the little garden earlier in the day seemed also to have been in a lively humor. But such distractions were rare. For the better part of the day the mosque was silent, save for the occasional murmur of a deep voice from the gateway, the slight rustle of the trees, and the light whispers of the wind in the minars.

At noon Soble came, bringing cold water from the well near the Nizam's bungalow, its coolness preserved by felt-covered water bottles. It seemed to us then the softest, purest, most delicious water we had ever tasted. The influence of nomadic and desert life was making itself felt in us, so that we were now beginning to be able to sample the flavor of water as a tea-taster will judge the fine leaves which give savor to his cup. Soble brought us all that was left in our stores in the way of eatables and then went away to pack us up. Alas, that evening we were to go back to the noise and clatter, the modernity, the almost intolerable sophistication and pressure of life in Aurangabad! After he had gone we lingered on as long as we could in our sweet retreat, reveling in every line, every curve, every shadow of the cupolas and minars, rejoicing in the benedictions of that peaceful day.

There was a little knoll near the fork of the road where the bus would stop and on it a few wide-spreading trees; here we hastened, that we might be shielded from the ferocious sun, which was soon to set and was making the most of its last blistering moments. The bus was (of course) late but its lateness was to our profit, as from this little rise of ground we could look down upon the small walled town of Khuldabad. While we sat there we saw two horsemen slowly pass beyond the walls and go down to a small lake to water their mounts, a scene wholly chivalrous. Where else today could it have appeared?

Soble and our baggage coolies sheltered from the sun under the low wall of a wayside tomb, squatting beside their loads. Time passed, but brought no bus with it. There were other hopeful passengers not far from us on the knoll and finally one among them came over and spoke to us—an elderly Muslim in a red fez and a long gray *sherwani*. He supposed that we had been looking up the Mohammedan monuments in the area and was perfectly horrified to find that we had not done so. "What!" he exclaimed. "You have been three days at Khuldabad and you have not seen the grave of Alamgir!" With that deep absorption in the Islamic world which distinguishes so many of the followers of the Prophet, he was almost unaware of the valid presence of any other sort of existence and could not conceive that we had been so long in the neighborhood without seeing the old Emperor's tomb. What, then, had we been doing? "Seeing the caves." Ah, yes, he *had* heard of them, but he cared nothing for the relics of any civilization other than his own. Had we at least seen some of the *durgas* and *macqbaras* of the district? Here we could reassure him and we calmed him by telling him that we were to visit Roza and see the tomb of his Alamgir. But in this we were wrong, for though we did not realize it then, Khuldabad is on the site of the old town of Roza and the tomb, such as it is, was almost before us at that moment—we had mistakenly thought that Roza, still bearing its ancient name, was near the fort of Daulatabad, which we were intending to visit the next day. Our friend did not enlighten us, not realizing our confusion. Though this tomb offers little to the eye, save the memory of Curzon's love for the old monuments of India—it is a memorial to him as well as to Aurangzeb—we have always regretted having missed it.

It was so hot and dry that we began to drink from our felt water bottles. Had we tasted of the well, the well on the plain behind us? That was fine water indeed, said our friend, and he told a boy who was with him to run quickly and draw us a bottleful. The boy spilled out what was left in our flask, making a little rivulet on the hard and dusty earth, and started off, but just at that moment the bus appeared, so we never tasted the water of that famous well.

By the time the bus reached us every seat in it had long been taken and dirty, ragged personages in huge turbans of every color hung onto every possible support like creepers in a jungle. The agonized driver and the harassed conductor swore that they would, could, *not* take any more passengers. We insisted on entering as we had reserved seats, knowing that in Hyderabad we had more prestige than in British India and our reservations would be honored. Places were immediately cleared for us and our servant by the seemingly impossible process of squeezing the creepers even closer together. We then struggled to get our friend of the roadside admitted; at last he, too, was jammed in. Such shoutings, imprecations, pushings, arguments, wrath, and emotion could never be surpassed, but at last all who could in any way be stuffed aboard were fitted in somehow and the groaning vehicle lurched up the glaring dusty road, past the stout walls and under the deep gates of Khuldabad.

Daulatabad

After the journey to Ellora and a few days resting in Aurangabad we hired a car and drove out to see the fortress of Daulatabad, the renowned fortress of Daulat. Rising straight out of the utter flatness of the plain, this great rock with its rugged palisades, its height, and its general air of ferocity is very striking. A white building seems to hang just below the summit, as though over sheer space, looking from a distance through the shimmering air like a little ivory jewel casket. Daulatabad is a sort of Gibraltar lying on the Deccan, a perfect natural fortress, at one time of great strategic importance.

The rock rises steeply to a height of some six hundred feet above the plain, on the south side forming natural cliffs which were a sufficient defense for that part of the citadel. On the other three sides the precipice is less abrupt but still formidable, soaring over a hundred and fifty feet from the inner moat, which is itself a natural ravine: here the barriers are artificially enforced. The garrison town and outer fortress zone lie on the plain on the northern, eastern, and western sides of the rock, surrounded by outer curtain walls which were once over two miles in circumference. Beyond this lay the glacis.

The history of Daulatabad is one of intrigue, treason, and war; many ancient kingdoms and conquerors struggled to possess it and

its present ruins go back beyond the Moguls to the Pathan rulers—
to Tughlaq and Allaudin. The King of Golconda was imprisoned
here and may have died in the little cell in which he was confined,
far up in the rock. These names convey little to the Westerner as
yet, but they are important to students of Indian history. The last
great commander does mean something to us all, for it was
Aurangzeb. Whoever held the Deccan had to be master of Daulatabad.

The fortress is not beautiful, Aurangzeb being the man he was,
but even he could not prevent it from appearing both fascinating
and romantic. The Mogul buildings were constructed of huge
stones, torn in haste from the Hindu temples which the conquering
Mohammedans demolished, partly in order to have materials for
their own fort. Aurangzeb would, no doubt, have destroyed such
shrines in any case—he had no tolerance in him for other faiths,
though it had been the tradition of his family to allow freedom
of worship. In much of the masonry of Daulatabad large sections
of carvings, clearly of temple origin, appear. The engineers seem
to have worked at careless speed—there was no strength in what
they built and little of the garrison town still stands. A few streets
have been cleared of rubble, showing the basic plan of the place—
these, ordered and military in character, lead past roofless barracks and offices. In its time the Mogul administrative machine had
a great reputation for efficiency. Standing in those sunny streets
among the ruins, the reality of the old empire forcibly impressed
me—how did it seem to the people who came to live in the garrison
town of Daulatabad? The garrison engineers, the petty officers, the
officers in command—how did they impress themselves upon the
local people? Daulatabad kept its silence but I felt in the air a maxim
I had heard from British Army officers: "Never explain, never
retract, never apologize."

The entrance is by a massive barbican with splendid round
towers and deep passages under the wall leading to a wide straight
road which runs to the heart of the ruined town. In this, the
outer fortress zone, is a superb minaret, called the Chand (Moon)
Minar, towering high over its mosque. It is a striking and lovely
tower, over three hundred feet high, covered with pale pink
plaster which has retained its harmonious coloring through the
centuries, and it is ornamented with sky-blue tiles—what a conceit
for the severities of a fortress! When we were there, there were
swarms of bees hanging in great bosses and clusters under the eaves

of a high upper balcony, effectively preventing anyone from trying to use the narrow winding stairs within.

The little mosque at the foot of the minar is unpretentious, but opposite it is a much larger one of an unusually complicated design, having galleries and columns, both intricately carved. Being built over the site of a Hindu temple, perhaps it had borrowed some of the features it found there. We lingered by the minar for a long time, looking up its slender shaft to the bright blue tiles and the dark clusters of the bees, both colors so strong against the rosy plaster and the pale though brilliant sky. It evoked so many unrelated, poetic images, quite out of the world of fortresses and harsh, proselytizing religions—it made one think of tulips and ballet, of model rooms in the Beaux Arts.

Further down the road we came to an enormous elephant tank, now dry, with grass-grown steps leading down to its depths. It must have been at least a hundred and fifty feet square and fifty deep. Daulatabad was now rapidly coming alive for us, we could begin to imagine the elephants coming down to the water, their *mahouts* on their backs. What problems they must have created for the Mogul Transport Corps! When the huge beasts were entering the water in the evenings, how often must the priests have been ascending the minar to the high upper balcony to cry out over the town:

LA ILLAHU ILLALLAH
   MOHAMET ER RASHOOL
   RASHADU AN LA ILLAHU ILLALLAH

We then went under the wall which contains the inner fortress zone. Here the ascent begins. Wide ramps or flights of stairs lead to the summit, past ruined buildings and fine old guns, many of European make. High up the hill we passed a massive round caponnier on which rests a very large bronze cannon with a ram's head at the mouth and two little lions crouching on the long shining barrel. On this is inscribed, in Arabic, "Mohammed Aurangzab Bahadur Alamgir." After this was a pleasant little building of arched recesses, which seemed to have been the officers' mess; separated from it only by a terrace was the prison where the King of Golconda had lain so many years.

Now we had finished with the first stage of the hill and the amenities, such as dining rooms and prisons, which went with it. The way led across a bridge which spanned the moat, here a deep ravine which had once been crossed by a drawbridge. The countryside was beginning to open out below us and we could already see far over the plain, which lay shimmering in heat, floating like a bubble, its soft dull tones broken only by the tiny white domes and walls of the *macqbaras*, while in the foreground the great height of the pink minaret with its dark apiaries stood out like the stalk of some huge magic flower.

We now entered the ultimate defenses of Daulatabad by plunging at once into a vast tunnel which goes up through the living rock for nearly two hundred yards. We were lit through it by a wizened old man who carried a flare which diffused a pleasant bouquet. Our distorted shadows mounted the damp, resounding walls—first the old man with his immense round turban, which seemed to occupy half the rock face, then Stanton, tall, striding on with an easy, steady gait, holding my hand and hauling me after him, while my meager shadow showed how my knees were trembling after these interminable upward flights. At the end of the procession came the lean figure of the sentry with his neat, close turban—even when caricatured by flare and shadow and cavern wall, he still looked a military figure. The way was steep and winding, cold after the outside air, but it was not stuffy and the passages were roomy. There were occasional chambers hollowed out on the sides, where Stanton concluded that as many as two thousand men might have sheltered. There was also a conveniently placed oubliette and near it a sinister grid for coals.

Once out of the tunnel we found ourselves well above the stone palisades which form the natural defense of the hill. Before the days of modern weapons the rock should have been almost impregnable, as it harbors plenteous springs of water, even though the garrison below might have been forced to surrender. Yet we were told that at the last it capitulated to the Mahrattas without a struggle. Treachery!

As we continued climbing the hill we came upon a very small mosque and more guns, some of Dutch origin, and passed under some very handsome gates. On one little terrace were two swivel guns, each forged with a dragon's head at the chase. How fascinating, how little known, are these old forts of India! Had Daulatabad been in Europe we would have known of its riches and vagaries from our childhood—now, how the mind was teased, how the eye was delighted, by this strange treasury, high up under the sun, in the world of the wind!

Soon after we arrived at the keep, the largest building of the citadel (that which from a distance had appeared as an ivory filigree casket lodged in a niche of the rock). This turned out to be a substantial building of great simplicity, centered around a large courtyard and as open as possible to the high air and the warm winds of the peak. It had enormous windows where there was a constant passage of light air, the whole was whitewashed (no bombs, no aircraft, no heavy artillery), there were stone benches and space—a pleasanter keep could hardly have been imagined. Just the place to laze away a summer afternoon, provided one was not a soldier of Alamgir.

The roof of this building is flat with a battlemented edge; leaning on the crenellations we studied the layout of the town and fort; looked across to the flat-topped hills, then down at the scorching plain, then back to the great gateways of the town, the elephant tank and the minar, all now seen in miniature. But this was still not the summit. On we went, up through a whitewashed passage which had wide benches for sentries (and, I trust, for exhausted messengers—I have no doubt it must have taken some time to send notes to the gates!), passing a gun which had three charming dolphins sporting on its back—what could have been more incongruous than this image here?

Just under the summit is an extraordinary and mysterious ruined shrine dug into the hill. A few rocky steps descend into a partly flooded dark cave. The roof of the shrine is too low to allow one to stand upright and the strange little place is evidently always at the mercy of its hidden spring. In the gloomy, dank cavern our torches caught in their thin beams of light two tiny pairs of stone feet, naked feet. The smaller pair was of soapstone, about three inches long, the larger some two inches longer, and of a red stone— they were to represent the footsteps of the Buddha. (When Buddha felt he was to enter Nirvana, he went, according to legend, to a place called Kusinara and stood on a stone looking southwards —this stone forever afterwards bore the impress of his feet. From this story grew the practice of reproducing stone footprints of the Buddha.) The temple must have antedated the fort and Daulatabad is, after all, not far in miles from the Buddhistic caves at Ellora— there must have been some centers of worship for the religion in the neighborhood at that time.

At the very top of the hill is another huge gun. Some of these guns were so large that they could not have been dragged through the twisted passage in the rock and must have come up via the outside of the cliff, handled by tackle and some sort of cranes. It is truly an amazing place, romantic and wild—but not admirable. Its history has little to record of courage, magnanimity, or virtue, and in comparison with other renowned Mogul forts, it has little beauty. It is in the little humble sepulchers of the plain that beauty lies, where modest shady verandas offer the pilgrims a refuge from the heroics, the martial trumpery, the ambition, and the treacheries of these old warriors.

Ajanta

It was primarily for the caves of Ajanta that we had wanted to visit Hyderabad—we expected to find them the climax of our journeys in the state. Because of this we prepared for this last trip with an added measure of enthusiasm, though wondering how any place could give more pleasure and interest than the Ellora district. We replenished our stores and then once again, with Soble, boarded a bus and went out into the country.

It was not till ten o'clock in the evening that we reached Fardapur, the town nearest Ajanta—these caves are much further from Aurangabad than are those of Ellora. In the darkness we were only aware of a dismal little village as we climbed down from the bus in the company of eight Indian students who were on the same quest as ourselves and were also expecting great things of the caves. An old *chokidar* had come down from the rest houses to meet us, carrying one solitary lantern by which he led us in a long file through a dusty black lane for several hundred yards. Then we found ourselves among the bungalows, of which there were a number. The Nizam's rest house and another large building were the most impressive, but the eight students and ourselves were hurried past these by the village porters and finally were all pushed into the same modest bungalow, half of which was allotted to the students and half to us.

The trip in the bus had lasted so long and we had been so depressed by the increasingly wretched appearance of the last villages we had seen, and we were so tired, that we did not protest much against this arrangement, though we felt we should have had a quiet night to ourselves. The *chokidar* was clearly making his duties as easy for himself as he could. We devoted our last energies to a great struggle to have lamps and pitchers of water brought in and in having the rooms cleaned out. Soble, with his usual calm air of having seen far, far, worse things than this, opened a tin of soup and produced some fruit out of his baskets. We could hear the eight students banging about on the other side of the thin partitions which divided the house into two and it all seemed a discouraging start to the great frescoes.

In the morning sunshine most of this was forgotten. The beds, from which in the dim light of the evening we had feared the worst, had proved uninhabited, the new home seemed passable and the eight students civil and unobtrusive. These youths had come from Bombay to see the caves and were doing it as economically as they could. They started off towards the caves on foot and reached them much sooner than we did, as Stanton thought that after the rigors of the past fortnight I should be pampered and engaged a bullock cart for me, a kind but disastrous gesture. The caves were over two miles from the rest houses and the day, of course, became extremely hot. Ajanta began to seem a great deal of work, but still we did not doubt that seeing it would be worth any effort. We found the *chokidar* and arranged to have the bullock cart washed and spread with rugs.

The cart took an hour to reach the caves. When the bullocks walked, their pace was so incredibly slow that we seemed to be going backwards, but when the aged driver who crouched in front poked them into a clumsy trot, I was almost shaken to pieces. The floor was made of bamboo poles laid lightly side by side and the wheels were wooden, so all the shock had to be taken by the luckless travelers. The sun beat down, the road was almost treeless, the fields were deserted, and the barren and rocky hills seemed to be in a conspiracy to keep the valley under a perpetual weight of hot, heavy, dry air. There was nothing for it but extreme patience. But I thought all this ominous and began to be more and more suspicious of Ajanta.

At last we arrived at the foot of the cliffs, where the mind is put in tune with what is to come by the sight of a fine Bô (Bodhi) tree which has been planted at the base of the ascent. It was under one of this fortunate species that Buddha received his final enlightenment, according to all the legends which surround him, and it was an indication of the care which was being taken of these caves that one of these trees should be there to welcome visitors. It is a distinctive tree, with large, curiously shaped leaves. We began to climb up towards the caves with keen anticipation—they do not

open out from the road but from a long line over a wild ravine and
a river. When the river is full and when a waterfall plunges over
the cliff, the site becomes very impressive.

These caves were discovered in the last century by an English
sportsman who was out after tiger. His quarry ran into one of the
caves, and when he went in after it, his boldness could only have
been matched by his astonishment. (This is, at least, the version
current when we were there. A recent book attributes their discovery to some British soldiers on maneuvers in 1817.) The caves
had been "lost" through complete indifference. During the centuries of silence and neglect irreparable damage took place—the
frescoes could not endure as did the sturdy sculpture of Ellora.
Bats and birds, insects, the rains, mildew, vandals, all played their
woeful parts—and at first their discovery almost ruined them. An
English curator, alarmed at their crumbling fragility, precipitately
started to varnish the walls, with the most horrifying results. Everything he touched turned brown. When we were there artists were
carefully cleaning and restoring the falling scenes, but most of the
walls are bare—the frescoes have long since become dust.

Once the initial effort in reaching them was past, these caves
were much less arduous to see than those at Ellora, being smaller,
simpler in construction, and each exactly adjacent to its neighbor.
As far as architecture goes, most of these temples are nothing more
than large caves hollowed out of the rock. Their sculpture and
carvings are crude and rough—in some cases repulsive. There are
a few *chaityas* but not one nearly so fine as Ellora's number ten.
The whole glory of the caves rests on their frescoes. Once that was
enough, for it is an astonishing conception. When the paintings
were fresh and whole, here in these remote chambers was a vast
treasury of some of the most beautiful frescoes the world has ever
known. But, alas, it is all so worn and defaced now, so blackened,
that one can see only a fraction of the exquisite lines once traced
here with unerring hand, only a hint of the colors. We had not
realized, before we came, how great a proportion of the frescoes
have faded or perished. The reproductions we had seen in Europe
had really raised our hopes too high—often they seem lovelier than
the originals.

These caves are very dark, as almost no skylights or windows
were excavated to light them. Electric lights had been installed,
which were in use during the rains and for which the sightseer had
to pay a considerable figure. When we were there, another device

was used. A man stood in the strong sunlight at the mouth of each cave, with a large mirror in his hands. Another, within the cave, holding up a sail of white cotton cloth, caught the rays of light as they were deflected from the mirror and threw them upon each section of the frescoes in turn. The idea was ingenious and the pure, entrapped light undoubtedly better than any other for seeing the true colors; but the coolies were slow and inept. There were long delays before each scene could be successfully illuminated, while the mirror was being shifted into its next position and the light entrapped by the man with the sail. During these intervals the mirror threw dazzling light fitfully all over the interior of the cave, seeming like a fugitive resisting capture, and half-blinding us. It all became very exasperating; with everyone shouting directions and waving their arms about it was difficult to recapture a mood of artistic receptivity. In the end we were given a bill, made out in English, charging us two rupees for "sunlight." In the past torches were taken in, and the artists themselves worked by the light of flares—long black streaks on the walls are supposed to confirm this story.

These Ajanta caves are all Buddhistic and exerted a great influence over like caves throughout the Far East—the cave temples of Ceylon and of China followed their tradition, or that of Ellora. They were executed between the first and the seventh centuries of our era: the most notable and splendid pertain to the Great Vehicle, or the Mahayana form of the religion, which developed after the Hinayana or Small Vehicle. The earlier and purer form was transcendental in concept and avoided the materialization and human compromises of the Mahayana. At first Buddha was considered only the Great Teacher. Later he was deified and the cult of Bodhisattvas, or intermediary saints, was introduced as something easier for the crowd to grasp—at this stage the artists found much to portray, much to symbolize. The devotees of the Mahayana reproached the Hinayana element with being cold and so absorbed in abstractions such as the pursuit of the absolute that their earthly life was of no good to anyone else. The Mahayana people laid great emphasis on compassion and altruism and it would seem that they were kind and gentle, but that, also, they often seemed to lose the essence of philosophy in their compromise with the world around them.

The caves here, inspired by the Mahayana doctrines, give a very favorable impression of that cult. Almost every picture is marked by an air of sweetness and purity, of gaiety, though not of worldliness. They differed very much from the Buddhistic caves at Ellora (aside from being sculpture and not painting) in that those had hardly been concerned with any personalities except Buddha and his disciples. Here we see the Buddhistic world—hundreds of persons crowding round the teacher. In the Hindu caves at Ellora the "common man" was often shown—as a childish and superstitious mortal, satisfied with his plethora of earthly-minded gods. Here at Ajanta he is held to be a different sort of being—aware of true values and virtues, he seeks the crowning blessing of spirituality.

The frescoes are on a small scale—about half life-size, though the principal figures, for emphasis, are larger. The majority of the men and women on the walls of Ajanta are between two and three feet in height and delicately formed, giving the caves an air of miniature perfection rather than the heroic treatment we had expected. The scenes are of the various Buddhistic legends, the interest lies with the representation of the crowd, as though the artists wished to present the effect of this faith upon its devotees rather than concentrate upon the Buddha himself. The men appear intelligent and restrained, the women lovely and deeply moved by the message they are receiving—throughout the tone is thoughtful, happy, dignified, and calm. The colors are very beautiful, delicate and light, like pastels or fresh watercolors. The flesh tones, the clear yellows and soft greens, and the pure whites are most remarkable. The best figures are familiar to anyone who has seen anything on the caves—these are not only the best, they are practically the only survivors. The great Padmapani, the lovely portrait of Buddha's wife, the Black Princess, leaning against her column, Buddha as a prince—all these are marvelous. There are court scenes, scenes of dalliance, and many odd fantasies, such as the famous study of fighting camels. One of the few personages unknown to us was a thin red-haired lady, carrying a handbag and dressed in a light, gauzy, pleated skirt. Stanton thought her the image of myself.

Only four caves of the twenty-seven have any considerable number of frescoes left. In the first is a beautiful coffered ceiling, like a Greek or a Roman ceiling. The medallions are of jocund floral design as well as of elephants and other animals, all cunningly fitted into the little squares. One study, that of the two fighting bulls, is a miracle of design—the heads down, the horns interlocked. Only four colors had been used here: a light turquoise green, white, burgundy, and orange—happily, this area had escaped the hand of the varnishers. The floral designs are still wonderfully fresh and lovely, and were possible to see through the light which streams through the wide entrance, uninterrupted by the coolie ballet. For a couple of hours in the middle of the day we lay under it, pursuing its themes with the greatest of pleasure. I suppose by now the caves have some more orthodox system of lighting in use and are much easier to reach. But then it seemed to us that the reproductions really gave a perfect idea of the originals and were sufficient —we regretted that we had left Ellora to come here and decided that we would not stay any longer but would go back to Aurangabad the next morning.

Our bus conductor, a handsome man in a saturnine Hollywood way, had told us that his bus left Fardapur at seven every morning. so the next day we rose before six, made up our bedrolls, drank our tea, and hurried out under the stars. Soble had porters waiting for our gear; they hoisted it onto their heads and we strung out in a long line going back to the village. To our disgust, when we arrived at the bus stand the driver and the conductor were still asleep inside the vehicle and in answer to our indignant banging on the shuttered windows replied that they were not going to leave before seven-thirty. It was then only six-forty-five. We walked up and down the road, which was dusty and dirty and had cows sleeping in it, while we watched the dawn coming. It was eight before the bus *log* had finally got themselves awake, dressed and washed (i.e. had run their fingers through their hair and assumed their fezzes), opened the bus windows (it was not swept or any such nonsense), and allowed the patient passengers to enter. By then we knew why the starting time had been put back an hour. A *tussuldar* and his suite were coming with us.

A *tussuldar* corresponded somewhat to a District Commissioner in British India; he was quite a great man in his own world and we were surprised that he would travel in such humble style even in wartime. We had known he was at Ajanta, as he had occupied the students' rooms on our second night there. The students themselves had flitted through the temples and disappeared into the wastes, and when we had come back from the caves, considerably more dead than alive, we had been surprised to see their old rooms brilliantly lit up. (Or so it seemed to us then, having become entirely oil-lamp-minded.) The *chokidar* told us that a *tussuldar* had come for the night and therefore especially good lamps had been brought in for him from the Nizam's guest house.

The great man's suite—about ten followers—had before eight that morning assembled at the bus stop in all the arrogance, importance, and busyness of the Shadow of Authority in the East. There were half a dozen peons in rather dirty but splendid uniforms—red, maroon, or scarlet coats worn very long, with tight white trousers, big red turbans, and any amount of gold braid and frogs. Dozens of pieces of luggage went up on the roof of the bus—tin boxes, wooden boxes, and lastly, a small hat box, just large enough for a fez. *Chattis*, the beautiful earthenware vessels with long necks and swelling bowls, fitted into large wooden traveling frames, were solicitously stowed away inside. When all this was aboard we went off to a stop outside the village where, attended by his secretary, the *tussuldar* was ready for us.

He was a big good-looking young Muslim, dressed in a gray *sherwani* and a red fez, as was his secretary. As soon as he entered the bus, the whole suite stood up: then began a remarkable journey. Everyone observed the most perfect manners. No one shoved, no one quarreled, no one crawled in or out of a window, no one spat on the floor, the conductor himself put away his old peremptory ways and became a cooing dove. At every stop village headmen came out to salaam and all the suite bridled and swelled. To the waiting would-be passengers the conductor (whom we called Basil, because he was the image of the actor Basil Rathbone) would observe with regret and sweetness that as we were full we could of course take no more and everyone beamingly acquiesced. When we were nearly in the city, at the request of the *tussuldar* a few persons were allowed to come in and sit, not stand, on the floor. The *tussuldar* had the manner of accustomed authority; he took it all as his due and appeared quite an efficient and effective man. I daresay that he milked his district as dry as the market would bear. Probably he was now in a position to offset any complaints about the bus service, if anyone had the temerity to complain, through what he had seen with his own eyes—courtesy and no overcrowding were characteristics of the route.

Secunderabad

We now had only a few days left before we must be back in Ambernath. The problem was, how to go back and yet not pass through Manmad; that would have meant changing trains there once more in the middle of the night and walking a long distance along the tracks in the dark—it seemed no Bombay trains ever went through that ghastly place by day. The alternative was to go hundreds of miles out of our way, traveling down to the southeast corner of the state to Hyderabad City, where we could catch a direct train to Bombay. Looking back on this dilemma from the cool climate and short distances of Europe, it is a little difficult to reconstruct our frame of mind. Then I remember the dirty waiting rooms, the lack of water, the flies of Manmad. No one in Jalna thought it in the least odd that we should add seven hundred miles to our journey in order to avoid Manmad—it was a local game to find an itinerary which left that junction out. As soon as we came to this decision, everything fell into place. There was some ordnance affair which Stanton could attend to in Secunderabad (which adjoins Hyderabad City) and the superintendent of one of the factories there offered to put us up. And of course we were delighted to have a chance to see more of the state.

We left the mission bungalow one night after dinner, in great style. Three *tongas* were summoned, one for our hosts, one for us, and one for the luggage. This cavalcade, with the shouting drivers and the nodding plumes of the horses' headdresses, seemed in the lamp light quite a spectacular affair. No matter how poor and old the horses, how shoddy the carriages, a few of them together embody a certain air and spirit. The horse still represents elements of chivalry and romance in our civilization—to approach him is enough to hear the jangling of the cavalry's stirrups and bits, to enter another sphere. You may despise it, you may love it, you cannot ignore it. Our *tongas* dashed through the narrow streets with their bells ringing and the *syces* shouting; the children's eyes shone with excitement. The roads were almost entirely dark save for the glow which came from the open shop fronts and from the little fires of the street restaurants. Now that it was night and cool, the world had come out to take the air and the itinerant cooks, who take with them little barrows, were busy frying pancakes and patties in the sputtering oil of large black iron pans. There were no sidewalks and I often held my breath as some leisurely old man strolled across the road, barely avoiding our high wheels.

The train, the stationmaster told us, was immensely crowded and there would be no possibility of giving us a carriage where we could be together; he would put Stanton in with some officers and the children and I must go into a *zenana* compartment. It was due in a few minutes and would barely stop—we must be ready to throw ourselves aboard.

The *zenana* carriage already held three women when the babies and I darted into it: a tall Sikh lady with her old woman servant and a slender Mohammedan, deeply shrouded in a *burqa* of soft, elegant material—even at that moment I recognized at once that the wearer of such a *burqa* must have some pretensions as to rank. A Muslim gentleman was rushing in and out of the compartment with his servant but with the most perfect courtesy, and in spite of the obvious need for the utmost dispatch on both sides, paused to introduce himself to me and to apologize for being in a ladies' carriage even for a moment. He was, he said, a *tussuldar*, traveling only a few stations up the line. Around his wife's feet they were piling bags, baskets of vegetables, bundles, multilayered picnic baskets, and tin boxes. As the Hindu lady had a similar array of baggage, and as my collection of suitcases, bedroll, dunnage bags, and water bottles was fast coming in too, the compartment already looked a perfect horror. Stanton and I bade each other goodnight; then he rushed down the platform to his distant carriage, followed by a red-turbaned porter who had his huge bag on his head. I leaned out of the window into the soft, black, troubled air, with the dim figures of other travelers hurrying to and fro on the unlit platform forming a sort of backdrop, and said goodbye to our cousins. The whistles blew and we were off. We did not meet again until the children were nearly grown up, long after the war and the independence of India.

When I turned from the window to the compartment, it all looked unbelievable to me: the small dimly-lit room with the black Islamic bundle on one bench, the Sikh lady stretched out on her couch, the personification of dark languor, while in a corner sat the old servant rolled up in her sari and eating a *chapatti*, while she stared at us out of small, curious black eyes. What was I doing here? The cheerful eagerness of the children was a touch of reality but for a flash of time even they surprised me. It was now years since I had traveled alone. I had scarcely been anywhere since my marriage without Stanton, always the most solicitous of escorts, and my mind went back to the days when I so often went so far alone—the beautiful little girls seemed part of the strange, dramatic group before me, of which I hardly felt myself a part.

Life, like a dome of many-coloured glass,
Stains the white radiance of Eternity.

Then Madame Tussuldar threw back the veil which enclosed her head, disclosing a beautiful face framed in black draperies, and by this action I at once found myself part of the little company. She had great dark eyes, fine aquiline features, and an expression which was gentle and sweet, but piercingly sad. A young woman, but so worn! She was of a pitiful gauntness and fragility, sitting perfectly still, just as she had been placed, smiling tenderly at the children. What could her lot have been like in purdah? I remembered the words of a mission padre in Mussoorie, a temperate, kind man, who never spoke carelessly: "The lives of the Mohammedan women in purdah are hopeless, desperate . . ."

The Hindu lady, on the other hand, seemed very free in her manner and easy in her mind. Judging by her dress (loose trousers, full at the knee, tight at the ankle, a long full shirt worn over them) I thought she must certainly be a Punjabi and probably a Sikh. She had thrown off her shawls and was enjoying the fan. Four more dissimilar women one could hardly imagine confined within that small space in the fast train. The solvent between us was the children. The Indians almost fell upon them, with cries of pleasure, petting them, laughing at their glee—for no one ever enjoyed traveling in trains at night more than these small persons.

After an hour the *tussuldar's* lady left, and soon afterwards the Sikh lady and her wrinkled crone, leaving us to a peaceful and restful night. Several times at stations soldiers, banging at all the doors of the train, hoping to find a niche, would attempt to open ours also. First peering out, to be sure that the man had no lady with him, I would shout *"Zenana!"* and there was never any dispute—these carriages were really respected.

When the morning came, bright and sunny, a pleasant Hindu lady entered the carriage, bringing with her her little boy, who wore a ring in his nose. They sat staring at us, while we stared out of the windows. Posy, looking out on the hard sun-dried landscape, summed it up when she said, "What huge rocks!" Enormous black boulders lay everywhere, tossed and tumbled on the flat hard ground and forming the salient feature of the whole area around Hyderabad City and Secunderabad. They are due, we were told, to desiccation, combined with wind erosion—the effect is most extraordinary.

On this weird lunar countryside lie several adjoining settlements: the old city of Hyderabad, which was built by the nizams (who were the provincial governors for the Moguls); Secunderabad, the largest British cantonment in India, comprising sixteen square miles, and garrisoned with great numbers of troops from the United Kingdom; and several large suburbs, of which Begum Pet was one. There was great wealth here—with beautiful homes and gardens and imposing government buildings—next to abject poverty, as everywhere in the East at that time. Secunderabad was of particular importance in the medical world of India. There were a great number of military hospitals here and a special emphasis was given to facial surgery, so that wounded soldiers were coming in constantly during the war. All these cities had expanded so much that they had run together—it was a place of vast distances and vast transport problems. We were to stay in Begum Pet.

We arrived in Secunderabad about nine in the morning and went out to the house of the generous bachelor who had offered to put us up—in fact he gave us his house while we were there, moving out himself. It was a strange and amusing place, a mansion which had once belonged to a Mohammedan family and had been arranged in a number of apartments to accommodate semi-separate establishments. Afterwards it had passed into the hands of an eccentric and lively Czech and his Japanese wife; they altered it extensively but made it no more orthodox. Then the British took it over to house senior personnel in the Ordnance, but it was too late to do anything with it—the place dominated its tenants, who laughed and wrung their hands and let it alone. It was by then an extreme mixture of ostentation, pseudo-luxury, comfort, ugliness, and the impressiveness which accompanies plenty of space. There were large handsome rooms, huge bathrooms, marble floors, fans everywhere, large sofas, heavy tables—and little connection between the various wide stairways, verandas, flat roofs, and terraces. But the garden was lovely, doubly charming after the inanities of the house. It had a beautiful long avenue of bougainvilleas—rose-pink, coral, salmon-pink, rose-purple. There was a maze and formal gardens, an oval swimming pool, and paths lined with hundreds of potted plants. After the little strip of watered earth in Jalna where the few roses and oleanders grew beside the well, this luxuriance was very inspiriting to us. Our lives had for so long been so austere, this opulence was exciting.

Hyderabad City has one particularly fine old monument in the bazaar area called the Char Minar, which is, as its name implies, a building made up of four connecting minars which bestride a wide street. The minarets are some hundred feet high and form the corners of a domed, arched, glorified guardhouse, of saffron-colored plaster, very delightful to see. Near it were the shops of the silversmiths and the jewelers, where merchants were reclining on their white mattresses. One of these men, noticing the Chinese aquamarines I was wearing, went to the back of his room and returned with his large brown hands cupped together and literally brimming over with these translucent green-blue gems, most of them as large as marbles. This was an Arabian Nights gesture—at last! handfuls of gems!

There is also here a very perfect little museum, devoted to a few remarkable collections: a section of old weapons, one of Chinese porcelain, and one for Rajput and Mogul prints, Persian miniatures, and ancient manuscripts of the Koran. The martial selection is considered the most important. Here are daggers and swords with damascene blades, splendidly displayed on velvet, the light falling on the gold and jewels of the rich hilts. Many favorite swords of great generals, Mogul emperors and Mahratta chieftains are treasured here, but the brilliant, decorated daggers dominate the collection. Their velvet and leather sheaths, crimson, emerald green, azure, scarlet and gold, were trimmed and tooled as though to hold the finest jewels. Among these the Mahratta daggers were unique, with their double-pronged hilt. There were, too, armor and lances—all the trappings of war.

The porcelains were extremely good: Sung celadon, green, gray, and creamy white, and ying ch'ing eggshell blue. There were also *sang-de-boeuf* vases from the Ming, and from that dynasty also trinkets, trays, and boxes.

One evening we drove outside the city to see the Fort of Golconda, one of whose rulers had been imprisoned in that small room in Daulatabad. Golconda lies on a low hill. These large ancient forts of India do not vary much one from the other, but they are all romantic and handsome and each has its own fascinating variations. The heavy walls and deep gates, the courtyards and ramps, the keeps, the red brickwork and the dryness, the sun, the slow ascent—what pleasure all this always gave us! Here under the main gate, if you stamp your feet on the keystone under the arch, you can set up a fine ringing echo. Halfway up to the keep is a remarkable sight: a small mosque, set about with minarets, stands next to a slight Hindu shrine. On the low painted wall of the latter is a truly striking insignia—the lion and the unicorn. Under them a lion's head is centered, below that again a double-headed eagle, holding a small elephant in each beak and another between its claws.

The keep is exceedingly large and windy, reached by steep stairs. From its huge windows we looked down upon a wide prospect: on every side the plain, the wall and the moat below us, and behind the fort three domes, each the tomb of some local grandee. These were quite pretentious—alas, what do we know of the renown of the great men of Golconda!

That night we had a long talk with our host's old bearer. We asked him the story of the young *missolchi* who helped him to serve our meals and who seemed a likable and lively youth. He had disappeared when the coffee had been brought in and we could see that he was of interest to his superior. The lad had been a homeless orphan when the *sahib* had heard of him, said the old bearer; he had brought him to the house to become a servant under the particular care of this old man, who had served his master for many years. The only difficulty, said the ancient, was that the boy was a Hindu. However, he continued cheerfully, this problem was quickly surmounted—in three weeks he had become a Mohammedan. This type of conversion must underlie millions of cases within the country—most of the Mohammedans were once Hindus, or their forebears were.

Early the next morning our train left Secunderabad for Bombay. Waiting for the car to come and fetch us, Posy and I went out into the garden to watch a dozen comely Mahratta women, their saris tightly molded about their pretty figures, water the potted plants and the tall ferns which hedged the paths. Drawing water from a stone tank, they filled their large earthenware vessels and passed rapidly up and down the walks, sprinkling the begonias, lilies, and palms till everything smelt of freshness and well water and sweet morning coolness. It needed the water to awaken these scents, which the aridity had locked away. It was hard to leave this quiet, fragrant scene for another dusty, noisy journey. Today I can scarcely recall anything of the next twenty-four hours, and yet I might have left that sweet-smelling, cool, dark green garden only a moment ago: I can still see the early sunlight falling through the long sharp fingers of the palms, dappling the ground, gilding even the coiled black hair of the swiftly moving girls.

XVI Jaipur and Agra

THEN THE SUMMER BEGAN—the summer of 1945. Germany was defeated. Though we did not know it, we were all now waiting for the atomic bomb. We were asking how long would it take to defeat Japan—two years, perhaps? Through the downpours of the monsoon this was the great topic of conversation and concern. Time hardly seemed to move. In Europe there was a sense of release, but for us the war continued to be just as pressing. The Indians felt differently—they were tired of waiting for time to move and did not intend to wait much longer. Then the bomb was dropped on Hiroshima.

The Japanese War, which had been going on since 1937, and the attack at Marco Polo Bridge were over! Through this fearful instrument, the atomic bomb, many months of war had been obviated, and possibly millions of lives saved. It was a dreadful thing for the Japanese—but one had to remember the years of destruction they had wantonly visited upon the unguarded, open cities of Asia. The sudden end of hostilities implied so much that I shall not attempt even to discuss it here.

Indian nationalism burst into fresh flames and the country was torn with daily riots, disturbances, speeches. The Congress and the Muslim League achieved no compromise but the temper of the people was such that some change was inevitable. Most of the Europeans longed ardently to leave the country before things got any worse, but there was very little transport available and that was mostly for the troops. We had to wait and take our turn.

In the fall of this year some inspection work was demanded in the native state of Jaipur, in Rajputana (now known as Rajasthan). We had any amount of leave due us, accumulated over the years—we had hardly taken any of it, due to the pressure of work and our lack of money. The pressure of work was now at least much less, and we decided that we must use this trip as a partial holiday and see not only Jaipur but Agra. Agra was included because there had been such a violent storm in October that great damage had been inflicted along the west coast and many miles of the Frontier Mail's line had been washed away in the state of Baroda. That was the train we should have taken for Jaipur and Rajputana—as it was we took the Punjab Mail, which meant changing at Agra. At last we could see the Taj.

At that time we felt particularly indignant about the state of Baroda, where the peasantry was wretchedly poor and whose Maharajah was so welcome at Ascot. He had recently been buying racers in England; one stallion had cost twenty-eight thousand guineas. This was strictly his own affair, as a native prince—his subjects could not rebel because the status quo was maintained by the dominant power. It did little to calm nationalist feeling.

The journey to Agra was enlivened by the presence of a genial Australian, an expert in agricultural equipment. He was on his way to Delhi to find out why his *zamindar* customers were being refused permits to buy the tractors they wanted and which the land so urgently needed, while permits were being issued for heavy types which were quite unsuitable. Weeks later, when we had all returned to the coast, we looked him up to ask him what he had discovered. He told us that the government insisted that the cultivators must wait till goods from the United Kingdom were ready for the market. (Even the Australians had no priority.) For at least two years only heavy tractors would be available from the "home" market and the Indians were being obliged to purchase these or nothing. Britain would not allow them to convert their sterling balances into gold to enable them to buy what they wanted at the time. It was on this meat that Congress fed.

All his stories were not so gloomy. He and his wife had recently been to the wedding of an Indian contractor's daughter in Jodhpur, a celebration which had cost the proud father some forty *lakhs* of rupees. Six hundred guests, including our friends, had been given their tickets from Bombay to Jodhpur and back, with their hotel bills and all their expenses paid—many stayed three weeks. Everyone had lavish presents and constant entertainment in the traditional style—dancing girls, theatrical troupes, music, banquets. In British India, during the war, such affairs were (in theory) not possible but there was more leeway in the native states.

Sometime during the second day an Indan naval officer, very smart in his white ducks, joined us. The men of the Indian Navy had a very attractive air of courteous reliability and one felt they would be good seamen; we were pleased when he came in. Our railway journeys gave us some of our most interesting hours in the country—it was then that we could meet people and talk to them. Our naval companion spoke freely about the state of his country and its partial estrangement from Britain, which he deplored very much. He attributed it to the type of person who had come out East for the last thirty years. "Always the wrong type of people," he reiterated, "self-seeking, often uneducated—or, if technically educated [and he included in this phrase the public schools], not genuinely educated—almost always arrogant, opinionated, callous." He thought that if Britain would make a clean sweep of most of the men from the mother country now holding office and readjust her policy to one more reasonable and less selfish, she might yet hold her position. We thought that possible in theory only. Where and how could she find such men?

About a hundred miles west of Agra the countryside becomes very romantic. The old forts of vanished kingdoms, little palaces, and ancient tombs rise from the barren ground, in the midst of long stretches of monotone brown soil where only a few wretched bushes could survive. The monsoon being just past, there was sometimes the faintest tinge of green on the few tilled fields we passed, where the hard dry earth had been sparsely planted and the wooden plows had scarcely broken the topsoil. The whole region seemed utterly deserted and I believe that during the whole day we spent going over the Deccan we did not see a single person, except in the stations.

The railway line passes directly under Gwalior's magnificent high golden walls. This is one of the most splendid forts in India, its crenellations surmounted by tempting glimpses of minarets and domes, its gates and cupolas the epitome of this type of architecture. Bitterly did we regret going on and leaving it unexplored. As the afternoon drew on towards evening and we approached Agra, the ground presented an astonishing effect. It is eroded into fantastic hills and valleys, with miniature mountains rising from tiny ranges, none over thirty feet high (most much less), of bone dry clay—a perfect maze. We could not discern a stone base and it seemed odd that, erosion having proceeded so far, the whole formation had not disappeared. The wild and mysterious contours vanished behind us and the train thundered on; we arrived in Agra and changed into another train which took us west into Rajputana.

The ruler of the state of Jaipur was a young and progressive Maharajah who, though a Hindu and controlling a population predominantly Hindu, had yet the imagination and good sense not to let his religion stand in the way of his employing good men to help govern the country. His Prime Minister was a Muslim, Sir Mirza Ismail. Before accepting this post, Sir Mirza had had a similar appointment in Mysore, another Hindu principality, where he had made a great reputation for himself. It was generally admitted that Mysore was the most advanced place in the whole of India, from the point of view of literacy, development, cleanliness, and progress, and the vigor and intelligence of this man were held largely responsible. Mysore had also an able and efficient maharajah and Jaipur was anxious to follow his example. (Both these states retained their rulers after Partition; when they were absorbed into India, these men were elected to office.) The harmonious progress in such states as these, resting upon real cooperation between Muslims and Hindus, made it obvious that these two communities could work and live together. We were not long within the borders of Jaipur before we began to hear of Sir Mirza's activities and aims. He was dealing drastically with the modernization of the capital. From the pictorial point of view some of these measures were to be regretted, but no one could seriously protest who had seen the terrible bazaar quarters of so many towns and knew what they implied in the way of living. He was substituting wide roads for the old lanes, demanding higher standards of public sanitation, and putting up better buildings.

Jaipur City is comparatively young. The maharajahs used to live in the mountain palace of Amber, a little distance from the present capital, with a modest town lying below it. Jai Singh II, the father of his people, a patriarch of great local renown, early in the eighteenth century decided to break out of this limited circle and transferred the court and the people to the new city on the plain.

We arrived at four in the morning when it was still dark and, to us, very cold—we shivered in our little-used sweaters. Some young men from the factory Stanton was to inspect had come to meet us. The chief of these strangers, we had been told, was exceedingly anti-British—a member of the Congress Party and an ardent nation-alist. His superficial politeness at that first meeting on the platform was accentuated by the biting scorn and resentment he automat-ically felt towards any persons who even in the most minor ca-pacity represented the hated Raj. But I was pleased to be met by anyone at all after our long journey, we were all happy and excited to be in Rajputana, and it would have taken a lot more than his icy manner to have dampened the enthusiasm of the little girls who were, indeed, completely unaware of it. A car was waiting for us and we were soon installed in a curious semi-foreign suite in the best hotel the little state could boast, the Kaiser-i-Hind.

Long years afterwards, when we were living in a small city in Germany as a part of the Control Commission, I talked a little of India to a lady whose husband had spent most of his career there and had left as a very senior member of the Indian Civil Service. I told her how curious I was as to what was happening there now, how I would like to go back and see. She told me she had no desire ever to see it again. Though she had loved it and had been perfectly contented with their lives there, she had no wish to return even for a short stay unless she were in a highly privileged position. She remarked that she liked being met on railway stations with the red carpet rolled out, and if that was not going to be done for her, she would rather never go. She did, I think, realize that this was an atti-tude difficult to defend on any ethical grounds, but she was none-theless very emphatic about it. She and her husband had many virtues and had received many honors—he had been knighted—but in their way they had no doubt contributed to the state of mind of our new host.

October is a good month to be in Rajputana—the sun is not too burning, the nights not yet really cold. After so many years of finding this month the most difficult of the year, it was a great pleasure to find in it again the bright and sparkling moon to which we had been accustomed before arriving in India. In most parts of China October is almost the best time of the year: the days of bright sunshine, the gardens full of gay flowers, the markets (in the old days) bursting with produce—pheasants and bamboo shoots, chestnuts and persimmons, chrysanthemums and cosmos. The nights were so crisp and clear after the summer heat, everyone felt invigorated. I had never become reconciled in India to the des-perate climate of this month. In Jaipur, once again, we could have the magic of autumn.

Jaipur and Agra

The city calls to mind the setting of a blithe ballet. Mirza Ismail had had all the municipal buildings and the booths and arcades of the bazaars painted a bright pastel pink—under the cheerful sunshine Jaipur could not have presented a more lighthearted, theatrical front. The citizens particularly loved a structure called "The Palace of the Winds," which is literally only a facade (pink, of course), just the high front of a plaster building which has neither back nor sides nor interior—or meaning, as far as we could discover. But this was the first "sight" we were shown—we were driven directly to it and helped out of the car that we might better admire it. I was already so delighted with the gaiety and freshness all about us that I became enamoured of this bauble at once.

The most charming feature of the city is the old wall, a low and ancient ribbon of creamy plaster. From the slits of its narrow, rounded crenellations falls a deep black line, the effect of weathering, which gives it the look of having black stripes, like a zebra. The stonework beneath the plaster is not massive and consorts well with the light and delicate graces of the town. Before this bizarre original wall and the pink structures which house the halls of justice and of government and the post offices pass the extravagant living creatures of Rajputana. It seemed too good to be true. Far down the wide road which encircles the wall go the Maharajah's elephants and strings of the proud shaggy camels from the desert, while everywhere along its length—on the ground, on the telephone wires, on the roofs—are the bold white sacred peacocks of the district. Troops of Mawari women walk by in the dust, the most pictorial of all the passersby. These poor girls of queenly bearing wore only the gaudiest colors, their full skirts swirling as they walked. I could hardly believe that so colorful and extravagant a city was not a mirage of the desert.

Mr. Lal, the young man who had met us so coldly at the station, showed us these things before taking us to the Palace, which lay at the heart of the town. Surprised by our interest, he began to forget his hostility and laid aside his grievances. He was, he told us, a Gujerati from Kathiawar and a scrupulously orthodox Jain. The Kathiawar states, in the peninsula north of Bombay, were at that time held by scores of petty rajahs and were miserably poor and undeveloped. A Kathiawari of any ambition, said Mr. Lal, was obliged to emigrate. There was quite a community of these people settled in Jaipur, which seemed a place more kindly to strangers than to its native sons—the state was anxious to avoid nepotism.

The firm in which we were interested was run largely by Kath-iawaris and our companion was evidently a rising star in their midst, but his gloom, from whatever cause, was patent. Our little daughters, having lost no time in penetrating his embittered Congress front, now lavished upon him their spontaneous demonstrative affection, which included everyone they met. Poor Mr. Lal! He had to desert his party line and like a British family! He told us that he was married to a beautiful girl and had many lively young cousins living in his household. They had come here from Kathiawar for their education. What were they studying? "Oh, the usual subjects—mathematics, history and languages." "What languages?" "Sanskrit, Hindi, and Gujarati," he replied, clearly surprised that I should ask anything so obvious.

While the men were busy, the children and I went to the zoo, where there were tigers, mongeese, and a whole family of mugger living in a stream. Much as I loathe zoos I did not feel I should deny the *babas* the chance of seeing these creatures before they in their turn would revolt against seeing them in captivity. We also visited the museum, where every attendant hastened to press peacock feathers upon us. I accepted them, thinking them a pretty present, until it dawned upon me that the donor of each feather expected an equivalent return in the shape of *baksheesh*. These long and beautiful feathers could be picked up off the ground quite easily anywhere in the city and there was no shortage of them at the zoo.

The hotel garden was also subject to the influence of the sacred bird—two of them lived in it and flaunted their white beauty on the lawns. The Kaiser-i-Hind (which is Hindustani for the Emperor of India) was a strange little semi-foreign hotel—it was tolerable for either Indians or Europeans but not wholly agreeable to either. In the evenings they turned on some little fountains which played in basins on the lawns. The best feature of the place, aside from the peacocks, was the veranda which ran along the front and was generally dominated by some merchant who had come up with a bundle from the bazaar. These local potentates took turns—one day it was a man with bejeweled slippers, their saffron or magenta toes sparkling with sequins (twenty-five years ago you never saw such things in the West though now every shoe shop in America has them), the next afternoon it would be a man with specimens of the inlaid brass which was a great specialty of the district. The man whose merchandise I liked best was a jewel merchant. He brought amethysts and white sapphires, topazes and opals—some set, some only as loose gems. These he laid out on the floor on a white cloth, their glowing surfaces making little pools of color, luminous and pure, to tempt the hotel guests. All of these vendors sat on the stone floor of the veranda, and in the afternoon hours when everyone was resting they would doze too on their little mats while waiting for their prey with all the patience which an absolute indifference to the passage of time can give.

Mr. Lal had arranged for us to visit the Palace, parts of which were open to an accredited public, even though the Maharajah and at least two of his Maharanees were in residence.

Within the precincts of the Palace is a small park, the setting of which must surely be the most fanciful and romantic observatory in the world, more so even than the old Mongol-Jesuit observatory in Peking. The Rajah Jai Singh had been so versatile a character that apart from his role as able and imaginative ruler, he was also an impassioned astronomer, a student of Ptolemy. With the help of a Bengali scholar called Dr. Jugernath he studied mathematics, astronomy, and the occult arts, and built four observatories in different parts of India, this one in Jaipur, in his own city palace, being the best. He believed that if possible astronomical instruments should always be made of marble, as he thought this substance more dimensionally stable and accurate than any metal. It is certainly more beautiful than most metals and the observatory on the green grass, bathed in sunshine under the luminous sky, hidden from the world by the walls of the Palace and again by the city walls, was of a surpassing charm and loveliness.

The instruments were locally known as the *junta munta* or "magic objects." At one end of the greensward and dominating the whole scene is the vast arc of an enormous equinoctial sundial. A prodigiously large marble crescent forms the scale of the dial, on which the sun's shadow is cast by a gnomon some sixty feet high—the span of the arc from horn to horn is at least eighty feet. The arc is made of marble blocks, each about five feet wide, perfectly white and intricately divided, showing every hair's breadth of shadow—providing a scale on which solar time could be read to the nearest second. Sunken marble stairs follow the curve of the crescent, becoming ever narrower and deeper as they ascend— deep enough to be safe for the observer, there is no need for a balustrade. The gnomon, the amazing triangle which bisects the arc, is of old yellow plaster, hard and fine, almost golden in shade, topped by a romantic little kiosk. This is reached by deep stairs which lead up the incline, affording at every step a more marvelous view of the two wide marble swirls which wing out on either side. The broad expanse of the golden wall of the gnomon is broken by large, balanced arches, calling to mind one of those great pictures of Roman aqueducts which Brangwyn painted—grandiose, sweeping, measured. This glorious instrument, this fantastic wonder, this queen of all the instruments that could ever be made, for any purpose, anywhere, is called the Samyat Yantra. Having once laid eyes upon it, it was for a long time difficult to see or to think of anything else.

Spaced on the lawns below this masterpiece are twelve much smaller marble instruments, each a suitably oriented segment of a disk, graduated so that transit observations could be carried out with them, and each marked with a sign of the Zodiac. To the ignorant eye (mine) they looked like twelve aureate pavilions, ornamented with marble in geometric style. The zodiacal signs were entirely familiar—these show, I think, no variation the world over —but they were amusingly interpreted, the Heavenly Twins being, for instance, particularly adorable little Rajputs. There are also celestial globes, equinoctial sundials, and altitude azimoths, some immense bronze disks, and other strange and fanciful conceits, strongly flavored with astrology and wizardry. Here Jai Singh and his associates, half-scholars, half-magicians, had measured the distances between the stars, observed the moon, calculated eclipses, foretold the future, and attempted to influence the affairs of state by making them subservient to these very stars. Beauty and mathematics Jai Singh loved; he could not resist dabbling in the mysteries of the occult—he was the child of his age and of his country.

We then entered the Palace, going through a fine old armory, its narrow rooms crowded with lances. Here the air was still and musty, no one seemed to have disturbed the quiet of the rooms for a long time. The weapons, once the pride and stay of their fiery owners, seemed peculiarly shadowy heaped in this forgotten corner.

In the arcade beyond we came upon the Palace quartet, who were practicing, sitting on the stone floor and resting their backs against the wall. The Jaipur quartet played without notes—though they had a large repertoire, they knew it only by ear. The music of the West was absolutely unknown to them. The drummer was lightly thumping his two little drums, using the palm of his hand and all his fingers. Beside him was the zither player, a man of great local renown. They were all poor men, unschooled and ragged, but clearly true musicians—their position was comparable to that of the gifted performers in the German courts in the eighteenth century. Mr. Lal told us that the outer world of Rajputana paid the zither player great sums for his occasional appearances but that his professional life was very difficult because he was obliged to be in the service of the Maharanee. Whenever she wished to hear him, he had to appear after only fifteen minutes' warning, and during that time he had to dress himself in resplendent livery.

The zither player, a heavy person in a shabby turban, was strumming his *sarangi* idly but as though he could not have it in his hand without conversing with it. I stopped and watched him, trying at last to play it myself. Though I could do nothing with it, he was delighted that I should try—at once there sprang up between us those ties which unite the lovers of music. The *sarangi* has a bulbous body, a long neck, large stops, and many spiderish strings which are pressed from *underneath*. It is a beautiful instrument but hard on the performer because of this strange necessity—the master's nails were broken and his fingers calloused through constant practice. He played us a few random bars which seemed to come from the same spring as the melodies of Rimski-Korsakov. Scheherazade herself belonged to the world of the *sarangi*.

Leaving these artists with regret, we went down a long stone corridor and out into a grassy court which contained a neat square little house. Downstairs this contained a library of precious books and upstairs an art gallery of Rajput prints. These included many portraits of Jai Singh and his descendants.

I was tired and sat down on the first chair I saw in the library, which was next to a table on which lay an immense illustrated book. The room was cool and shady with many windows and, happy to be again in the precious atmosphere of a library, I pulled the book towards me and began to turn over its enormous pages. As I came to a particularly curious picture Mr. Lal came across the room and looked over my shoulder, explaining to me the legend it illustrated. It was about a famous lover's trial. The suitor, in order to win his lady, had been given a number of Herculean tasks in

Rajput form; on this occasion he had to put out the eye of a gold-fish using a bow and arrow and being allowed only to see the reflection of the fish in a bowl of boiling water. In the picture the small and unfortunate goldfish was hanging well above a large cauldron, under which a fire crackled, while the young hero gazed earnestly into the troubled waters, his bow drawn for action. It made William Tell's feat look ridiculously easy.

Mr. Lal had told us that we were also to see the elephants of the Palace stud and all morning the poor children grew progressively desperate as they saw more and more time wasted on observatories, libraries, armories, and musicians. From their point of view (five and three years old) the whole purpose of the expedition was to see the elephants and here were the adults rooted to one spot after another, ruining their lives. They were well-mannered and restrained themselves as long as they could, but at last the breaking point was almost reached and we left the art gallery and started towards the stables.

At that time the Maharajah had eighteen elephants. Their upkeep was very expensive and was causing some anxiety to the palace accountants, which was in itself a sad reflection on the times. I was glad, as I listened to all this, that I had never had to worry over the maintenance of my elephants. It was necessary to the Maharajah's prestige that he keep this stud—all the other rajahs round about had elephants and they were a *sine qua non* in all state processions. An elephant then cost at least twenty thousand rupees (well over a thousand pounds) and the daily expenses of each animal were about one hundred rupees. (For purposes of comparison, an *ayah* in a European household at that time drew thirty-five rupees a month—in an Indian establishment she was paid much less.) Each elephant required four attendants and then there was the problem of their food. Sugar was rationed, yet each beast had to have a minimum of eight pounds of *ghur* (the unrefined native sugar) every day. It is never possible to pass judgment on what constitutes an unjustifiable luxury to other people—no doubt very many Jaipuris considered these elephants worth whatever they cost. Any state which maintains a court and goes in for pomp and display can do this only so long as the people (ultimately) will pay for it. Certainly during our short stay we had great pleasure in the elephants, but we saw them more advantageously than most people in the state ever could.

The elephants and their *mahouts* were in an enormous cobbled courtyard where there was both hot sunlight and deep shade from some large trees—it all gave very much the traditional idea of India. The animals, so dignified, so individual, gave an impression of sapience. It was a new thing for us to come upon so many of them together and they were so intelligent and so calm that we felt as though we had come to call on, not to "see," them.

Two were having their baths at a well, standing quite still while their attendants doused them with water. Servants were drawing up skinfuls from the depth and it took an immense number of these before one elephant became even wet, let alone washed. Others were resting under the trees, looking as though they were composing their memoirs. As we passed by, their *mahouts* would ask them to salaam to us—each time the elephant in question raised his trunk and with the greatest courtesy gave us his salute.

All of them were then in the process of being decorated for the coming Dussehra Puja when the whole town would be *en fête*. Many were already stained a bright cobalt blue and some had had their ears gaudily painted with large red and yellow flower patterns (the Puja would not start for several days but they had to start early with this elaborate making up). The animals looked very charming in this guise and offered great scope to the imaginative artist—one was immediately full of ideas on how to paint and decorate an elephant. I felt my horizon widening very rapidly.

One elephant was unable to join his fellows in the courtyard— alas! he was in chains. He had belonged to the Maharajah of Ajmeer and in a fit of madness, some four months previously, had killed his *mahout*. For this he would have been destroyed, had not Jaipur happened to be in the state at the time; pleading for his life, he received him as a present. We went to see him in his covered stable. They had secured his hind legs and made him stand with his back to the courtyard and his head to the wall, that he might better meditate upon his sins. He was now mild enough to allow himself to be painted blue and was to take part in the celebrations. His keepers did not seem at all afraid of him and he was already an accepted member of the community.

A very thin, very old *mahout* then climbed upon the neck of his charge, who was resting under a tree, and made him get upon his feet. While this was going on—an elephant does not rise quickly— Rosalind was handed up to his back and together she and the *mahout* made a stately tour of the courtyard. "Mr. Lal," inquired the little girl on her way home in the car, while she held her victim's hand, "how would you like to be an elephant?" By this time Mr. Lal was more than ready to be anything she liked.

One night we went to an entertainment at the factory where all the audience sat on the grass and were amused by conjurors and singers and speeches. In the front were the women and children, very fine in gauzy saris, gold embroidery, and white coats for the little boys. The conjuror delighted us with his first trick, which was to shoot the eye out of a goldfish by looking at its reflection in boiling water!—the details of this impossible feat being slightly modified. He lamented to the audience that he ought to receive a fair princess but knew very well he would in fact get nothing. The long arm of coincidence! Had I not happened to have seen just that one picture in the library that morning, I would never have heard of this *tour de force* before, and from that day to this I have never come across any reference to it.

The children had one experience which I envied them—they were invited to lunch with the Lals. Mr. Lal asked us in an impromptu fashion, evidently never dreaming that we would accept, and his extreme pleasure and surprise that we did was sad. The children accordingly vanished into the purdah part of his square house, which stood in a neat, uncommunicative lawn ornamented with four severe little rose bushes. They came out cheerful and happy in the course of time but did not tell me very much about it, except that there was a grandmother and that they had had curry.

Our last expedition in the state was to the old Palace of Amber. We drove out to it in a small car, into which squeezed Mr. and Mrs. Lal, two grown-up cousins, four of us, the driver, and our poor *ayah*, who was made to sit on the floor beside a large bundle of fruit. How this was accomplished I do not know, sometimes the impossible is achieved. After we left the city we found ourselves once more in the sere, romantic countryside we loved so dearly, where the crumbling ruins of many an old palace, with its arcades and cupolas, appeared here and there in the dry hard fields. Deserted, unidentified, these faded evocative fragments persist all the way to the hills and the palace-fortress itself. Amber still seemed full of life—it was in good condition, its village still inhabited, and the sprightly quality innate in Jaipur was to be felt here also. Its cheerful golden-yellow walls are to be seen from afar, overhanging a well-kept palace garden. In the courtyard of a lodge below the fortress our valiant car drew up; waiting there were two elephants from the Jaipur Palace who were to take us on up to Amber, an arrangement of Mr. Lal's, whose one idea in life now seemed to be to give us every possible pleasure.

The Lal family installed themselves on Goulab Peri ("Rose Nymph"), who was handsomely clothed in red, while we climbed up a stepladder to the *houdah* of Mohum Lal ("The Necklace around the Neck of Lal"), a stylish creature who was wearing a saffron-colored garment besprinkled with huge red roses and enriched with a deep red and saffron fringe. The Necklace then lumbered to his feet, giving us the sensation of being in an earthquake. *Ayah*, terrified, clung to me, while I seized the children. They had nothing to hold on to, as the *houdah* was a sketchy affair without sides—only footrests, which their legs could not reach. Also, alas, it had no awning.

The Nymph and the Necklace filed majestically out of the courtyard and passed along the road towards the village, where they turned as sharply as was possible for creatures of their prehistoric build and began the ascent to Amber. At that dusty corner, which we so slowly negotiated, was the most romantic vehicle in the world of today, waiting for us to pass. It was a bullock-drawn carriage *circa* 1400. Narrow, long, and high (something of the proportions of a lady's pump), partially screened by canopies and curtains of faded rose brocade, it was crowded with the ladies and children of some country gentleman's *zenana*, reposing on carpets. They looked up at us with avid curiosity in their great black eyes, while I gazed down on them equally eager, equally curious. Then we lost each other forever. The carriage started forward on its high wooden wheels, its dusty draperies trembling slightly, while we went our way past the lake which lies at the foot of the hill. Where were they going and whence had they come in their fantastic carriage? They were like persons in a dream to us, vivid, but almost meaningless—as, no doubt, we were to them.

The Palace extends along the higher levels of the hillside; for a longish distance you must go under its glowing ochre walls, passing through high gateways. Below lie the village and the lake, above, high on the hill, are watch towers, bastions, powder magazines, all of the golden color so characteristic of Rajputana. The elephants' "eight times as slow" movement was still too fast for me, so fascinating was every single scene upon which our eyes rested. On one stretch of the road we were so fortunate as to meet a string of camels, whose scorn we could for once return from our greater dignity on the backs of the Rajah's household elephants. To meet camels while in a mere car can be terribly humiliating. They curl their lips and look down their noses.

There are gardens planted round the lake, as well as projecting into the water, very quaint and artful in design, geometric and complicated. The tense formality of the rococo gardens, patterned after Versailles and found in so many small European courts, was after this order, but here it was even more like a fretted puzzle. Fitting well into this severe and studied setting, large monkeys whose extremely thin tails were neatly curled at the very ends walked on the shore or swung themselves up the hillside through the large trees. On our right was the long expanse of the yellow walls, high and strong, broken by splendid gateways, fretted windows, and captivating balconies.

When we descended from the Necklace and the Nymph and went through the wide and sprawling Palace, we found it a warm, intimate place, more plaster than marble, more light than shade with many cheerful, insouciant kiosks and balconies. It was of a feminine persuasion, in keeping with Rajput history where women have ever played a significant role. High up on the immense flat roof was a platform for dancing girls, where they performed by moonlight before an audience lounging on divans. There were some walls inlaid with tiny bits of broken mirrors whose sparkling facets gave back distorted images. The Kathiawar Lals proved sufficiently under Rajput influence to find this rather meretricious decor exquisitely lovely. Under one beautiful gateway we all sat down to refresh ourselves with pomegranates and conversation; there were hardly any other visitors, we almost had the whole Palace to ourselves.

Near the entrance and holding pride of place was an active Hindu temple, while high up in one of the courts was the dining room of a particularly zealous rajah, who had had the walls painted with pictures of the Holy Cities that he might worship them all, especially Benares, before he broke his fast. The other palace-fortresses we had been seeing were all Muslim—here one did not forget for a moment that Rajputana was Hindu territory. But the striking thing about the little dining room was to find any apartment actually designed for *eating*, which is such a complicated and awkward activity for most Hindus. This one was very small, and the rajah had always dined alone with his naive and primitive little frescoes.

When Indians wish to give presents it is very difficult to say them nay. We had had several years experience in refusing every gift ever offered us, which was, of course, essential procedure for people in the Inspectorate. Mr. Lal could not endure this, in the end I broke down and accepted two little brass finger bowls and two little brass leaves; he was upset that they could not be a dozen. By the time we left Jaipur we could hardly recognize this young man as the same person who had met us at the station, not many days before. The train for Agra was late and an attentive station-master had large chairs drawn up for us on the platform while we waited. Mr. Lal held one of the children; it was late and she fell asleep in his arms. He looked down on her fairness, saying, with tears, "For her there is no caste, and no color."

Agra

In his august personal appearance, he [Akbar] was of middle height but inclining to be tall; he was of the hue of wheat; his eyes and eyebrows were black and his complexion rather dark than fair; he was lion-bodied with a broad chest and hands and arms long. . . . His august voice was very loud and in speaking and explaining had a peculiar richness. In his actions and movements, he was not like the people of the world, and the glory of God manifested itself in him.

Jehangir

There exists a bond between the Creator and the creature which is not expressible in language.

Akbar

The glories of Agra—the Fort, the Taj, the tomb of Itmad-ud-Daula, the old pleasure gardens—lie along the banks of the Jumna. Splendid and beautiful as these all are, the Taj yet stands alone, without a rival—the travelers' tales do not lie. No panegyric, no praise, can do it justice, so enchanting, so pure, so absolute is this marvelous building.

We saw it first at midnight. The heat of the day had vanished, all was hushed, silent, and almost deserted. There is a long approach to the gardens of the tomb, by a tree-lined avenue past deep arcades, wrapped at that hour in vague shadows. The high dome of the gateway was lit by an immense lamp of copper filigree whose strong, mild flame was fed by oil, giving just the right degree of illumination for this entrance chamber. It, and another within the Taj itself, were gifts of Curzon. Even though it was so late there were still guardians there, and while I gazed at the intricate shadows thrown by the lantern onto the large stones of the floor, Stanton arranged with one of the men to take us out into the park.

He led us along a dark waterway, lined with cypresses, to the upper terrace which holds the square pond. Not a ripple moved the water, the trees did not move in the still air, there was no murmur from any voice. Even the gentle glow of the copper lamp had been enough for a time to render us incapable of making out anything at all in the darkness—we could only distinguish the lines of the pools, which reflected a shimmer of starlight, and sense the tall sentinels beside them, till from the terrace we could begin to see the dim outlines of the tomb ahead, which is too white to be quite hidden by night. Here our guide stopped us and made us take off our shoes. The attendant who kept the box of slippers had gone; Stanton had socks on, but I was obliged to go up barefoot like a true pilgrim. The smooth hard marble, still slightly warm from the long day's sun, was delicious to feel under my feet and I felt at once a contempt for the bondage of shoes.

A short stairway, sunken in the wall, leads up to the wide terrace which surrounds the majestic building. It was much lighter here than down among the cypresses by the pools, but we still could not gain much more than a shadowy impression of the great size of the shrine. From within came the soft gleam of the lamp, the companion to the one of the gatehouse, which hangs over the two sepulchers; this we followed till we saw the tombs, enclosed in a fantasy of soft wavering shadows which were cast by the screens of marble filigree which surround them. The guide, picking up an oleander flower from among the petals which lay scattered on Mumtaz Mahal's grave, presented it to me with a somber and practiced courtesy—he knew how to enhance the spell of the hour and the darkness—and, moving away a little distance, tilted back his turbaned head and called loudly towards the dome so that we might hear the echo resounding in the vast, dim, empty marble chamber. "A—llah! Al-lah!"

Mumtaz Mahal's grave lies in the exact center of the building, which is itself centered on a line from the gatehouse—everything is mathematically perfect, even the cypresses seem to match each other in every nuance across the pools. The only asymmetry in the whole design rests with the tomb of Shah Jehan, who lies here beside his love. He had not meant this to be so, but had intended, when he buried his Begum, to make for himself another, identical, tomb across the river, confronting this one. His was to have been of black marble—what a conceit that would have been! A replica of the white marble image which the world has so long loved—but black, with black minars, beside its own pools and cypresses! But there was no filial son to carry out such plans. Aurangzeb killed his brother Dara and seized power—he was the last person who would have emptied the treasury by building yet another great tomb. Jehanara, the cherished favorite daughter who had tended her father to the last, could do nothing. Nor indeed, could such a building have been justified—except that Aurangzeb himself wasted his people's monies with his endless wars and the traditional Mogul heritage of fine building did, ultimately, give back something to the nation.

The next time we went back was in the bright light of an afternoon. The terrace which holds the main building has, at each corner, a minar—I wondered if the whole might not have been more beautiful without them. From a short distance the faint lines between the great blocks of marble composing these towers are slightly visible, giving an heretical effect of giant blocks, and the severity of the four straight masts is the more marked because they are so near the flowing curves of the central structure. They are traditionally correct and no doubt the artists concerned felt they lent emphasis and strength to the whole design—anyone capable of planning the Taj could not, I told myself, have erred here.

That afternoon, our shoes properly wrapped up in immense slippers, we padded about everywhere, giving the minarets particular attention as we strolled on the terrace above the river. Finally we followed the narrow winding stair up the heart of the right-hand minar on the Jumna side to gain a view of the gardens. Behind us, on this ascent, came a whole flock of Muslim ladies, their colored satin *burqas* streaming behind them. I left the procession at the first small circular balcony, where I sat down on the floor, looking straight across at the marble domes of the tomb itself, one pure curve after another, mounting into the vivid and cloudless sky as though they were themselves cumulous clouds. Below on the terrace in a little patch of shade sat our *ayah,* amusing Celia. The baby was barefoot, as there were no slippers small enough for her feet and we had not thought of bringing socks for her; in that heat children hardly ever wore them. Above me, high in the sunlight rose the white shaft of the minar and as I watched I saw Stanton and Rosalind with their escort of lady Mohammedans come out on the second balcony. Even where I was there was a fair view, the park spread out, green and inviting, with people coming and going in an easy and animated mood. The Indians loved and appreciated their Taj, approaching it with respect— but they also came to see it for pleasure, bringing their children with them, and resting beside the pools as they went through the gardens.

Our last visit was when the Dussehra festival was in progress and the Hindus celebrating riotously in the town, but the lights and the shouting did not extend to this pure shrine. That night the moon was half-full and the marble and mosaics gleamed in the soft and tender light more beautifully, it seemed to us, than they could have done under the sharper, rather cold, illumination of the full moon. It is one of the witcheries of the Taj to make you feel, every time you go there, that she has never been so lovely before. When I saw it that night from the arch of the gateway I literally started—it seemed a vision, an angelic mirage floating in the soft azure sky, which acquired a new depth in supporting this white dream. The long, dark, narrow pools in the stillness of the evening reflected in their depths the noble dome, as white as a swan on the water. The bolder stars were still visible, despite the moon, and the jewels on the facade answered them, sparkle for sparkle. We felt that we could not bear to leave such loveliness and turned again and again for a last lingering glance. Then our old *tonga* carried us slowly under the walls of the Fort, where we could now hear from far away in the bazaars the sounds of revelry. We did not want to hear—we had seen the palace which the genii created for the prince.

The crenellations and bastions of the Red Fort command a long section of the river bank some distance from the Taj. From above the encircling wall, little windy pavilions, the most famous of which is the Jasmine Tower (the Samman Burj), overhang the Jumna. From it one has a fine direct view of the tomb, as well as a miniature image which is reflected in a particular jewel set in a wall panel and which acts as a tiny mirror. It was to this little kiosk that Shah Jehan was carried in his last hours that he might look once more on the place he loved. During the last seven years of his life, when he was a prisoner in the Fort, he lived in fairly luxurious but close confinement. He had a terrace and a few rooms, as well as a small and perfect mosque of absolutely white marble where he was allowed to perform his devotions.

When as a prince Shah Jehan was conspiring against his father, Jehangir, he once asked the Portuguese to supply him with arms from their establishment on the Hooghly. Unwilling to stake their fortunes on this young pretender, they refused. He never forgot this slight. After he had secured the throne he expelled them from their position in Bengal (in 1631) and pulled down the Catholic churches which the Jesuits had erected in Agra and Lahore.

There is a legend to the effect that when Shah Jehan's favorite daughter was almost fatally burned she was only saved through the skill of an English surgeon, Gabriel Broughton. She was going through some arcades in the Palace at night and tripped over a thread, which was attached at one end to a candle, placed in a niche—these rows of candles were the usual and very beautiful illumination. The princess was wearing a gauzy sari, and in a moment she was wreathed in flames. After her mother, the Mumtaz Begum, had died she was the greatest consolation to her father and when she was so injured the Emperor was in despair. When the doctor was asked, after the recovery of Jehanara, what he would like as a reward, he is supposed to have petitioned on behalf of his countrymen for trading rights in Bengal. If this be true it was a modest and fortuitous way to lay the foundation of an empire in India which would be even greater than Shah Jehan's.

Lying above the wall of the Fort is an immensely wide, long marble terrace on which two platforms face each other—one of white, one of black, marble. From this vantage point the nobles would watch elephants fighting in a deep pit beside the wall below them. Behind this vast promenade, high above the level of the city, are gardens and pools, one of which has in its center a stage, so that the lovely girls who danced there could be reflected in the waters. The *zenana* quarters, which are further back from the wall, retain some little traces of the strangers who lived there— the Rajput princesses had their rooms adorned with that inlay of tiny fragments of glass, the type of decor we had seen at Amber.

This great fortress of red sandstone, so intimately bound up with the long era of Mogul power and supremacy—with Akbar, Jehangir, and Shah Jehan, with Dara, Jehanara, and Aurangzeb—is a small kingdom in itself, with special gardens (one for growing grapes) and private palaces, with courtrooms and prisons, and even a little marketplace. In the *Akbarnamah*, Akbar's autobiography, there is a picture of the building of the Fort which shows materials coming up the river to the water gate and the laborers carrying beams, mixing mortar, unloading camels, all with the greatest energy. (The print is in the Victoria and Albert Museum in London.) In front of the Diwan-i-Am, the Hall of Public Audience, set into the paving of the courtyard, is perhaps the most surprising feature of the whole fortification—a fussy Victorian sepulcher, the grave of the Honorable J. R. Colvin, the Lieutenant Governor of the North Western Provinces who died in the Fort in the dread year 1857.

The city which harbors the Taj suffers the disadvantage that nothing else can hold its own beside that pearl—everyone must always be hastening back to it. The other buildings lie within the common sphere of discussion and criticism, while the Taj rests on another plane. Yet it has serious rivals. Further down the river, past the Fort, is another near-miraculous tomb, that of Itmad-ud-Daula, the maternal grandfather of Mumtaz Mahal, the father of Nur Jehan, who was the wife of the Emperor Jehangir. Jehangir had fallen in love with Nur Jehan as a young man, when he somehow had occasion to catch a glimpse of her, but his father disapproved of the match, as she was not highly born, nor rich. He therefore had her married to the Governor of Burdwan, one Sher Afgan.

It was this very father whom Akbar thought unworthy to be a member of his family who lies buried here in this beautiful building, erected by his daughter, who in spite of Akbar became the Empress—and a very dominating one indeed, she was the stronger character of the imperial pair and greatly feared. Jehangir, cruel and treacherous, yet able and a connoisseur, was no match for her. There is a posthumous portrait of him by Bichitra (also in the Victoria and Albert) painted about 1645, showing him as the glass of fashion and the mold of form—with a string of pearls round his neck, wearing a flared skirt of a stiff green, a green turban, and holding a jewel. He was then still a prince, not yet an autocrat.

The Empress's father had been a Persian adventurer called Mirza Ghyas Beg (or Uddin) who, unable to make his way in Teheran, decided to come to the court of the Great Mogul Akbar to seek his fortune. He had a terrible journey across the desert, with only his wife and a small son, as they had not been able to travel in caravan, being destitute. A child was born on the way, a daughter, whom the father decreed must be abandoned—he saw no possibility of caring for her, their own survival was doubtful. The mother was in despair. As they turned away from the baby a huge serpent suddenly appeared, making straight for the infant. Mirza Ghyas Beg, more pious than compassionate, took this as a sign that Allah willed the child should be saved. At last, after many vicissitudes, they arrived in Agra where they prospered greatly, Mirza receiving court appointments and becoming Itmad-ud-Daula, or Prime Minister—a title conferred upon him by Jehangir.

Nur Jehan had married the Emperor in 1611. The prince never forgot her and when he came to power he caused her husband to be killed in battle. Mihar-un-Nisa, as she was then called, could not resist his command that she be installed in the imperial harem, but even in that environment she observed full mourning for her husband for six whole years, refusing even to see Jehangir. Nur Jehan means "Light of the World" and it is certain that the Emperor was captivated by the lady always, though their life together was stormy.

Itmad-ud-Daula died in 1622. Nur Jehan commenced building his tomb at once and it was finished after six years. The mosaics and inlay, the perfection of workmanship of this building, no doubt had great influence on the Taj, which was erected later—probably some of the same craftsmen were involved.

The sepulcher is in a large, perfectly square garden which runs down to the banks of the river and is of a severely simple basic plan—everything foursquare. There is the usual deep gateway, the pavilions at each corner of the wide lawn, with the tomb at the river end of the garden, resting on a marble terrace which has minarets at the corners. What makes this shrine so rare is its extreme delicacy—it gives the impression of a jewel casket. The walls are either unadorned white marble or inlaid with the most exquisite mosaics. These are in conventional designs but each separate panel is so beautiful, graceful, and poetic that it is a treasure in itself. The themes are floral arrangements or the rose-water bottles and incense burners that signify the final parting. The lower story is paneled with these charming studies; above, where are the tombs of the Prime Minister and his wife, the walls are entirely of marble filigree, the intricate patterns worked out with great harmony of conception, resulting in a lacy perfection. Sitting on the floor and studying these fretted walls, through which a gentle light, tempered and shady, comes into the cool room, one senses a sweet contentment and tranquility in the mood of the place hard to understand. The persons of the drama were not gentle or sweet but, leaving and looking back upon the flawless elegance of the tomb, the impression of dulcet charm was deepened. Nearby is the Chini-ka-Rauza, so called because this old tomb was once covered with tiles in the Chinese manner—but the tiles were actually of Persian inspiration and now most of them have fallen off and broken. It is only a modest tomb, in a small deserted corner; it is half-forgotten and crumbling away but there is an eloquent though fading charm about it—it plays its modest but distinguished role here among the greater splendors of this once lavish river bank. We saw it just before sunset, in a moment of poetic melancholy which consorted well with the old dome and the swift shadows which were lengthening on the warm white dust of the road. It is the memorial and sepulcher of a poet of Shiraz called Shukrullah, who served both Jehangir and Shah Jehan.

Beyond the Chini-ka-Rauza are some lovely old gardens, neglected, almost deserted, quiet; they seemed still to hold a certain wise charm and a gentle melancholy. Members of the court came here in search of simplicity and privacy. There is one now called the Rambagh, which is overgrown and rambling, leading past untidy bushes and great trees by unswept paths till the Jumna is reached. It was a retreat for the noblewomen of the court who could fish here in a deep square pool and loiter unobserved in the shade of the trees. The Rambagh is reputed to be one of the oldest places in Agra which came under the care of the Moguls for, according to legend, Baber himself had it laid out and loved it, making it an oasis for himself in the desert of Hindustan. It may even have been inspired by the renowned gardens in Kabul, the Bagh-i-nur-Afshan. The Moguls were homesick for Afghanistan; Baber was never reconciled to living in India. "Bagh-i-nur-Afshan" is the prettiest name in the world for a park—it means "the Garden of Spangled Light."

One day we went out to see Fatehpur Sikri, the city Akbar built as his capital outside Agra, and abandoned after having lived there a few years. In spite of the favored rival city, Agra flourished, even building its Fort at the same time that the severe red sandstone palaces of Fatehpur Sikri were going up on the plain far from the river. Ralph Finch, the English traveler, wrote of these two places: "Agra is a very great city and populous, built with stone, with a fair river running by it. It hath a fair castle with a large ditch. From there, we went to Fatehpur Sikri, which is the place where the king kept his court. The town is larger than Agra but the houses and streets are not so good. The king hath in Agra and Fatehpur Sikri, 1,000 elephants, 30,000 horses, 1,400 tame deer, 800 concubines and such store of leopard, tigers, buffaloes, cocks and hawks, that it is very strange to see. He keepeth a great court. Agra and Fatehpur are very great cities, either of them much greater than London."

In spite of the careful records kept of Akbar's reign, it is not clear why he felt the necessity of building the new capital and then of abandoning it in 1585. After that he often administered his great nation from Lahore but in 1600 he returned to Agra, living in the Fort where he died in 1605. It may be that it was founded primarily with a religious motive or that possibly he wanted to uproot his nobles from their old seat of power. Perhaps it was the result of a grandiose vision, which only an oriental potentate could put into effect.

There was originally at this site the little village of Sikri, the home of the holy man Salim Chisti. Akbar, with his passionate interest in religion and philosophy, had made a friend of Salim Chisti to whom he confided his dismay that though he was the father of many daughters he had no son. Salim Chisti offered prayers on his behalf, and when the Hindu Empress Maryam-uz-Zaman had a boy the Emperor called him Salim in gratitude. This was the prince who afterwards took the imperial name of Jehangir and who probably gave his father much more sorrow than joy. It was after this birth, which seemed then so auspicious, that Akbar decided to develop Fatehpur Sikri, a city which was always deeply involved in religious ideas and religious controversy. It was here that the Emperor and his counsellors worked on the problem of a composite religion, a blend of Mohammedanism and Hinduism which would help unite the country through all men embracing one faith. It is extraordinary that a man so intelligent and practical as Akbar could have even imagined that such a thing might be possible; yet, compared with the outlook of nearly everyone in contemporary Europe, it was an advanced concept. Akbar was a truly tolerant man at a time when most of the civilized Western world was convulsed with religious prejudice and bigotry. Fatehpur was always full of holy, and not so holy, men, many of them intensely ambitious and longing to go in for empire-building in their own way; there was constant discussion and argument over religious affairs and principles. It may be that one reason why the city was finally deserted was that the priestly caste became over-bearing, aware of its privileges, taking advantage of the ruler's inclinations. Perhaps Akbar came to realize that no effective religion could ever be born there and wished to escape from the pressure of the charlatans around him. There was undoubtedly something wrong about the place. He himself espoused his own new faith (Din-i-Ilahi) but exerted no pressure on others to worship with him or join him—this was probably the most remarkable and admirable act of his life.

The city was built entirely of red sandstone, not a very beautiful material. Having been abandoned when everything was still new and always having been perfectly maintained, it was not in the least worn or shabby and the climate has aided in its preservation. This contributes to an extraordinary effect. You go out expecting to see a vast, princely shell, magnificent and romantic after the Mogul manner, full of imperial glories but of a tragic and mysterious mood—the deserted city, the enigma. But what you find is something severe and practical—almost a "utility capital," as Stanton remarked. It is the very antithesis of such a place as Ankor Wat, for instance.

The entrance, however, is very fine. Here is the immense Victory Gate erected to commemorate conquests in the Deccan, the Buland Darwaza, nearly 180 feet high and reached by a very high flight of stairs. This leads into a large and well-proportioned court-yard, in one corner of which is Salim Chisti's tomb and beyond that a mosque—the religious issue is immediately apparent. The ornamentation is drawn from both Muslim and Hindu motifs throughout: there are carvings of lotus and parrots, as well as the Muslim decor which one would expect. It is slightly ornamented, however, compared to most of the great cities—it was evidently intended to be rather simple and straightforward.

As we entered the courtyard we were seized upon by guides, many of whom claimed at once to be direct descendants of the saint. Indian guides seemed to suffer from most of the occupational drawbacks of their Western colleagues, but they were even more of a trial because they were generally almost wholly ignorant of their subject. Their chief function seemed to be that as they knew their way through the courtyards and up the ramps of the various buildings, they could at least insure that their clients did not get lost. Those at Fatehpur had two claims to distinction: first, their descent, and second, the number of titled visitors whom they had shown over the city—the names of whom they were only too eager to relate. Happily Fatehpur was an obvious sort of place and (surprisingly) well sign-posted, so we refused to allow any of the gadflies to attend us.

The saint's tomb was oppressive with incense and pious horrors, as were the dozens of other graves sunk in the ground or lodged in a mortuary building nearby. This was the only Mohammedan burial ground we had come across which gave this horrid impression of churchyard mold—was this because of the perversion of faiths which had taken place here and the dubious nature of the whole experiment? We were glad to press on into the town.

The Town Planning Committee, starting work early in 1570, had thought of everything and the building was rushed through in a few years (the Victory Gate was added later). The capital was enclosed by a wall on three sides; on the fourth was once a lake. The perimeter of the city was six miles long. Halls, courtyards, apartments for the Emperor and the harem, pavilions for poets, lairs for saints, an elephant tower (which was stuck full of great spikes like an enormous pineapple) and long rows of stables, a musicians' gallery and a mint were all constructed of the same material—red sandstone. It had been taken into consideration that the royal city must have its fantastic elements and many amusing conceits had been elaborated, such as the courtyard marked in squares like a giant chessboard, on which the pieces were to be dancing girls. There was also the unique Hall of Audience in a small kiosk. In this, the entrance vestibule formed the lower story while the room upstairs, directly over it, was formed like an "X"— two narrow passages crossed each other diagonally, while at the meeting point was a small circular space just large enough to hold a modest throne; the diagonals were like little bridges thrown out over the vestibule. On these narrow lanes sat the petitioners, ministers, and secretaries, while Akbar held the center. It must have been cool, suspended over the deep well of the vestibule, and perhaps any possible danger of assassination was lessened in this small and curious conference chamber.

In spite of these extravaganzas we found Fatehpur unutterably dull. Whether we would think so today I do not know; at any rate it was the only one of these famous places that did not please us. The Victory Gate was different, but it was not built as part of the "package" and had its own individuality. None of the buildings in the city, with their monotonous finish, seemed to us beautiful and we concluded that the court, like ourselves, had been so bored there that they had at last been eager to abandon it to the wilderness and the panthers, which reputedly infested the neighborhood, and to return to the delights of Agra.

Even the floors of the pavilions were of red sandstone—the floors, the walls, the ornamentation. The quarters allotted to Birbal, the poet, were alarmingly similar to the stables—the material was the same and the same department had clearly approved the plans. The screens and lattices of the harem might have been machine made in their rigid symmetries. There was one curious building, the Panch Mahal, five stories high and each receding from the other, but it was no good—it had no charm, it was too deliberately worked out as an eccentricity straight from the factory. There were legions of little cupolas stuck on the roofs of the city, looking like baubles filched from a Victorian railway station in the Midlands. I felt sure that the artists, the fops, the ministers, and the literati—everyone but the priests—in Akbar's court had felt the same way.

There was at least one exception in this great and lamentable waste of time, labor, treasure, and enthusiasm: the courtyard of the palace designed for Jodh Bhai, Akbar's Rajput wife. It is not certain that it was finished in time for her ever to occupy it but such an air of sweetness hangs over it that I thought she must have lived there, or else have loved it while it was building. The courtyard, so wide and calm, might almost have been part of a palace in Peking—everything four-square with just a trace of turquoise glazing left on a few roof tiles. The perfection of its proportions gave it such grace that it reduced the rest of Fatehpur to more of a mockery than ever. There was here a true feeling of integrity and content. This modest court and the Buland Darwaza alone, in our eyes, gave Fatehpur any true value.

On the road between Fatehpur and Sikri is Sikandra, Akbar's tomb, which is also in absolutely atrocious taste. The great art which we associate with the Moguls, with Shah Jehan and Jehangir, did not come from Akbar himself. The gateway here is handsome and strong—these people's instinct for the fortress gate was too sure ever to falter—but the main building is like an overloaded red and white Hindu wedding cake. The actual sepulcher is hidden at the end of a deep dark passage in the heart of the building; on the roof amidst spurious marble trifles is another monument, bearing at its head a small column carved in the form of a lotus. In the heart of the lotus once reposed the Kohinoor diamond, before it was borne over the sea, as almost priceless loot, to Queen Victoria.

The passage of the Kohinoor from Akbar's tomb to the hand of Victoria was not entirely smooth, if the story told of its seizure is true. A party of horsemen, among whom was John Lawrence, secured the jewel at some date after the Mutiny; Lawrence then thrust the bauble in the pocket of his riding jacket and forgot all about it. When he remembered it, a few hours later, he was appalled—he knew that the coat would have been sent away to be cleaned and would have passed through the hands of at least two servants. He groaned over his own carelessness. Indeed, he was not a careless man, in any respect, but jewels could have had little if any significance for a person so dour and so severe. He summoned his bearer and asked without emphasis if he had noticed anything in a pocket of the jacket he had worn when riding that morning. "Yes, *Sahib*, there was a large piece of glass." "Have you still got it?" "Yes, *Sahib*." "Then bring it to me." It may be apochryphal but I hope not, as it puts Lawrence in a human light, which was rare with him.

Our journey back to the Bombay Presidency was memorable for our fellow travelers—it was the last long journey we made in India, the last time we had this brief and easy intimacy with persons we could not otherwise have met. Yet I remember that we were still so stupid that for a moment we were dismayed to find our carriage so full. The judge and his wife from Gwalior and the young man who had been in England for eight years, part of that time at Cambridge, were so agreeable that I remember them vividly today, after thirty years. We talked till eleven that night when the Pauls, the legal family, got off the train at Bhopal.

The young Indian was interesting, civil, and alert, though disturbed by the difficulties he was having in trying to settle back into Indian life. He had had various jobs in England after he had finished his education; now, after six months in India, he still could find nothing to do. The English firms had nothing to offer him, the Indians found him too expensive and highly trained—a familiar story. He had no pull. His people lived in Gwalior, which he thought an impossible one-horse place. He had been to Delhi looking for work and was now going to Bombay to try his hand there.

His very elegant, sweet-faced mother, all in snow-white and scarlet, had come down to the station to see him off and to give him his dinner, which she had cooked herself and arranged in a pyramid of fitting dishes. This meal he later shared with us and it was extremely good.

Mr. Paul, the judge, had lived contentedly in Gwalior for many years. He and his wife were Christians—she was strikingly beautiful, much younger than he. Their seventeen-year-old son saw them off. Mrs. Paul told me she was only thirty-five and that this young student son was leaving Gwalior a little later in the day to return to his college in Delhi. He obviously adored his lovely mother. She was delightfully talkative. She soon told me that she and her husband had married for love, actually chosen each other, which they could do as they both came from Christian families. They were quite evidently happy together. She had been to a famous missionary school in Lucknow, the Isabella Thobourne College, and spoke of it with the greatest affection. But, she said, it was hard for her to make friends, as her religion created a barrier. Living in Gwalior she seldom came across Christians. Most of her Hindu and Mohammedan acquaintances, she sighed, were very limited in their outlook and interests and I could well believe it! Of course, too, they could never eat together. There were a few exceptions to this dearth, here and there someone who was "enlightened." Her friends, being women, had in general had so few opportunities for education—the men fared rather better. Besides they had their work as an interest.

I asked her what she did with herself. She was domestically inclined (fortunately for her, life is easier for such women) and did much of the cooking and the tending of her household. She and her husband belonged to a small club, where she was the only lady member. There she played tennis and badminton. I asked her what she wore for sport, as my eyes traveled over the pale lemon yellow georgette sari trimmed with silver which she had chosen for the journey. This sari, she explained, was a little old, so she was wearing it on the train. It looked very expensive to me and I cast down my eyes at my coarse *dasuti* slacks and bush shirt (also old). She told me that when she played games she wore Punjabi dress—the loose trousers and long tunic. She looked like Scheherazade—a little heavy, but then perhaps even Scheherazade changed as the years passed.

Everyone talked about India. The Cambridge youth said he

didn't care who governed it—English, Muslim, anyone—if only it were properly done. There was a long conversation about Indian women. The young man was exasperated because he never met any socially. Mrs. Paul deplored the absence of romance in Indian women's lives—no sweetness, no thrill, no memories. Her husband, smiling (it was clearly an old argument between them), took an old-fashioned view and said that as things were in India it was still better for the parents, who have the girls' interests at heart, to arrange their marriages. Most of his family were in educational work and he spoke of the problems which were arising in the universities in this line of country. The girls were pressing forward for university education—even Mohammedan girls who, during these four years, would throw their awful *burqas* aside—and then go back to them! This influx could not be absorbed by the few over-crowded girls' schools and consequently the maidens were entering the men's universities, despite protests all round. Terrible things were happening. Quite recently there had been a scandal in a university of which he knew. A youth had quite simply, in public, *kissed* a girl. He later explained that he had felt he had to. This was, of course, no excuse at all.

Most of the luscious young girl students had never seen any men except their fathers and brothers and the result was that young hearts beat fast and the atmosphere of the schools was disturbed by elopements. Mrs. Paul, the young Indian, and I all thought this symptomatic of a difficult transition phase but we approved in principle. Mr. Paul was against it. The young Indian reiterated that he could *never* even *meet* girls. Mr. Paul was worried and fussy; Mrs. Paul insisted that the dreadful repression of women must stop. She spoke of the Maharanee of Gwalior, who while in Bombay flashed about like lightning, doing as she wished, but when in Gwalior was in such complete purdah that she even had to watch the Dussehra festival from behind the fretted screens of the harem lattices. I was immensely pleased with Mrs. Paul's liberality—the Indian women were generally even more conservative than the men. Bombay, we all agreed, was the freest place in all India for women, due to the influence of the Parsees. Mrs. Paul sighed in envy of the lucky Bombay girls. Today she must be glad that so many other cities have come round to this point of view.

XVII The Last Months in India

Lied vom Winde

Sausewind, Brausewind!
Dort und hier!
Deine Heimat sage mir!

"Kindlein, wir fahren
Seit viel vielen Jahren
Durch die weit weite Welt
Und möchten's erfragen,
Die Antwort erjagen.

MÖRIKE

IT WAS STILL OCTOBER when we came back to Ambernath, back to the shade of our vines, which had become thick screen shading the verandas, back to the roses and the lilies, the chameleons and the desert heat. The factory now seemed strangely purposeless. We began to make plans for leaving India. The Ordnance Service would continue under whatever government there would be and many of the permanent members of the organization would stay with it, but few of those who had been blown in with the war wished to remain. We had not found the Raj a good employer and we did not think an Indianized service would do more for its staff. We longed to return to the West and begin again far from the field of weaponry. We could not know, then, in the fall of '45, that a year later we would have only exchanged the work of building up the armament factories of India for destroying their tremendous counterparts in Germany.

It was clear that it would still be some months before we could go: there were so many civilians awaiting passages and so few ships—besides the priority given the military. We all had to wait our turn, according to carefully computed governmental lists. The sick, the Important Persons, those with the longest-overdue home leave (for, of course, everyone was now due that leave), felt they must go first. Nearly everyone had reasons for special treatment and most of them were valid, but they could carry little weight. We ourselves entered into a long dispute about pay, which we lost. We had been assured, when we left Hong Kong, that eventually our fares would be paid back to London, as that would have been guaranteed had we stayed in China. No document was signed, but in the urgency of the war and the surge of patriotism we had no thought of haggling over such a paper—we were naively confident of fair play. Passages were being handed out by the tens of thousands but in our case now the government insisted that we were only due our fares to Hong Kong, which, of course, was in a state of semi-devastation, the Japanese having just left. We had no idea of returning there. In the end the government won and we had to pay a substantial part of our fares—the normal rate minus the fare to Hong Kong.

The enormous army which was foreign to India was being moved out as fast as was practicable. Troop ships, crowded to the gunwales, went out of Bombay harbor every week but no one coveted passages on them, as the accommodation was as uncomfortable and as regimented as it could possibly be. It was, however, risky to refuse any passage, as one was not soon offered another, and many civilians did leave the country on troop ships, sending back dismal letters about the overcrowding, the queuing for bad meals, the separation of families, and the communal cabins. How quickly we all forgot to rejoice that the seas had become safe!

Having put our names down in all the requisite places and visited all the harassed gentlemen who were trying to control this vast exodus, we settled down to that winter of '45–'46 to possess our souls in patience. It was a hard period to sit through quietly. It seemed then, from week to week, from month to month, as though the country would burst into flames, so great was the political pressure, the public unease. The fierce impatience of the Indians to be freed from the yoke of a foreign government and the intensity of their apprehension that even now Whitehall might not honor its promises gave cause for constant demonstrations. The old bone of contention, the Muslim-Hindu impasse, seemed as insoluble as ever—

Wavell, still the Viceroy, set his face against Partition as resolutely as in the past. While feeling great sympathy for everyone concerned, it was impossible for the transient not to wish that he could be safely out of the way before the balloon went up.

Being quite uncertain when we might get a ship (sometimes a passage was given one very suddenly), we thought it wise to fold up the house as far as possible and be at least partly ready for a summons, so we went in search of packers. Unfortunately nearly everyone had the same idea. We were all selling off our furniture, we were all packing—no one wanted the first and the demand for packers far exceeded the supply. None of the big firms in Bombay would even consider our china and glass—they were all booked up for months ahead. Finally Stanton went down into the bazaar area near the Crawford Market, determined to find someone who could do the work, and unearthed two "experts," claiming wide and successful experience, who agreed to come out to Kalyan on the following Sunday morning. He paid them their traveling expenses on the spot and arranged to have a *babu* from the office meet them at the railway station, engage a *tonga*, and escort them to our bungalow.

Early on Sunday morning I had boxes and straw, newspapers and nails, and our dishes, glass, and curios all laid out on the veranda so that no time would be lost. The two gentlemen arrived at the appointed hour and started about their task at once with a great show of energy. Lightly strewing the bottom of our largest packing case with straw, as a flower girl might scatter roses at the feet of the bride, they arranged a number of plates and soup bowls upon it without one shred of paper or straw which might even hold them in place, let alone protect them. Then they asked us to approve this much before they went further. It was like a comic opera, except there was no light gay music coming from the garden and there was nothing gay, indeed, in the way we reacted.

But *they* were indignant at our horror. We tried to explain to them what happened to packing cases that went halfway around the world on ships, in a world which had just had a war, where cases were roughly handled even if they were marked "Fragile." They knew nothing about anything being marked in any particular way. Who could have read it? *But*, they insisted, if we would only tell them how we wanted the thing to be done, they would then pack extremely well and they would *guarantee* that not a single article would be broken. Not a written guarantee, of course. Exchanging wounded looks, beyond words, we parted. They went back to Bombay, while we took everything off the veranda, feeling that after five years in the country we really should have been past such nonsense. What they felt remained a mystery, but I believe that they actually considered that we were of all beings the most unreasonable and mistrustful.

We persevered. We still felt we could not do it ourselves. We did not know where we would go when we left India, we were fairly sure we would have long sea voyages and many changes, we did not want to lose our Chinese treasures through breakages. Finally we found a little old man in a Gandhi cap, very much like our dear old Barrackpore *darzi*, Cassim—he was a denizen of the same bazaar as the rascals, but of very different metal. He came out, looked over our packing materials and what was to go in them, and began his labors with the authority and swiftness of a master. We had no doubts at all as to his capability when we saw him first soak the straw, then carefully wrap each plate in wads of newspaper, and deftly wedge everything into the cases with calm, dexterity, and concentration. Over a year later when they were opened in Kiel, having made many journeys, and having been roughly handled in many ports, we found only one dish broken.

We rolled up the Chinese scrolls, packed the books, folded the carpets, and sold what was left to a rascally Parsee auctioneer in Bombay, whose goal, as we were to discover, was not to auction anything of ours until we had sailed and were not in a realistic position to collect what he owed us. We then had three or four months to pass in an almost empty bungalow: in its lean and barren state, with its bare gray stone floors, it was unexpectedly pleasing— it took on the aspect of a caravanserai. We had left out only a picture or two, a rug, and a huge flat round basket which served as a tea table. All the Chinese tables were crated and sent away into the city, to be put on the first boat which would take them. The extreme simplicity, the essential clarity of outline in which we now lived, made us feel that we should never put into a room more than a Ming lady and a Persian carpet, a long table and a pile of books, with plain curtains which would rise in the hot wind over the floor. That floor, so constantly and so vainly swept against the active wind, those rough stones of pinkish gray, took on a new importance, no longer subordinated to many chairs and tables but significant in itself. The bedrooms, holding only beds and mosquito nets, with tin trunks spaced about the walls and the *punkahs* whirling overhead, were entirely true to any tale of India. Here in a sort of suspended animation we read, talked, and observed, through the long days of uncertainty, rising passion and near-mutiny.

During that last winter when we had so much leisure, the Royal Asiatic Library became more than ever important to us. They were a generous institution, allowing us to take out seven books apiece at once: if our passages had been delayed a little longer than they actually were, we should probably have got through *Paradise Regained* and the whole of Gibbon. As it was Stanton read the whole of the *Morte d'Arthur* aloud to me, while I knitted. As a rule I share Florence Nightingale's horror and disgust at the idea of adults being read to, but it was a palliative to the imbecile activity of knitting. I cannot read and knit—reading is too absorbing, I read too fast, the knitting goes into incurable confusion. We had been so long in the heat that we had practically no warm clothes at all, and the children literally had none. Wool was rationed in Bombay but one could buy so many ounces at a time, enough for my progress. Small kilts, pullovers, and socks piled up as the world of Mallory became more vivid to us than our tenuous present. Beaumains, the comic antics of Gawain, the tragic strivings of Launcelot, the almost total inadequacy of the knights who set forth after the Grail, most of them having no idea of what they sought or how to find it—how absorbing these tales were! The bravado, the aspirations, the humor; Elaine stepping out of her hot bath as naked as a needle, and the music that came out of the chapels, Launcelot jumping out of a high window, maddened by his own failure—when I think of these I remember our little drawing room and its soft shadows, I feel the hot air spiraling down from the fan onto my cheek and hear my needles against the gentle stillness of the night, their low sound against the melodic measures of Mallory's wonderful prose, read by an English voice.

We were as though in the center of a typhoon, but there were others like us—for instance the Khan family.

A Mohammedan foreman, whom we had known in the Ishapore Inspectorate, was at this time transferred to Ambernath, to be ready to take over some of the work as the Europeans left. Mohammed Iqbal Khan was a genial, competent Punjabi, a man of parts, and we were glad that he was joining our small forces in the wilderness. He had left Ishapore some two years before and had been since stationed in the Central Provinces at another remote and lonely ordnance factory. Before bringing his family, which consisted of his wife and eight children, the eldest twelve years old, to the new post he came first by himself on a quick trip to Ambernath, looked over the work, and saw the small bungalow he would be given. He accepted its limitations with the cheerful and philosophic calm which was characteristic of him and the administrative officer assured him that the house would be ready to receive the family by the following Sunday. He then returned to Cattney to collect Mrs. Khan, Modh Iqbal, Khalid Latif, Delshad Akhter, Lafar Iqbal, Naseem Akhter, Saluaddin, and the twins, Javed Iqbal and Saleem Ahmed, who were seven months old, the servants, and the baggage. Hardened traveler as I was, I trembled when I thought of this move and I pitied Mrs. Khan from the bottom of my heart. Six of the eight children were boys—it was a true Punjabi family with a preponderance of men—but that would certainly not make things any easier. (The two daughters were Delshad and Naseem.)

On the Saturday the Inspectorate was notified by the administration that it would not be possible, for various unconvincing and fatuous reasons, to have the Khans' bungalow ready for them in time and they would therefore have to stay in the *dak* bungalow for a few days. The *dak* bungalow was just like all the other military huts in the station, neither more nor less uncomfortable, but it meant that the family would have an additional move and a further delay in getting settled. I thought of the babies and three-year-old Salauddin and expended more sympathy on the trials of the Khans.

On Sunday evening we went down to the *dak* bungalow to call. On the way I considered the probable state of mind of an English or American mother of eight who had just passed twenty hours in a second-class carriage, which would no doubt have been crowded even without her own plethora of children, the thermometer over a hundred, and everything perpetually covered with sifting dust. The combination of extreme heat, clouds of dust, and eight children under twelve was, I felt, too horrible to contemplate without emotion and I longed to bring comfort to her wounded soul.

The *dak* bungalow presented its usual air of calm, but not of lifelessness. The lights were all on and we felt its new vitality from afar—but its animation was in harmony with the hour, tranquil and unhurried, quiet, shadowy. The sun had gone down and the welcome darkness had enveloped the station, cooling us all, taking away the harsh outlines of the little houses. The great stars of the tropics were coming out—it was one of the best moments of the day and we rejoiced in it, as always. As we came up to the veranda a *babu* from the Inspectorate appeared, also on his way to welcome the Khans. He had, he told us, intended to meet their train but had missed the lorry which was being sent for their trunks and on which he had expected to make the journey to Kalyan. The *babu* evidently took a more liberal view of that flexible commodity, time, than did the driver of the lorry, who seemed to have been more corrupted by Western influence, but in any event the incident had not disturbed the *babu* in the least.

As we went up the steps onto the veranda, Mr. Khan appeared from a doorway, calm, unruffled, untired. Several viewers from the Inspectorate were strolling about, each carrying a small, grave, calm child. More children came into view, all Khans, all perfectly composed and amiable, freshly bathed and in clean clothes. The viewers were presenting themselves in a favorable light to a new officer and appeared to be as equal to the task of dandling babies as to inspecting cartridge cases. Through the open windows we could see people at work, putting up the mosquito nets. It was a Mohammedan clerk from this Inspectorate who had so pleased us when he was being tested for the post, by handing in a précis which was longer than the original article. He was more at home in the world of the Khans.

At the time of the Cattney move Mohammed Iqbal Khan had been perhaps thirty or thirty-two. He was thinner then, but even now when the supple grace that had been his had been transmuted into the larger mold of maturity, he was an arresting figure. A Muslim from Rawalpindi, he had the height and commanding build of the Punjabi, with large, melting brown eyes and black hair —he was a very model for a Mogul print. Even in European dress he was handsome, but when he changed to the greatly preferable costume of a Mohammedan gentleman—the long fitted jacket, jodhpurs, and leather slippers—he was more than that. His good looks were something of a legend in the Inspectorate. While probably aware of his charms, he carried them lightly, having a cheerful, mild presence. He was one of those rare persons who never appear anxious. To have eight children on the salary of an Indian foreman, in a country ridden by inflation, would have been enough to have tormented most fathers. Perhaps his calm was bolstered by the backing of his family in Rawalpindi, who may have been landlords or merchants.

We all sat down on cane chairs on the veranda and tea was brought. Mohammed Iqbal put our three-year-old Celia on his knee, her infantile fairness a foil to his dark grace, and talked to her in Urdu, a language which she understood perfectly. One might have thought that he would have had enough of children by this hour! But no—the Easterner has some secret about him which we have not fathomed. During their conversation we leaned back in the darkness and watched them. He sat thus in shadow, caressing Celia and sipping strong tea, while he told us that they had had "a good journey" in a train so crowded that he had had to put the family in a purdah carriage and squeeze himself in elsewhere; that they had been some hours late both in leaving and in arriving; that they had taken their food for the trip with them; that the heavy luggage and the furniture was already on the way here; that two of the children—the two eldest—had been dispatched to Rawalpindi to stay with his father; and that Mrs. Khan was bathing and would be with us in a few minutes.

This was a fair amount to have been dealt with in so short a period, and from Mohammed Iqbal Khan's manner and appearance it all seemed to have been carried through without the least fever or fret. But, I thought, he has been able to rest during the journey, as he could dispose of the entire family in the purdah carriage. What a golden vista that opened up for fathers! It was Mrs. Khan who had had to bear the heat and burden of the day—no escape for her within the neat arrangements of Mohammedan society! I felt at that moment the keenest sympathy for the purdah *log* of all countries, abandoned to their lot, while the liberated spouse beguiles himself with joyous conversation. My heart swelled with righteous indignation for the downtrodden women of India—though I knew that Mr. Khan was the soul of good nature and clearly incapable of treading his wife down. He began to talk to us of his favorite poet, the Persian Iqbal.

The process of my inward indignation was interrupted by the arrival of the lady herself, a plump, good-looking girl who in that half-light did not seem to be much over twenty. She had been washing her hair and its dark abundant mass was hanging loosely over her back and shoulders—against it shone the little sequins which ornamented the gauzy scarf she wore. Greeting us with greatest composure, she sat down in a chair beside me and took up her cup of tea, smiling upon each of us in turn. She knew no English but seemed in no way abashed on that score. She was dressed in a loose tunic and jodhpurs, her feet were bare and her soul was free. Alas for my great fund of overflowing sympathy! Mrs. Khan would not have known what to do with it. She was the personification, the very embodiment of placidity, of calm, of serenity, of ease. How, then, had she effected the heroics of the last days? Who had been responsible? The one servant who had accompanied the family looked as insouciant as they did. The children, who had by now drawn ours away into their circle, were revealing themselves as a merry lot, quite unburdened.

Already the bungalow was full of helpers. A viewer whose normal work was inspecting bullet cups was feeding one of the twins, while the other baby awaited its turn with quiet confidence. The children fitted easily into the scheme of things—civil, unobtrusive without being subdued, they enacted their proper roles in the family theatre. The huge mole hills I had built up for this family did not exist for them. They were to a great extent free from the bondage of possessions, they were not troubled by the passage of time, they took things just as they came, they were not demanding. Their reward was not what many would call a high standard of living, but it was something more remarkable—an ease of spirit. There was no need to apologize for and lament the dilatory conduct of the administration—they did not mind that their bungalow was not ready, they had dismissed the entire affair from their minds.

We made our adieux and walked slowly home through the sweet-smelling darkness under the stars. I laid down the burdens I had been creating for the Khans and saw them vanish away; as I remembered the paraphernalia I felt essential for even one baby I felt like the Duchess rocking the pig-baby before the fire, while the Cook filled the kitchen with pepper and with song.

There is an old Chinese poem on "Tranquil Repose" which contains the lines:

> Meeting by chance, it seems easy of access,
> Seeking, we find it hard to secure.

From Day to Day

One morning going out onto the veranda before breakfast, Stanton's attention was attracted to a solitary man, walking slowly out into the large tract of wasteland directly in front of the bungalow. The autumnal fires had not yet burnt the high grass away and

until that happened this section was always deserted, as it was
known to be the haunt of cobras, kreits, Russell's vipers, and
scorpions—no one crossed it carelessly. But this man was wandering about amongst the reeds in a vagrant, unconcerned fashion,
though his actions were deliberate enough to make it clear that he
was there for a purpose. He held his arms out as he moved and
occasionally uttered a loud peculiar cry. Suddenly his turban disappeared and he was lost to sight in the grass. When he stood up
again he had in his right hand the head of a king cobra with the
long, angry, writhing body lashing out into the air around him.

Holding his captive fast, he made his way back to the lane in
front of our garden, where he was met by what passed in our
desert for a crowd—a score of people, who were astir and had
noticed him and were eager to see his prize. The Indians feared
their snakes but they were fascinated by them. When he reached
us we saw that he had been bitten on the hands and his wounds
were bleeding, but he himself was obviously not the least disturbed by them. Asking Stanton for a razor blade and forcing open
the serpent's mouth with one hand, he cut out the two little white
poison sacs which lie at the back of a cobra's fangs, his every
gesture dexterous and sure, contemptuous of his captive's wrath.
For these sacs, he told us, he could get a sum worth over a pound
sterling from any serum laboratory. He then thrust the creature
into a bag made of gunny and proceeded to attend to his own
injuries. From a fold in his turban he took a small root, with which
he rubbed his cuts. Then, squatting down, he placed the poison
sacs on his hands in such a position that the sun would shine
through the little white bags into his wounds, asking us to stand
back that we might not intercept the rays. After a few minutes
he felt his cure complete and got up. One could see from the
many scars on his thin brown hands and arms that he had been
bitten many times; it was evident from his whole manner that he
was quite unafraid of anything any snake could do. To amuse us
he now opened his bag and let out the furiously angry cobra. The
snake coiled himself up in the dust and raised his great marked
hood, hissing and darting out his fangs—did he not realize that no
one was afraid of him now? The snake *wallah* said that he would
sell him too, but that he was of less value than the poison sacs.

He was so sure of himself, so much the master of his curious art,
that we asked him to examine some deep holes in the garden which
we suspected were inhabited by snakes. He looked down them in a

347

professional manner, found the egress, and said that he would get the snake out for sixteen rupees. We decided to keep our unobtrusive serpent or serpents rather than pay such a price to a man who would quite likely only slip a cobra down his sleeve and then introduce him to us as our ex-tenant. We had never been anxious about snakes, though they were, we knew, always neighbors. During the fires that year we found the remains of a Russell's viper just outside the fence and a man who lived just behind us always claimed that he had shot one as it was gliding over the veranda, a story which was locally received with a good deal of mild skepticism and suggestions that he take more water with it. Our decision to leave well enough alone proved wise, our unknown cobra remained very discreet and we never disturbed one another.

Government regulations annoyed us a great deal more than any cobras—we were frequently tormented by the edicts of a system of administration which had become the victim of its own paperwork. It was in Ambernath that we had a supreme example of this, which had to do with the interior walls of the bungalows.

A few people disliked the rough colorwashed bricks enough to have had their drawing rooms plastered and distempered at their own expense, but to most it was a matter of supreme indifference. We ourselves liked them—we thought them suitable for a desert, in keeping with the monastic little houses, lending themselves to our tropical decor. We would have liked other amenities such as bathtubs, refrigerators, basins, garden taps, transport to the bazaar, telephones, but whether or not our walls were plastered was a bagatelle, particularly in the rains when the ceilings became watersheds. If they had suggested making the roofs watertight, it would have been another thing. However, in the spring of '45, when we all knew that the European war was practically over, when we hoped that the Japanese war could not last more than eighteen months at most, we were surprised to hear that at some high-up administrative level it had been decided that two rooms of every bungalow in Ambernath were to have their walls plastered and distempered. The government would defray the cost as it was their decree, and it was said this would amount to some five hundred rupees per bungalow. The wretched houses were so infirm, though they were hardly three years old—every roof needed repairing, that was patent, and entire window frames often came out in our hands, the fences were collapsing round the compounds—but these trials were ignored and we were to be given the plastered walls of two rooms.

The plastering and colorwashing of a bungalow took about six weeks. The occupants of the house had to clear everything out of the two rooms, pile the furniture up on the veranda, where it blistered in the sun and became half-buried in dust, or else squeeze it into the other rooms, where the congestion made the little apartments seem hotter than ever. Some families had only four rooms, accepting this as a wartime necessity. Now, during a long period in the worst of the heat they had to eat and live in one room and share a communal dormitory in the other—all for nothing.

An army of Mahrattas would invade a bungalow, bringing along their small children and babies, both men and women being employed in the highly unskilled labor of the task. They were noisy, dirty, and inclined to be thievish. First they scraped the walls, then sluiced them with water, then slapped them with putty, and as an accompaniment to each process they shouted, screamed, rested, took the air, cooked, ate, and slept, making themselves absolute pests. For long periods each day they would study the walls, standing back and gazing at them with half-shut eyes, like artists, and then conversing loudly about them. No one knew what they were saying, none of us knew their language. Sometimes as much as four whole days were spent throwing bucketsful of water on the walls, after the putty was on. The walls were small, too, and much broken by doors and windows—yet the contractors contrived to make them the agent by which scores of people were employed, and a considerable amount of money changed hands, no doubt at several levels. At last, when the flattish, plastered walls had been covered with streaky coats of paint of the regulation shade of yellow, it was time to put back the electric light wires, leading them down the fresh surfaces, so that there were everywhere trails of dirty fingermarks. The wretched occupants could not escape the confusion, noise, and dirt in any way, except that the exasperated man of the house could at least flee to the factory and describe his sufferings to his colleagues, who were anticipating the same fate. Authority's idea was that we were not to reason why.

Nearly every household did its best to avoid this "amenity," to the surprise of those directing it, who thought we ought to be grateful. House after house, family after family was conquered in turn. We ourselves resisted stoutly to the end, continually refusing to clear our rooms and make way for the invaders. Several times I shooed away the workers myself as they advanced in hordes in the early morning light. In the end Stanton wrote a strong letter of protest which was designed to go up the echelons to the fountainhead of the problem, where it would be, we knew, looked upon with heavy frowns. We were paying rent for the quarter and felt we had certain rights. The letter was indeed received with deep indignation. Protests were something the authorities in India could not endure—particularly Military Authority, and the Ordnance personnel came under their aegis. Furthermore, it was wartime and only a cad would complain. It was the time to endure. Apparently this included compulsory house decorations.

After a long interval spent in contemplating this impasse, the Ordnance decreed that the plastering must not be interfered with by anyone in the Inspectorate (we were the only ones who had spoken out), as this would have a bad effect upon morale and interfere with the cooperation which should exist between that service and the factories. The line between cartridge cases and the plastering of drawing rooms was evidently very finely drawn. Stanton was called up to the headquarters at Kirkee and had an unfortunate interview with an irate brigadier. (He had had some words with this man once before over the subject of salaries and the inflation, and the officer had remarked *en passant* that his wife banked and drew her income from a certain source—he was independent of ordinary cares.) I continued to refuse the Mahrattas entry, and in spite of having apparently lost both our oral and verbal battles, *mirabile dictu*, we won. One day the Mahrattas disappeared like an ill wind, never to return, and without having touched our bungalow. We never heard an explanation but we rejoiced in our brick walls and the cause of liberty.

It was that winter that our bearer developed a strange nervous complaint which made his right arm twitch violently, an impossible ailment for him long to endure—it interfered with everything he did and he was afraid to wait at the table. We asked him if he would like to try the British Military Hospital at Ambernath; he went there and received injections, but was no better afterwards. Then, without a word to us, which was most unlike him as he was a conscientious man, he disappeared for a whole day. Late that night he returned, bearing an enormous flat round basket in which fluttered and cooed eight pigeons. He had been to Bombay where he had consulted an Indian doctor of the old school who had told him that he must eat a pigeon a day for eight days. Even though, to a Hindu, this involved the horrifying expedients of both taking life and eating meat, he was prepared to risk anything to regain his health. It was, moreover, a costly cure, as the poor birds were not sold at less than a rupee apiece—it meant a whole week's salary. However, he solemnly ate one after the other during the next week, and at the end of it was perfectly recovered. Watching his victims as they cleaned their feathers in the sun and walked about, we observed that their sharp wing movement was very reminiscent of the jerk he had had in his arm . . .

> There are more things in heaven and earth, Horatio,
> Than are dreamt of in your philosophy.

Mounting Tension

The last months of 1945 and the beginning of 1946 were marked by political storms of ever-growing intensity, of which the trial of the leaders of the Indian National Army was the most dramatic and alarming. Many had not even known of the existence of such an army until the press was allowed to tell the public that the leaders were to be tried for treason.

The trial took place in Delhi in the spring of '46. The four principal figures of the INA were charged with having been false to their oath of loyalty to the King Emperor, of having fought with the enemy and against the Allies in Burma, and having been guilty of grave crimes in torturing and coercing their fellow Indians to join the movement. Such was the fever of nationalistic feeling in the country that they were considered heroes by the vocal section of native public opinion. Even some of our clerks, sober and loyal persons in themselves, not anti-British nor volatile in character, told us that these men were to them the George Washingtons of India.

By bringing these turncoats back to Delhi to be tried instead of holding court-martials on the spot, the government played into the hands of the experts in political propaganda. The traitors were made to seem martyrs in the eyes of the public—and certainly, to many Indians, they had a case. It was felt that they had been compelled to take up arms in a war in which they had no wish to fight, and that they had joined their friends, whose slogan "Asia for the Asiatics" understandably had seemed reasonable to them. The men could, of course, have left the army had they felt morally unable to support the British cause, but this was ignored. From the point of view of the British, these two divisions of the Indian National Army who had actually joined with the Japanese and fought against us in Burma were guilty of treason. There was no question on this score. Yet as the trial developed and it was evident that they were guilty of this act, it became equally apparent that they could not be sentenced. The danger that the country might rise if they were made to suffer for their acts was too great. There were not enough police to maintain order, nor troops who might justifiably be called in to help, and the possible consequences of India in flames against the Raj that spring after the end of the war were too frightful to contemplate. Justice had to be waived; that of itself further weakened the prestige and position of the British. Wavell was still the Viceroy. A little later, when Lord Mountbatten was in charge, he openly admitted that administrative control had virtually broken down. We were ourselves so constantly exposed to the hostility of some of the population that we were well aware that this was the case.

Even in our little station there was a series of incidents, which were multiplied a thousand times all over the country. Bricks were thrown at Europeans in the dark, windows were smashed, women's handbags snatched and thrown away, and most of these acts were unpunished. In the military hospital which belonged to our transit camp an English nurse had her face slapped by a sweeper in full view of an Indian ward—and the authorities dared do nothing. Any spark, it was thought, might start a conflagration. The army was enormous and unoccupied, but it was an army raised and trained to fight a foreign foe. There could be no question of a civil war or a war of Indian against British—the cost in lives and principles would have been too great to justify any arguments.

Allowing those accused and found guilty at the trial to go unpunished had further repercussions when it was realized that in this way the whole service was cheapened. The loyal soldier who had scorned to go over to the enemy, even enduring torture to stand by his oath, felt now that his allegiance was not valued, that it meant nothing. The position of the Raj was intolerable, there was no respect left for the authorities. After the ringleaders of the INA were freed they made matters worse for the government by touring the country and giving speeches, being met everywhere with the greatest enthusiasm and praise. There were enormous gatherings in their honor—near us, at Dada, Shah Nawaz Khan, one of the foremost INA "heroes," spoke to an impassioned crowd of two hundred thousand, flying to and from the meeting so that he could fit in all his engagements—which was something quite new for Indians. The theme of all these talks was everywhere identical— freedom from Britain.

The name of Subhas Chandra Bose, the Congress leader who had lived in Tokyo and had been killed in an airplane crash at the end of the war, still exerted a certain magic. Most Indians seemed to think that he was still alive, that the disaster had only been a newspaper story, and that he would return to help them free themselves from their bonds, as they sometimes put it. He had for years been one of the most important figures in Congress and he was not forgotten. That he had worked with the now defeated Japanese did nothing to detract from his prestige. One of Stanton's best clerks, a man of whom we were genuinely fond, who was both intelligent and good and who was personally always friendly to the British as individuals, told us that Subhas Chandra Bose was the George Washington of India; he had in his house, hanging on the wall, pictures of the Indian National Army leaders, whom he regarded as great men, giving their all for their country.

At that season men like Nehru and Patel were constantly moving about the country, urging the immediate end of British rule and everywhere drawing large crowds who were totally in sympathy with what they said. Patel's birthday fell on a winter's day when we happened to have gone into Bombay, only to discover that in his honor the Indian shops were observing a *hartal*, a boycott against the English, and therefore no one would serve us. It was unpleasant to stand waiting in an open shop and find ourselves studiously ignored. Then we were not accustomed to the slights which fall upon the more-favored nations today—the burning of American and British libraries abroad, the stoning of embassies, were not frequent events, to be philosophically endured. It was a painful shock to confront a hostility which had in it so much unreason.

Still, in that period directly after the war, as long as the Conservative Party held the reins in England and Lord Wavell was the Viceroy, there was always the same reply to the Indians: Congress must come to terms with the Muslims, who whatever they might or might not do seemed always to be the favored minority. The Raj would not split the country, which they felt would be a moral crime, a geographical disaster, and an economic folly of the first magnitude. Yet it was obvious to nearly everyone that there was no compromise, no reconciliation, possible between these two major groups and that as long as this impasse continued Britain must retain her supremacy. The princes, well knowing that their only hope of continued power and privilege lay in the maintenance of the status quo, did nothing to help the country reach any solution, remaining solidly and selfishly behind the Raj, defending their stand with grandiloquent bogus speeches in which they protested their disinterested loyalty. These gave comfort and pleasure to a large section of the British, who often reviled the rest of the country but would repeat, "The Princes are loyal."

Fiery orators, defying reason with the intensity of their prejudice, violent in their denunciations of British rule, in which they could admit no element of good, no benefit to the country in any respect, went from city to city, making increasingly inflammatory speeches of a kind with which the modern world is only too painfully familiar. Mrs. Asaf Ali was one of the more successful of these, forgetting that to her sex at least the British had brought not bondage, but freedom. What is so fatally easy as destructive criticism of another race, another country? It was true that the British in India had laid themselves open to such attacks by the insolence, ignorance, and callous indifference of some of their nationals and a desertion of the principles they knew to be just—but this was by no means a balanced picture, and the Indians really knew that. In these last crucial years, by and large, the government was judged by the actions of its inferior nationals, while those who had lived in the country with modesty and magnanimity were overlooked. If there had been more of the latter sort the story might have been different, but human nature seldom comes out very well in such a test, and now the issue had gone beyond personalities—India was determined to govern herself whether well or ill, free from supervision, and could not be gainsayed. What arguments were used were really only by the way.

The importance of the Islamic world affected the Muslim League's struggle for the partition of India. The precarious balance of international affairs, the necessity of remaining on tolerable terms with the Near East, the question of oil, all were cogent reasons which enabled the proud, arrogant, bitter, brilliant, difficult Mr. Jinnah to be uncompromising, to break up negotiations, and yet always to be sure of a hearing, always to be received with respect. At the Simla Conference, on which so many hopes were vainly pinned, he appeared to hold all the cards in his insistence on Pakistan or nothing—no Hindu was ever humored to this degree. Yet, in spite of this personal indulgence, the Raj still would not consider partition. The wire stretched and stretched till it was so taut that it did not seem possible that there would not be revolution unless someone gave way.

That winter there was a great celebration in Bombay for the jubilee of the Aga Khan, the spiritual head of the Ismaili sect of Mohammedans, and for political as well as for religious reasons this was made a tremendous event. The chief feature of the rejoicings was the presentation of a spectacular gift from the faithful of his sect, as well as from prominent Mohammedans everywhere: he was given his weight in diamonds. As he was a very heavy man, this offering was of great financial value, truly a lavish and oriental gesture of homage and respect. Having been weighed in a balance against thousands of these gems, he then presented them to his church, by which he was held to be quite above the ordinary ranks of mankind. The Muslim religion recognizes only one supreme deity, but in the case of the followers of the Aga Khan, this tenet seemed to be obscured. To the Ismaili country folk he was indeed held a god. Someone once questioned a loyal devotee how this was compatible with the Aga Khan's passion for the turf and received the indignant reply: "And why should not a god go racing?"

For many days this jubilee held pride of place over all local affairs, while every detail of it was discussed with pride and joy and really deep feeling by the Mohammedans. The ceremonies themselves were long and impressive, attended by vast crowds as well as by many distinguished guests, some from abroad. The press made much of it and Bombay became for a season a rallying ground for all Muslims, whether Ismailis or not, rich or poor, pious or only nationalistic. It was a good opportunity for them to wave the green flag with the star and crescent, to show how much of a nation the Indian Muslims already were. The Hindus behaved well during these days—there was no special communal strife, as though to make it clear that this was often only the result of fanatical propaganda, which with a modicum of good will could be avoided.

The greater part of the anti-British demonstrations came from the Hindus. The Muslims were seldom actively hostile as they did not feel the necessity to exhibit such a sentiment. The Hindus, on the other hand, felt themselves very much alone in the world. It had not always been so. During the Mutiny the greater part of the combatants had been Mohammedans and over the last decades of the nineteenth century they were to bear the onus of British disapproval because of this. They were, also, the poorer and more ignorant part of the population (speaking generally—of course, the vast majority of both faiths were both extremely poor and extremely ignorant) and so they remained. The fact that so many of them were converts from Hinduism contributed to this as, naturally enough, it was the more hopeless and wretched Hindu who was ready to abandon his faith for one which would offer more, apparently, both in this world and the next. That is to say that most of the converts were from the ranks of the untouchables.

It was hard to realize in our time in India that during the first years of the British Raj the "gentle Hindoos" were the favored sons. We came when no one ever spoke of them as "gentle" or thought of them in that light, yet it is true that early writers often found these people mild and tractable. After the establishment of the country as a part of the British Empire, they at once took advantage of what the British offered them in the way of education —they flocked to the schools and colleges and from their ranks came the legions of *babus* who did the clerical work of the country; those who could afford the training became lawyers and doctors. They prospered as merchants, for which calling they had special aptitude. Their downfall from this happy position of favor came with the growth of nationalism among them, their patrons being either unable or unwilling to understand that this development was both desirable and inevitable. It was foreseen by men like Munro and Macauley and without dismay, but their outlook was rare. At the turn of the century with the dawning of nationalism in the East, it was the better educated, more intelligent, more sensitive Hindu who began to long for his country's independence which, he thought, would also contribute to his own advancement. He read marvelous statements about liberty and self-government in his textbooks and began to take them literally. As the movement began to grow and wax strong, the Hindu came to be regarded with dislike by the Raj, which had found the old status quo very comfortable, and accordingly the loyal, conservative, slower-witted Muslim took his place as the good child of the family. The landowning class among the Muslims, the *zamindars*, had always had much in common with their English counterparts, and between the soldiers of the Punjab and of the Northwest Frontier Provinces and the British regiments there was great natural sympathy. The British officers loved these men of what they liked to call "the martial races," and there was probably more true friendship between the Muslims and the English as individuals than there had been between the English and the Hindus.

In these later years of happier relationships, however, the Muslims did not recover the ground they had lost (or, rather, had failed to gain) in the educational world. The Hindus had universities in all the great cities of India and there were hosts of students eager to go abroad for further study, despite the religious problems this step entailed. In all of what is today Pakistan there were, up to Partition, relatively few schools of higher learning. (These statements can only be taken generally, as there were countless exceptions to prove the rule on both sides. Mr. Jinnah, for instance, was a brilliant lawyer. The Hindus who lived for generations in the Punjab were often highly educated, as one can discover from Tandon's absorbing *Punjabi Century*. But by and large the country was divided to some extent, as by a horizontal line, into two zones of lesser and greater educational zeal and achievement.) The very cleverness and intellectuality of the Hindu often served to make him more anti-British than to produce other, more constructive characteristics. He found too small a field for his talents—he could not bear to accept the eternal poverty of his village. The public school attitude of the English administrators made them mistrust so much book learning and glib argument. The Hindu therefore often became more ardent in the pursuit of political freedom than in other less spectacular goals and was held to be disloyal and a nuisance. Nehru's great intellectual prowess did not necessarily endear him to many Western officials who had not been so liberally endowed, and his avowed republicanism was often construed as an affront to a people extraordinarily sensitive to the claims of monarchy.

The Muslim religion presents fewer barriers to ordinary friendship than does the Hindu—though some few Hindus laid aside their rules and prejudices when they were with Europeans. Untouchability, however, renders the whole Hindu system of thought unhappy and suspect—anyone who can accept it in theory or practice seems on a different plane from non-Hindus. It is also very difficult, on a mundane level, to be socially easy with people with whom the whole question of eating is so complicated that one can almost never have a meal together—so many foods are taboo and then there is the caste problem, the anxiety over the orthodoxy of the cook. Even for Hindus themselves these barriers make it difficult to sit down easily for a meal together. The situation did not arise with Muslims. These strictures are loosening—today it must be far less awkward for these societies to mingle if they so wish. Before we left India we had dinner in a restaurant with an Indian colleague who went so far out of his way to put us at our ease and to make it clear that he was not bound by the outward signs of his faith that he actually ordered (and ate) veal. He was a man of the greatest sensibility and it must have cost him an effort, as no doubt it disgusted him, but he wished silently to explain to us that his principles were not offended, if his taste was.

That spring of 1946 there were many provincial elections, offering another good ground for rioting. The voting was divided on a communal basis and though the intent of the system was probably reasonable and honest at the outset, the effect was, naturally, to divide rather than to unite public opinion. The policy was adopted in 1909 in response to a strong Mohammedan demand and once put into action was not recalled. All this was easy to understand but unpleasant to experience. In that dangerous and turbulent period every day seemed to bring fresh news of ugly scenes of mob violence in Calcutta or Bombay, Allahabad or Cawnpore. Among the demonstrations against the Raj, the communal riots, the enormous meetings called for one reason or another, the opportunities for the agitator, the frustrated student, the malcontent, were legion, and many thousands of young men felt deeply convinced that throwing a rock was accomplishing something, no matter where it fell or whom it hurt. Lawlessness steadily gained the upper hand.

Rajagopalacharia, the moderate Madrassi, had been too good a friend of the English, too ready to compromise, to take, in these last hours of the old system, a commanding position in the estimation of his compatriots, but the presence of Gandhi,* pacific and anxious to avoid bloodshed, was a great boon to the country. This strange figure, so little understood abroad, had often played a de-

---

* To discuss the character and career of Gandhi is beyond the scope of this book—it would take more pages than have already been written here. In his defense of the untouchables, in his march to the sea in protest against the salt tax, he showed himself beyond reproach. His political life partook of the nature of politics; many examples of the manner in which he worked could be cited to illustrate my thesis, and can be found in any dispassionate history.

vious game—sometimes he had been a crafty, clever, unprincipled politician, sometimes a genuinely religious personality, devout, kind, careless as to his own fate. The younger and more sophisticated men in the Congress would not follow him blindly, as did the great bulk of the people, but they valued his influence in the country, admired him personally, and wanted him as a fatherly patron. If, instead of standing apart in a visionary role, he would only come back and stand with Nehru and Patel as a practical leader, they thought all would be well. For the poor, the humble and the desperate he was by far the greatest figure of them all; the vast majority of the Hindus loved him as their hope and guide. It was he who now restrained them, and had he not been on the scene, affairs would undoubtedly have been much worse. He had himself come to realize how difficult it is to rule and was sincere in his wish to lift the country not only out of its miseries but also out of its baser impulses. It is true that in spite of his past trickery there was something of the saint in him.

Another element in the conflict, beyond that of the Hindus, the Mohammedans, the British, the princes, the international balance, was that of a very numerous and potentially important group within the country—the untouchables, led by Dr. Ambedkar. There were some sixty million of these unfortunate people, bound by their imaginary chains which no one seemed able to break. How many of them were conscious of being part of a political unit, or even how many were cognizant of what Dr. Ambedkar was trying to do for them, it was impossible to say. He was himself of that caste—that is, an outcaste—but through his own ability and his good fortune he had become highly educated and was devoting his life to the cause of his own kind. It seemed best to him that they should form a separate party and through it attempt to raise their status, economically and socially. In this he was the antagonist of Gandhi, who wished to help the outcastes by absorbing them into the Hindu block and constantly playing down their differences. Gandhi was keenly aware of the problem and genuinely anxious to undermine the iniquitous system which insisted upon the suppression of millions on the false and fictitious grounds of birth, but to Ambedkar it seemed that Gandhi's stand made it more difficult—that they needed a separate political formation to fight for their interests as a group. Obviously this caste could never be freed by political means alone and Gandhi probably thought he could influence the Hindus to accept their co-religionists by other and more lasting means. Both men were sincere but their differences made for ill-feeling between them, each accusing the other of playing for power. Ambedkar, who had personal experience of this cruel yoke of untouchability, had no faith in persuasion, influence, time, and speeches—he wanted action.

That spring saw also the Indian Naval Mutiny played out in Bombay and Karachi. The naval ratings were dissatisfied with their pay and their conditions of service, which compared unfavorably with the terms under which British seamen served. The pay of Indian officers had lately been increased but the lower deck seemed to have been forgotten. Their discontent was increased by the tactlessness and overbearing attitude of certain British commanders and by the fact that the men were expected to mess together regardless of caste or religion. All these factors were skillfully manipulated by agitators, including communists as well as purely nationalistic agents, but there was more than a little justice in many of their grievances—the problem could not honestly be laid upon the agitators' shoulders. The ratings, who had at first never wished for or advocated a mutiny, had for a long time been writing letters and signing petitions—moderate and civil documents—asking for adjustments; but Delhi had often not even answered them. The same tactics were employed which had been used during the mutiny at Spithead, and with the same results. Exasperated beyond bearing that they should continually be ignored, the sailors could see only one course to follow.

The general public knew nothing whatever of the impending storm until suddenly the mutiny was upon us. There was a gun battle in Bombay and another in Karachi, with mutineers parading the streets and rendering both cities unsafe for several unhappy and disordered days. The agitation did not last long—in a week order was restored and the long, slow business of trying to repair the damage began. Most of the requests were found to have been reasonable and were granted. It transpired at a moment when India was receiving much praise for her war effort abroad—chiefly in the Italian theatre—and no one wanted to call any more attention than was inevitable to so unfortunate an incident.

We ourselves inadvertently went into Bombay on the second day of the mutiny, before the morning papers had arrived in Ambernath bringing the news of the disturbances of the previous day. (Neither we nor our neighbors had radios.) To our astonishment and concern we found Victoria Station full of indignant ratings, bearded and swarthy, in disheveled white duck and shouting "JAI HIND!" in a ferocious manner as they moved along the platforms on their way out to the squares and streets of the city, where they added to the general uproar. It was already unsafe to move about the city in any ordinary capacity and most of the shops had their shutters up. We were particularly dismayed over this catastrophe, having an affection for the navy and regretting that affairs should have been so mishandled that seamen should have felt constrained to resort to violence. It all added to the mounting tension, to the strains and fears of that uncertain and unhappy period, when it was clear that the government would go but there seemed nothing ready to take its place.

Returning troops often added their share to the anxieties of the times. Regiment after regiment, even including the Gurkhas whom everyone admired and respected, broke up in disorder and bad feeling—in a spirit which verged on mutiny. It was a time of divided loyalty for Indian soldiers and the trial at Delhi had confused most of them very much. Their economic situation rendered them uneasy about their future. They had become, in these few years of service, used to secure employment and wondered where they should turn now. Sensing that it was going to be difficult to find other work as lucrative and rewarding as they had been enjoying, they were in a mood which was quick to feel resentment and government regulations and discipline did little to ease the strain.

It was a tradition, for instance, that the Gurkhas were always allowed to keep their uniforms on retiring from the army—they were proud of their battle-stained dress and eager to show it in Nepal. But now, according to all reports, the Accounts Department decreed that they must turn in their clothes. In consequence they mobbed one of their officers. The army had become so large and had drawn so many of the poorest men in the country into it (it had seemed so comfortable and safe a career) that its swift decline made a sharp impact all over the land. As soon as the men came to the end of their service, life changed abruptly for them— unnecessarily so. The officer commanding the transit camp next to us at this junction was an example of a certain type of proud and unimaginative, insensitive soldier. He told us one day, with great disgust, that some returning Indian troops who had fought in Italy had objected to their quarters in the camp. They felt they were being ill-used and said, among other things, that they ought to have sheets on their cots. They had become accustomed to having sheets and abroad had drawn them in the ordinary way. The commanding officer was incensed. "Sheets! Why should they have sheets?" he shouted. "They never had sheets before in their lives!"

The Indians would have felt less angry if they realized how common this attitude was among the British towards their own less privileged stratas of society. A couple of years later I often heard senior personnel grumbling in the Occupied Zone of Germany when humble persons asked for cars or wanted to buy cars (there was often no other means of transport). "Why should these people have cars? They never had cars before in their lives!"

There were too many irreconcilable points of view on every hand to be absorbed in the tenor of living. To add to everything else in our poor station, the Honorary Secretary of the Club chose this moment to embezzle the funds—some thousands of rupees, filched from our only mild amenity. He calmly admitted what he had done. Yet the prevailing opinion in the station (the club was ninety-nine percent white) was that he must not come up for trial, as the nearest district magistrate who would hear the case was an Indian and "the white people must stand together." The Indians who fumed and castigated such a point of view did not seem to realize how many of us shared their feelings.

Everywhere we went we saw chalked on the walls "Quit India"—and we longed to do so.

A Strange Story

Stanton's successor at the Inspectorate was to be a pleasant Hindu gentleman from Madras called Mr. Sen. We had known each other in Bengal, since when he had had the experience of being sent to England under a scheme which was intended to acquaint Indians with Western methods and processes in industry. He was quite modern in his outlook and friendly with Europeans; after six months in the West he became even more so.

When we were in Ambernath he was connected with a Bombay office of the Inspectorate and had made his home in the city; he did not now intend to uproot his family and bring them out to our desert wastes. The pressure of work was no longer heavy and he expected only to stay in Ambernath himself when it was imperative. He automatically would fall heir to our (unplastered) bungalow and while discussing household details with him, as to what furniture he might like to keep and such trifles, we asked him also if he would not perhaps take over some of the servants. They were finding it hard to get other work and the cook was especially worried—could I not prevail upon him to take at least the cook? I was so anxious not to leave them unemployed.

Mr. Sen had had lunch with us on the day this subject came up. It had been a strictly vegetarian meal to conform to his orthodoxy and he was on the point of returning to Bombay when I made my appeal. He looked at me in a peculiar way and, leaning against the veranda door of the drawing room, replied, "No, no, not the cook—I could not change my own cook." His matter-of-fact Western air fell away from him at once, and in spite of his Western dress and his admirable command of English, he could not have seemed more Oriental, more mysterious, more melancholy than he did at that moment. The Madrasi is apt to be gentler, more suave than his northern counterpart—there is that curious similarity between southerners of all continents—and our guest suddenly evoked, at this moment when he was making his adieux, an atmosphere of deep concern over the hidden facets of man's life. With the most earnest and searching glance, looking straight into my eyes, he asked, "Do you believe that a person can be possessed?" Then, a true Oriental, disdaining the waiting car (the car allowed him by an impatient and begrudging factory administration), careless of train times, of appointments in the city, he put down his hat, sat down again, and told us this tale:

When they had first arrived in Bombay from Madras the Sens had taken a large old house in something of a hurry—they had four small children and felt they could not afford to wait long before settling somewhere. Mrs. Sen did not like the place but houses were hard to come by, the city was extremely crowded, and they had so much to arrange with the children's schooling and Mr. Sen's work that they moved in and started to furnish it without more ado. She was particularly unhappy with the bedroom in which she slept, being one of those persons who are strongly susceptible to "atmosphere" and sensing here some past wretchedness. Like her husband she was a Madrasi but unlike him she had had little contact with the West or anything modern—she was very much the sheltered, conservative Hindu wife. She was, moreover, pious and orthodox, not ambitious to enlarge the scope of her life, and could speak only her own language, which was Telagu, a notoriously difficult tongue and very different from either Urdu or Hindi.

The Sens had not been long in their new home when they went one evening to see the film of *Dr. Jekyll and Mr. Hyde* (with Indian subtitles) which was very popular in Bombay and drawing great crowds. The morning after, to the astonishment, alarm, and dismay of her family, Mrs. Sen awoke with the delusion that she was a Mohammedan. With this her whole character and feelings changed. She conceived a strong aversion to her husband and took no interest in her children, whom she had always loved with true maternal affection. And, strangest of all, from that hour she was quite unable either to speak or to understand her native Telagu—instead she spoke in Urdu, a language she had never known, and which no one in the house, except the cook, could speak. Like many Hindus they had a Mohammedan cook, who could not complicate the household catering with any caste problem, and in this painful dilemma he became the poor lady's interpreter. Mr. Sen, in the greatest anxiety, took her to European doctors, to Indian doctors, to psychologists and psychiatrists, but none of them could help her. She remained a victim of her conviction that she was a Mohammedan woman.

Meanwhile her dislike of the house, and of her room in particular, was intensified by her strange mania and she was determined to discover what had happened in it to render the place so unhappy. Ready to do anything to humor her, Mr. Sen asked the landlord if anything untoward had ever been known about this property, but the man knew of nothing. Mrs. Sen received this report with contempt and insisted that a former landlord be interrogated—she said that she was sure that the present owner had not had the house very long. And she was right; the former landlord confirmed her suspicions. Long ago a Mohammedan woman and two servants had been murdered in that very room which possessed for this nervous tenant such a troubled air. Mr. Sen did not know how his wife could have been sure about the two landlords but he did see that (if one took any credence in such things) she seemed to have taken upon herself the nature of the unfortunate woman who had suffered there. And then there was this extraordinary evidence of the change of language.

For six months, with scarcely any interruption, the obsession continued. The only times Mrs. Sen came to herself were when her husband managed to take her to a Hindu temple, a pilgrimage she was most loath to make. Once within the gates she became at once her normal self—gentle, pious, affectionate, and Telagu-speaking. The moment she came out she fell once more under her strange spell.

By Christmas of 1945 Mr. Sen was in despair—it seemed to him that there was no way out of this misery. In that month, however, it happened that old Mr. Purwani, one of the owners of the copper firm we had visited in Jaipur, came on a visit to Bombay and in the course of his work met the disconsolate husband. He knew of the Sens' trouble and was ready with advice. Being a member of the Kathiawar community, he was a Jain and very pious. He recommended that Mr. Sen write at once to a holy man living on Mount Abu who, he was sure, would be able to help him. Mr. Sen was skeptical—he was not a Jain, had no dealings with gurus, and did not see what good this distant man could possibly do. "Only write him," urged the old Kathiawari, "and tell him exactly what has happened and he will cure your wife. I know of his success in these matters." Mr. Purwani was so kind, so reassuring, and Mr. Sen had come to such a pass, that he concluded that he would follow his counsel and that evening he wrote out the whole story for the guru and posted the letter.

On the very day the letter reached the guru—an hour after he had received it, as they later realized—Mrs. Sen came to a decision. "Let us part," she said to her husband. "I don't like you and you don't like me. Only get me now a black sari, some black bangles, and a few plantains for my journey." Mr. Sen had no idea what she intended to do, but he perceived that the guru was at work and these simple but rather dramatic articles were at once fetched from the nearest bazaar.

Then, standing before her husband, the lady began to take off her jewelry, the heavy, valuable ornaments which represent so much to an Indian family—the gold and silver bangles, the elaborate earrings, the necklaces, the rings. She stripped off her rich sari and put on instead the plain black one they had brought her and the black glass bangles—startling attire in that country where the women nearly always wear pale colors to set off their dark skin. Then, picking up the little bundle of fruit, she said, "Now I am going." First, however, she went to bathe, as though to wash the whole experience of her life in that house away; after this ritualistic ablution she fell down in a deep swoon, which lasted for thirty-six hours.

When she awoke she was perfectly restored, with no recollection of her long madness, once again a loving wife and mother and unable to speak or understand one word of Urdu.

A few days later a letter arrived from the guru, saying that the whole affair was over and they would never again be troubled by it. Her cure had begun almost as soon as he had read Mr. Sen's letter.

Our friend assured us that he had previously always laughed at such stories but now, confronted by this evidence, he was quite at a loss as to what to think. He was deeply glad and grateful that his wife had been restored to him; otherwise the whole trial had been to him simply a mystery, tormenting and unresolved. It had descended suddenly and inexplicably and disappeared in the same manner. Being an intelligent man he was now consumed with a vast unsatisfied wonder. We felt his deep, searching curiosity, his reluctance to let the matter rest till he could understand it—but we could not help him. Shaking his head, he rose to say goodbye and went slowly out into the sunlight.

Goodbye to India

In the middle of March, when the great heat was again coming upon the land, we were told that we had been allotted passages on a ship sailing early in April. She was a civilian packet,* and we were given two cabins, amidships, on the starboard side, the favored position for the homeward journey through the Red Sea and a marvelous privilege at that time, so our long long wait had at least had good results. It proved to be a halcyon journey with pleasant company, under almost prewar conditions—stewardesses! good food! plenty of service! The majority of civilians leaving India now (and, of course, the military) had to put up with great discomfort. Our little ship had two hundred passengers, of whom seventy were children—it followed that most of the adults were parents, so we were indulgent with each other. The railings of one of the rail decks were lashed and the children played there, while for some hours of each day the water in the canvas swimming pool was kept at a level suitable for babies. The sea was perfectly smooth till we

---

* It was this vessel, *The City of Exeter*, which had carried the British delegation to Russia in June, 1939, in a vain attempt to attain agreements which would prevent a rapport between Nazi Germany and the Soviet Union.

had passed Gibraltar. In a lifetime of long sea voyages this is the one I like most to remember.

Before we left Ambernath the Inspectorate gave us parties and presented us with garlands of marigolds and lilies and with brass vases and books about Gandhi. The clerks came with gifts, their eyes full of tears, the tears of affection which came easily to them—they had never been schooled to reserve. We gave them all the plants from the garden—our successor did not intend to live there regularly and would not care for them—so they came with their parcels and flowers and went away with roses and lilies. On the last morning I divided the stores I had saved for the servants, the last of the rice, the sugar, and the tea, the *dal* and the salt—and, finally, we distributed our mosquito nets. Then I realized that we really were going—it had been years since we had slept without a net over us.

The boat was to sail early in the morning and the last night we spent in Bombay, taking our last *ayah*, dear Rai, with us. She was bathed in tears and we, too, were sad. We loved her and we also knew that of all the servants and all the amenities of India it was she whom we would miss the most. The children were three and five and she had long been their faithful shadow. She had been to Jaipur with us and had ridden upon the Necklace round the Neck of Lal under the walls of Amber; though she had a child of her own, she looked upon these two as almost hers. She had never been difficult, always patient and good.

We reached the docks before nine in the morning, to be surprised and touched to find all the other servants there waiting for us. They had risen at dawn, to get to the city in good time: the bearer (he of the pigeons), the cook, the sweeper, the *dhobi*, the old Bengali gardener, even the little tailor who had sometimes sewed for us—they were all there, holding garlands in readiness, the long, sweet-smelling garlands of ceremony and affection.

The ship did not put out to sea for many hours, even after the passengers had been escorted through the Customs sheds and had gone aboard. Through the heat this little knot of melancholy and loyal servitors waited, joined by several clerks from the office and by Mr. Sen, till at last, late in the afternoon, the ropes were cast off. As the blue gap between us and the pier widened, in that slow inexorable way which has intensified so many a parting, they called out to us again and again, begging us to come back and let them be with us once more, till at last they faded away into the soft vague outlines of the shore. The ship turned out of the harbor into the sparkling waters of the Arabian Sea and set her course towards Aden. India fell below the horizon.

> Let us go. Come;
> Our separation so abides, and flies,
> That thou, residing here, go'st yet with me,
> And I, hence fleeting, here remain with thee.
> Away!

Glossary

apsaras—a woman water sprite, attendant upon deities.
ata—flour.
baba—a baby.
babu—a clerk.
baksheesh—a gratuity, a present of money.
bhisti—water carrier
budmash—a bad, difficult, or troublesome person.
burqa—the Muslim covering for women, a long garment covering the wearer from the crown of the head to the feet, with slits for the eyes.
chaitya—a hall of worship with an arched roof in Buddhistic architecture.
chapatti—a thin cake of unleavened bread.
charpoi—a bed made of a wooden frame laced with rope.
chatti—an earthenware water bottle or pitcher.
chokidar—a caretaker.
chokra—a boy.
chota hazri—an early, first, breakfast (*petit déjeuner*).
dacoit—one of a class of criminals who rob and murder in roving gangs.
dak—mail, the post.
dal—pulse, lentils.
darzi—tailor.
dhoti—a long piece of cloth, so worn as to form men's trousers.
dudh—milk.
durbar—a great ceremonial display, generally military in nature, a show of power. Governing body of a native state. Also a formal reception of native Indian princes given by the British government; a court held by a native prince or a festive recep-

tion given by a maharajah for his subjects at which they pledged fealty to him.

durga—the shrine of a Muslim saint, a place of religious resort and prayer.

durwan—a doorkeeper, sometimes a porter.

dvarpala—"Guardians of the Gate" of Hindu temples.

ghat—a landing place, a bathing place on the bank of a river.

ghur—unrefined sugar, brown sugar.

godown—a warehouse (where people once went down), used in India as a term for the servants' quarters.

gompa—a Buddhist temple in the Himalayas generally of the Lama sect.

hammam—a bath.

hartal—a boycott.

houdah—a litter carried by an elephant, often with a canopy and railings.

jaghir—land or villages given by the government as a reward or fee for services; a freehold.

jemidar—a native officer in a sepoy regiment ranking under a subahdar, i.e. a lieutenant. Also a rank in the police and civil departments; and, lastly, a servant—of low degree in our time—the sweeper.

khud—a precipice.

knol khol—knol is an obsolete word (sixteenth-century English) for a turnip; this delicious vegetable is like a cross between a turnip and a cabbage.

kukeri—the Gurkha knife.

lakh—100,000.

lingam—phallic symbol.

log—people.

macqbara—a Muslim tomb.

mahout—elephant driver or groom.

maidan—a common.

maila—a fair.

mali—a gardener.

memsahib—feminine form of *sahib;* lady or lady of the house.

mendong—a Buddhistic monument made of loose stones, set off by prayer flags, found in the Himalayas.

missolchi—the second bearer.

mistri—a carpenter.

mulk—a country.

nundies—bulls (sacred).

pailow—a ceremonial arch (Chinese).

pan—a small package made of betel leaf, in which are dabs of lime, areka nut, etc., which is used as a masticatory.

panchayat—a village council.

pani—water.

puja—religious festival, celebration

punkah—fan.

pushta—terrace.

sarangi—a stringed instrument like a lute.

sherwani—Nehru jacket.

sirdar—an official, a person of rank or responsibility.

stupa—a Buddhist monument, an ancient structure partly in the form of a dome; sometimes Buddhistic relics were preserved within.

suji—fine wheat.

syce—groom.

taluqdar—big landowner, a potentate.

tazia—a tall, painted structure paraded by the Shia sect at the Muslim festival of Moharram, representing the mausoleums of the martyred Ali, Hasan and Husain.

Thugs—a sect devoted to ritual murder to propitiate the goddess Kali; an association of professional robbers and murderers in India; thieves, swindlers.

tonga—a carriage.

tussuldar—a tax collector.

vagra—thunderbolt.

veda—one of the ancient sacred books of the Hindus.

wallah—equivalent of the suffix "er," connected with, or, a man (e.g., *dudhwallah*, the milkman).

zamindar—a landowner/tax collector.

zenana—harem, women's quarters.

Index